Integrated Business Communication

Integrated Business Communication in a Global Marketplace

Bonnye E. Stuart

Marilyn S. Sarow

Laurence Stuart

BICENTENNIAL
1807
WILEY
2007
BICENTENNIAL

John Wiley & Sons, Ltd

Other Wiley Editorial Offices

John Wiley & Sons Inc., 111 River Street, Hoboken, NJ 07030, USA

Jossey-Bass, 989 Market Street, San Francisco, CA 94103-1741, USA

Wiley-VCH Verlag GmbH, Boschstr. 12, D-69469 Weinheim, Germany

John Wiley & Sons Australia Ltd, 42 McDougall Street, Milton, Queensland 4064, Australia

John Wiley & Sons (Asia) Pte Ltd, 2 Clementi Loop #02-01, Jin Xing Distripark, Singapore 129809

John Wiley & Sons Canada Ltd, 6045 Freemont Blvd, Mississauga, ONT, L5R 4J3

Wiley also publishes its books in a variety of electronic formats. Some content that appears in print may not
be available in electronic books.

Anniversary logo design: Richard J. Pacifico

Library of Congress Cataloging-in-Publication Data

Stuart, Bonnye E.
  Integrated business communication in a global marketplace / Bonnye E. Stuart, Marilyn S. Sarow,
Laurence P. Stuart.
     p. cm.
  ISBN: 978-0-470-02767-7 (alk. paper)
1. Business communication.   I. Sarow, Marilyn S.   II. Stuart, Laurence P.   III. Title.
  HF5718.S78 2007
  658.4′5–dc22   2006034928

A catalogue record for this book is available from the British Library

ISBN 978-0-470-02767-7

Typeset by Thomson Digital, New Delhi, India
Printed and bound in Great Britain by Bell & Bain, Glasgow

This book is printed on acid-free paper responsibly manufactured from sustainable forestry in which at least
two trees are planted for each one used for paper production.

Contents

About the Authors

Bonnye E. Stuart is an instructor in speech communication and mass communication at Winthrop University. She holds a graduate degree from the University of New Orleans and has worked in advertising, marketing and public relations for small businesses and non-profit organizations. She has taught both in the USA and in France and is the author of several historical books.

Marilyn S. Sarow is an associate professor of mass communication and coordinator of the integrated marketing communication programme at Winthrop University. She holds a PhD from the University of South Carolina and has authored several books. She has worked in public relations and marketing in higher education and in the medical field.

Laurence Stuart is founder and CEO of College to Career Seminars. He speaks on college campuses across the USA about how to use effective communication skills in the job-seeking process. He holds a journalism degree from Louisiana State University and has authored several motivational books. His marketing career spans 30 years in executive management in the retail sector of Corporate America.

Preface

This book is the culmination of many years of working in the communication field for all three authors. Collectively we have over 65 years of professional experience and 32 years in academia. We each were driven to complete the book for individual reasons. Here are our stories.

The idea for this book came about more than five years ago. I was talking to my son, an MBA student, about the concepts I was covering in my public speaking and persuasion theory classes. He had never been exposed to the concept of a "communication process" or that communicating effectively, how and why, could be taught or learned. He told me he thought all business students should be required to take a communication course, and even arranged for me to guest lecture in some of his classes.

Since that conversation, I have spoken to many college students who have expressed the same unfamiliarity with the discipline of communication. Just yesterday, a business student I told about almost finishing the book said, "Great, we need to learn about communication in the business department".

And so I hope this book helps as you enter the business world and in some way propels you toward the attainment of your career goals.

Bonnye Stuart

Executives report they look for employees who can think across disciplines and work cross-functionally. After more than 15 years coordinating an undergraduate integrated marketing communication programme, I am more than convinced the first step in that process is to tear down the walls separating academic disciplines. We cannot expect our students to think in new ways if we continue to maintain the silos of academia. This book illustrates the power of sharing information.

I believe business students need to have a basic knowledge of communication theory and practise to become leaders in the global workplace. Furthermore, students should understand how the practice of communication must be integrated across organizations, a considerable challenge in a flat world.

Much of the information in this book is based on our knowledge of professional communications, our professional experience and the joy we feel in collaborating with students. We believe in two-way communication and encourage your comments, anecdotes or criticisms.

Marilyn S. Sarow

Fifteen years ago, as a top executive in the corporate world, I couldn't even "sign on" to a computer terminal, but I knew if I was to continue to be an effective communicator (I now conduct motivational seminars for university students) I had better learn some computer skills quickly!

You see, whether you are young or old, verbal and non-verbal language requires learned skills, especially to communicate ideas, a point of view, an emotion, belief, anger and disappointment, excitement and joy, or simply to ask someone to do something and respond the way you intend.

More importantly, to be the best communicator and conduct business the world over, you have to master and use appropriate communication skills in order to deliver your message with total clarity, understanding and sensitivity. Leaders continue to learn, no matter their ages or positions.

The name of our book is *Integrated Business Communication in a Global Marketplace*. Enjoy it and learn the skills you need to succeed in your chosen career.

Laurence Stuart

Acknowledgements

Writing a book of this scope requires the input and support of many friends, colleagues, institutions and professional contacts too numerous to mention individually. You know who you are ... we're grateful to have you in our corner.

We extend heartfelt appreciation to our "Learning from Others" contributors. Their expertise brings a professional and thoughtful perspective and adds value to the learning experience. Contributors include Bill Belchee, Beacon Small Business Solutions; James Bernhard, Shaw Group; Geoff Cox, New Directions, Ltd; Elizabeth Dougall, University of North Carolina at Chapel Hill; Despina Kartson, Latham & Watkins; Charles Lankester, Asia-Pacific, Edelman; Kristi LeBlanc, Nosal Partners, LLC; Padmini Patwardhan, Winthrop University; Theresa Thao Pham, Teachers College of Columbia University; Jen Ross, journalist; Stephen Salyer, Salzburg Seminar; Alan Stine, Eaton Corporation, Heavy Duty Transmission Division; Elnora Stuart, American University, Cairo; Jean Watin-Augouard, Trademark Ride; Arthur Weise, Jr, Entergy Corporation; and Katherine van Wormer, University of Northern Iowa.

Designers took our ideas and created understandable models. They worked on short deadlines with congeniality and willingness to make changes. We are indebted to Barbara Aubin, Ben Bôhly and David Stuart.

The work of translators added to the international flavour of our book. Thanks go to Maria Clara Kulmacz, Aurélie Muret and Capt. D. M. Patwardhan.

Photographic resources were contributed by Susan Stine, Lawson & Associates, and by Les Winograd, Subway Restaurants.

Other individuals offered expert advice and subject matter. We are grateful to Gelson Kawassaki, Daquiprofora; Sayward McInnis, Winthrop University student; Bunny Richardson, BMW North America; and Rebecca Bernhard, Shaw Group.

Thanks for business examples and anecdotes go to David Stuart, Elizabeth Gorman, Jessica Ambrose, Christian Stuart, Jessica Bishop and Rick Vogler.

Appreciation for believing in this manuscript is extended to Stan Wakefield. Editors Sarah Booth, Anneli Anderson and Emma Cooper, Paul Curtis, Mark Styles and Neetu Kalra and the support staff at John Wiley & Sons encouraged us to continue writing and provided technical assistance. We credit them and the many reviewers whose feedback was invaluable to the finished book.

Our colleagues, faculty, staff and students at Winthrop University inspired our efforts, tolerated our ravings and allowed us to test our ideas.

Special thanks go to Roger Sarow for his contributions to the manuscript, including interviewing, editing, photography, ideas and all-round faith in the project. Without his behind-the-scenes support, we would not have ice cream sundaes with raspberries for dessert.

Introduction

Regardless of your degree discipline, as you enter the workplace and progress in your career you will be required to share information, follow instructions, direct and lead projects, instruct personnel, persuade colleagues, clarify misunderstanding and gain respect for your knowledge and expertise.

You will do all of this and more through the power of communication.

This book first introduces you to the process of communication and how it is used in daily life. Next it moves into the business arena and explores standard practices of communicating with personnel and management. Finally it tackles the cutting-edge world of the global marketplace and the communication challenges it presents.

The language and tone of the book changes as we advance from everyday experience to the workplace. We hope this illustrates the inherent differences between everyday conversation and the information-sharing processes that occur in the workplace. Language gets more complex and the tone becomes more professional.

In this book, you will be exposed to specific information covering a variety of topics.

PART 1 Communication in Daily Life introduces the foundations of the communication process and attempts to explain the role of communication in everyday life. It lays the groundwork for our discussion of business communication.

Chapter 1 The Building Blocks of Communication gives an overview of communication and its processes. We present our version of the transactional communication model as a basis for the communication concepts presented in this and future chapters.

Chapter 2 The Complex World of the Sender explains effective messaging by focusing on the sender of verbal and non-verbal messages. It covers encoders of information and the factors influencing effectiveness in the communication process.

Chapter 3 Knowing the Receivers of Your Messages examines ways to learn more about the receivers of your messages. It suggests theoretical and practical methods for "reading" an audience, and how to use this information to reach receivers better.

Chapter 4 Breaking Through the Noise explores the effect of clutter and message bombardment on the understanding and interpretation of meaning. We look at internal and external noise, selective filters and the differences between hearing and listening.

Chapter 5 Communication Channels analyzes communication's progression from spoken to written language and from printed to electronic forms. It includes examples of messages, guidelines for effective presentations and tips for channel selection.

PART 2 Towards Integrated Business Communication explores the various roles communicators play as they create and maintain successful businesses. It establishes a basis for the discussion of communication in the global marketplace.

Chapter 6 Business Communication, Public Relations and Integrated Marketing Communication covers the development of communication as a business discipline. We emphasize the growing need for knowledgeable communicators who can reach both external and internal publics.

Chapter 7 External Communication: Messaging to Your Publics focuses on the external communication efforts of an organization and the importance of reaching various publics. It considers messaging from an organizational perspective and includes external relationships and protecting brand image.

Chapter 8 Internal Communications: Messaging Within Your Company centres on the influence of effective communication on the productivity and performance of employees. It looks at various internal communication formats including meetings, videoconferencing, company newsletters and blogs.

Chapter 9 The Importance of Effective Communication in the Workplace uses two-way communication as a model for effective messaging to and connecting with a changing workplace. It investigates the importance of sharing knowledge and encouraging innovation as well as the need for employee training.

Chapter 10 Issues of Organizational Leadership looks at executives as leaders and the role communication plays in developing leadership skills. It brings ethical, cross-cultural and legal issues to the forefront of our discussion of leadership challenges in the workplace.

PART 3 Integrated Business Communication extends our discussion of communication to the global marketplace and focuses special attention on the integration of messages throughout all levels of an organization.

Chapter 11 Global Communication Expands ventures into the changing marketplace and addresses diversity and stereotyping in traditional and emerging markets. It introduces the world of social media and other communication phenomena, such as communicasting and datacasting.

Chapter 12 Communication in the New Management World examines the role of the executive in strategic communication management. It explores the executive as team builder, mediator, negotiator, educator and facilitator of creativity and innovation.

Chapter 13 Emerging Issues Affecting Communication Strategy addresses the communication gaps among executives and employees and customers and highlights the issues management and crisis management processes. Trendwatching adds a futuristic dimension to the discussion.

Chapter 14 New Focus on Responsible Communication probes integrated marketing communication and outlines its influences on IBC. Social responsibility, as a civic expectation, adds to the public's perception of an organization.

Chapter 15 Looking Ahead prepares students for a flatter world that will include shifts in people, place, time, information and technology. Finally, it challenges future business leaders to seek innovative ways to achieve integrated business communication in a global marketplace.

We encourage you to read the essays and interviews in the "Learning from Others" sections. These experts offer personal, professional and scholarly insights into business communications. Each essay should stimulate further discussion and study.

Case studies, class exercises, action plans and websites will help you apply and synthesize the material presented in the chapter. Many of these activities have been used in our own classrooms.

We believe our discussion of integrated business communication in the global marketplace is relevant to your career in business and, more importantly, encourage you to develop your own style of communication as you become a leader of tomorrow.

PART 1

COMMUNICATION in Daily Life

CHAPTER 1

The Building Blocks of Communication

Executive Summary

Communication always has been a prime human objective. Grunts and gestures used by humans in the Stone Age have advanced to complex meanings and nuances. Communication today is not simple. To be an effective communicator, you must know how the process works and how your skills add to or detract from effective communication.

Communication theories help to interpret the communication challenges of a new millennium
Our transactional communication model shapes the business communication discussion in this book.

How a message is shaped is called framing
Framing also determines how a message is interpreted or evaluated by others. Such factors as how concepts are communicated by leaders and the media, and how they are accepted by the culture, form an important role in the adoption process. How management views the communication process and shapes its messages has a significant impact on how the public views an organization.

Why a person listens to or understands one message rather than another depends on the communicator's knowledge of the many complex elements involved
For example, non-verbal language is more difficult to read, is culture bound and requires rigorous attention to interpretative meanings. In addition, listening is not necessarily hearing, and barriers reduce the number of messages that influence us.

Communicative skills are vital to sending and receiving messages
Today's business world requires an understanding of modern communication principles and ultimately their application to create effective messages. ■

The Building Blocks of Communication

In this age of audience fragmentation, global presence, data overload, niche marketing, downsizing, reorganizing and accountability, effective oral and written communication skills are in demand.

Introduction to Integrated Communication

How important is effective communication in your daily business and personal life? The answer is obvious; without effective communication even everyday tasks are difficult, if not impossible. The average person takes messages at face value without evaluating the true meaning and intent of the communication.

Here's a quick scenario. You didn't quite understand what the weather man predicted this morning on the radio and, because you didn't take your brolly or mackintosh, you are now soaked. You were focused on your wet shoes and hair when you ordered lunch at the local café, and consequently you are eating a sandwich with mustard. You hate mustard. You received a low grade on your class report because your professor said you didn't address the issue (you didn't tell her you couldn't read your rain-soaked notes). Your boss at your part-time job got angry because you didn't say you would be running late (you had to change out of your wet clothes before going to work). Your car battery went dead because you left your lights on in the parking lot after driving in the rain, and you missed meeting your friend for dinner. When you finally arrived home and collapsed in a heap on the sofa, you rued the horrible day that you had experienced. How could everything have gone so wrong?

If you were to think back over the day's events you would see that, because of one simple misunderstanding, the rest of the day's events were affected by your failure effectively to receive, interpret, understand and evaluate the meaning of simple daily messages.

Now let's consider the consequences of poor communication in terms of a catastrophic natural disaster.

In late August 2005, as water poured into the US city of New Orleans and thousands of citizens began to evacuate the low-lying areas of the region, many people received mixed messages. Some understood that the Superdome, a huge sports arena near the centre of the city, was the emergency shelter. Others heard reports that they were to assemble at the Convention Centre on the edge of the Mississippi River.

Conditions were difficult for those who made it to the Superdome. There were just a few doctors on hand, limited supplies, little food or water and the authorities were keeping a tenuous peace. It took several days for these people to be boarded on buses and helicopters and evacuated out of the city.

Meanwhile at the Convention Center there was total chaos: no organization, no ruling authority, no food or water, no medical services and no communication.

News crews from around the world covered the unfolding story both at the Superdome and at the Convention Center. The reporters made passionate on-air appeals for help at the Convention Center.

Why the disparity between conditions at the two sites?

After three days of chaos, and in spite of the worldwide distribution of photos and video footage of the awful situation at the Convention Center, the head of the US Federal Emergency Management Agency claimed on camera, "I didn't know they were there until today".

Where was the communication? How had his team, trained to respond to emergency rescue procedures, missed the hours of continuous media coverage of the people at the Convention Center?

It was ineffective communication on the part of many coordinating agencies that did not know what their counterparts were doing.

Communications is at the root of everything you will do in your personal and professional lives. Consequently, you need to master and use communication tools effectively and strategically.

Silo mentality

In the past, organizations have suffered from a **"silo" mentality**. A silo is a huge, vertical container used to store grain. When people in a given part of an organization such as a department have information and refuse to share it with others, they reinforce the walls of their silo. Historically, this was thought to give that department within the organization additional power as it had control over information that other departments didn't possess.

In these vertical silos, it is also difficult to share information from the top of the organization to the bottom, and vice versa. This makes it unlikely for everyone in the organization to be "on the same page", resulting in less effective communication, loss of time, lack of quality performance and ultimately the loss of potential profit.

Today we believe sharing information, rather than hoarding it, makes the total organization stronger. Cooperation encourages connections between ideas and actions by drawing information from across the organization.

To clarify the concept of shared information, think about your favourite sports team. When specific plays are designed by the coach, each team member has specific duties to perform for the play to work successfully. If one person fails to do his or her part, the play can fail, and the end result will be a loss for the team. The same is true for effective business communication. If only a select group of people know the information and keep it to themselves, the other players within the organization don't have all the facts to make responsible decisions.

One of the leading cultural management firms in the European Union had this to say about informational silos:

> Even functions, once regarded as monolithic silos, standing proudly on their own, are in need of reconciliation. Time was when the workplace simply manufactured things that the sales force then tried to sell to customers. But the modern corporation cannot be like that. Increasingly we have customized workplaces, customized to not just what customers are asking for, but to what growing, learning, ever-more-complex employees seek to learn, to discover, and to express. The boundaries between functions are dissolving into integrated capabilities (Trompenaars & Hampden-Turner, 2004, p. 14).

How do you use communication to gather, interpret and synthesize information? How do you communicate this information to receivers? How do you evaluate your message? How does the message find its meaning in and through various environments? How do you employ strategy to ensure communication success? How do you evaluate your message to see if it was indeed received as you intended?

These are just a few of the questions that need to be addressed. And we hope that by now you see how complex the idea of communication can be. If you do a simple Google search of "communication", you will get 619 million hits. While much communication occurs outside business, it is often difficult to draw a definitive distinction. But Google "communication business" and you will receive 245 million hits. Change the words around to "business communication" and you will get 262 million hits. There is much to know, and much to learn.

Why Does Integrated Business Communication Work?

In this age of audience fragmentation, global presence, data overload, niche marketing, downsizing, reorganizing, research demanding and accountability, communication has to work. It must be strategically employed to achieve measurable results. Everyone has to be on board, everyone has to buy in. Engagement is the key. Only by totally integrating all business communication from department to department, division to division, employee to executive, president to branded image, engineer to customer, retail to mail order, and advertising to the CEO's appearance on a talk show can you make the most of your communication resources. Making sure your company speaks with one voice is the challenge of the future. It will take understanding and a coordinated effort by everyone, but especially by young, fresh executives like you who will be running the companies of the world far into the future.

Creating and sustaining an integrated business communication programme must be a priority in today's business climate. As the *New York Times* columnist Thomas L. Friedman reminds us, around 2000 the world entered a new era of globalization where the playing field is level (Friedman, 2005). Your success in what has become a small world, owing to instant communication access, demands that you are able to communicate and compete with people in literally every corner of the globe. So let's prepare for your future in this global marketplace. We'll start with the communication approach that, if practised skillfully, will help you build strong linkages to customers, employees, stockholders, financial institutions, suppliers and other stakeholders.

Our collective practical experience in a variety of market sectors convinces us that a planned communication approach that considers the goals and values of an organization, the needs of its stakeholders and the demands of a changing marketplace will help ensure profitability and institutional success in a global environment.

To learn how to use integrated business communication practices, you must first understand how this process of communication works from the bottom up. So we will embark upon a journey of breaking up, investigating, probing and reconfiguring the communication process so that you will be able to construct a viable world of integrated business communication that will be useful in whatever career path you take and in whatever part of the world you choose to go.

What Is Communication?

Communication is simply the sending of a message from a source to a receiver. But history shows that communication is never simple – from medieval coded messages that prohibited the messenger from knowing what the message contained to the misinterpretation of Japan's answer to the US demand for unconditional surrender before dropping the atomic bomb toward the end of World War II, you will recognize the need for clear, accurate communication.

Perhaps because the warning (to surrender unconditionally) was only a general statement, the Japanese ... chose to ignore it, employing the ambiguous word mokusatu, which means literally "to kill with silence"... Tokyo radio used the word, saying the government would mokusatu the declaration and fight on. The English translation became "reject", and the president took it as a rebuff (Ferrell, 1960).

The first communication models sought to explain how a message is sent and received. They tended to concentrate on one message being sent from a sender to a receiver who in turn then sent a return message.

This was soon seen as too simplistic. As the field of communication took root in academic disciplines, the early linear models fell short of modern findings. Those who began to study this science of communication asked the following questions:

- Is just one message being sent at a time?
- Does the receiver wait for the completion of a message before he/she sends a response?
- Do messages have a distinct beginning and ending?
- Why do different people interpret the same message differently?
- Are non-verbal messages being read and what is their influence on the verbal message?
- What factors interfere with communication?

Communicating is not simple. Once we accept this basic fact, we can begin to think not only about how and why we communicate, but to whom and in what manner we do so. Getting our message across in the way in which we want it to be received takes time and effort. This realization opens the gate to developing successful communication techniques.

Strategic Thinking

Effective communication is crucial, especially when lives are on the line.

The European Commission report on the "Impact of Multicultural and Multilingual Crews on Maritime Communication" (MARCOM, 1998) cites the following example from *The Ethnography of Communication* that occurred when relationships between Egypt and Greece were strained.

Egyptian pilots radioed (in English) their intention to land at an airbase on Cyprus, and the Greek traffic controllers reportedly responded with silence. The Greeks intended thereby to indicate refusal of permission to land, but the Egyptians interpreted silence as assent.

The result of the misunderstanding in this case was the loss of a number of lives when the Greeks fired on the planes as they approached the runway. (Buck, 2002).

The Development of Theory

Communication theory is important to the study of communication and its role in business in the global marketplace. The history of communication theory begins with the social sciences but today can be found in many other disciplines such as media, organizational development and mathematics.

The boom years

The 1930s was a **boom decade** for communication theory. One of the names you should be familiar with during this era is Sigmund Freud whose new theories of psychoanalysis coloured the communication landscape. You should also know the name Edward Bernays, the public relations guru and nephew of Freud. Bernays, who died in 1995, furthered Freud's studies in the USA by incorporating them into the new ideas he was using to promote goods and services across the country.

In 1948, political scientist Harold Lasswell described communication as *who* says *what* through *which* channel to *whom* and with *what effect*.

The study of communication grew rapidly both in academic circles and in the professional arena. Advertisers helped speed the development of communication theories. Ever ready to consider a new theory or idea that would help sell their products or services, advertising agencies began to employ social and behavioural scientists to help them communicate messages to consumers about their products.

Dig Deeper

Modern communication models to read about: visit www.ccms-infobase.com.

The Lasswell formula deals with components: communicator, message, channel, receiver and effect.

The Osgood and Schramm circular model presents communication in a circular pattern including elements of encoder, decoder, interpreter and message.

Gerbner's general model shows communication as a dynamic event with a focus on the communicating agent. He is known for his theories on violence in the media.

Ronald B. Adler's transactional model is perhaps the most practical model. It is the one we have used as a basis of our model for discussion of effective communication.

New terms were introduced and studied:

- Feedback made senders play a role as receivers of information.
- Communication was seen as simultaneous and continuous.
- Encoding became a point of study.
- Decoding was deconstructed and analysed.
- The medium or channel took on characteristics that added complexity to the communication model.
- Noise was defined as external or internal.

What became important was not just communicating, but communicating effectively. A new definition was created: effective communication is when a message is understood by the receiver in the manner in which it was intended by the sender.

For example, I explain to my friend how to get to a certain store. I use the directional phrase, "It's a way down the street". Now in my mind that means 15 blocks or so. But effective communication doesn't hinge solely on what I mean, it also depends on the receiver's interpretation of "way down". If we disagree as to what the actual distance is, then my friend may think I have given him wrong directions. He may begin to look for the store by the third or fourth block and perhaps will continue looking for a few more blocks. But, confused and now assuming he received the wrong message, he may give up altogether, well before he goes 10 blocks further.

Communication education today

Today, universities are revamping their curricula to reflect the need for greater communication skills in the business world, but there is a debate about how much focus should be on theory and what concentration should be placed on practicality. In "Teaching Communication to Business Management Students", Laurie Cohen, Gill Musson and Susanne Tietze explain that most business students are not educated in communication-related study, "the area seems to have remained curiously untouched and … more practically, there is an apparent need for competent communicators in all sectors of our economy" (Cohen *et al.*, 2005, p. 281). The authors, citing Cameron (2000, pp. 180–181), contend that "a competent communicator is someone who exercises choice and judgement" and understands "how her choices will be received and interpreted" (Cohen *et al.*, 2005, p. 286). They conclude: "Understanding how language works in the construction of social and organizational realities is fundamental to management practice. To deny students of management access to these theoretical ideas simply perpetuates the theory and/or practice divide so characteristic of management education" (Cohen *et al.*, 2005 p. 286).

Most business schools have a full timetable teaching management, marketing, sales, accounting and other necessary courses. Communication is often an optional course in another department, if at all.

But that is changing. Once thought to be the domain of public relations or human resource departments, communication is now being valued across the multilayered spectrum of business. Many employers are demanding that recruits be well versed not only in practical presentation skills but also in the theoretical realm of what constitutes sound communication principles and how they can be applied to changing situations. Business students are expected to be effective communicators with the ability to analyse, evaluate, adapt and connect to a changing business landscape and a multinational workforce.

> ## Definition of Discourse
>
> A connected set of statements, concepts, terms and expressions which constitute a way of talking about a particular issue, thus framing the way people understand and respond to that issue (Watson, 1999).

> The study of semiotics has led to an emphasis on the receiver's role in meaning-making. Understanding that "meaning systems are arbitrary, culturally mediated and operating at a largely subconscious level" and knowing that receivers "influence how a text is decoded and understood" is a valuable management skill (Cohen *et al.*, 2005).

Forms of Communication

In this text we will introduce you to intrapersonal, interpersonal and mediated communication. Our primary focus, however, is on business communication.

Intrapersonal communication

Intrapersonal communication is communicating with ourselves. That little voice we consult before we ask a favour from a friend, plead for an assignment deadline extension from a professor or request a promotion from a boss is invaluable as a sounding board. We all talk to ourselves, some of us more than others. And that is a good thing. Hashing over available options is part of a self-monitoring mechanism that allows us to evaluate and correct our behaviour both before and after our actual performance.[1]

[1] Donna Vocate addresses some of the theoretical thinking behind this type of communication in *Intrapersonal Communication: Different Voices, Different Minds* (Vocate, 1994).

Therapists explore the workings of intrapersonal communication and usually adhere to the school of thought that says individuals can enhance their self-esteem by talking to themselves in a positive manner. So instead of saying, "I was awful in accounting, no one will hire me", individuals should turn the negative into a positive and say to themselves, "I didn't do so well in accounting class, but I can be of great value to a company because of my financial analysis skills". Many experts believe that what people say to themselves ultimately affects their feelings of self-worth.

Interpersonal communication

Interpersonal communication, the exchange of information between two or more senders and receivers in a casual context, is a science unto its own. Interpersonal communication is neither always personal nor always private. It is about real relationships that take root through communication between and among individuals, verbal and non-verbal. Scholars began to consider components that affect communication as closeness of the parties, context (business or personal), length of contact (momentary or extended), friendly or adversarial tone, etc.

Scholars took up the discipline and theories were formed: social exchange, uncertainty reduction and reward theory.[2] Julia Wood suggests that interpersonal communication exists on a continuum from extremely personal to extremely impersonal (Wood, 2000). The information available regarding interpersonal communication is extensive. We will cover some of the relevant components to our discussion of business communication, but for a more detailed study you can search the Internet or your library for sources.

Mediated communication

The mass media developed their own communication models. Communication researcher Wilbur Schramm and psychologist Charles E. Osgood created the circular model. In their model, the sender becomes the encoder and the receiver is the decoder. They were concerned with why individuals receiving identical messages interpret them differently and what happens when feedback is delayed. For example, if a newspaper prints a story, it may take time to receive reader feedback. Of course the Internet enables nearly immediate feedback as viewers and readers are directed

[2] See Thibaut & Kelly (1959). *The Social Psychology of Groups*. New York: John Wiley & Sons.

to websites to express their opinions, vote for a favourite singing idol, access more information on a story or log on to receive free soap opera updates. Some theorists like David L. Evans who has studied stereotypes in the media (Evans, 1995) and A. Silverblatt who has explored media literacy issues (Silverblatt, 1995) are important figures in **mediated communication** research. George Gerbner, the guru of media analysis theory, identified the "three Bs" of television's impact on society: blurs, blends and bends (Gerbner, 1990).

Media richness

With roots in computer-mediated communications, **media richness** theory is built on the assumption that organizations select a form of communication based on their ability to reduce uncertainty and equivocality (Daft & Lengel, 1986). Some scholars describe media richness as the ability to carry information, defined as its data-carrying capacity and its symbol-carrying capacity (Daft, Lengel & Kiebe, 1987). Using these two criteria, some media are classified as more effective in meeting specific communication objectives than others.

Media can be ranked from "rich" to "lean" on the basis of the following considerations:

- Interactivity or speed of feedback. Face-to-face conversations would be considered rich media in this case, whereas email would be rated low or lean. In face-to-face communication the message can be adjusted quickly if the sender believes that the message is not being accurately received.
- Multiple clues. Rich media provide a variety of verbal, kinetic and spatial clues. Again, face-to-face would be considered a rich medium, whereas a videoconference or text-based chat would be less so. When the sender and receiver can "read" each other through both verbal and non-verbal cues, the message has a greater chance of being understood.
- Message tailoring. Rich media enable the sender to shape the message to the needs of the receiver, whereas lean media, such as databases, restrict the sender's ability to tailor the message but also leave little room for ambiguity.
- Emotions. Some media allow the sender to infuse personal feelings and emotions into the message. Face-to-face meetings allow the sender to show, both verbally and non-verbally, what she or he feels about a particular message or situation, whereas an annual report leaves little room for emotion (Daft & Lengel, 1986; Daft, Lengel & Kiebe, 1987).

In an effort to attract readership, traditional newspapers are encouraging journalists to post supplemental writings on weblogs. They hope this will establish a dialogue with new techies. The French *Le Monde* provides weblogs to selected subscribers to "create a club of bloggers" and increase loyalty. "The reader is a partner, not a passive audience", says Stephane Mazzorato, editor and publisher (World Editors Forum, 2006).

Business communication

Business communication falls somewhere in the middle of the continuum with intrapersonal communication at one end and mass communication at the other.

Business communication refers to the transfer of messages that pertain to the world of business, from personal email, office memos, sales presentations and conferences to daily greetings, departmental meetings and corporate branding strategies. Of course, there is much intermingling of message types in the workplace. A study by Ted Zorn investigates the communication among "bosses and buddies" in the office (Zorn, 1995). It uncovers numerous ways that people cope with the uncertainty of contradictory messages as messages are sent among friends, co-workers, bosses and subordinates.

Integrated business communication

Integrated business communication in this book refers to *the process of planning, executing and evaluating unified messages that create stakeholder relationships and build brand recognition.*[3]

In this book, the model of transactional communication forms the basis of our discussion on how organizational communication works and the role of integrated communication in that process.

Communication continuum

Figure 1.1 Intrapersonal communication is at the far left of the continuum and is an internal communication process. Interpersonal communication involves two or more people, but usually involves small groups where members interact with one another. Business communication reaches both small and large audiences, all of which have something in common – a stake in the organization. Mass communication is on the far right, reaches an impersonal public audience.

[3] This definition is based on Tom Duncan's definition in *Advertising & IMC* (2005) but views business communication in a broader perspective.

Understanding What This Means to You

Understanding communication and how it works in the business world is crucial. Not only is the way we communicate changing, but people's expectations and standards of that communication are also changing. Businesses are both senders and receivers of messages. As such they must communicate both horizontally and vertically within and outside their organization. A "this is the way we've always done it" won't work in the global marketplace. Because communication needs to be integrated into every facet of the organization, informational silos, the tall vertical depositories of information, are out. Horizontal seas of information shared between various departments and management levels, consumers and employees, shareholders and stakeholders are the new ideal.

So let's look at a model that depicts many of the elements involved in effective communication. We will call it the 'transactional communication model'.[4]

Consider the components of the transactional communication model.

The **sender**, also called the encoder, is the oval on the left. The sender's mission is to compose a message embedded with meaning from his/her world, while considering the interpretative resources the receiver, the oval on the right, will use to decode the

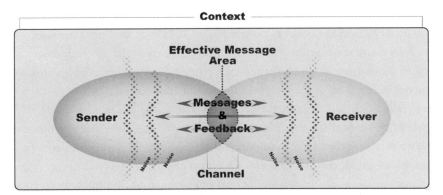

Figure 1.2 Transactional communication model, illustrating the communication process.

[4] There are other models that focus more or less on various components. Sometimes they are called transmission or transactional models. Leading theorists in the field are Shannon and Weaver, Adler, Lasswell, Osgood and Schramm, Berlo and Gerbner. There are critics, too: Ang, Cherry, Reddy and Underwood, to name just a few. For more information, see Baran and Davis (2000) and Lowery and DeFleur (1995).

message. Let's say this in another way. The sender must formulate a message based in his/her own world which includes such factors as education level, socio-economic status, prejudices and cultural concepts, among other considerations, and then relinquish control of that message as it enters the world of the receiver.

The **receiver** then has to decode the message and give it meaning, but that is not so easy. Judgements have to made on the basis not only of the actual words the person is hearing but also of an infinite number of subtle cues, such as tone of voice, a smile, a handshake, a furtive eye, ambiguous word usage, etc. The receiver's world is individualistic and thus different from that of the sender. We will talk about how we perceive and try to understand the world of our receiver later.

The **channel** is how the information is being sent: face-to-face, email, phone, fax, text messages, advertising, group presentation, etc. While this may sound like the easiest element of the model to understand, there is much to think about when selecting a channel. Marshall McLuhan's *Understanding Media: The Extensions of Man* introduced the concept "the medium is the message" and directed scholars to focus on how content is influenced by what a medium "says" (McLuhan, 1964). Why do we choose to call a friend to impart bad news, rather than write an email? Why is a story broadcast on the evening news more believable than a story in a tabloid newspaper? Is a television commercial just an ad with motion? Each channel has not only certain requirements inherent in the medium but also implicit expectations on the part of both senders and receivers.

An **effective message** is not just *any* message. While we may get a message across, perhaps even many messages, they would not be considered effective unless they are received in the manner in which the sender intended. The level of effectiveness depends on the overlapping areas of the worlds of the sender and receiver, the union set of the two ovals; the bigger the overlap, the better the chance of a message being effective. In other words, the greater the extent to which a sender and receiver share commonalities, the better the chance they have to understand one another. However, no amount of common background, culture, religion, education or shared experiences can ensure success, but "being on the same page" at least opens the door for understanding to occur.

Noise is just that – noise that interferes with the transmission of a message. It can be external (a sudden loud noise, a sneeze, a power shortage, etc.) or internal (lack of education, prejudice, stubbornness, etc.).

Feedback is made up of all the verbal and non-verbal messages sent back and forth between sender and receiver as communication proceeds. It may or may not be noticed, heard or understood, but it exists nonetheless and often determines the future direction a message will take.

Context refers to the occasion, time and place of the communication. It comprises all the underlying and overarching factors that impact a message. The phrase, "come and see me" has different meanings when said by a sister, professor or boss. Likewise, its meaning changes if it is received by a lover, truant or employer. Its meaning is dependent on where it is said, by whom, at what time and on what occasion.

Simultaneous and continuous describe actions in the communication process. Many messages are sent simultaneously in the guise of a smile, toss of the hair, accent, nod, furtive eye or yawn. Messages are also continuous; even though words have a starting and an ending point, non-verbal messages do not. They never stop.

This transactional model is used throughout our discussion of integrated business communication in the global marketplace. Think about the various components and how they influence effective business messages.

Shaping the Communication Process

Now that you have been introduced to our transactional communication model used in this text, let's examine other concepts that influence the **communication process** and that are important to your understanding of the role of integrated communication in the business sector. You will encounter these concepts in future chapters of the book.

Dig Deeper

There are varying statistics on how people learn information. Lee and Bowers used university students to determine learning performance (Lee & Bowers, 1997). Lawrence Najjar compiled a literature review of research-based learning principles and applied these to website construction (Najjar, 1998). You can find many other studies by searching the Web. Faraday and Sutcliffe tracked eye movement patterns during multimedia sessions and documented these tips for improving learning performance (Faraday & Sutcliffe, 1997):

- Spoken words reinforce an image.
- Symbols direct attention to specific objects and locations.
- Object motion can attract attention.
- Revealing information systematically controls viewer attention.
- Concurrent presentation of several pieces of information hinders viewer focus.

Framing

As we have discussed, the effectiveness of a message depends on many factors including whether the sender and receiver understand each others' spoken language. The context of the message or the frame used in shaping it contributes to how the message is interpreted, and thus understood.

Suppose you missed a class and sent your instructor an email with the following message: "Did I miss anything important today in class?"

How might your message be interpreted by an instructor who had spent time and effort in preparing the day's lecture? How will the instructor's answer be framed? Will it be tongue-in-cheek? Serious? Sympathetic? Angry?

Can you see how your choice of language influences the instructor's response?

Robert Entman defines **framing** as "selecting and highlighting some facets of events or issues, and making connections among them so as to promote a particular interpretation, evaluation and/or solution" (Entman, 2004).[5]

Consider this example of how a major world leader framed his response to a national crisis. On 7 July 2005, the British Prime Minister Tony Blair was attending the G8 Summit in Gleneagles, Scotland, when he received word that terrorists had bombed London's Underground as well as a double-decker bus. Blair used the backdrop of this meeting of world leaders to frame terrorism as "not an attack on one nation but on all nations and on all civilized people everywhere" (Associated Press, 2005).

Would Blair have framed the event in similar terms had he not been hosting world leaders? Did the circumstance of the meeting make his message all the more poignant? It seems clear that the militant group who carried out the bombing chose that particular day because it knew its cause would be a featured topic in worldwide media.

Organizational leaders from politicians to CEOs to managers to shop supervisors knowingly – or unwittingly – frame their messages to address issues of strategic and tactical importance. How the media choose to use the message, or, in this case, frame the event, shapes how the public perceives it.

If you understand the communication process, you will have a clearer idea how best to communicate a message. The frames you choose in that communication process may determine how well your message is understood and ultimately accepted by the audience you are trying to reach. In Chapter 2 we will further

[5] Framing has been studied across many disciplines from issues of risk such as a fire and explosion at an oil refinery (Hornig, 1992; Duhé & Zoch, 1994/1995) to political and health issues (Clarke, 1992; Lupton, 1994).

examine framing as it applies to integrated business communication in a global marketplace.

How we frame messages is of key consideration in how the message is processed and received.

Diffusion of innovation

Organizations that create a climate where creativity and innovation are encouraged and supported will have a stronger chance of surviving global competition. Change is the key word in today's business climate. To understand the process of change and the role of communication in that process, you need to understand the theory of **diffusion of innovation**.

Diffusion theory grew out of the high rate of change occurring during the Industrial Revolution. In the 1890s, French sociologist Gabriel Tarte wondered why some innovations succeeded while others failed. Tarte posed a theory of imitation based on psychological concepts, but his theory failed to see the connection between the adoption of innovation and the power of the mass media to stimulate awareness (Lowery & DeFleur, 1995, p. 117).

British and German–Austrian scholars noticed that the process of adoption seemed to follow the S-curve or the standard normal curve. In other words, when a new product became available, it was slow to take off. Eventually the product would be adopted by the mainstream. However, some individuals simply ignored the invention altogether.

It wasn't until American rural sociologists Bryce Ryan and Neal Gross published their important article on the diffusion of the practice of using hybrid seed corn in two Iowa communities that social scientists began to understand the role of communication in the process of diffusion (Lowery & DeFleur, 1995).

Ryan and Gross discovered that adopting the practice of planting hybrid seed corn did not happen overnight but was influenced by both interpersonal contacts and the attention of mass media.

For example, you need to convince your employees to adopt a new standard of practice or perhaps you have a revolutionary new product to introduce in the marketplace. You will want to know how long it will take to implement your new ideas or to make a profit on your innovation.

Words are framed by their history and use. Retronyms are words adapted to explain the past in terms of the present. These words are usually due to new innovation or increased specialization (Dalvi, 2003).

What was once called:	Is now referred to as:
A book	A printed book
Mail	Snail-mail
A fireplace	A wood-burning fireplace
A phone	A landline phone
Coffee	Regular coffee
Airline ticket	Paper ticket
Reality	Real reality

Many factors influence effective messaging. The role of diffusion of innovation in the marketplace is crucial to the success of an organization.

We will explore how these forces affect the integrated communication process in a later chapter.

Opinion leaders

The diffusion theory points out not only the role of the media in influencing the adoption of new ideas but also the importance of intervening publics or opinion leaders. Business decisions are influenced by a variety of factors including those individuals to whom we turn for advice on particular issues. **Opinion leaders** include politicians, business leaders, religious figures and other individuals we deem experts. Indeed, our very definition of "expert" will vary depending on the issue and circumstance.

Your company wants to buy property in an area with easy access to transportation, connection to public utilities, an available labour force and a positive business climate. Who would you consult? A likely first choice is an estate agent who deals in industrial development. However, your search for expertise needs to extend beyond the real estate broker to education officials, government bureaucrats and politicians. Who are the leaders in the community whose opinions on economic development are valued?

As a future business executive you will need to analyse and evaluate the role opinion leaders play in the decision-making process.

Chapter Summary

In this chapter you were introduced to the concept of integrated business communication and its vital role in the global marketplace. The transactional communication model components – the sender or encoder, receiver or decoder, channel and the effective message, plus noise, feedback, context and simultaneous and continuous actions – influence how the message is received.

Several concepts – framing, diffusion of innovation and the role of opinion leaders – will underscore much of our discussion. As a future business leader you need to consider how you frame messages as well as how they have been framed for you.

The survival of organizations in a global society depends in part on how well companies adapt to competition and change. The theory of diffusion of innovation helps you to understand the role of mass media and opinion leaders in influencing the change process.

Effectively communicating may be a complex process, but communication is more an art than a science. ∎

Learning From Others

Despina Kartson is Chief Marketing Officer for Latham & Watkins, a global law firm with over 1800 attorneys with offices in the UK, USA, Singapore, France, Belgium, Germany, China, Italy, Russia and Japan. The firm has received the highest honours from industry watchdogs in areas such as "associate relations" and "openness regarding finances".

Kartson is charged with furthering the company's global business developmental initiatives and will coordinate her efforts with the Marketing Strategy Committee. She shares her insight on some of the global communication issues addressed in this textbook.

Q. How important is integrated business communication in a global marketplace?
A. Integrated communication is critical in a global marketplace as the need for regular and consistent information delivery can positively impact the organization's business model and client relationships.

Q. With whom do you communicate on a regular basis?
A. My daily communication is with firm leadership, department personnel, media, outside vendors, clients and prospective clients, located literally around the world. Internal communication covers topics from planning and organizational matters to policy issues and client concerns. Much of my daily external communication is in the broad area of public relations which includes media alerts, press releases and case notes.

Q. What communication issues do you face when dealing with different cultures?
A. As a global firm without a headquarters location, we are extremely sensitive to the use of terms that are too US-centric. For example, we do not refer to our European and Asian offices as "non-US" or "foreign". Instead, we refer to them as European, Asian or US, as appropriate. We also steer clear of colloquialisms that would not be understood outside the US.

Q. How do you ensure that your messaging is heard the way you intend?
A. If possible, we test market our communication prior to finalizing it. For example, we send communications to appropriate staff in the receiving market and ask them to confirm the message they receive.

Q. What are your thoughts on the importance of effective corporate leadership?
A. As a leader, it is critical to listen to superiors and other leaders, to peers, to subordinates, to constituents and to key influencers. Equally important are effective communication skills. Many college graduates have weak communication skills – they

cannot craft a compelling written piece or cover letter and generally lack the ability to communicate their thoughts. A solid communicator who can write clearly and present effectively is respected and well regarded.

Q. How important is teamwork to an organization?
A. Teamwork is very important, especially in a global organization. Most initiatives, projects and day-to-day assignments require participation by multiple individuals, and are rarely done solo.

Q. Finally, integrated business communication uses multiple channels of communication effectively to reach audiences with one voice/one message and works to ensure that messages are received the way they are intended. Do you think it is important for students to understand this concept?
A. Integrated business communication is important in the global economy of which many students will likely be a part. Understanding the differences in learning styles and knowing how to reach receivers on many levels with meaningful messages will make our students effective leaders in the future global marketplace.

Case Study – Simultaneous Message Systems (SMS)

Does the innovation of Internet messengers, mini-homepages and simultaneous message systems (SMS) signal the death of email? If young people in Korea are seen as early innovators, it may.

A poll of 2 000 middle, high school and college students in Gyeonggi and Chungcheong provinces, conducted by a professor at Chungbuk University in October 2004, reported that two-thirds of the respondents "rarely used or didn't use email at all".

Why? Email was viewed as too much like a chore.

In addition, they noted that it is impossible to tell whether the respondent receives the message if the reply is not immediately forthcoming.

One communication executive observed: "Email efficiency fails in terms of promptness, convenience and credibility".

Professor Lee Ok-hwa who conducted the survey said, "The new generation hate [sic] agonizing and waiting and tend to express their feelings immediately".

Koreans are considered early adopters in integrated technology. Do you think this trend is a prediction of the future? What might hinder the acceptance of Internet messengers, mini-homepages and SMS messages? (Ki-hong, 2004). ■

Class Exercises

1. Think about a time when you misunderstood a set of directions, a procedure, a recipe or a task. Try to pinpoint which element in the transactional communication model went wrong. What could have made the communication more effective?

2. With a partner, agree on a person (famous or a professor) that you both think is an effective communicator. Separately make a list of why you each think so. Compare your lists. Where do you agree or disagree? Why do you think you and your partner are able to agree on certain points and disagree on others?

3. Do some Web research and see if you can find an organizational leader, politician or corporate executive who has framed a business message in such a negative way that he/she has jeopardized his/her reputation. Check out CNN.com, 18 February 2004; Conan O'Brien apologizes to Canadians. Available from `http://www.cnn.com/2004/SHOWBIZ/TV/02/18/leisure.obrien.reut` (CNN.com, 2004).

Action Plan

In an essay called "Innovation Diffusion" for TechnologyReview.com, Michael Schrage makes this statement: "The big lie of the Information Age is that 'nothing is more powerful than an idea whose time has come'. What nonsense. In reality, nothing in this world is more powerful than an innovation that has diffused to the point where it enjoys both global reach and global impact. Ready access to ideas promotes awareness, but ready access to innovation promotes empowerment and opportunity" (`www.technologyreview.com/articles/or/12/schrage1204.0asp`) (Schrage, 2005).

Explore with your classmates the differences between ideas and innovations. Can you give examples? Then take either side of this argument and prepare an oral or written argument to share with your classmates.

Websites

Research any of these concepts that are of interest to you:

Find out how psychology impacts communication at `http://psychclassics.yorku.ca/topic.htm` (Green, 2006).

Learn about Edward Bernays, the father of modern public relations and some of his theories at `http://www.prmuseum.com/bernays/bernays _ 1915.html` (Public Relations Museum, 2006).

How important are innovations to companies? Look at the corporate website from Pella, a manufacturer of windows and doors, at `www.pella.com/about/history.asp/` (Pella Corp., 2005).

References

Associated Press (2005) Text of Blair's remarks on London explosions, 7 July 2005. Available from: http://npr.org/templates/story.php?storyId-4733076 [Accessed 5 October 2005].

Baran, S. & Davis, D. (2000) *Mass Communication Theory: Foundations, Ferment, and Future*, 2nd edn. Belmont, CA, Wadsworth Publishing.

Buck, V. (2002) "One world, one language?" Association Internationale des Interpretes de Conference, April–May 2004. Available from: http://www.aiic.net/ViewPage.cfm/page732.htm [Accessed 22 May 2006].

Cameron, D. (2000) *Good to Talk? Living and Working in a Communication Culture*. London, Sage.

Clarke, J. (1992) "Cancer, heart disease and AIDS: what do the media tell us about these diseases". *Health Communications*, **4**(2): 105–120.

CNN.com (2004) "Conan O'Brien apologizes to Canadians", 18 February 2004. Available from: http://www.cnn.com/2004/SHOWBIZ/TV/02/18/leisure.obrien.reut [Accessed 28 June 2006].

Cohen, L., Musson, G. & Tietze, S. (2005) "Teaching communication to business management students". *Management Communication Quarterly*, **19**(2): 279–287.

Daft, R. & Lengel, R. (1986) "Organizational information requirements, media richness and structural design". *Management Science*, **32**(5): 554–571.

Daft, R., Lengel, R. & Kiebe, L. (1987) "Message equivocality, media selection, and manager performance: implications for information systems". *MIS Quarterly*, **11**(3): 355–366.

Dalvi, M. (2003) "Retronyms: looking back on progress". Indus, May 2003. Available from: http://www.stc-india.org/indus/052003/mdalvi.htm [Accessed 6 November 2005].

Duhé, S. & Zoch, L. (1994/1995) "Framing the media's agenda during a crisis". *Public Relations Quarterly*, **39**(4). Available from: http://0web27.epnet.com.library.winthrop.edu:80/citation.asp?t...h+op%582+%5B1+%2DAnd+op%5BO+%2D+D851&cfr=1&cf=1&fn=11&rn=12 [Accessed 05 October 2005].

Duncan, T. (2005) *Advertising & IMC*, 2nd edn. Boston, McGraw-Hill.

Entman, R. (2004) *Projections of Power: Framing News, Public Opinion and US Foreign Policy*. Chicago, University of Chicago Press.

Evans, D. (1995) "The wrong examples". In *Foundations: a Reader for New College Students*. Belmont, CA, Wadsworth.

Faraday, P. & Sutcliffe, A. (1997) "An empirical study of attending and comprehending multimedia presentations". *In Proceedings of the Fourth ACM International Conference on Multimedia, Boston, MA*. Available from: http://portal.acm.org/citation.cfm?id=244225&coll=portal&dl=ACM [Accessed 10 June 2006].

Ferrell, R. (1960) "Truman and the bomb, a documentary history. Chapter 7: The Potsdam Declaration, 26 July". In *Foreign Relations of the United States: The Conference of Berlin*, 2 vols. Washington, DC, Government Printing Office, 1960: 147–1476. Available from: www.trumanlibrary.org [Accessed 18 November 2005].

Friedman, T. (2005) *The World is Flat: a Brief History of the Twenty-first Century*. New York, Farrar, Straus and Giroux.

Gerbner, G. (1990) "Epilogue: advancing on the path of righteousness (maybe)". In *Cultivation Analysis: New Directions in Media Effects Research*. Signorelli, N. & Morgan, M., eds. Newbury Park, CA, Sage.

Green, C. (2006) "Classics in the history of psychology", 6 February 2006. Available from: http://psychclassics.yorku.ca/topic.htm [Accessed 26 June 2006].

Hornig, S. (1992) "Framing risk: audience and reader factors". *Journalism Quarterly*, **69**(3): 679–690.

Ki-hong, K. (2004) "New forms of online communication spell end of email era in Korea". Boz/Tech. Available from: http://English.chosun.com/.w21data/html/news/200411/200411280034.html [Accessed 24 October 2005].

Lee, A. & Bowers, A. (1997) "The effect of multimedia components on learning". In *Proceedings of the Human Factors and Ergonomics Society*: 340–344.

Lowery, S. & DeFleur, M. (1995) *Milestones in Mass Communication Research: Mass Effects*, 3rd edn. White Plains, NY, Longman.

Lupton, D. (1994) "Femininity, responsibility and the technological imperative: discourse on breast cancer in the Australian press". *International Journal of Health Services*, **24**(1): 73–89.

McLuhan, M. (1964) *Understanding Media: The Extensions of Man*. New York, Signet.

MARCOM (1998), Final Report, "Impact of multicultural and multilingual crews on maritime communication". Available from: http://europa.eu.int/comm/transport/extra/final_reports/waterborne/marcom.pdf [Accessed 16 September 2005].

Najjar, L. (1998) "Principles of educational multimedia user interface design". *Human Factors*, **41**(2): 311–323.

Pella Corp. (2005) "Innovations". Available from: www. Pella.com/about/history.asp [Accessed 5 October 2005].

Public Relations Museum (2006) "Edward Bernays". Available from: http://www.prmuseum.com/bernays/bernays_1915.html [Accessed 28 June 2006].

Schrage, M. (2005) "Innovation diffusion". Available from: http://www.technologyreview.com/articles/04/12/schrage1204.0.asp [Accessed 10 October 2005].

Silverblatt, A. (1995) *Media Literacy*. Westport, CT, Greenwood Press.

Trompenaars, F. & Hampden-Turner, C. (2004) *Managing People Across Cultures*. Chichester, West Sussex, UK, Capstone Publishing.

Vocate, D., ed. (1994) *Intrapersonal Communication: Different Voices, Different Minds*. Hillsdale, NJ, Lawrence Erlbaum.

Watson, T. (1999) "Beyond managism: negotiated narratives and critical management education in practice". Paper for the First International Conference on *Critical Management Studies*, 14–16 July 1999, University of Nottingham. Available from: http://www.mngt.waikato.ac.nz/ejrot/cmsconference/documents/Management%20Education/TJW.pdf [Accessed 28 June 2006].

Wood, J. (2000) *Relational Communication: Change and Continuity in Personal Relationships*. 2nd edn. Belmont, CA, Wadsworth.

World Editors Forum (2006) "Creating loyalty with weblogs". Available from: http://wef.blogs.com/editors/2004/11/creating_loyalt.html [Accessed 2 November 2006].

Zorn, T. (1995) "Bosses and buddies: constructing and performing simultaneously hierarchical and close friendship relationships". In *Understanding Relationship Processes*. Wood, J. T. & Duck, S. W., eds. Thousand Oaks, CA, Sage: 122–147.

Bibliography

Baran, S. (2004) *Introduction to Mass Communication*, 3rd edn. New York, McGraw-Hill.

Cutlip, S., Broom, G. & Center, A. (2000) *Effective Public Relations*, 8th edn. Upper Saddle River, NJ, Prentice-Hall.

Rogers, E. (1995) *Diffusion of Innovation*, 4th edn. New York, Free Press.

Underwood, M. (2003) "Transmission models – criticism". Communication, Cultural and Media Studies. Available from: http://www.ccms-infobase.com [Accessed 2 December 2005].

Wilcox, D., Cameron, G., Ault, P. & Agee, W. (2003) *Public Relations: Strategies and Tactics*. New York, Allyn & Bacon.

CHAPTER 2

The Complex World of the Sender

Executive Summary

Senders of messages must understand how language, verbal and non-verbal, affects the effectiveness of communication. Some messages are deliberate and well developed; others are instinctive and subconscious.

Verbal and written messages use words that frequently mean more than their dictionary definitions

More important than what a specific word means to you is what it means to the receivers of your message.

Paralanguage concerns the vocal but not verbal aspects of communication meaning

This includes rate of speaking, silence, accents, etc. Non-verbal language elements are communication components that are not verbal or vocal, such as a yawn, a nod, poor posture, blinking eyes, a smile. Some are controllable; others are uncontrollable. Although paralanguage and non-verbal communication are culture bound and often difficult to interpret, some experts say they are 10 times stronger than verbal language.

The study of persuasion is rooted in the teachings of the Greek philosopher Aristotle

Learning how to use ethical persuasive tactics to ensure that a message is received and interpreted the way it was intended can lead to successful communication.

It is important to consider the different interpretations of a communication

Using concrete words, explaining abstract concepts, employing bias-free language and making sure facts and statistics are presented ethically may prevent misunderstanding. Being audience centred is vital to effective messaging. ∎

The Complex World of the Sender

> **In an 1888 letter, Mark Twain explained: "The difference between the almost right word and the right word is really a large matter — it's the difference between the lightning bug and the lightning".**
>
> *Mark Twain, 1888*

Introduction to the World of the Sender

Communication is transferring a message effectively from one person to another. We spend about 80 % of our lives communicating information and ideas to others. This information may be encoded and decoded in a variety of ways that will ultimately affect the meaning of the message.

Consider the following example of how the sender's message was interpreted differently by the receiver to the way it was intended by the sender.

Samuel C. Pulitzer, founder and CEO of Wembley, a necktie company, told a story in his book *Dreams Can Come True* about selling ties from town to town in the USA in the 1920s.

In one small town, he spent an hour carefully showing the owner every sample tie he had. At the end of the presentation, the owner said, "Sam, you have some nice stuff. But I make it a rule never to buy from a salesman on his first visit. So the next time you come in and see me, I will buy some ties".

Sam packed up his sample cases, loaded them into his Model A and took off down the street. He had a brainstorm and immediately circled back to the men's store and went inside.

"What are you doing back so soon?" asked the owner.

"Well, sir", said Sam, "you said the next time I came in you would buy ties from me. So here I am".

The owner bought ties from this innovative young salesman who had interpreted the owner's message to fit his own purposes.

In this chapter we will look at how senders encode their messages both verbally and non-verbally. We will also explore paralanguage, silence and empowerment.

Messages sent via a communication process are divided into two types: verbal and non-verbal. In a world increasingly complex, the division is rather simple. Verbal messages use words. Non-verbal messages do not.

Understanding Verbal Language

Let's look closely at verbal communication messages.

Verbal or written messages use words. These words take thoughts formed in the sender's mind and encode them into a message to be transmitted across space and time. However, there are numerous variables in the process.

Language is an arbitrary yet structured system of coding that, once agreed upon, allows members of the society using the specific language to understand one another. However, understanding the words does not mean understanding the message.

Word choice

Consider the difficulties of **word choice** for internationals working abroad. English-speaking natives may know what the "full monty" or "hotdesking"[i] means, but do most internationals? The Internet site of the BBC offers the latest English slang and tips to improve working English vocabularies (BBC, 2006). This site not only promotes programming but helps the BBC build a relationship with potential users of its Web and radio services.

Words mean more than their dictionary definitions. Searching for just the right word can be frustrating and time consuming, but effective communication without it is impossible. The same word may vary from culture to culture or geographic region to region. For example, the English word "dinner" means a midday meal in some parts of the Midwestern USA, whereas in other locations, such as Britain, it means the traditional evening meal.

> Semantics is the study of the meanings of words, phrases and texts. For example, in the sentence, "He ate some game", the meaning of the word "game" to include animals such as deer or rabbits can be clearly distinguished from "game" as something played, such as chess or checkers.
>
> Syntax, in contrast, deals with the arrangement of words in a language. For example, in English, adjectives are usually placed before a noun (the white house), whereas, in French, adjectives usually follow a noun (la maison blanche).

[i]You may associate the phrase "full monty" with a 1997 British film about a group of unemployed men who decide to take off their clothes to earn some money. But the BBC site says the phrase dates from the 1980s and may have originated from a clothing manufacturer called "Montague Burton". Today, the word has evolved into meaning "everything that you need" or "is appropriate" (BBC, 2006, p. 3).

The term "hotdesking" refers to the practice of sharing workspaces or desks among employees. The practice is common in operations with rotating shifts or in companies where employees work from home or on the road and so come to an office irregularly; thus, they have no need for a desk. The meaning, of course, implies that much energy flows from the desk (BBC, 2006, p. 18).

For more words consult http://www.bbc.co.uk/worldservice/learningenglish/

Strategic Thinking

Word choice in the international marketplace is sometimes a nightmare for advertising copywriters and translators. Urban myths abound about the selection of brand names that, when translated, have negative meanings or connotations. Pepsi's slogan "Come alive, you are in the Pepsi generation" was reportedly translated as "Come out of the grave" in German and "Pepsi will bring your ancestors back from the dead" in Taiwanese.

Enron, the international energy company, whose trading scandals made headlines in 2000, launched its famous E logo in the late 1980s to much fanfare. Branch officers and customers around the world received faxed copies of the new design. What Enron management failed to realize was that the yellow middle prong of the E completely disappeared in the faxing process. The resulting symbol became a rude gesture to many receivers in the international arena.

How can a brand maintain consistency when language and cultural differences often prevent a global approach to advertising? Most multinational companies use a two-tiered integrated approach to marketing communications. It is an adaptation of the "think globally, act locally" philosophy – the global headquarters of a brand determines the overall strategy for the campaign, and a country or regional organization implements the plan to fit local needs (Duncan, 2004).

We must evaluate our vocabulary choices carefully before we speak. The larger our repertoire of choices and the better our ability to choose the correct word, the more probable it is that we will send a message that is received as we intended.

What is paralanguage? Should I care about it?

Let us now explore **paralanguage elements** which include rate of speaking, silence, volume, pitch, stresses on words, accents, disfluencies and vocalizations. As humans we have many tools we can control and use to our advantage when trying to formulate an effective message.

Rate of speaking

Consider the **rate of speaking** – too slow or too fast can undermine an effective message.

Dig Deeper

If you are interested in the study of semantics and syntax, here are some names to investigate further:

- Leonard Bloomfield – early twentieth-century linguist influenced by behaviourism*
- Noam Chomsky – wrote *Syntactic Structures*, a book that revolutionized linguistics (Chomsky, 1957)
- Robert B. Lees – reviewed Chomsky's book and began serious study of semantics
- Yehoshua Bar-Hillel – suggested that logics play a part in language semantics
- Richard Montague – his complex study was interpreted by scholar Barbara Partee
- Donald Davidson – credited with "event" semantics
- Greg Carlson – uses his study to exhibit various levels of significant meaning
- Gilles Fauconnier – current expert and author of *Mappings in Thought and Language* (Fauconnier, 1997).

The human brain gets distracted easily. When listeners and readers become bored they shift their attention to other matters, because they feel they can listen to or read the message while taking care of other pressing mental matters. Often they miss the message. Did you ever attend a lecture when the speaker spoke so slowly that your mind began to wander?

Speaking too fast brings about the same result, a missed message, but for other reasons. Rather than being bored, the brain feels it has to work too hard to listen or read and so jumps to other more interesting and pleasurable topics to contemplate, such as menu choices for your evening meal.

Silence and pausing

At this point we also need to take a look at the roles silence and pausing play in transmitting an effective spoken message. As you cannot say more than one word at a time and each word follows the next, words, phrases and sentences have distinct beginning and ending points. The spaces between these words can also communicate.

Silence accomplishes two ends. Firstly, it can be interpreted as non-response. The interpretation of that non-response can be read in different ways: not interested; too busy; still thinking about it. Secondly, silence can be interpreted as "your turn to respond". This also has various decoded meanings: give me an answer; provide me more information; prompt a response from me.

Silence has cultural meaning as well. Native American Apaches have a strong sense as to when it is best to be silent or "to give up on words", as tribe members would say. Keith Basso spent 18 months living among tribe members and discovered that silence is used in various contexts as a communication tool (Basso, 1990). His study underscores how silence and the rules governing verbal and non-verbal behaviours vary according to culture. For example, the Western Apaches do not typically introduce those who are unknown to each other. It is assumed that they will introduce themselves when they feel it is the time to do so. "Outside help in the form of introduction or other verbal routines is viewed as presumptuous and unnecessary" (Basso, 1990, p. 308).

Pausing can be one of the most effective tools in our speaking arsenals. **Pausing** gives listeners the time to absorb what the speaker is saying and to internalize the message and make it their own. Read the next five lines as quickly as you can:

> The wild horses of Russia used to number in the thousands. They roamed the vast open steppes, uniquely connected to their homeland. Today there are fewer than a thousand of the animals and most of them are in zoos. Something must be done to save these horses because if we don't our children and our grandchildren will never have the opportunity to learn about these wonderful creatures.

What did you absorb? More importantly, what did you feel? How engaged were you in the topic? Was the message effective?

Now slow down and read the same lines again, mentally pausing (count one, two, then continue) where indicated:

> The wild horses of Russia used to number in the thousands. (pause) They roamed the vast open steppes, uniquely connected to their grassy homeland. (pause) Today there are fewer than a thousand of the animals (pause) and most of them are in zoos. (pause) Something must be done to save these horses (pause) because if we don't (pause) our children (pause) and our grandchildren (pause) will never have the opportunity to learn about these wonderful creatures.

Now, what did you feel? Did you get a more engaging message? Even those of you who don't have children felt the loss future generations would experience if the wild horses were not preserved. Now that's an effective message!

Volume, pitch, stressed words and accents

Volume is how loudly or softly you speak. One problem with delivering an effective message is speaking loudly enough. Some people are embarrassed to ask for a message to be repeated. This is especially true if the message comes from a superior. Others won't admit they have not heard a message if they are in a group with peers who seem to have heard it.

Pitch has to do with the high or low tonal qualities of your voice. High-pitched, squeaky voices are generally read as weak and unimportant. Very low voices can be read as slow and dim-witted. You can change the pitch of your voice by working to raise or lower the vocal tone. Variations in pitch keep listeners interested and engaged.

Disfluencies are the "not fluent" words or sounds that we intersperse in informal conversations, such as "ah", "um", "like", "you know", "well" and "okay". They make a speaker seem natural and spontaneous when used in moderation. However, in the business world, using too many disfluencies makes the speaker appear unprepared and unprofessional (Bortfeld *et al.*, 2005).

Vocalizations

Vocalizations occur when we imitate a sound or laugh, moan, cry, etc. They can be useful when we want to add drama or understanding to a message. For example, a car mechanic might ask you to imitate the strange noise that you hear when you start your car.

Strategic Thinking

In today's workplace, voice = empowerment. You need to develop verbal skill strategies that allow your voice to be heard at appropriate times by the right people. Review the tools covered in this section and evaluate your own strengths and weaknesses. Work to eliminate any disfluencies in your speech patterns. You want to appear businesslike, knowledgeable and in control. What can you do to improve your ability to send effective messages?

Strategic Thinking

Here is a little *unscientific* test for you. First assess your own paralanguage skills, and then have a classmate evaluate these same skills. You may be surprised at how much difference there is in the two evaluations.

On a scale of 1–5, with 1 being low and 5 being high, rate your level of competency in using the following:

Paralanguage element	Your score	Classmate score
1. Varying your rate of speaking	( )	( )
2. Use of silence and pausing	( )	( )
3. Using volume for emphasis	( )	( )
4. Varying pitch from high to low	( )	( )
5. Eliminating disfluencies	( )	( )
6. Using vocalizations for interest	( )	( )

Non-verbal Communication is Complex and Ever Changing

Non-verbal communication is often taken for granted because it is second nature to us. We learned how to smile, frown, shake our head or point a finger well before we studied verbal language in a formal school setting.

But which is the more powerful? Verbal or non-verbal language?

A research study by Michel Argyle and Florisse Alkema of Oxford University and Robin Gilmour of Glasgow University suggests that non-verbal language is more than 10 times stronger than the verbal language accompanying the message (Argyle, Alkema & Gilmour, 1993). And, they said, "When verbal and non-verbal signals were inconsistent, the performance was rated as insincere, unstable and confusing" (Argyle, Alkema & Gilmour, 1993, p. 387). In other words, we believe non-verbal behaviour over verbal language.

Here's a quick example. You see a friend who is dragging her heels, shoulders slumped, face drawn. You ask, "What's the matter?" She replies, "Nothing." What do you believe? You know something is wrong, her body language told you so.

Non-verbal communication includes facial expressions, eye contact, tone of voice, body posture and motions and hand gestures. It also may include physiological elements such as blushing, twitching, shaking, stuttering, etc.

Two problems with non-verbal language for you as a business executive are:

• Non-verbal language is difficult to interpret.
• Non-verbal language has to be consistent with the verbal message.

Firstly, let's examine the problem of interpretation. Non-verbal language may have many meanings and, although we may feel we interpreted the behaviour correctly, that may not be the case. If you see someone yawn during your presentation, is that person tired or bored? Is she drowsy owing to medication? Add individual and cultural interpretations to this mix and the difficulty in reading non-verbal language is apparent.

Non-verbal messages are not always consistent with verbal messages. When faced with inconsistency, listeners rely on their reading of a speaker's non-verbals first and may, consequently, misinterpret the content. A study by Harald G. Wallbott at the University of Salzburg suggests that "posed" emotions are seen as less powerful than truly expressed emotions (Wallbott, 1998, p. 883). Listeners can sense insincerity through nonverbal body language and this insight can obscure verbal messages.

Body language

Non-verbal language, body language, tells as much about speakers as the words they choose to use. For example, a group of students told one of the writers of this book that they always knew what points in a lecture they should remember by the way she batted her eyelids.

Speaker credibility will be enhanced by learning how to use body language to communicate confidence to listeners. Posture, rate of delivery, eye contact and use of language indicate to the audience that a speaker believes in his/her message (Beall, 2004).

Motivational speakers are used in corporate meetings to rally employees to action. These master communicators use body language, hand gestures and pauses, along with verbal skills, to connote their expertise and credibility. Invariably they know little about the company's product or services, but their dynamic and inspiring non-verbal presentation, coupled with their choice of words, makes them persuasive speakers.

In the global marketplace, effective, culture-sensitive non-verbal communication is essential. *CNN Money* says, "In the high stakes world of international business ... the most innocuous of gestures – when misinterpreted – can wreak havoc on business negotiations" (Helenius, 2000). The surest way to end negotiations in Bangladesh or Nigeria is to give the "thumbs-up" hand gesture. While most of the world sees this as a friendly "all is set" sign, some countries view this signal as a "you're full of nonsense" message. Hilka Klionkenberg, international protocol consultant, advises keeping choppy and frequent gestures at a minimum when dealing with Asian nations. This is seen as "idle chatter" in a non-verbal format (Helenius, 2000). Ignorance of another culture is not a sufficient excuse for using inappropriate gestures in our information-rich world.

For example, a businessman visiting Tokyo was invited to attend a cocktail party at the home of the chairman of the board of a company to which his organization was trying to sell additional products. It was the organization's largest account in Asia. The businessman showed up for the evening in a lightweight summer suit, open-collared shirt and loafers. Everyone else in the room was dressed in dark suits, dress shoes and ties. The damaging effect of this insensitivity to Japanese formal business culture affected the relations of the two companies. The executive was reassigned. Simple research into the appropriate attire for an evening business meeting would have avoided such a cultural blunder.

The issue of touching – who, where, when and why – possibly causes more anxiety in overseas business than any other non-verbal issue. Sheida Hodge, author of *Global Smarts: The Art of Communicating and Deal Making Anywhere in the World*, notes that generally people in Southern Europe and the Middle East are more physical than North Americans (Hodge, 2000). In Muslim countries, social contact between the sexes never takes place (Garfinkel, 2004).

Persuasion as a Communication Tool

Persuasion theory originated in Greece with Aristotle, called the "father of persuasion". He put forth his rhetorical ideas based on the elements of ethos (the speaker), pathos (emotion) and logos (logic). He saw the speaker's charisma, credibility, expertise and skill as the most powerful element in persuading an audience. Even with distorted or non-existent information and few emotional ploys, speakers were able to win their audiences over to their side. A speaker's effectiveness was inexorably tied to his verbal and non-verbal skills.

> What are the social rules for riding elevators? Try this experiment. Next time you are on an elevator, turn and face the back. Observe how the people in the elevator respond to you. What does their body language tell you about their comfort zone? Write down the meanings you assigned to their behaviour and report them to the class.

Aside from a speaker's ethos, rational arguments (logos) and emotional appeals (pathos) are effective elements in **persuasion**. Some people are swayed more by reason, others by emotions. There are many persuasion theorists researching this subject today. But persuasion theory also plays a practical function in today's business setting. Advertisers use persuasion to sell products. Innovators and opinion leaders rely on persuasive powers to influence followers. Politicians frame their stand on popular issues to persuade voters to support them.

Executives must work to exude confidence, leadership and credibility when they speak, whether to one person in a face-to-face situation or to a large conference group. How the receiver decodes a message depends on how it is encoded, not just in words but in body language and style. Getting others to accept your ideas will depend on your powers of persuasion.

Physiological barriers do not have to prevent individuals from becoming persuasive speakers. US President Franklin Delano Roosevelt was stricken with polio, but being restricted to a wheelchair did not prevent him from becoming a powerful world leader. Steven Hawking, world-renowned scientist and author of *A Brief History in Time*, among other books, can neither speak nor walk, but he addresses mass audiences through computer-aided speech technology.

An executive from one of the largest US retail chains motivates and inspires more than 6 000 employees who respect his judgement and knowledge in spite of a noticeable speech impediment.

Choosing emotions, logic or both as the basis of an argument is fundamental, but what the receiver thinks of you and your ideas can mean the difference between being perceived as simply adequate or as a powerful executive.

Dig Deeper

Persuasion theory is the study of the various ways to get attention, motivate to action and influence feelings and attitudes.

Here are some of the concepts used today to persuade others. You can begin your study of the following theories with *Mass Communication Theory: Foundations, Ferment, and Future* (Baran & Davis, 2000):

- agenda-setting theory
- assimilation theory
- cognitive dissonance
- impression management theory
- one-sided messaging
- opinion leader theory
- personalities theory
- reference group theory
- reinforcement theory
- selective perception
- social impact theory
- source credibility
- subliminal persuasion
- uses and gratification theory.

Using persuasive tactics to reach your audience

When you begin to formulate your message, consider incorporating listener relevance and speaker credibility components into your planning process.

The "listener relevance" component is the WIIFM factor – What's in it for me? Because we have more things to do than time to do them in, we have to choose what we take in and what we shut out. It's a matter of, "If I find no relevance in a particular topic or subject matter, I have lots of other things I can think about".

So, if you are talking about the safety features of your company's baby prams to a group of men and women of all ages, how do you provide listener relevance? What if you said: "I know some of you may not have small children, but do you have grandchildren? Or are you looking to buy a gift for a niece or nephew? Or perhaps you have often watched new mothers in your neighbourhood push prams past your house, never thinking the little ones might be in danger because of the lack of safety features".

You have just made your message about baby prams relevant to more of your audience members. It is incumbent upon the speaker to make the audience understand what is relevant to them. Point it out! Don't assume they will get the connection.

Speaker credibility is a second component that can influence your audience. Where listener relevance is "Why should I listen?", speaker credibility is "Why should I listen to you?".

In business you will be expected to make group presentations. Let's say you are presenting a problem–cause–solution case to management on what to do about excessive product damages. Instead of "This is Mary, that's Steve and I'm Joseph. We're going to talk to you about …", try this: "This is Mary. She works in product design and has been studying the problem of product damages for the past six months. This is Steve from the training department; he has surveyed some of our employees to see what they think about product damages. And I'm Joseph; I have spent 16 years in the field selling to our customers and now head up the task force that has been looking into some of the problems of product control".

Using speaker credibility allows your audience to make a connection with the group members. They not only can relate a name to a face, but they now know something about that person. By the time Mary or Steve get up to speak, the audience will feel they already know them and feel vested in what they have to say. Your inclusion of a credibility factor frames group members as experts.

Speaker credibility and listener relevance are two persuasive tools that can help you to send an effective message.

Figure 2.1   Four cultural non-verbal symbols. The thumb touching the forefinger sign means okay to Americans but is an obscene gesture in other countries. Snakes are viewed as sneaky in some cultures but represent rebirth in others. Baring one's teeth is associated with anger or rudeness. Flags are revered in some countries and not usable in commercial advertising.

Language in the Global Setting

In a global marketplace messages have a greater probability of being distorted. You should evaluate all messages before they are sent. Here's some information you need to know.

Words both denote and connote information

Denotation is the standard definition of a word. Denotative meanings are usually easily understood. If you don't know what a word means, you look it up in a dictionary.

But does this ensure that you will understand a specific word and what it means?

No. The meaning of the word depends largely on the **connotation** and the subjective meaning within and surrounding a word. It is dependent not only on who uses the word but also on who interprets the word as well as such factors as culture, background, educational level and the occasion.

The request "I'd like the report ASAP (as soon as possible)" can be understood in many different ways. Each word can be looked up in a dictionary for its definition, but that doesn't mean the report will be on your desk in an hour, by the end of the day, tomorrow morning or next week. Likewise, it doesn't mean the report will be detailed enough or in the format you want, or that the "like" is interpreted as a request or a demand by your employee.

Strategic Thinking

The concept "clarity of instruction" means the ability to communicate your wants, needs, desires, ideas and directives in both speech and the written word and have receivers interpret the same meaning as you intended when you sent the message. This ability clearly to convey your directives fosters an atmosphere of trust and security for your team. It gives them confidence they are working at maximum efficiency. The term "a well-oiled machine" refers to organizations led by effective communicators.

Share with the class an example of when you completed an assignment or task that was not acceptable because of your misunderstanding of the professor or supervisor's instruction. How did this affect your trust level of your understanding of future assignments?

When you begin to formulate your message, think about the connotation behind the words. As the head of a department, you think everyone under your leadership agrees on the meanings of certain terms. You may assume when you talk to your employees about dedication to the company and working hard to protect its brand image that they are getting your message. They know what dedication means and they can look up brand image. But what do you mean by dedication to the company and what does your average employee understand about protecting brand image?

Strategic Thinking

Look at the language of a Greenpeace UK press release: "At 5:15 am today in a peaceful direct action, a Greenpeace decontamination unit removed genetically modified pollution from the third farm-scale experiment to be disrupted in the UK over the last eight weeks".

The *National Post* conservative Canadian newspaper asks: would the release have connoted a different idea if "trespassing on private land and ripping up crops" had replaced "peaceful direct action", or if the word "destroying" had been used instead of "removed" or if the phrase "the science of transgenics" had replaced "genetically modified pollution" (Fumento, 1999)?

The language used to convey a message is important to the effectiveness of the communication. Word choice is one of the tools we use to "frame" our messages in order to persuade others to agree with our way of thinking. What words would you use to tell the story of the Greenpeace action?

Using concrete words

Using concrete words will help clarify meaning. **Concrete words** refer to tangible objects such as a table, a car or a computer program, and are usually understood. However, you can be even clearer by using more specific words such as lunchroom tables, Toyota and Microsoft Word.

As an example of how being concrete and specific can lead to a clearer message, let's look at the following example:

The dog bit the man.

What dog did you see in your mind? Come on, you did see a dog. We see words in images. It might not have been a distinct type of dog, but you didn't see a blob. You saw something and we bet it had four legs, a tail and a head. So some of you saw a Pit Bull, others saw a Doberman Pincher or a German Shepherd. Did you feel any sympathy for the man?

Well, we didn't send a very effective message because the dog we were talking about was a little, fluffy, white, miniature poodle. Oh, now you see what we wanted you to see.

So we send the message again:

The little, fluffy, white toy poodle named Fifi bit the man.

How about the man? What type of man do you see? A big strapping man? A man tormenting poor little Fifi? And has your sympathy switched from the man to poor, little, innocent Fifi? Well, once again we have not been very clear in our message. The man we wanted you to see was a man in a wheelchair. Do you see him now? And have we turned your sympathy back to the man at whom Fifi was yapping so hard that he could hardly move his chair along the street?

Sending complex messages to people who know little about the topic we are discussing or who are in different environments requires spending time to perfect our messaging skills.

Using abstract words

Abstract words, the opposite of concrete words, pertain to ideas and concepts. They are harder to comprehend and usually require more explanation. These are words like truth, honesty and love. Certainly, ideas surrounding love differ considerably, and, if you asked 20 people to define love, you would get 20 variations. As an effective communicator, you must ensure that the idea you encode is, in fact, the message receivers decode.

Let's go back to the message you sent your employees about commitment to the brand image. What exactly do you mean by commitment? Commitment is an abstract word that has various meanings. You will have to explain your intended meaning by using analogies and employing specific language before you and your receiver can agree on the basics of what you are trying to say.

Metaphors and idioms also fall into this category of ambiguous language.

Metaphors

Metaphors are shortcuts to understanding and compare a complex subject to a simpler image. For example, an employer who wants her employees to stay with her during the bad times the company is experiencing may gather her executive team together and say, "Right now our company is like a ship on rough seas. We've been thrown about a little, but there are blue skies and smooth sailing ahead". Comparing the company to a ship in bad weather creates a palpable image that others can easily picture and understand.

Idioms

Idioms are sayings that mean more than the actual words. For example, to most people in the USA over 50 years old, the meaning of the idiom "She is the apple of her father's eye" is clear. To others, whether outside the country or in a younger demographic, even looking up the individual words in a dictionary will not yield the culturally agreed upon meaning of the statement. The meaning is dependent on the saying as a whole and what the words together convey. (The idiom means the father would do anything for his daughter.)

Jargon

The technical language of a specific industry is called **jargon**. If you are talking to or writing a message to someone who is not in the industry, you should steer away from jargon. If you have to use it, define and explain the terms you use. If you are communicating to people within the industry, your credibility and expertise can be enhanced by your skillful use of jargon.

Slang

Informal language used by and understood by a specific group, **slang** is really too informal to use in business communication. Of course, if you are speaking to teenagers, your use of slang might provide credibility in their eyes.

Euphemisms

Euphemisms are inoffensive words used in place of more unpleasant words. We use them all the time. We say "passed away" instead of "died." We might say "sales consultant" instead of "salesman" which, besides being sexist, is a term that may connote some negativity.

Notice how euphemisms may portray a negative word in a positive manner:

Negative word	Euphemism
Used car	Pre-owned vehicle
Pollution	Run-off
Overweight	Big-boned
Wild two year old	Hyperactive
Sweating	Glowing
Blind	Visually impaired
Toilet	Ladies' cloakroom
Crippled	Handicapped
Old	Mature
Poor	Low income
Vomiting	Yodelling on the lawn

Barriers to direct and ethical language

Choice of language and use of facts and statistics can act as **barriers** to understanding. As senders, you are responsible for making wise choices in accommodating the needs and expectations of your receivers.

Relative words

Don't assume your listener or reader will understand a vague or **relative word**. Take, for example, the word "tall". "Tall" to a small man or woman would not be the same as "tall" to a 6'6" professional basketball player. Other relative words include rich, small, few, many and soon.

Biased language

It will take a conscious effort on your part to view your communication from your receiver's perspective. We are often unaware of our own bias, usually deep rooted and existing well below our conscious level. Much of our bias was formed when we were young and persists because we surround ourselves with those who are like us. However, it is incumbent upon the speaker or writer to adapt to audience needs and concerns, not the other way around. Most of us do not want to offend any co-worker, superior or supervisee. **Biased language** occurs because it is easy and familiar, and we often justify our use of it with "I didn't know". Reading popular magazines, trade journals or worldwide newspapers and listening to news reports from other cultures and countries opens our eyes to proper, acceptable and inoffensive language. Pay attention. Look over your message from your receiver's point of view. It could make a difference in the audience's perception of your credibility.

Misleading facts and statistics

Facts can be slanted, skewed, omitted, restated and interpreted to suit your purposes. Unethical accounting reporting practices, such as those used at Enron/Anderson, ultimately bankrupted dozens of global companies and affected the lives of employees, stockholders and local communities, as well as world markets. Ethical use of **facts and statistics** builds a track record for your viability and believability.

Inaccurate statistical reporting or bias is a favourite topic on blogs and the Internet. Sites reporting unethical practices are often equally guilty of misusing information. Consider these criteria in citing secondary research, or developing in-house reports – sample size, methodology for gathering data, unit of analysis, statistical confidence level, industry standards and practices and the context of the research study. Here are some examples of faulty research practices:

- A magazine published an article that rank-ordered the number of bags lost per airline. The numbers were accurate but failed to take into account the number of passengers on each of the airlines involved. A comparison of baggage lost per number of customers would have been a more accurate statistic.
- An employee survey regarding a proposed dress code for nurses sampled only nursing supervisors on two shifts. The survey failed to take into account non-supervisory staff and those on the third shift – individuals who often feel as though they are overlooked

in the decision-making process. Hospital officials took the results of the survey and proposed a new uniform policy. Staff nurses organized a unionization effort because they felt left out of the decision-making process.

- A follow-up study on the number of women entering the national ranks of chief executive officers failed to sample the same population as used in the first study. Sampling techniques were flawed and reported an inaccurate picture of the true labour profile. Had women made progress? It was not possible to tell from the survey results.

Misrepresenting facts damage credibility with those you most want to influence. The best way to persuade someone is to establish irrefutable credibility. Then, when a legitimate mistake is made, it will not reflect negatively on your character.

Knowledge of survey research methods and statistical practices is a core skill for anyone entering the employment market. On the global stage all errors are magnified.

Chapter Summary

The sender is a complex element in the communication model. Through both verbal and non-verbal messages, the sender transmits clues as to the message he or she is trying to communicate. Senders must be aware that these cues provide a subcontext to their message. Receivers will interpret and apply this information to the meaning they give the message.

Understanding messages requires knowing not only how words affect interpretation but also how the delivery of those words impact upon meaning. The use of jargon, abstract words, slang, biased speech and relative words may confuse the message. Likewise, paralanguage, including the pace of delivery, volume, voice quality and disfluencies, also shapes the interpretation the receiver gives a message.

The union set of a sender's and receiver's understanding and agreement of the message, as illustrated in the transactional communication model, may be severely compromised by verbal and non-verbal language that is easily misinterpreted, misunderstood or offensive to the parties involved.

Since the Golden Age of the Greeks, the rhetoric of persuasion has been debated and studied. The ability to persuade an audience to accept your point of view, use your service or purchase your product is connected to your ability to formulate an effective message that incorporates listener relevance and speaker credibility components into the message.

In the global setting, you will need to be even more conscious of connotative and denotative meaning of the words you choose to use. Effective messages often require the use of concrete words and bias-free language.

Remember that the sender, as the originator of the message, has the power to determine, in part, how that message is received. You can take advantage of that power by thinking critically and analytically about message content, language and delivery. ■

Learning From Others

Katherine van Wormer is professor of Social Work at the University of Northern Iowa. She has studied and taught in the USA and Northern Ireland and is the author of 11 books, including *Social Welfare: A World View* (1997) and *Confronting Oppression, Restoring Justice: From Policy Analysis to Social Action* (2004). She has co-authored a new book, *Human Behaviour and the Social Environment Macro Level: Groups, Communities, and Organizations* (2006).

Van Wormer studies human behaviour around the world and its complex layers of understanding and interaction. She shares some of her views with us in the following essay.

How Cultural Values Affect Communication

Values go deeper than manners or mannerisms and may boost or impede the business process. Comparative studies are in general agreement that one of the primary US values is work. Through one's occupation or profession, an individual gains status and a sense of self-importance.

This notion of the work ethic encompasses the traits that the typical employer desires: punctuality, efficiency and productivity. Workers deficient in these qualities will be eliminated.

According to international economic sources, Americans average just under 2000 hours of work per employed person annually to just over 1500 in Germany. The work weeks in the United States are longer and vacations are considerably shorter. The explanation is often that large pay disparities in the United States lure workers to work harder for a chance of advancement. My argument is that the very value system encouraging the wage differentials and rewards for the long hours are part of the cultural pattern.

Before I visited Korea, I generally agreed that the American work ethic was the strongest in the world. Then I learned of a land so competitive that children rarely play and are tutored during most waking hours until their education culminates in rigorous university entrance exams.

Consistent with the Korean work focus is that of Japan. An English teacher (Butler, 2003) from Texas who lives in Yamogota, Japan, observes: "It's fair to say that Japanese people are unbelievably busy. Working ten hours a day, and often coming in on days off, they rarely take a vacation of more than three or four days. A straight week is a hedonistic luxury. Students have less than a month for summer vacation, and even then they have all kinds of assignments to do" (Butler, 2003, p. 65).

Norwegians are also an industrious people, but much of their work is done off hours – building cabins in the woods, training and grooming dogs and washing windows. Many jobs are only six hours per day; little work is done at Easter, Christmas and in July. The right to leisure is fiercely guarded. As a supervisor of a counselling staff, I had to justify my expectations accordingly.

The non-collectivist cultures of the UK, USA and Germany are task oriented and have no problem jumping into business discussions with people with whom no relationship has been established; it's considered insulting in most other parts of the world, such as in Latin America and the Far East, to begin negotiations before socializing and first establishing trust (Brandel, 2006).

The first prerequisite for engaging in business abroad, therefore, is not to memorize the nation's rules of etiquette, or practise phrases in the nation's language, but critically to examine the uniqueness of the culture.

In this age of globalization, one of the biggest enemies of multicultural communication and team-building is denial of the reality of cultural difference and lack of awareness of one's own cultural uniqueness within the broader context.

Case Study – **Greenpeace**

Greenpeace is a multinational organization with offices in 24 countries. Its aim is to draw worldwide attention to environmental causes through non-violence, research efforts and political lobbying. The Greenpeace website says the organization "depends upon the rapid transmission of information and images across the world". Greenpeace relies on the "many to many" model of communication, "massive numbers of people broadcasting to massive numbers of people". Greenpeace engages in interactive communication which makes its readers and listeners actively involved in world events rather than passive participants.

Greenpeace started its website, www.greenpeace.org in 1994 and today it averages 150 000 hits per week (Greenpeace, 2006).

The first campaign designed specifically for the Internet was the Climate Campaign of 1995, launched just prior to the Climate Summit in Berlin. It contained press releases, in-depth reports, an interactive quiz for viewers and a click-through button to send a fax to officials for those concerned visitors to the site who wanted to take some action.

Here's another example of Greenpeace communication from its website: According to its website, "We put on the site pleas for people to fax President Chirac to urge him to end nuclear testing in French Polynesia. Within 24 hours the fax lines to Chirac's office were totally jammed and he's had to change the telephone number – we received a leaked memo which was from the President's office addressed to French Telecomm which gave the reason for the need for new numbers as 'electronic pollution from Greenpeace'".

Do some more research and see why Greenpeace is so successful in communicating with its supporters. What specific words does it use to encourage action? Does it rely on abstract or concrete words and images? What tools of persuasion does it employ? How does it communicate effectively with globally diverse supporters? What does the *Rainbow Warrior* and the tag line "you can't sink a rainbow" say about the organization? ■

Class Exercises

1. Read the front page of a major newspaper and a front page of a small, local newspaper. Look for examples of ineffective word choice such as sexist language or evidence of biases. Try to locate at least 5–6 instances where the words chosen reflect poor decision-making on the part of the reporter. In groups, share your newspaper findings and discuss their results. Are some people offended by certain words while others are not? Why? Should the feelings of other people determine the words a speaker chooses to use? What if the speaker thinks the receiver is too sensitive and should not be offended by the language?

2. Each student selects one of the "persuasive" theories listed in the chapter and finds a journal article discussing the concept. Find out who was the first theorist to come up with the idea, as well as who is studying that concept today. Illustrate how this type of persuasion could be used to sell a product in the global marketplace. Try to adapt the theory first to a generic product such like "apples", then see how the theory could also be applied to promoting a niche product like "ski vests". (You can also make up your own products.)

3. What euphemisms might you use in the following messages?

She died.	Her haircut is terrible.
He's fat.	My brother can't seem to keep a job.
He's a janitor.	She's a housewife.
My daughter is wild.	He's ugly.

Action Plan

You have been appointed the chairperson for a company-wide drive to raise money for Children's House, a local orphanage. Your CEO is a member of this agency's board of directors. The drive to raise funds has been successful in the past. Your task is to write a letter to colleagues within the company, asking them to support the charity with a monetary contribution. What type of facts and figures would you need to support a rational approach? What emotional appeals would be appropriate? What tone of voice (serious, humorous, demanding, dutiful, etc.) would you use?

Websites

See how South Korea makes it easier for foreigners to access information at `http://www.seoulsearching.com/assistance/` (Seoul Searching, 2006) and `http://www.kois.go.kr/news/news/newsView.asp?` serial_no = 20051030006&part = 109&SearchDay = (Korea.net, 2005).

This site is designed to help US business people identify best practices in international trade relations. Read about "the ugly Americans" in World Resources for Teens: `www.businessfordiplomaticaction.org` (Business for Diplomatic Action, 2006).

References

Abbott, B. (1999) "The formal approach to meaning: formal semantics and its recent developments". *Journal of Foreign Languages*, **119**:1: 2–20.

Argyle, M., Alkema, F. & Gilmour, R. (1993) "The communication of friendly and hostile attitudes by verbal and non-verbal signals". *European Journal of Social Psychology* 1(3), pp 385-402. Reprinted in: *Experiments in Social Interaction*. Aldershot, England: Ashgate Publishing, LTD.

Baran, S. & Davis, D. (2000) *Mass Communication Theory: Foundations, Ferment, and Future*, 2nd edn. New York, Longman.

Basso, K. (1990) "'To give up on words': silence and Western Apache culture". In *Cultural Communication and Intercultural Contact*. Carbaugh, D., ed. Hillsdale, NY, Lawrence Erlbaum Associates: 303–320.

BBC (2006) "Learning English". Available from: http://www.bbc.co.uk/worldservice/learningenglish/radio/specials/1728_uptodate//page3.shtml [Accessed 8 June 2006].

Beall, A. (2004) "Body language speaks". *Communication World*, **21**(2): 18–20.

Bortfeld, H., Leon S., Bloom, J. *et al.* (2001) "Disfluency rates in conversation: effects of age, relationship, topic, role, and gender". *Language and Speech*, **44**(2): 123–147.

Brandel, M. (2006) "Culture clash: closing gaps between different worlds is crucial to building team trust". *Computerworld*, **40**(8), 26–30.

Business for Diplomatic Action (2006) Available from: www.businessfordiplomaticaction.org [Accessed 16 May 2006].

Butler, L. (2003) "Living on Tokyo time". *Utne Reader*, **65**(January/February).

Chomsky, N. (1957) *Syntactic Structures*. Berlin, Mouton de Gruyter.

Duncan, T. (2004) *Principles of Advertising & IMC*. New York, McGraw-Hill.

Fauconnier, G. (1997) *Mappings in Thought and Language*. Cambridge, Cambridge University Press.

Fumento, M. (1999) "Biotech crop-busting comes to Canada". *National Post,* 27 December 1999. Available from: http://64.233.187.104/search?q=cache:DsBB1MYgAvsJ:www.fumento.com/cancropbusters.html+Fument [Accessed 3 December 2005].

Garfinkel, P. (2004) "On keeping your foot safely out of your mouth". *The New York Times*, 13 July 2004: C8. Available from: Custom Newspapers: Thomson Gale document A119211131 [Accessed 8 June 2006].

Greenpeace.org (2006) Available from: www.greenpeace.org [Accessed 26 June 2006].

Helenius, T. (2000) "Body language savvy". *CNN Money*, 3 May 2000. Available from: www.money.cnn. com/2000/05/03/career/q_body_language [Accessed 16 September 2005].

Hodge, S. (2000) *Global Smarts: The Art of Communicating and Deal Making Anywhere in the World.* New York, John Wiley & Sons, Inc.

Korea.net (2005) "Seoul City to open French, Spanish web site", 31 October 2005. Available from: http://www.kois. go.kr/news/news/newsView.asp?serial_no = 20051030006&part = 109&SearchDay = [Accessed 28 June 2006].

Seoul Searching (2006) Seoul Help Centre for Foreigners. Available from: http://www.seoulsearching.com/assistance/ [Accessed 28 June 2006].

Twain, M. (1888) Letter to George Bainton. *Directory of Mark Twain's Maxims, Quotations, and Various Opinions.* Available from: www.twainquotes.com/Lightning.html [Accessed 18 November 2005].

Wallbott, H. (1998) "Bodily expression of emotion". *European Journal of Social Psychology*, **28**: 879–896.

Bibliography

Beebe, S. & Beebe, S. (2005) *Public Speaking Handbook.* New York, Allyn and Bacon.

Lucas, S. (2001) *The Art of Public Speaking*, 7th edn. New York, McGraw-Hill.

CHAPTER 3

Knowing the Receivers of Your Messages

Executive Summary

Attempting to determine the characteristics of the receivers (decoders) of your messages is crucial in the global marketplace where barriers to effective communication loom in inconspicuous places.

Verbal language differences are one obstacle to communication barriers
Cultural non-verbal language, diversity in needs and wants, individual values, beliefs and behaviours, cultural norms and corporate and personal agendas also must be considered.

Stakeholders have an interest in your message and include consumers, employees, shareholders, competitors and potential customers with their own special sets of wants and needs
To be audience-centred you must critically analyse the receivers of your business communications.

The more information you collect, the better prepared you will be to create an effective message
Information-gathering tools include interviewing, focus groups, ethnography and researching secondary sources.

By applying Maslow's hierarchy of needs, profiling techniques and narrowcasting, you can formulate messages that will be understood by receivers in the way you intend
It is important to remember that some audiences are voluntary while others are captive. Some may be eager to hear your message, while others are resistant.

Receivers of business messages make up culturally rich and diverse market segments
If you want your messages to be effective, you must know your audience. ■

Knowing the Receivers of Your Messages

> " *The "global village" might be a reality soon, but it will not be a homogenous entity. It will be diverse and profoundly individual, both within an organization and with stakeholders outside the company.*
>
> *Anonymous* "

Introduction to Understanding Receivers

In our communication model, we refer to "**receivers**" as "decoders". Who are decoders? What do they think and why?

Successful communication takes place when a sender's message is decoded in the way the sender intended. A message may be sent, but if it is not the "right" message, or the message the sender wanted to get across, then it is not "effective communication".

Let's take the case of a retail store that sells hiking equipment and is ready to send out its first direct mail catalogue. There are so many decisions to be made even before the catalogue is created. Where will the store get the names and addresses of potential customers? Does it have a database of present customers to use? Will the store buy a list, from whom and of what target audience? Will it be targeted at consumers in close proximity to the retail stores or will the objective be to get new customers from across the country?

In creating the catalogue, what colours will be used to depict the store's products? What tone and language will the catalogue use? How can the store make a consumer want to open the catalogue and buy a product? How can ordering be made easy?

But consideration of the customers receiving the catalogue does not stop here. How about customer service, product guarantees and ease of returning merchandise? Above all, how does the store build a long-term relationship with every new customer that will lead to brand recognition, continued loyalty and more sales?

In global communications, the accurate decoding of a message is a vital element that requires study and thought. The originator of a message must do everything possible to ensure the message is received as intended.

Also, remember that there is a relatively small area in our communication model where the sender's world overlaps the receiver's world. This union set is where effective messaging will take place in our model, and the union set becomes smaller as we go beyond our own country and cultural borders.

For global businesses to operate successfully, it is imperative that communication be integrated not only throughout the corporate culture of the business but also through any and all communications with those outside the home country and culture. The cultures touched by your business both internally (a diverse workforce, culturally and ethnically) and externally (multicultural suppliers, international customers) should be a major concern of every executive at every level of the organization.

The way a receiver decodes a message is influenced by his or her communication style and culture. Communication problems do not necessarily stem from cultural insensitivity but rather from a lack of awareness of the cultural environment of senders and receivers.

Culture is an invisible field in which we live, work and play. We often do not think about why we act in a certain way or behave in a certain manner, and the same can be said for the receivers of messages. Culture exists so deeply within everyone's every day experiences and knowledge that it becomes invisible.

Looking at a Global Audience

An audience-centred approach helps communicators frame messages to meet the needs of targeted receivers. To be audience centred you have to be able to look beyond your own biases and see the world from a different perspective. In a global perspective of integrated communication, organizations and individuals need to be aware of their own **ethnocentricity**, the opinion that one's own world is superior to that of another's.

Globalization and localization

There is a consensus that multinational companies should follow the advice: "think **globally** and act **locally**". In other words, they should have a global vision but communicate that vision from a local perspective. The "global village" might be a reality soon, but it will not be a homogenous entity. It will be diverse and profoundly individual, both within an organization and when dealing with stakeholders outside the company. Let's look at how these two concepts play out on the international stage.

Strategic Thinking

USA Today published an interview with David Novak, CEO of Yum Brands which owns KFC, Pizza Hut, Taco Bell, A&W and Long John Silver's. When asked about doing business in China, where the company opened its 1 500th KFC franchise in Shanghai in 2005, Novak admits having a "visible brand" helps with consumer recognition and acceptance in this market, the key strategy for success being that "we have Chinese people running our business".

Novak believes in acting locally. He said, "Any company that wants to do business with another country is always better off with people from that country". When it comes to direct management communication, Novak applauds the Chinese team led by Sam Su, soon to be inducted into the Yum Hall of Fame. Novak said, "Last year, I made the decision that China was so self-sufficient that Su should report directly to me".

In a *Newsday* interview, Su said, "In many parts of China, the local municipal governments actually view the arrival of a KFC as a sign of the city coming of age" (Jones, 2005).

What does this case say about both globalization and localization when it comes to marketing brands?

Diversity and individualism in the workplace

Communicating effectively with your workforce is a necessity. Tommy Kennedy-Bartshulkoff, formerly of Volvo and co-owner of the European branch of Praendex, the Swiss business management workshop and seminar company, employs a predictive index (PI) that uses verbal one-to-one feedback to match the person with the job and "foster better communication and management within a multicultural workforce" (Van der Boon, 2005).

Acknowledging that everyone is unique, whether in learning, management style, or conflict resolution and negotiation skills, is a first step. It gets more complicated, of course, but researching and preparing for differences in your employees is the first important step.

Diversity and individualism in stakeholders outside the workplace

Certainly, in the global marketplace you will deal with many diverse people, from suppliers and shareholders to concerned citizens and government bodies. Don't get caught assuming that everyone does business in the same way. The motivation to succeed and personal agenda priorities are not the same across the globe.

Mary van der Boon, intercultural trainer, says, "Multicultural teams need extensive training on the principles of intercultural adjustment and management" (Parfitt, 2005).

Because of the concern for, and the awareness of, the difficulties in accurately communicating on a global stage, an entirely new industry has been born to prepare business executives to operate successfully in the new world marketplace.

Van der Boon has outlined the 15 states of the European Union (EU) according to values, sense of humour, hierarchy and business communication, among other characteristics. She points out that there are no set "European values" or "European culture". Like the rest of the world, each EU country is culturally diverse and individual.

For example, she cites Austrian values as hospitality, nostalgia, cleanliness and charm, while the British value tradition, restraint, courtesy and politeness. She characterizes Flemish business communications as informal and factual and notes that the Danes prefer a modest and low-key approach, marked by humour and goodwill.

German employees tend to favour written communication, and their correspondence usually opens with a reference to the business relationship and closes with a kind word about continuing, or hoping to continue, that business relationship. Japanese writers are usually slower (according to the opinion of Westerners) in coming to the point. They may discuss the weather or inquire about your health at the beginning of a letter.

Of course, email is becoming more acceptable and usable as an everyday form of business communication, and that means new communicative styles are in the making.

What is important to remember from all these examples is that individual preferences for receiving communication messages run along a continuum. Generally, Germans may prefer written communication, but some prefer to speak face to face. Some US employees might feel at ease in heated debates with co-workers or even superiors, but others will not enter into confrontation at all.

You have to find out what the receiver of your message is comfortable with and adapt, within ethical bounds, of course, to that style. Diversity will be further explored in a later chapter.

Saving face

Face is the public image a person wants/needs to maintain. This is an important consideration for both decoders and encoders. Some cultures place emphasis on

Dig Deeper

Ben & Jerry's, the ice cream brand built on social responsibility, has experienced a decline in the public's perception of its adherence to that social consciousness. CEO Walt Freese admitted recently that Ben & Jerry's has lost some "face".

In 2000, Ben & Jerry's Homemade, Inc. was purchased by Unilever. The terms of the sale were unique. Ben & Jerry's was to operate separately from Unilever's other American ice cream products and operate with an independent board of directors which was to focus on providing leadership for the company's social mission and strong brand equity.

As a Unilever executive said at the transaction announcement: "Much of the success of the Ben & Jerry's brand is based on its connection to basic human values, and it is our hope and expectation that Ben & Jerry's continues to engage in these critical, global economic and social missions" (Ben & Jerry's, 2000).

Unilever also agreed to make a one-time $5 million gift to the Ben & Jerry's Foundation, a one-time $5 million gift to the new Social Venture Fund, run by Ben & Jerry's co-founder, Ben Cohen, plus a contribution of $1.1 million (subject to annual sales and inflation) to be maintained for 10 years (Ben & Jerry's Foundation, 2002).

Ben and Jerry's owners' vision to influence the corporate giant Unilever to be more socially conscious may have failed to come about. An article in *The Guardian* (Walsh, 2006) noted that a recent social audit of the company cited "disappointment" with the lack of social initiatives and "poor morale" among employees. It questioned whether the company was "simply a Unilever marketing operation using the brand's reputation for social responsibility to promote sales" (Walsh 2006).

What about other mergers of so-called socially responsible companies such as Body Shop or Green & Black? Have mergers hurt or helped their brand images?

maintaining "face". Koreans, for example, prefer an indirect business style, avoiding face-to-face criticism that might seemingly threaten a person's "face".

Business organizations also have "face" or, to put it in Western terms, "reputation".

In other words, brands have their "image", businesses have their "reputation" and people have their "face".

Knowing Your Audience

Evaluating your targeted **audiences** and stakeholders, knowing who they are, adapting to their communication style and considering their values, beliefs and attitudes are critical in getting a clear and acceptable message across.

Defining stakeholders

Stakeholders are individuals or entities that have an interest in your company: government, customers, employees, financial institutions, media, scholars, industry leaders, interest groups, communities, distributors, trade and professional organizations and competitors (Gronstedt, 1996, p. 291).

As mentioned earlier, targeting these groups with effective messages gets complicated, however, because they all have their own specific, and sometimes adversarial, agendas.

For example, company executives may be pushing for a new plant to be built overseas in a remote Indian village so the company can capitalize on low construction costs; shareholders, on the other hand, want the new plant's plans to be rushed through and approved so next quarter's stock will go up; local community members want the new plant to be built in their own town so they can take advantage of job openings; the media, looking for story angles, may be concerned with an "exploitation" issue of cheap labour in a poverty area, while consumers may be looking for a less expensive version of your product, and, if moving the operation to India brings down the price, they will be happy.

Let's look at stakeholders in order to understand who they are, and what is important to them? Various audience segments can be analysed using the "graphics" approach:

- demographics
- geographics
- psychographics
- sociographics
- usergraphics
- webographics.

Demographics

A **demographic** is something that can be measured or verified. For example, a demographic characteristic is that a person is 35 years old and has a college degree. It's not a relative evaluation, such as "she is rich". The fact that she makes 50 000 is a good example of a demographic. What distinguishes a demographic from other values is the **measurability** of the characteristic.

Demographics are germane to understanding your audience. If you sell high-priced hiking boots and need to communicate with your customers, it may be useful to know their age, education level and economic status before sending them a brochure of your new products. Why?

Knowing their age and education level will affect what words you use, the degree of complexity in sentence structure, your use of slang or analogies and your use of examples. Knowing your target audience's economic status will determine to whom you send the high-priced product information.

Geographics

Geographics pertain to place. In the context of knowing our audience, geographics refer to where a person lives, works, goes to school or plays. Our connection to various places not only dictates our level of interest but also determines our viewpoint of those places.

Let's go back to the high-priced hiking boots example for a minute. To communicate with 25–30 year olds who make upwards of 25 000, who are permanently employed and who have some college education, it might also be useful to know where these people live, work or play. Do they live in cities or rural areas? Do they commute long distances? Do they take short weekend trips or enjoy longer outings? Do they do a lot of hiking around their home town, or are they occasional users who hike on holiday in exotic places?

Why would this information be useful in sending out a brochure to these stakeholders? Because it will dictate the selling language used and the visual appeal employed to display the boots in settings that will "capture the imagination" of the target audience. They will "see" themselves wearing these boots.

Psychographics

Psychographics are what receivers "think about". What are the attitudes of receivers towards societal issues? What are their personality traits? **Psychographics** segment groups and individuals by their values, attitudes, interests, opinions and activities.

So when we again think about our potential hiking boot user, it might be useful to isolate what is important to this person. Does this person value his or her time? Does this person value money? Does this person value leisure time? Are environmental issues important to this person? Does this person think hiking through the countryside is the best experience ever? Does this person like hiking but rather be skiing? Psychographics help us get into the head of the receiver of our communication message.

Strategic Thinking

A provider of psychographic segmentation information in the USA is SRI Consulting Business Intelligence (SRIC-BI) which developed the values and lifestyle (VALS) system (SRIC-BI, 2006). The VALS segmentation divides US adult consumers into one of eight groups based on their responses to a questionnaire.

VALS might be used by an organization that wishes to conduct a direct mail campaign to encourage participation in a particular environmental programme. By identifying the types of personality that might be interested in this cause, the organization can better select the appropriate types of individual to target, thus making the campaign more effective.

European organizations that offer values research include Basisresearch GmbH in Frankfurt, Cofremca in Paris, Sifo AB in Stockholm and DemoSCOPE Markforschungsinstitut AG in Bern.

You can find out more about VALS consumer groups by going to `www.sric-bi.com/VALS/types.shtml` or reading a chapter on marketing and opinion research from the *ESOMAR Handbook of Marketing and Opinion Research*, written by Hans L. Zetterberg of City University of Stockholm and ValueScope AB (Zetterberg, 1998).

Sociographics

Sociographics are characteristics that have to do with what receivers do in society or with other people. Does a potential customer hike in groups or alone? Do these people hang out with friends and talk about new products available in the market? Do these customers read travel magazines or belong to a travel club?

This information would be useful to know and would be helpful in framing a brochure, not only in the language, style and tone used but also in the very nature of the promotion itself. Should the retailer offer a 25 % discount, a 30 rebate, a two-for-one train ticket or a free hotel room as a further enticement to buy?

Usergraphics

The term **usergraphics** defines how customers use a product. Again, using our hiking boots as an example, a usergraphic value of importance might be that our target market wears our boots every weekend, whether on a hiking trip or raking leaves in the backyard. Or it might be that our boots are so special and prized that they are only used for hiking excursions, with all the necessary precautions taken to ensure they are cleaned, rubbed down with protective coatings and carefully stored. Knowing how our customers use our boots will dictate all sorts of communication messages from ads to promotions, from pricing to loyal customer databasing.

The usergraphics model is used in the technology field. TechTV, a technology news outlet bought by Comcast, relies on usergraphics to describe how its customers use its media. For example, a report on TV viewers by Fulcrum Analytics in January 2003 lists TechTV.com usergraphics as follows: "TechTV.com visitors are loyal to the site. 79 % of TechTV.com users visit the site at least once a week. TechTV.com delivers experienced technology users; nearly seven out of ten TechTV.com visitors give more technology advice than they receive" (Rogers Media, 2005).

Webographics

This is a new technique developed to look at the profiles and interests of people visiting websites. **Webographics** include a user's webographic profile, usually offered voluntarily by the visitor to the site. In order to enter a protected website, it may be necessary to fill out this profile information before gaining access to the information you need. Some profiles require only basic information such as name and email address. Other sites, however, such as airline personal accounts or message boards, give users the opportunity to input more personal information, from mobile phone numbers to convenient airports near your home, vacationing likes and dislikes and seat preferences.

While users are volunteering some information, the Web is also collecting information that users do *not* volunteer.

Webographics can record which platform a user has, such as a Mac, Unix or Windows, as well as which browser, year model and connection speed (Dynamic Storefront, 2005). These factors have an impact on a user's experience while visiting websites.

For example, will your communication be effective if it includes so many graphics that it will take your visitors too much time to upload? Or do your customers have high-speed and high-tech equipment that welcomes cutting-edge, technological messaging?

Webographics also include Web user information on surfing patterns and online shopping habits, perhaps vital research in determining when and how you speak to the Internet citizen.

Webographics will expand in importance as companies continue to collect, evaluate, analyse and use information gleaned from their websites to enhance communication to and from web page viewers.

Qualitative research

Qualitative research helps identify impressions and trends and suggests areas or issues that need further clarification. Let's examine some qualitative techniques that researchers use to collect data about audiences:

- interviewing
- focus groups
- ethnography.

Businesses use these tools to understand their stakeholders and their needs, and then integrate this information into their business message development.

Interviewing

Interviewing can be a powerful tool for gathering information about audiences. Reporters, public relations professionals, human resource managers and market researchers all know the value of effective interviewing to obtain vital information about an audience.

The formal interview process collects information from individuals face to face, over the telephone and, increasingly, by email. Compilation of interview materials yields valuable primary research about the receivers of your messages.

Marketing research firms conduct structured personal and telephone interviews for clients with end-users of their products and services and those of their competitors. They develop case histories and profiles of potential customers based on these interviews. This type of information helps businesses position their products on the basis of documented audience needs.

Informal interviews are often used to obtain valid first-hand information from audiences you will be addressing. Successful public speakers like to talk with audience members before their presentations. This gives them a chance to gather information that will help them get their message across.

Focus groups

Focus groups constitute a qualitative research technique designed to gather information about the receivers of our communication messages.

Focus groups have been widely used and abused in audience research. This technique involves putting together small groups of individuals with similar demographic or psychographic characteristics to test new ideas, evaluate services or validate that receivers are decoding the intended communication message. Researchers vary on the ideal size of focus groups, but generally 8–12 people is an ideal number of participants. In public health, for example, much smaller groups are sometimes used.

Key points to remember about focus groups are:

1. They function best as exploratory or confirmatory resources.
2. Participants are compensated for their participation.

For example, in an exploratory stage, focus groups might be used by radio stations to help gain insight into programme formats. Likewise, in a confirmatory stage, a radio station might test changes in format by using focus groups.

Generally, focus groups are 60–90 min sessions facilitated by trained, impartial leaders who use a series of structured questions to elicit insight from participants.

As consumers become more market savvy and technology opens new possibilities for connecting with a target audience, research firms are adapting focus group techniques. Online focus groups had a surge of popularity in the USA prior to the bust of the dotcoms in early 2000–2001, but researchers found that they did not produce the synergy inherent in real life groups. Allison Stein Wellner, reporting in *American Demographics,* notes that online bulletin boards are gaining in popularity (Wellner, 2003). Using an online moderator, a single question is posed to Web users who have the opportunity to answer the question in depth.

Focus groups work well in cultures where the meaning of the language is explicit and where an open sharing of opinion is valued. In Asian culture, for example, group harmony is an important quality. This may inhibit individuals from expressing their opinions, making the focus groups less effective. Even in cultures where context is of less importance, focus groups should be structured according to specific criteria and visually recorded so that body language and other subtleties can be filtered into the analysis of the group's reactions.

Ethnography

With its roots in anthropology, **ethnography**, the study of people and their cultures, is a qualitative research tool widely applicable across organizations. Ethnography provides organizations with insight that is beyond the scope of a focus group. In 2001 the Gillette Company launched its Venus razor targeted at women simultaneously in 29 countries. It did so after conducting ethnographic research in the bathrooms of women across the world to see how they shaved, how they used their razors and where they stored them. For example, North Americans stored razors in their baths or showers and the spare blades in other locations, whereas Europeans did not keep either the razor or the blades in their baths or showers. As a result of this insight, Gillette designed a special carrying case for its razors so that those customers who wanted to could store the razors in baths, and adhesive strips were attached to the case so it could be hung in showers (Spethmann, 2001).

Ethnography involves participant observation, immersion in the setting and informal and in-depth interviewing. Industrial anthropologists are now employed by companies such as General Motors, Intel and Nynex to study customers, employees and management practices. As the observation is done in the workplace or in the home, participants yield reality-based information.

Interviews, focus groups and ethnography are the primary qualitative tools used to understand your audience.

Quantitative research

Another research tool is quantitative research which, if properly conducted, provides information that may be accurately applied to a population. **Quantitative research** involves surveys or questionnaires administered face to face, by mail, online or on the telephone. Such issues as the size and type of sample, the wording and structure of the survey instrument and procedures for administration must be considered in formulating research procedures.

Quantitative research is often used to measure the impact of communication on organizational performance. Such issues as trust of management, understanding of company goals, employee attitudes, evaluation of work environment and job satisfaction are communication issues that can be measured (Williams, 2002).

It is important to understand that effective research plans should include both qualitative and quantitative research. Focus groups (qualitative) might be used to identify employee issues regarding the implementation of a new policy or procedure, whereas a questionnaire (quantitative) might be administered to explore those issues further.

Reaching Your Audience

Now that we have discussed some of the ways you can characterize the receivers of messages, let's look at how we can take the information and make sense of it.

Abraham Maslow and the hierarchy of needs

In the 1930s psychologist Abraham Maslow began formulating a hierarchy of needs theory. While many of the early psychological and sociological theories have been disproved, fallen by the wayside or used as an early platform from which to formulate more modern theories, Maslow's hierarchy of needs theory is stronger today than it was in its infancy over 70 years ago. His theory says that we as humans have certain needs, some more demanding than others. Our need for water takes precedence over our need for shelter; our need for security is more basic than our need for a promotion at work.

Maslow used a pyramid to depict his theory. At the bottom of the pyramid are physiological needs for air, water, food, shelter from the cold, etc. Maslow also noticed that only when our basic needs (those from a lower level) are satisfied do we look to fulfil the needs of a higher level.

If we don't have food or clothes, we will not worry about our safety. For example, some people have risked imprisonment, while others have dodged enemy bullets, to get food for themselves or their family. However, once we feel fairly certain we will have food on the table and a roof over our heads, we begin to think about safety concerns. Locks on a door are not needed if you do not have a house or possessions to protect.

As we move up the pyramid, meeting all the needs of each level, we take on new challenges to meet those higher needs. Status becomes important; for example, the kind of car we drive may fill our need to "be cool" or "look important". An executive title or accolades from our manager (esteem needs) may become a demanding need. But when one of the lower needs risks being unfulfilled, we regress down the pyramid to attend to that need. This was evident in the terrorist attacks across the globe in 2005. Millions of people who had never felt insecure before now felt vulnerable and exposed. Dinner plans were cancelled and meetings were called off; our need to belong to certain groups or clubs that seemed so important one minute were now inconsequential.

After the natural disasters of the tsunami in Indonesia and Hurricane Katrina in the USA, people who had thought they needed a gold bracelet or a swimming pool suddenly found their needs focused on food, water and a dry bed.

At the top of the pyramid are self-actualization needs. When all of our needs are met – physical, safety, belonging, esteem – the self-actualized person turns around and reaches back, lends a fellow man a hand, tutors a small child, becomes a philanthropist, helps others, contributes creative works to the culture, etc.

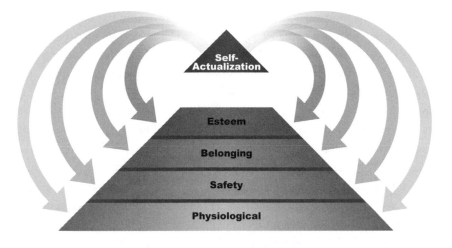

Figure 3.1 Maslow's hierarchy of needs.

The floating cap of the pyramid is meaningful. Once thought to be the pinnacle of the totally fulfilled person, theorists have pointed out that self-actualization can function at any level of the pyramid. For example, in the aftermath of Katrina, people who had few belongings and no homes of their own were helping others in need of food and water. Another example is the number of people who used their creativity in some fashion even while in concentration camps. Viktor Frankl developed his approach to therapy and Anita Lasker performed as a cellist in Auschwitz.

Maslow's model is a way of "reading" your audience, trying to understand what their needs are and then using this information to frame your message to fulfil those needs.

Now you have some options for "reading" your audience and looking at their values, where they live or work and their needs. Let's see what we can do with the information using some of the following techniques.

Profiling and narrowcasting

Audience **profiling** is a systematic way to look at all the information you have gathered about your audience, evaluate it and make a composite picture of your audience members. Profiles are used in databases to identify target consumer characteristics.

Meghashri Dalvi, documentation executive with Savvion India, Ltd, a management software company, says that audience profiling is "a brief description of the characteristics, needs and interests of your target audience". She says profiling helps in "presenting communication in the way the target audience will identify with, listen, understand and appreciate" (Dalvi, 2004).

Information for developing an audience profile can be gathered in a number of ways, such as surveys, interviews, focus groups, secondary market research, ethnography and face-to-face assessment, among others.

Marketers, advertisers, public relations professionals and communication executives can collect an infinite amount of information about those who purchase or use their products or services, as well as profile potential customers and their competitors' customers.

For example, grocery stores scan UPC and EAN codes while checking out a customer's purchases, and, while they do not necessarily have the names of the individual attached to their purchases, they can collect and store information on the types of purchase, the frequency of purchases, individual brand purchases and even coupon use for products.

It is said that grocery stores have so much stored information they cannot use it all. The information is databased and stored until the market research can be used to profile

Strategic Thinking

New marketing research technology is not without its problems. Frequent user clubs have been the target of fraud. Ill-meaning people with little software expertise can reproduce coupons and stamps, filling the necessary quota of purchases to get a free product.

Subway, with 26 342 sandwich outlets in 85 countries (as of August 2006), was forced to cancel its Sub Club programme in which customers would get a small stamp with every sandwich purchase to be pasted in the space provided on the card. When the card was filled with stamps, customers could get a free sandwich. That system is gone; too many people were printing bogus stamps.

But don't despair. Subway has a new reward programme. A magnetic Cash Card system will be more flexible, enabling customers to store money as a prepaid credit card usable in the stores or as gift certificates, which in paper form were more susceptible to counterfeit abuse. The Cash Card can also be used as a reward card, allowing customers to trade reward points for cookies and other foods at participating locations.

The new card can be managed online, and the information gathered about a consumer's purchasing behaviour will be part of Subway's customer database. The electronic card will make counterfeit hacking of the customer database difficult (Ogles, 2005).

a company's present customer base and its competitors' customer base. In the USA in 1978, less than 1 % of grocery stores nationwide had scanners. By 1984 it was 33 %, and today more than a million companies in over 140 countries across 23 industries use barcodes as a form of data collection in the grocery store business (GS1 US, Customer Services, 2005, private communication).

The Danish Ministry of Employment uses an information system to profile new unemployed workers in the country. The information compiled can predict whether registered applicants will be unemployed for more than six months and may determine how the cases will be handled so that the needs of the unemployed worker are better served (Rosholm, Svarer & Hammer, 2005).

Target audience profiles (TAPs) are used to gather information about target audiences and potential customers, and it has been found that valuable insight can be gained by analysing customers' characteristics, attitudes and behaviours (Microsoft Office Online, 2005; Microsoft Office Online, 2006).

Subway, the fast-food sandwich chain, recently switched to a magnetic cash card/gift certificate programme. Subway's original paper stamp programme, which gave customers credit towards future sandwich purchases, wasn't capable of collecting database information; however, the new Subway Cash Card will have this feature. *Wired News* points out the importance of customer

Figure 3.2 Subway Restaurants cards. Subway Restaurants switched from a paper stamp reward programme to an electronic cash card in 2006. Photo by permission of Doctor's Associates, Inc.

information-gathering programmes, saying that, while the upfront cost "might be high, it may reap larger rewards for the companies in the long run. As grocery stores have learned, the market research gleaned through establishing databases while handing out discounts can turn swipe cards into a winning formula very quickly" (Ogles, 2005).

Narrowcasting is another way of looking at the receivers of your business messages, whether individuals or a customer database.

The term "narrowcasting" was first used by the mass media industry to mean the opposite of broadcasting. It references information, programming or advertising cast out to highly audience-specific segments. It began when audiences for network programming began to dwindle as more viewers tuned in to cable channels and signed up for satellite service looking for specific-interest formats.

The term "narrowcasting" has also been used by other industries. It applies to defining your audience using narrow terms rather than broad characteristics. Narrowcasting allows you to "zero-in" on target audiences, reaching their individualized needs with specific language and format.

The Internet uses both a broadcast and a narrowcast model. Generally, websites are considered broadcast models as anyone can view the sites. A site that uses a log-in feature to be completed before its content can be viewed is a narrowcast model, as is a subscription website.

For example, for reporters to access media news from CBS television online, they have to register and provide credentials. A site that requires you to be part of a particular group such as a university student body or a club roster is casting to an even narrower target audience. An email list where messages are sent only to individuals who subscribe to the list is a further example of target narrowcasting.

The book publishing industry is searching for a way to capitalize on the trend by narrowcasting to specific audiences. Fabrizio Cardinali, CEO of Giunti Interactive Labs and one of Europe's main eLearning standard experts, addressed the eLearning conference in Brussels in 2005, saying, "Location-based and context-aware digital information delivery, personalized to users' abilities, competencies and portfolios, is the next frontier; narrowcasting to a community of interests is again becoming economically sustainable after the abnormalities of mass communication affecting the economics of publishing over the last 50 years" (Cardinali, 2005).

Developing a message with specific characteristics of your audience in mind and evaluating how you can send a relevant and meaningful message to that audience can result in successful narrowcasting of your message.

Cultural Influences Affect Receivers of Messages

Though globalization affects the way we do business, our cultural and social heritage determines how we perceive business messages. In his book *The Geography of Thought*, American psychologist Richard Nisbett illustrated the differences in Eastern and Western thought with this simple experiment (Nisbett, 2003).

Using Japanese and American students, a researcher showed groups of Japanese and American students eight animated underwater scenes. At the centre of each scene was one or more rapidly moving fish against a background of plant and animal life. The students viewed each scene twice for 20 seconds each. Participants were asked to record what they saw. The rapidly moving fish, the focal point of the scenes, were mentioned by both groups of students. But the Japanese students made 60 % more references to the background elements and twice as many references to the relationships of the elements in the scenes to each other than the Americans (Nisbett, 2003, pp. 89–90).

The experiment illustrates a principal difference between East and West cultures: Asians see the world in holistic terms – the big picture. Westerners, on the other hand, think analytically and are more interested in individual objects or differences.

University of Chicago anthropologist Edmund Hall was one of the first social scientists to study cultural differences in terms of space and interpersonal distance. His theory, called **proxemics**, describes an individual's use of space in the cultural context. Although his work has sometimes been criticized for the simplicity of his experiments, sweeping generalizations and cultural stereotypes, Hall was a pioneer in cultural research. He conjectured that the concept of distance in both non-verbal and verbal behaviour is culturally defined and determined. In other words, we each have a zone of personal space that we will allow others to enter into without harm, but these space definitions will differ between cultures (Hall, 1966).

Arabs, Latinos and Southern Europeans are "contact" people where touching and close distances in conversation are expected. Hall argued that Northern Europeans, Americans and Asians prefer non-contact. Thus, to non-contact people, individuals who get too close in a conversation are "invading our space".

Our comfort with distances is governed by many criteria including familiarity, the subject of the conversation, the sex of the receiver and the perceived status of the receiver, among other issues.

Others have expanded upon Hall's research. Argyle and Dean developed the **theory of equilibrium** which states that there is an inverse relationship between mutual gaze, a non-verbal cue signalling intimacy, and interpersonal distance and space (Argyle & Dean, 1965).

Suppose you are walking along a corridor in a busy airport and make eye contact with the person walking next to you. Your mutual gaze lasts only several seconds, and you move on. But suppose the gaze lasts longer than a few seconds, turning into a stare from the other individual. If you feel that this non-verbal action is inappropriate, you will increase the distance between yourself and the other individual.

Hall also introduced the concept of context in conversation. **Context** is the information surrounding an event that helps determine its meaning. A high-context message is one that we already have the information in words, pictures, etc., to process, whereas a low-context communication is just the opposite. Much of the information is in the message itself (Hall, 1977).

Context varies between culture. Low-context cultures demand more explicit verbal context. In his book *Marketing Across Cultures*, Jean-Claude Usunier cites the Swiss as an example of a low-context culture with a reputation for demanding preciseness in language and behaviour. For example, when a meeting time is set, the Swiss expect those who attend to be punctual. The British and the French are considered to fall in the middle range between low- and high-context communication styles. Japanese, Arab and Mediterranean cultures are examples of high-context societies. In their conversations much of the information needed is already perceived, and thus they do not require, nor ask for, details or background (Usunier, 1996).

Cultural differences affect the way messages are received and acted upon. Much has been written about the customs and practices of various cultures in conducting business. A plethora of websites, articles and books describe differences among cultures, from the bear hugs and kisses expected as greetings from Russians to the use of only the right hand for greetings in Egypt.

Dr Daniel Kealey, a leading Canadian psychologist and expert in intercultural studies, advises the Canadian government on the hiring of government employees for foreign service. Kealey, in an interview for *InterCulture Magazine*, noted that simply knowing a list of dos and don'ts may not be the way to do business in a foreign culture. Good business relationships are built on understanding and sincerity.

> ...in a foreign culture, people aren't expecting you to know all the rules and the issues and what's taboo. It's not critical; what is critical is how genuine you are, what your capacities are, and that you really want to learn about the culture. And they'll know that you are not faking that; there is no way you could fake that. I heard many, many stories about people who were told

Dig Deeper

Intercultural writing and speaking tips:

1. Be aware that there are differences in written communication styles.
2. Be sensitive, do not pass judgement on your audience.
3. Learn about the communication preferences for the culture with which you are trying to correspond.
4. Adapt your style to meet their expectations.
5. Use simple words. Use easy-to-pronounce words.
6. Be sure you are using the correct forms of address. Cultures vary a great deal in this respect.
7. Use transitions, signposts, when switching from one point to the next, making sure you are taking your reader with you as you progress through the correspondence.
8. When writing, use numbers (102) rather than words (a hundred and two) to express quantity. If speaking, consider visual aids or handouts for hard-to-remember figures and concepts.
9. Read your message from the point of view of your receiver. Does your message contain any bias or sexist language? Does it conform to cultural standards?
10. Edit and revise your message until you are confident that the message you are sending will be received successfully by your audience in the way in which you intend it to be.

certain things about how to behave and then they take it as the absolute truth. It sets you up; you get caught up in that circle of misperceiving and misjudging" (Dr Culture, 2005).

Kealey's point is important – knowing the culture is the key to understanding your audience.

Types of Audience

Another way of evaluating your receivers is to determine their listening agenda or motives. This information will determine how you frame your message. It is important to remember that receivers exist on a continuum between each extreme. They will not be either one type or the other, but rather make up both extremes and the wide range between them.

Interested/disinterested

Interested receivers are ready to listen to your message. It will take little work to get their attention.

Disinterested audiences will need an attention-getter to get them to listen and a listener relevance component to make them want to listen to what you have to say.

No matter how easy or difficult it is to get an audience's attention, both interested and disinterested audiences will require you to work hard to keep them engaged throughout your message.

Voluntary/captive

Voluntary audiences want to hear what you have to say. They are listening (or reading) of their own free will. But this does not mean they will continue to stay focused if your message is not clear and relevant; however, you don't have to work too hard to get their attention.

Captive audiences are those required to be in attendance. They may be physically in attendance (or required to read a report), but mentally they may be a million miles away. You will have to do something significant to get them to listen to you; you will have to be engaging and accommodating.

Eager/resistant

Eager receivers are easy to reach. They want to hear what you have to say and will actively try to understand your points.

David Stuart, president of College to Career Seminars, describes the students who attend his seminars to learn how to get a job as eager listeners. He says, "They want all the help they can get. They want to learn, and learn quickly" (Stuart, 2003).

Resistant receivers are hard to reach mentally. They are wary of you and what you have to say. Developing an opening that warms them to your message is sometimes crucial. You have to show that you understand their wants and needs and are sincere about imparting your message.

Chapter Summary

To be successful in the global marketplace, you must understand your audience. This means you must identify your stakeholders, recognize that they may think differently from you, respect those differences and learn to adapt your communication to fit that reality.

However, to understand your audience segments, information and insight concerning their demographics, geographics, psychographics and sociographics are necessary. If you are analysing customers, knowledge of how they use products, usergraphics, and how they search and use the web, webographics, will give you additional information on their needs and how you must tailor a message to address them.

Background information on your audience is the first crucial step in knowing who they are and how they function within their culture. An understanding of their needs is the next step in the effective communication process. Maslow's hierarchy of needs provides a framework for that process. Qualitative research tools such as focus groups and ethnography are frequently used techniques that will help you test your audience analysis. Quantitative tools will help you expand upon qualitative research. Audiences will differ as to intent and agenda.

Proxemics theory, the theory of equilibrium and cultural differences in terms of context help us understand audience differences. As you learn to analyse the receivers of your message, you will begin to understand how using the tools outlined in this chapter will make you a better communicator. ■

Learning From Others

Theresa Thao Pham is an applied anthropology doctoral student at Teachers College of Columbia University. She is currently conducting her dissertation field research on Moroccan immigrants in Spain. She specializes in migration, social and cultural incorporation and kinship studies, and has conducted anthropological research in Morocco and Vietnam.

Pham holds a master in Clinical Social Work from Smith College, Northampton, MA, and was a practising clinician for seven years.

Her essay provides a real-life example of cultural misunderstanding and how a common practice can be viewed from multiple perspectives.

Cultural Discrepancies in Business Communication

Moroccan organizational behaviour may reflect the traditional and cultural importance of the charismatic central person. In Morocco's case, the king, though not currently "dictator", solely rules this Arab country. Unlike the American

merit-based corporate culture, familial and political connections weigh heavily in business connections with influences centring upon one person, usually a man.

One example of this cultural practice can be observed in a renowned language school located in Fez, Morocco's cultural capital. Although the current director of the school is an expatriate American, everyone knows that the daily operations of the school and its influence in the community come from the Moroccan coordinator, Mr Ali.

As a special service for the foreign students, Mr Ali coordinates and reserves hotels through his personal connections in the Moroccan community. Even though students acknowledge that the school may be benefiting from their hotel stays, many were unaware of Mr Ali's personal cut. The clandestine connection was revealed only when the conventional person-to-person communication was disrupted with the globalization of new technology: online shopping.

One student booked her hotel reservation online from the USA and was given a better rate than her classmates who had consulted with Mr Ali. When her classmates discovered the online deal, they notified Mr Ali so he could inform other students of the special offer. Instead of being grateful, Mr Ali was enraged and dashed to the hotel where the student had stayed. He demanded that the hotel owner give him his cut of the referral, despite protests that he was owed nothing since the student had booked online. Mr Ali threatened to pull out his business connection from the hotel, and, with that threat, the hotel owner and manager gave Mr Ali a monetary cut for the student.

Mr Ali returned to the school and complained to staff, teachers and students how Moroccan business owners should not be trusted. The school staff and teachers had known that Mr Ali had been profiting from these business dealings, yet they nodded in agreement. Many foreign students, however, felt disappointed with Mr Ali's behaviour and deemed his business practices "corrupt" when compared with American business practices. The discrepancies in interpreting Mr Ali's business transactions may derive from the cultural differences in business communications.

Case Study – **The Smart Car**

DaimlerChrysler launched the first Smart car model, the City Coupe, in Western Europe in 1998. The market objective was to offer young people an affordable car. The ForTwo car, a hybrid two-seater, led to the Crossblade, ForFour, ForMore, Smart Roadster and Roadster Coupe. The company seemed to do well in the European, Japanese and Canadian markets.

Company president Ulrich Walker announced in 2005 that the Smart car would enter the US market. But suddenly things began to go wrong and

DaimlerChrysler chairman Jurgen Schrempp acknowledged that the company might discontinue the Smart car.

What could have gone so wrong that a successful car model found itself on the execution block?

Here are some possibilities:

According to Marl Landler, reporting in the *Taipei Times,* "DaimlerChrysler racked up years of losses as it struggled with Smart's high production costs and cumbersome distribution network" (Landler, 2005b).

Ferdinand Dudenhoeffer, Director of the Centre for Automotive Research in Gelsenkirchen, said, "To make a two-seat car, stripped down for urban environments, was an absolutely great idea, but then they made a lot of mistakes and wrong decisions".

An auto analyst at Dresdner Kleinwort Wasserstein in Frankfurt said, "This [shutting down Smart] is the easy solution for Schrempp, and a bad solution for shareholders".

The company said, in reference to meeting US road and safety requirements, "Smart's problem is its high cost, not lack of appeal".

Critics say, "Part of the problem is price. At 9 000 euros ($US 11 664), the Smart is not cheap for its size".

Analysts say that, since 1998, competition has increased, "Their competitor is a Fiat, a Peugeot, a Toyota".

Auto critics "derided the Smart car as looking like a toy".

The company considered a Smart sports utility vehicle as an entry model for the United States. To critics this seemed to go against Smart's appeal, which is its compactness. A Smart-based SUV concept vehicle was pulled from the 2005 North American International Auto Show at the last minute.

Some say the failure goes back to the initial merger between Daimler and Chrysler. It was called the "merger of equals" in all communication to the public and shareholders. When things went bad and Chrysler seemed to be subservient to Daimler, Schrempp told the *Financial Times* that "the merger of equals was all a sham". He went on to say, "If I had gone and said Chrysler would be a division, everybody on their side would have said there is no way we'll do a deal". In *Ward's Auto World*, Drew Winter says, "Mr Schrempp and his entire management team now have a king-size credibility problem in North America". Chrysler CEO James P. Holden was "stunned and embarrassed by Schrempp's comments". Employees lost confidence in Schrempp's leadership and stakeholders were confused by his contradictory statements (Winter, 2000).

In August 2005, Schrempp tendered his resignation. Since then other high-ranking company executives have resigned (Richter, 2005). The US Justice Department and the Securities and Exchange Commission are investigating the company on bribery charges in a dozen countries and insider trading charges (Landler, 2005a).

Do some more research on the company. Can you isolate any communication failures on the part of executives as they sent messages out to the public, their shareholders, potential customers or other receivers? ■

Class Exercises

1. Which lower- and which higher-level need will be fulfilled using the Maslow hierarchy of needs for the following example? You are trying to sell a frozen food dinner product. In your television commercial you feature a group of men. They are hungry and heat up frozen dinners to eat while getting comfortable around the television to watch a football match. What two needs are tapped for your consumer?

2. You want to interest your company in developing a new type of ergonomic backpack to be marketed to students as a book tote. You will be meeting college students in focus groups to see what information you can learn that will help you make a strong case to your boss. Conduct a demographic and geographic audience analysis of your fellow classmates (who share similar characteristics with the focus groups you will be meeting) to determine how to "frame" your introductory message to make your focus group participants eager to participate and provide feedback.

3. Continue the above scenario. Compile questions that would provide you with psychographic and sociographic information.

Action Plan

Make a list of the findings in the two exercises above that will be useful for your presentation to the focus group of college students that you want to question about their likes and dislikes regarding backpacks. Now prepare a two-minute introductory speech that relates to your focus group audience and motivates them to participate in your research. How much information will you provide? Can you establish "common ground"? How can you get reticent participants to speak up? Did the preresearch with your classmates help formulate this speech? Do you think you will gather the concrete information you need from the focus group to put in your report to your boss. What was the most difficult part of writing this speech?

Websites

Microsoft Office Online profiling page gives lots of information and tips for profiling external and internal audiences: `http://office.microsoft.com/en-us/FX011405101033.aspx` (Microsoft Office Online, 2006).

CAP Ventures offers information about narrowcasting on its website. Search for the term at `http://www.capv.com/home/Press/2001/11.8.01` (Cap Ventures, 2002).

Read about the future of barcoding and the information collected on the MIT Advertising Lab "Blog on the future of advertising technology" at `http://adverlab.blogspot.com/2005/03/paperclick-fcb-tie-barcodes-and.html`

Intercultures, diplomacy, language and the selection of personnel for international assignments are the focus of the website of the Foreign Affairs Office of Canada. Look for its online magazine and excellent list of terms at `http://www.dfait-maeci.gc.ca` (of course, the site is in both French and English).

References

Argyle, M. & Dean, J. (1965) "Eye-contact, distance and affiliation". *Sociometry*, **28**: 289–204.

Ben & Jerry's (2000) "Ben & Jerry's & Unilever to join forces" (press release, 12 April 2000). Available from: www.benjerry.com/our_company/press_center/join-forces.html [Accessed 26 June 2006].

Ben & Jerry's Foundation (2002) A statement from Ben & Jerry's Foundation, 27 March 2002. Available from: www.benjerry.com/foundation/funding/html [Accessed 26 June 2006].

Boeree, C. G. (2005) "Abraham Maslow". Shippenburg University. Available from: www.ship.edu/~cgboeree/maslow.html [Accessed 6 November 2005].

Cain, G. (2003) "Forget the sharks – swim with your own fish!" *Quirks Marketing Research Review*, May 2003. Available from: www.quirks.com [Accessed 14 September 2005].

Cap Ventures (2002) "Narrowcasting in public spaces: the outlook for out-of-home television and digital signage". Cap Ventures, Inc., March. Available from: http://www.capv.com/home/Multiclient/Narrowcasting.html%20 [Accessed 6 November 2005].

Cardinali, F. (2005) eLearning Conference, Brussels, 19–20 May 2005. Available from: http://elearningconference.org/key_speaker/cardinali.htm [Accessed 29 June 2006].

Dalvi, M. (2004) "Profiling audience, STC learning session". Available from: http://www.stc-india.org/learningsessions/MumSessions/ProfilingAudience.ppt [Accessed 5 November 2006].

Dr Culture (2005) An interview with Daniel J. Kealey. *Intercultures Magazine*, Summer 2005. Available from: http://www.dfait-maeci.gc.ca/cfsi-icse/cil-cai/magazine/magazine-en.asp?txt=1-3&lv=1 [Accessed 19 October 2005].

Dynamic Store Front (2005) "Webographics definition". Available from: http://dynamicstorefront.com/Glossary_Webographics.asp [Accessed 9 October 2005].

Gronstedt, A. (1996) "A stakeholders' relations model". In *Integrated Communications: Synergy of Persuasive Voices*. Thorson, E. & Moore, J., eds. Mahwah, NJ, Lawrence Erlbaum Associates: 287–304.

Hall, E. (1966) *Hidden Dimension*. New York, Doubleday.

Hall, E. (1987) *Hidden Differences*. New York, Doubleday.

Jones, D. (2005) "Putting brand on China success".*USA Today*, Sect. 4B, 17 October 2005.

Laks, S. (1989) "Music of another world". Translated by Kisiel, C. A. Available from: www.ralphmag.org/briefsZM.html [Accessed 6 November 2005].

Landler, M. (2005a) "Mercedes faces bribery inquiry and leadership void". *International Herald Tribune*. Available from: www.iht.com [Accessed 2 December 2005].

Landler, M. (2005b) "Minicar makes automotive giant look dumb". *Taipei Times*, NY News Service, Frankfurt, Germany. Available from: www.taipeitimes.com [Accessed 2 December 2005].

Microsoft Office Online (2005) "Profiling your target audience". Available from: http://office.microsoft.com [Accessed 6 November 2005].

Microsoft Office Online (2006) "Discover the importance of target audience profiling". Available from: office.microsoft.com/en-us/FX011454641033.aspx [Accessed 29 June 2006].

Nisbett, R. (2003) *The Geography of Thought: How Asians and Westerners Think Differently … and Why*. New York, Free Press.

Ogles, J. (2005) "Fraud sinks Subway's sub club". *Wired News*, 21 September 2005. Available from: http://wired-vig.wired.com/news/print/0,1294,68909,00.html [Accessed 11 June 2005].

Parfitt, J. (2005) "Working in the global village: managing and working with a multicultural team". Goinglobal. Available from: http://www.goinglobal.com/hot_topics/parfitt_inter_team.asp [Accessed 28 October 2005].

Richter, P. (2005) "Germany: DaimlerChrysler CEO suddenly resigns". World Socialist Web Site. Available from: www.wsws.org/articles/2005/aug2005/germ-a17_prn.shtml [Accessed 3 December 2005].

Rogers Media (RMITV) (2005) "TechTV (US) advertising research". Available from: http://rmitv.ca/techtv/advertising/stats_us.shtml [Accessed 9 October 2005].

Rosholm, M., Svarer, M. & Hammer, B. (2005) "A Danish profiling system". IDEAS, RePEc. Available from: http://ideas.repec.org/p/aah/aarhec/2004-13.html [Accessed 6 November 2005].

Spethmann, B. (2001) Venus rising. *PROMO*, **4**: 52–61.

SRIC-BI (2006) "The VALS™ segments". SRI Consulting Business Intelligence. Available from: www.sric-bi.com/VALS/types.shtml. [Accessed 29 June 2006].

Stuart, L. (2003) "How to get the job you want: an interactive CD that prepares you for the career of your choice". Available from: www.collegetocareerseminars.com [Accessed 21 August 2006].

Usunier, J. (1996) *Marketing Across Cultures*, 2nd edn. Hemel Hempstead, UK, Prentice Hall Europe.

Van der Boon, M. (2005) "Working in the global village: managing and working with a multicultural team". Goinglobal. Available from: http://www.globalcareerguide.com/hot_topics/parfitt_inter_team.asp [Accessed 28 October 2005].

Walsh, F. (2006) "When big business bites". *The Guardian*, 8 June 2006. Available from: http://www.guardian.co.uk/ethicalbusiness/story/O,,1792797,00.html [Accessed 26 June 2006].

Williams, J. (2002) "Linking communication to organizational performance: advanced research that measures the impact of communication in an organization". Working paper, Joe Williams Communications, Inc.

Wellner, A. S. (2003) The new science of focus groups. *American Demographics*, **3**: 29–33.

Winter, D. (2000) Editorial. *Ward's Auto World*.

Zetterberg, H. (1998) "Cultural values in market and opinion research". In *ESOMAR Handbook of Marketing and Opinion Research*, 4th edn. McDonald, C. & Vangelder, P., eds. Amsterdam, The Netherlands, ESOMAR. Available from: http://64.233.167.104/search?q=cache:6U_CMU913VMJ:www.zetterberg.org/Papers/ppr1998d.htm+VAL...[Accessed 29 June 2006].

Bibliography

Kane, K. (1996) "Anthropologists go native in the corporate village". *Fast Company*, **5**(October/November): 60. Available from: http://www.fastcompany.com/online/05/anthro.html [Accessed 14 September 2005].

Trompenaars, F. & Woolliams, P. (2003) *Business Across Cultures*. Chichester, West Sussex, UK, Capstone.

CHAPTER 4

Breaking Through the Noise

Executive Summary

Noise affects our ability to determine the meaning of a message.

Noise or static includes any physical, semantic or contextual action that distorts the receipt of a message
External noise is outside the personal world of the receiver and inhibits our ability to hear the message. Internal noise is the reaction of the sender to a particular message, based on such factors as culture, ethnicity, religion and class. Semantic noise refers to the meaning and value placed on language.

Selective filters work towards protecting us from information that we are uncomfortable knowing or remembering
Cognitive dissonance involves the process of accepting or rejecting information on the basis of how well it conforms to or reinforces our pre-existing attitudes or beliefs.

The "rings of defence", including selective exposure, selective attention, selective perception, selective retention and selective alteration, explain how we process information
These filters illustrate the complexity of the communication process and the many barriers that must be overcome to reach a receiver.

The electronic age forces business professionals to work more smartly and quickly while maintaining quality in the workplace
This often results in information overload.

Our ability to listen is a test to the filtering process
Identifying the types of listening patterns and the barriers to listening will help business professionals become more effective communicators. ■

Breaking Through the Noise

> **" **I hear and I forget. I see and I remember. I
> experience and I understand.
>
> *Confucius* **"**

Introduction to Message Perception

Our transactional communication model shows that noise, both physical and psychological, affects a sender's message and distorts a receiver's interpretation of that message. Based on the level of noise, miscommunication could result because of difficulties in listening, causing problems for both senders and receivers.

From prime ministers and presidents to shopkeepers and customers, no one is exempt from the root causes of noise. In January 2006, 13 miners were trapped in a US mine. The governor of the state of West Virginia received a cell phone transmission from rescuers on the scene. He subsequently told reporters and the families of the trapped miners that all but one of their loved ones were safe.

At 11:59 pm the Associated Press announced to the world that 12 miners were alive. Newspapers around the country, eager to get the story in their morning papers, printed headlines such as "Families Say 12 W. Va. Miners Found Alive".

But by 3:06 am the story had changed to 12 miners were *dead* – the revised report came too late to change the morning headlines. The rescue reports had somehow been misheard. While this is an extreme example, it is clear that our lives are governed by actions and reactions that often prevent our messages from being clearly received.

People perceive messages differently, for a variety of reasons, and these interferences are referred to as internal noise. A German couple, working for a brief time in a US-based division of a German manufacturer, was told by a fellow American worker, "We must get together some time". The couple read the message as "Where shall we meet this evening?" and were embarrassed to discover that the American didn't intend to make a social date, but was merely exchanging greetings or pleasantries. Cultural differences may create noise in the communication process.

As the transactional communication model and the examples above illustrate, multiple factors interfere with receiving an effective message. This chapter explores how external noise and internal psychological and social factors influence effective listening.

We will look at how technology can add to miscommunication. In addition, we will explore the value of listening in facilitating effective communication.

What is Noise?

Noise is defined as any physical, semantic or contextual action that detracts from or distorts the receipt of a message. Often referred to as static, noise comes from both external and internal sources. In the workplace, noise may take many forms, from Intranet information overload to poor lighting.

Noise grew out of the early mathematical theory of communication (Shannon & Weaver, 1949). This theory was developed by engineers who were concerned about interruptions in the flow or signal from one channel to the next. Each element in the flow was referred to as an information bit, or a digital bit. Any differences in the way the signal was sent and how it was received were referred to as errors or noise. The theory also introduced the concept of channel into the communication equation. The

Figure 4.1   Photo of workplace. Television studios are vulnerable to information overload. Good lighting, well-placed monitors and functional space planning are crucial to breaking through noise barriers. (Reproduced by permission of Lawson & Associates Architects.)

channel capacity may be quite high, thus allowing for a strong, accurate signal to be communicated, or weak, when noise interferes with the transmission of the message. Radio static, for example, is a form of noise.

In many instances noise can simply be the misreading of a message. For example, read this next paragraph and note how many F's you see:

> FINISHED FILES ARE THE RESULT OF YEARS OF SCIENTIFIC STUDY COMBINED WITH THE EXPERIENCE OF MANY YEARS.

How many Fs did you find? 3? 4? ? 6? 7?

If you counted 6 Fs you are correct, and no doubt blocked out all internal and external influences as you focused your attention on solving the problem.

In group training seminars, however, when this little exercise was conducted to emphasize the importance of paying attention to details, more than 70 % of the audience polled could only come up with 3 Fs, especially when a 15-second time limit was imposed.

It was further discovered that the power of suggestion could also play a role in the number of Fs found by the audience. Printing the same paragraph on paper of different sizes and shapes led participants to believe that their paragraph was different from others. If they found three Fs but their neighbour found four, they concluded that they had different paragraphs.

Obviously, the size and shape of the paper had nothing to do with the actual printed paragraph. However, the differences sent mixed messages and created enough noise to influence the outcome of the task.

External noise

External noise is physical activity, external to the source, that inhibits the communication process. It is often beyond our control. Physical noise such as the sound of a plane or the slamming of a door may literally prevent a receiver from hearing a clear message. A noisy crowd at a soccer or football match may prevent you from hearing your friends' conversation.

Did you ever attend a cinema where malfunctioning equipment forced the operators to start and stop the film several times? Such a break in the flow of the storyline detracts from the meaning of the film and the experience of cinema-goers.

Our reaction to noise is a biological stimulus that affects the senses – taste, touch, hearing, vision and smell. Our nervous system reacts to changes in the environment, our external noise. We give meaning to this stimulus on the basis of personal internal factors (our experience, emotions, etc.) and external factors.

People living under the flight path of airplanes grow accustomed to the noise; in fact they may find the silence of a country getaway almost too quiet. The airplane noise for these people may be viewed as comfortable and normal, quite a different experience from those who find it annoying and distracting.

Many experienced human resource executives, before making a final offer to new employees, insist on giving recruits a tour of the area where they will be working. It would be important feedback to note if an employee expresses concern over the small cubicle in the windowless basement of the building where he will be working. The external noise of this claustrophobic environment might affect his performance.

Internal noise

Internal noise is found in the mind of the receiver and how he or she reacts to the message as well as to the messenger.

Suppose you are listening to a city leader address a civic group, and the speaker continues to mispronounce a word. While his or her mistake may seem trivial and could be excused as the result of nervousness, you brand the leader as uneducated, uninformed, ill-prepared or unpolished. Your reaction to the speaker's flaw is internal noise and acts as static to your perception of the message.

Differences in culture, ethnicity, religion and class, as well as such factors as sex and age, can also alter the perception of a message.

Women interpret messages differently to men. A superior's demand for longer hours, perhaps understood by men as a path to promotion, may not be viewed as a necessary step to advancement by women who may place a higher priority on their personal and family time.

Semantic noise

Semantic noise, or the meaning and value of words, also differs according to the sender's or the receiver's perspective. For example, your meaning of what constitutes URGENT may not be the same as the sender's. Some experts suggest that the practice of labelling email correspondence as URGENT – when it often is not – may have changed the meaning of the word for many people.

The same is true of the acronym ASAP (as soon as possible). What does ASAP mean to a receiver? Is the message urgent? Something to be done today, tomorrow or next week?

For example, a budget director, faced with submitting an annual budget request for all departments by the end of the month, sends out the following memo:

DATE: 3 November 2006

TO: All Department Heads

FROM: Budget Director

SUBJECT: Annual Budget Reports

Please be aware that the final budget report requests for fiscal year 07 must be submitted to corporate for inclusion and approval by 30 November 06.

I know you are all swamped with end-of-year sales reports, but, using the templates provided, please submit your 07 budget requests to my attention ASAP.

Many thanks.

While the budget director was displaying empathy for the busy times the department heads were having, her message did not emphasize the importance or deadline of her request. To some receivers of the message, the deadline seemed to be 30 November when actually she needed their numbers immediately (ASAP) in order to prepare and submit her budget request to corporate by that date.

The lack of clarity and using ASAP sent mixed messages to the receivers of the message.

Filtering Out Unwanted Noise

In the Information Age, we can find out just about everything we need to know, 24/7, in a multitude of places. The problem is that it is impossible to see, read and know everything accessible to us.

Receivers, in order to alleviate the frustration of not being able to address all the messages that come their way, employ certain mechanisms that limit the amount of manageable information they take in. Senders of messages work to break through these filters, continually striving to find new ways to make receivers pay attention to their messages.

Cognitive dissonance

In the 1950s, psychologist Leon Festinger introduced the **theory of cognitive dissonance** (Festinger, 1962). In his study he recognized that individuals seek out or readily accept information that conforms or reinforces their attitudes or beliefs; they do not seek out dissonant information, which results in uneasiness or doubt. He also believed the only way to get individuals to look at opposing perspectives is to confront them with compelling reasons to look at issues differently.

Thus, advocacy groups trying to get teenagers to confront the effects of drunk-driving might display a wrecked car in which someone died as the result of a drunk driver. The image of a smashed vehicle might create cognitive dissonance in teens by making them doubt their beliefs that nothing will ever happen to them when they drink and drive.

Festinger's theory led to the development of "selective filters" – ways that we subconsciously protect ourselves from overexposure to information that can lead to cognitive dissonance. Psychologists call this ability selectively to process messages "rings of defence".

Selective filters

Selective filters are a series of barriers that receivers employ, often unconsciously, to prevent information from bombarding them. Senders have to understand how these filters work in order to circumvent their gatekeeping function.

Selective exposure

Individuals look for information that reinforces existing values or beliefs, resulting in their **selective exposure** only to certain material. From a communication perspective, it is almost impossible to expose individuals to other points of view if they already have made up their minds. If I subscribe to the ideals of the Conservative Party, I am not likely to read the platform of the Labour Party or listen to the views of any other political group. By this avoidance, I protect my way of thinking and do not risk cognitive dissonance.

Selective attention

People give **selective attention** only to those messages or communications that they are interested in or that are in agreement with their values or belief system. They tune out those messages that conflict with their beliefs. In 1890, the psychologist William James defined the concept this way: "Millions of items of the outward order are present to my senses which never properly enter into my experience. Why? Because they are of no *interest* for me. *My experience is what I agree to attend to.* Only those items which I *notice* can shape my mind – without selective interest, experience is an utter chaos" (http://psychclassics.yorku.ca/James/Principles/prin11.htm).

As James noted, there are many stimuli demanding our attention – we choose to consider only those that our experiences tell us are of interest or benefit to us at that moment. As a result, two people viewing the same research may notice different aspects of the findings, depending on what information they choose to give their attention.

Selective perception

In 1958, Donald Broadbent, the British cognitive psychologist, identified the concept of **selective perception** when he noted that our human perceptual system has limitations.

When collecting information (selective exposure) from different channels through our senses, we choose to process only that which is most pertinent or related to our interests (selective attention) and consistent with the way we view the world and compatible with our values and beliefs (selective perception).

In this stage, perceptions can be classified as low-level or high-level issues.

Consider this example of a low- and high-level classification. While driving on motorways, we selectively filter out any stimuli that might confuse our driving and focus on the cars immediately surrounding us. If we were to focus on every car on the motorway, we would quickly lose concentration.

Subconsciously, we classify the behaviours of drivers off in the distance as low-level stimuli. However, if we see bright, flashing lights many kilometres ahead, we shift to a high-level classification of an outside stimulus and immediately become more alert to what is happening.

A variety of experiments have illustrated how selective perception works. One of the most famous experiments involved a study on rumours (Allport & Postman, 1945).

The researchers showed study participants a picture of a group of people aboard a subway train. In the picture, a white male, casually dressed and holding a razor, stands next to a black man dressed in a suit, tie and hat. Participants in the study were asked to describe the action in the picture and then to pass the information on. Most respondents described the razor in the hand of the black man. While the study was conducted in 1945, it nevertheless reveals that "what was outer becomes inner; what was objective becomes subjective" (Allport & Postman, 1945, p. 81).

How we see the world affects how we interpret it. A utility company may view the building of a nuclear power station in a rural community as a way to provide safe, economical and relatively clean energy. Local politicians may view the same project as a source for new jobs and as an additional revenue stream. Environmentalists may see the power station as a blight to the landscape and a danger to wildlife. Homeowners may see it as a devaluation of their property.

Selective retention

Selective retention refers to the tendency to remember information consistent with our values and beliefs. Psychological factors inhibit our retention and block out information that is disagreeable. Recall rate varies among witnesses who view the same criminal act, for example.

Selective alteration

As we move further away from an event, the information we have remembered undergoes increasing alteration. We immediately begin to use **selective alteration** to alter and adjust what we saw or heard. Detectives know it is best to interview an eyewitness to a crime as soon as possible. The longer they wait, the more likely it is that the story will be altered by the individual as a result of his/her selected attention.

We are constantly changing our perceptions on the basis of new experiences, additional information, input from friends, what is in our best interest to remember and the importance of the memory. Often our memory of an event is altered to maintain our beliefs and biases.

These filters, also referred to as rings of defence, illustrate the complexity of the communication process and how noise can impact effective messaging. Understanding these difficulties can help the sender of a message comprehend the many obstacles that

Information decay and forgetting

Doris Graber, author of *Processing the News: How People Tame the Information Tide*, explains that managing information involves cleaning the mind of no longer needed information, and says forgetting is due to memory decay over time and problems in locating stored information. Her study also showed that "the ability to retain stories in memory and retrieve them varied widely, depending on the nature of stories, the use of visuals, and the concerns and life style of the audience" (Graber, 1988, p. 115).

must be overcome in order to have the message received in the manner in which it was intended.

Information overload

In the information systems business, information overload is known as content switching. Communication experts view information overload as:

- the amount of information or the quantity of information presented;
- the rate or speed at which the information is delivered and received;
- the complexity of the information (Farace, Monge & Russell, 1977).

Information overload is a serious threat to receiver comprehension. Consider the case of UK cabinet ministers who were reportedly given 2500 pages of Treasury documents about the euro to read and absorb over one weekend (Lewis, 2003). Across business sectors, employees at all levels receive dozens if not hundreds of emails each day. Employees have to decide which mail to read, when to read it, which to save for future reference or which to autodelete without so much as a glance. The extensive amount of information received forces employees to make important communication decisions quickly. The receiver is often expected to make an instant decision in order to make an instant reply. Consequently, complex messages may not get the necessary thought and attention they deserve.

Multitasking as noise

In the 1980s and 1990s, multitasking was considered the ideal way to work faster and more competitively in the marketplace. The practice became the norm in many business sectors; technology facilitated multitasking which today has reached a new level.

Here's one example. A young bank executive juggles her management duties at work with her school studies in an executive MBA programme. During class breaks, she toggles back and forth between an Intranet Web chat room of fellow employees to find out what's happening at the office and accesses her email account for customer updates. At the same time she retrieves messages from her cell phone. Because of all the information she has to process in a short amount of time, she runs the risk of information overload, misunderstanding and misinterpretation.

With the acceptance of multitasking activities, many companies saw a way "to do more with less", meaning they could hire fewer people and assign them more responsibility. **Multitasking** has become a buzz phrase for job-seekers who give interviewers examples of multitasking experiences in which they were able to take on, accept and accomplish more tasks.

Conversely, a study on multitasking found that shifting mental processes costs subjects time, and such costs were even greater when subjects switched to tasks that were less familiar. The authors of the study were particularly interested in the potential impact of shifting mental processes of those involved in vehicle and aircraft operations (Rubinstein *et al.*, 2001).

For example, when people drive and talk on their cell phones at the same time, they are using their executive control processes, or the brain's prefrontal cortex

Strategic Thinking

The framing of a message may be an impediment to understanding what the sender of the message truly meant. Framing studies are generally in three fields: the use of framing by the media and how they influence news coverage or production (Gitlin, 1980); the public discourse or social movement, such as how the development of nuclear power as a source of energy was framed in its early days (Gamson & Modigliani, 1989); and the media effects theory (Lupton, 1994; Iyengar, 1991).

However, the media are not the only organizations that use framing (they just have been studied more by scholars than other groups). Business, government, social agencies and social movements use framing to shape messages to achieve their own ends. For example, a company is forced to lay off workers. In its public announcement, it emphasizes how it will help displaced workers to find new positions at other locations or new jobs in the community. In choosing this frame, the company hopes to negate some of the publicity about the closing of the plant.

An energy company emphasizes how it has worked to preserve wildlife and waterfowl in an area where it is exploring for natural gas. This choice of frame, accurate as it may be, is designed to portray the company as an environment-friendly and responsible organization.

and other neural regions such as the parietal cortex. This portion of the brain determines mental priorities and allocates mind resources. It involves two distinct, complementary stages: goal shifting (I am going to do this project now and do the other one later) and rule activation (I am turning off the thinking process concerning that activity and turning on the process for this activity). This shift in process takes several tenths of a second – time that might be crucial in a life or death situation.

Information overload and multitasking have the potential to paralyse analytical skills, making decision-makers less effective in the information selection process and affecting the quality of work output.

Hearing Versus Listening

Hearing is not listening.

Hearing is the biological process of sound waves striking the inner ear bones and turning the waves into vibrations that the brain can decode.

Listening, on the other hand, involves making sense of the messages that the brain is receiving. It involves analysis, evaluation and judgement based on individual capacities. It is influenced by a person's background, gender, education, agenda, values, beliefs, attitudes and an infinite number of individual determinants, all of which will affect the meaning of the message. It is subject to our mood, physical well-being, emotional state, perception of the speaker and time of day.

Most people are poor listeners. Some professions, particularly those involved in health and social services, train practitioners to be active listeners. Physicians often determine the causes of patients' illnesses or complaints within several minutes of examining them. They are trained to ask key questions, observe patient responses and then, through a process of elimination, determine the cause of the complaints.

Listening is a crucial factor in effective communication. We are taught in the home and in school how to speak and how to read and write, but not how to listen. We work to perfect our basic communicative skills. Reading and writing skills progress from creating simple sentences to composing complex research reports. Speaking skills are considered important communicative skills, and college students are often required to take public speaking courses. But we are never formally taught to listen.

Our knowledge of the listening process and our skill in managing the complex elements in that process are vital to effective communication.

The complex listening process

Listening is difficult. If you've ever attended a day-long conference or had to take three classes back to back, you will remember how exhausted you felt by the end of the day. Why were you so tired? All you did was sit for a few hours and listen.

Effective listening takes great effort and concentration. You have to work hard not only to hear but also to analyse, evaluate, internalize, digest and make sense of the various messages – both verbal and non-verbal – that are entering your brain simultaneously and continuously.

All receivers do not "listen" to the same message. Listeners receive different messages from the same speaker using exactly the same words. Scholars have identified four stages of listening, and at every stage the message can be understood and misunderstood in myriad ways.

The four stages of listening

Listening is a four-stage process:

- *Attending.* In this stage you have crossed from just hearing to "listening up". You are beginning to take in the message.
- *Understanding.* In this stage you try to make sense of the words and non-verbal language. There are many factors, both internal and external, that will affect the message you receive. We make inferences, associations, formulate questions, look for clarification, etc.
- *Responding.* In this stage there is an exchange of feedback which can indicate understanding or confusion.
- *Remembering.* As we retain little of what we hear, in this stage it is vital to pay strict attention, concentrate on what is being sent and employ written notes or visual aids.

Barriers to effective listening

What makes listening effectively so difficult? Listeners often engage in faulty listening behaviours, both conscious and unconscious, and the use of any one of these behaviours dramatically affects the reception of a message:

- *Pseudo listening.* These listeners pretend to listen. They give the appearance of listening, nodding and smiling at the right times, but they are not really listening.
- *Selective listening.* Some listeners hear only what they want to hear. Teenagers, notorious selective listeners, hear "You can go to the party" but do not listen to "be home by midnight".
- *Insulated listening.* These listeners feel the message is not relevant, important or worthy of their time. They may find the speaker annoying or boring. They can find many reasons to insulate themselves from the message. They will remember little, if anything, of what was heard.
- *Insensitive listening.* These listeners can't find meaning beyond the speakers' words. Non-verbal and environmental cues that could add to the substance of a message are ignored. These low-context listeners rely on a literal interpretation of words and ignore the subtleties of language and expression that also carry meaning.
- *Ambush listening.* These listeners are actually paying very close attention … in order to collect information to use later to attack you. Prosecution attorneys listen to eyewitness accounts carefully, looking for information they can use later to discredit evidence or a reputation, cloud an issue, create doubt about an identification, etc. When Mary asks John why he didn't invite her along when he went to a local pub, John replies, "You said you didn't like going to Harry's Pub". John successfully manipulated his way out of being accused of neglecting his girlfriend for a night out with his friends.
- *Stage hogging.* Stage hogs don't listen at all. When they are not talking they are thinking about what they will say. They enjoy being in the spotlight and find a way to get there by interruption and exaggeration. Their project is more exciting, their work is harder and their story is more compelling. If they overhear you say how tired you are, they'll interrupt with, "You're tired? You don't know what tired is, let me tell you about my day!"

People engage in faulty listening behaviours everyday, in every country and in every company. Look at your own listening behaviour. If you see yourself here, try to cultivate more effective listening behaviour.

Good listening leads to good decision-making and will help you become a better communicator and a more effective executive. We can think much faster, some experts say six times faster, than we can hear. Our mind has lots of time for gathering information and making complex evaluations based on the incoming information.

Types of listener

Listeners process information on the basis of a variety of factors such as ability, experience, and motive. Here are some "types" of listener found in the business world:

- *The passive listener.* Listeners of this type think that silence indicates listening. They remain quiet while others talk. They are not actively involved in the communication process. Instead they are listening to their own mental processes, judging the speaker and the message on past knowledge and experience. They are listening, but not fully or effectively. They do not seek clarification, definition, illumination or interpretation, and so are processing what they hear on the basis of limited and limiting information. As many of us have been taught to be quiet while others talk, or not to ask too many questions, we often fail to find out what we want or need to know about an issue. This failure often leads to poor decision-making. Human resource specialists lament the fact that many interviewees, when asked, "Do you have any questions?", have nothing to say. Their passivity may be interpreted as lack of interest or preoccupation with other issues.

- *The obtuse listener.* Listeners of this type focus on the literal meaning of a message. They are insensitive to the subtle cues that surround and frame the words and expressions used. Educated and experienced people know reading these subtleties can impact upon the meaning of a message. These listeners take the message at face value without giving careful consideration to what the speaker meant or intended to say, the circumstances surrounding the event or various other interpretations. Not taking into account that your manager is stressed out may lead you to label her "difficult to get along with". Not understanding that an employee may not have the language skills to express an idea can lead you to believe a person is not a loyal worker. "I don't care what he meant, that's what he said" is the mantra of an obtuse executive.

- *The agenda-setting listener.* Everyone comes to the communication table from a different place. It is very difficult to avoid listening from your own individual perspective. When the company's CEO reports that sales are down, employees are listening to see if jobs might be cut; executives are concerned about departmental figures and bonuses, and salespeople may be listening for new marketing incentives. Everyone has his or her own agenda. People listen to messages that are most relevant to them; often their agendas are "hidden". When John Hoffman hears about sales being down for the quarter, he wonders if he should take that job offer at the La Crosse Garment Company and Mary Meyers decides that now is the time for her to get her MBA. Who knew the decline in sales would lead to employees leaving the company?

- *The active listener.* These listeners have mastered the art of listening. They know that effective listening will lead to effective communication. They understand that listening is not a one-stop, one-size-fits-all end in itself, but a complex process of understanding the speaker, the intent of the message, the required action and the desired results.

Executives who want to be effective listeners need to address many issues:

- What do my employees know?
- What is their understanding of the issue?
- What do I need to know about them to understand what they are trying to say? What are the internal and external factors affecting their understanding and response?
- What questions do I need answered to communicate my message better?
- How can I put their minds at ease?
- What actions do I need to take, and how can I get them to take these actions?

Active listening requires work and practice. Activities such as paraphrasing other's remarks, giving feedback and asking appropriate questions can help you become a more effective listener.

Chapter Summary

Effective listening takes effort and concentration. Noise, physical, psychological and semantic, can impede listening. Everything from prejudice and educational level to a grumbling stomach or wind rattling a window can prevent us from listening effectively.

Communicators need to be aware that thinking in new and different ways is impeded not only by cognitive dissonance but also by selective filters or "rings of defence".

Information overload, too many messages in a short period of time, can distort listening. We listen to very little and remember even less. We can think faster than we can hear, and that leaves time for mental distractions. It's hard to get back on track once you have deviated from the issue at hand.

Faulty listening behaviours can alter how receivers interpret and misinterpret communication messages. Lack of information, monotonous delivery and irrelevance of subject matter lead to boredom. When faced with boredom, we inevitably switch our thoughts to something more interesting, even if it's only what to plan for dinner. ■

Learning From Others

Charles Lankester is Managing Director, Corporate Practice, Asia-Pacific, of Edelman, the world's largest independent public relations firm. Edelman has 45 offices worldwide with 2000 employees and was named the best PR firm on *Advertising Age*'s "Best Agencies" list. *PR Week* awarded Edelman its "Editor's Choice" distinction in 2006.

Lankester specializes in corporate communications, reputation management and crisis leadership. He headed his own corporate communications consultancy, Limehouse Partners, and has held senior management positions at Financial Practice Europe, Weber Shandwick, Burson-Marsteller and Ogilvy & Mather. Here's his insight into crisis management and the barriers to creating effective lines of communication in a crisis.

Who's in Charge of Crisis Management?

Surveys consistently show that almost half the companies in Europe and the United States have no crisis management planning in place. Where plans do exist, they are often no more than a comfort blanket: useful to allow a risk management box to be ticked, but untested and uninvested. And thus ultimately unreliable.

A significant issue, therefore, is where does crisis management responsibility fit within an organization? Unlike more traditional business functions, such as finance, human resources and marketing, crisis management has yet to find a functional home.

When crisis management resides with security or health and safety, the focus is usually on the operational details of implementing emergency plans, with less on reputational issues such as business continuity, crisis management and crisis communications. This "emergency service" approach is very good at the "What do we do?" but doesn't help with the "What do we say?" part. Operationally rich, reputationally poor.

When the public relations/communications function is responsible for crisis management, the focus tends to be on corporate responsibility and crisis communications, but often with insufficient attention to emergency planning implementation. Terrific at the "say" part, but lacking in the "do".

Ultimately, successful crisis management encompasses all aspects of business, including operations, marketing, communications, distribution and legal. However, programme components are often developed in a piecemeal manner by the individual groups responsible for them, without the appropriate planning and higher-level oversight needed to ensure a cohesive, comprehensive programme.

What happens when a fire means you can't access your offices? Your IT department has the data backed up, but there is no way of retrieving it. All your email addresses are inaccessible.

You haven't considered alternative workplace facilities. You have a great crisis communications plan. But no way of using it.

Crisis preparedness and crisis management should be considered as much part of modern business as marketing, finance or HR and will incorporate the planning, implementation and control of activities in all these areas. In fact, the very terminology is shifting. Less crisis management. More crisis leadership.

Case Study – BrightHouse Neurostrategies Group

Seven hundred new products are introduced every day. In 2004, 26 895 new food and household products hit store shelves around the world.

Why does a consumer choose one brand over another? How can you use current findings on consumer behaviour to extend your brand and circumvent the noise in the marketplace.

Neuromarketing is a new marketing tool that uses magnetic resonance imaging (MRI) to study how the brain functions in buying behaviour. Using brain scans, scientists document the effects of advertising on various parts of the brain (Hotz, 2005).

This pioneering work has led to the growth of new businesses such as BrightHouse Neurostrategies Group in Atlanta, Georgia, USA. These types of companies help clients determine how to use messages effectively to influence customer buying habits.

Other institutions are also using MRIs in advertising research. The Open University in Britain and the London Business School have recorded the brain waves of shoppers at a virtual store. They have reportedly identified the portion of the brain that becomes active when shoppers decide to buy a particular brand.

DaimlerChrysler Corporation and Nikon University in Japan are also using scanning to identify customer buying patterns. DaimlerChrysler found that "reward centres in male brains responded more distinctly to sportier models" (Parapiboon, 2006).

Explore neuromarketing. What do you think are some of the ethical issues involved in using brain scans for advertising research? What do you think the future holds for the BrightHouse Neurostrategies Group?

Consult the Web for contradictory responses to the ethical dimensions of this research.

For more information on neuromarketing consult: www.stanford.edu/- dgermain/buyButton.htm ∎

Class Exercises

1. Suppose you work for the airline industry. Ethnographic studies and focus groups have reaffirmed the industry's concern that passengers pay little attention to the safety information presented before each flight or the seat cards spelling out the safety information of each type of airplane. Analyse this pattern using the selective theories.

2. Try to recall an everyday-life scenario when your attention was threatened by cognitive dissonance or selective perception. Write up the scenario as if it were a scene in a play or a television advertisement.

3. Think about information overload in the workplace. Talk to family or friends and get them to describe any incidences of information overload in their place of business. Ideas to be explored might include the influences of email on productivity, overly long meetings or assessing the validity of information in the Internet world.

Action Plan

You have just learned that an article about your snowboard company, written by your public relations department, will appear in a small Swedish monthly magazine devoted to extreme sports. The article will undergo some editing by the magazine's staff, but you are excited because now many people will hear about your company and the great products you manufacture.

But will they? Are your expectations too high? Develop your personal selective filters list and determine how a consumer like yourself may or may not even see the article. Will you pick up the magazine in the first place? Will you read the specific article? Will you think the company is great? Will you remember the company's name or will you focus on some other information like the name of the local distributor? Will you alter your opinion after reading additional articles or seeing other manufacturers' ads for snowboards in different magazines? How can the company use additional communication efforts to try to break through the consumer's selective filters and get you to buy the magazine (exposure), read the article (attention), get a positive image of your company (perception) and remember the necessary information about the product (retention), even weeks or months later when you may be ready to buy a snowboard (alteration)?

Websites

Access the business listening reference site at www.businesslistening.com and explore some of the advice it gives concerning "Listening Strategy and Skills" (BusinessListening.com, 2006).

You can take listening tests at http://www.esl-lab.com/index/.htm (Randall's ESL Cyber Listening Lab, 2006) in easy, medium, difficult and very difficult levels. This site, designed for English as a second language (ESL) speakers, also links to other websites that address accents and slang language.

You can learn more about cognitive dissonance and how it works from Changing Minds, an organization that boasts being the largest site in the world on all aspects of changing minds, at http://changingminds. org/explanations/theories/cognitive _ dissonance.htm (Changing Minds, 2006).

References

Allport, G. & Postman, L. (1945) "The basic psychology of rumour". *Transactions of the New York Academy of Sciences*, **8**: 61–81.

BusinessListening.com. (2006) Available from: www.businesslistening.com [Accessed 14 August 2006].

Changing Minds (2006) Available from: http://changingminds.org/explanations/theories/cognitive_dissonance.htm [Accessed 14 August 2006].

Farace, R., Monge, R. & Russell, H. (1977) *Communicating and Organizing*. Reading, MA, Addison-Wesley.

Festinger, L. (1962) "Cognitive dissonance". *Scientific American*, **107**: 93.

Gamson, W. & Modigliani, A. (1989) "Media discourse and public opinion on nuclear power: a constructionist approach". *American Journal of Sociology*, **95**: 1–37.

Gitlin, T. (1980) *The Whole World is Watching. Mass Media in the Making and Unmaking of the New Left*. Berkeley, CA, University of California Press.

Graber, D. (1988) *Processing the News: How People Tame the Information Tide*. New York, Longman.

Hotz, R. (2005) "Searching for the why of buying", 27 February 2005. Available from: latimes.com/news/science/la-sci-brain27feb27,0,3899978.story?coll=la-home-headlines [Accessed 30 August 2005].

Ivengar, S. (1991) *Is Anyone Responsible? How Television Frames Political Issues*. Chicago, IL, University of Chicago Press.

James, W. (1890) The principles of psychology. Available from: http://psychoclassics.yorku.ca/James/Principles/prin11.htm [Accessed 5 Dec. 2005].

Lewis, C. (2003) "Ready, steady, read". *Training Journal*, September 2003. Available from: http://www.trainingjournal.com/articles/archive/article.jsp?ref-135&page=34&topic=0&keyword=&issue=&order=issueref_label&direction=desc [Accessed 6 April 2006].

Lupton, D. (1994) "Femininity, responsibility, and the technological imperative: discourses on breast cancer in the Australian press". *International Journal of Health Services*, **24**(1): 73–89.

Parapiboon, P. (2006) "Pushing the buy button". *Stanford Scientific Magazine*. Available from: www.stanford.edu/~dgermain/buyButton.htm [Accessed 14 August 2006].

Randall's ESL Cyber Listening Lab (2006) Available from: http://www.esl-lab.com/index/.htm [Accessed 14 August 2006].

Rubinstein, J., Meyer, D. *et al.* (2001) "Executive control of cognitive processes in task switching". *Journal of Experimental Psychology – Human Perception and Performance*, **27**(4), 763–797.

Shannon, C. & Weaver, W. (1949) *The Mathematical Theory of Communication*. Urbana, University of Illinois Press.

Bibliography

Alder, R. & Rodman, G. (2002) *Understanding Human Communication*. New York, Oxford University Press.

Bivins, T. (2005) *Public Relations Writing*, 5th edn. Boston, McGraw-Hill.

Glaser, J. (2006) "Precision listening". Available from: www.benchmarkcommunicationsinc.com [Accessed 17 Feb. 2006].

CHAPTER 5

Communication Channels

Executive Summary

Channels are the modes by which communication is transferred. The selection of the appropriate channel is fundamental to reaching your audience. The evolution of communication channels corresponds to the development of spoken, written and printed languages and more recently to electronic language. The speed and interactivity of computers and technology are reshaping communication methods.

Oral communication – face-to-face communications, speeches and meetings – is less formal and the most personal form of communication
We can see the messenger, hear the message with a minimal amount of noise and ask for the message to be repeated if necessary.

Written communication – letters, memos and reports – is more explicit and can be accessed again and again and stored indefinitely
While less personal, the tone of the communication offers the reader clues about the sender.

Well-designed presentation materials reinforce message content, and listenability and readability of messages are important considerations

Electronic communication – email, faxes, instant messages, teleconferences and presentation software – continues to evolve in style, structure and format

Organizing information is fundamental to effective messaging, regardless of the communication channel
Subject material should fit your audience and include key elements to attract and hold the attention of the receiver.

Effective oral communication is an art and can be learned with practice and attention to delivery styles and methods
Your choice of delivery channel must meet the needs and expectations of your audience. ■

Communication Channels

> *When we make ourselves understood, we always speak well.*
>
> *Moliere*

Introduction to Message Delivery

An important component of our transactional communication model is the channel. A **channel** is the mode by which a communication is transferred. This chapter examines how channels influence message delivery in spoken language, written language, printed language and electronic language.

In the communication model below, messages and feedback travel along arrows that represent various transmission channels. There are many channels: face-to-face meetings, seminars, newspapers, radio, billboards, company newsletters, email, letters, memos, brochures, annul reports, phone calls, body language, books, tabloid magazines, respected journals, employee presentations and so on.

Each channel requires a specific format and language. Your choice of channel should add to the efficacy of your message. Using the appropriate transmission channel is important for business communicators and can establish your reputation as an effective communicator.

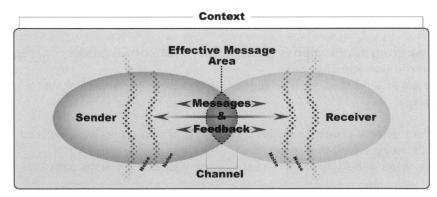

Figure 5.1 Transactional communication model. Notice that communication channels are represented by double-headed arrows that reach senders and receivers and provide a means of transmitting both messages and feedback.

Consider this example. A new employee for a food manufacturer began her career in a small community, but she wanted a more cosmopolitan territory. When her local team travelled to a larger city for a district meeting, the supervisor requested a presentation on selling to small grocery chains.

The young woman sensed her opportunity and volunteered. Instead of a simple verbal report, she decided to prepare an electronic presentation that included pictures of store layouts and charts of product shelving options. The regional vice-president who was at the meeting was so impressed with her presentation that he invited the woman to the regional meeting.

She was excited about a free trip to a vibrant metropolis, but, more than that, she felt empowered and in control of her career. At this regional meeting, she met another executive who would soon request her transfer to his team.

Within six months of joining the company, the young woman gave up her apartment in the small country town; she had been relocated to one of her dream cities.

A sender should select a channel on the basis of the receiver's needs and expectations as well as the content of the message itself. Channels may be divided into oral and written methods of delivery. Oral channels include person-to-person communication, phone conversations, small group discussions, speeches, teleconferencing, etc. Written channels are email, letters, advertising, newsletters, brochures, etc.

Let's first look at the beginnings of communication for a perspective on the various forms of communication used today.

Spoken Language

Early humans tried to communicate orally. Grunts eventually became a **formal language** with rules and structure. People communicated not only basic needs and wants, but also complex concepts that transcended local boundaries. The early history of civilization records the political and philosophical influence of great orators such as Aristotle and Demosthenes in Greece and Cicero and Cato in Rome.

Written Language

While spoken language was being codified, a **written language** also was being developed. The Sumerians used a cuneiform or pictograph script on commerce tokens, and the Egyptians used hieroglyphics to depict sounds.

Dig Deeper

We can learn from famous speakers of the past and present. Here are a few names you should be familiar with – if you are not, we suggest you find out not only who they are, but why they are considered great speakers.

- Mark Anthony – Oration on the Dead Body of Julius Caesar
- Martin Luther – Before the Diet of Worms
- Giuseppe Garibaldi – To His Soldiers
- W. E. B. DuBois – Behold the Land
- Winston Churchill – Their Finest Hour
- Otto von Bismarck – War and Armaments in Europe
- Nikolai Lenin– The Dictatorship of the Proletariat
- Susan B. Anthony – On Woman's Right to Suffrage
- Dag Hammarskjold – Values of Nationalism and Internationalism
- Golda Meir – The Gaza Strip Speech
- Pope Pius XII – Appeal for Peace.

Popular speakers today include:

- Zig Ziglar – See You at the Top
- Stephen Covey – Eight Discernable Characteristics of Principled-Centered Leadership
- Olli Rehn – Cyprus: One Year After Accession.

The Chinese, Mayans and Olmecs also had early alphabets. The creation of the first modern alphabet is usually credited to the Phoenicians of Western Asia who developed a limited alphabet around 1700 BC.

The Greeks took this alphabet, added vowels and began recording the events of their time and culture. The Romans and Etruscans also adapted the alphabet and used it as they traded and travelled throughout the civilized world. The written word has since been used to inform, persuade and entertain.

Printed Language

The next new "language" that developed was the **printed language**. Somewhere around 1450, some scholars say it was more than 20 years before this widely accepted date, the printing press was invented. While the Chinese had a method of printing more than 400 years earlier, it was Johann Gutenberg's use of movable type that ensured the success of the printing press.

Historians have also credited Dutchman Laurens Janszoon with the invention of movable type and believe he may have preceded Gutenberg. However, Gutenberg won his place in history as the inventor of the printing press allowing the printed word to be recorded in book form for the common man.

Reading and writing were no longer reserved for the wealthy who could afford to educate themselves or for religious figures who could spend years pouring over manuscripts, interpreting their meanings and recording books by hand. In Western civilization, the Protestant Reformation and the Age of Exploration owe their origins to the versions of the Bible and the tales of wondrous lands across the sea that the printing press put into the hands of everyday people.

Electronic Language

Now we are in a new "language" era, the **Electronic Age**. Computers brought about new forms of communication, and with those new forms came new sets of rules. Some rules are still being codified and what was considered a correct form yesterday may not be proper today.

Just a few years ago, email was not an accepted form of business correspondence, but today it is more pervasive than the paper interoffice memo. What was initially an informal communiqué has gained new stature, and with this commercial usage have come formal rules. Emails, which were initially sent to friends and buddies and contained lower-case "i" or smiley faces, have now taken on an appropriate seriousness for the office and adhere to grammatical and spelling standards.

However, not everyone is excited about, or rushing to embrace, this form of communication. Critics suggest email threatens the richness of our language and predict abbreviated word usage, iconography and loss of creativity.

Charlene Spretnak, an ecological and social critic, points out that an average 14-year-old's vocabulary has declined from 25 000 words in 1950 to 10 000 words today (Spretnak, 1997). This decline in the working vocabulary of a teenager is related to a significant decrease in the capacity to think analytically and critically.

Paul Hawken, environmentalist and educator, makes the analogy that young people can recognize over 1000 corporate logos but can name only a handful of garden plants or animals (Hawken, 1993). This, however, could be viewed as a positive sign by marketers of these branded products.

Other scholars differ from this view, saying that vocabularies are not declining but merely changing. People are becoming bilingual, speaking a new language called technology. Dictionaries publish additional words every year as new words and expressions are needed to communicate in a new world.

A school in the USA prides itself in its adoption of technology in the educational arena. A technology curriculum begins in preschool, and an objective for the second grade reads: "Begin to develop a vocabulary of technology terms". This objective is carried forward each year, moving into developing a working vocabulary of technology terms in the fourth grade and an introduction to Internet terminology in the seventh grade. By the eighth grade, students will "continue to develop a technology vocabulary" and will incorporate "the Internet in their five-page paper" (Rhodes, 2006).

A recent debate centres on whether email with its short-cut punctuation and language will bring the demise of written communication as we know it. Will potential wordsmiths be snuffed out in their infancy? Will the craft of letterwriting die in our lifetime? Will history no longer benefit from the individual perspective of those who put their thoughts to paper?

Many critics say email is an assault on proper language. Others say it just adds to the informality of language brought on by television, catchy song lyrics and pervasive ungrammatical advertising slogans.

The lack of facility with the process of formal writing has spawned a new industry. Firms like Business Writing at Its Best (BWB) charge top dollar to teach business executives, attorneys, doctors and other corporate bigwigs the art of writing, a skill many admit they didn't learn in school. BWB calls itself the "Rolls-Royce of business and legal writing workshops" (Agress, 2006).

Advantages and Disadvantages of Oral and Written Channels

If communication is the life blood of good business, then one of the first things a new executive must understand is that clear and effective communication is necessary to meet objectives because misdirected or confusing communication results in unresolved problems.

While some communication messages demand a specific channel over another, channel selection is often a judgement call. Making the right decision about which one to use is crucial because the channel itself brings added meaning to the message.

Oral communication

Oral communication is more personal and less formal. It conveys sincerity for the message and respect for the receiver. For example, if bad news is to be imparted, face-to-face oral communication is usually seen as most respectful. Face-to-face communication allows us to use all of our senses – we can see the messenger deliver the message, read his or her body language, hear the message with a minimal amount of external noise, ask for a repeat of the message, if necessary, and assess the tone of the message. It continues to be the most personal form of communication.

Sometimes, however, oral communication is not personal at all. Have you ever broken up with someone via phone voice mail? It might have been easy on you, but the person receiving the message probably would rather have received an explanation in person or at least in a personal phone conversation.

Recently, a student reported he had been fired by email. The student felt this method of letting him go was an added insult. "Why didn't he just tell me himself?" he asked.

Disadvantages of oral communication are misinterpretation of words, misread meanings, unrecorded facts and figures and lack of remembering. Of course, technology increasingly enables oral communication to be recorded and reaccessed.

Types of oral business message

More traditional forms of oral business communication include face-to-face meetings, one-on-one conversations, small group presentations, oral reports, videoconferencing and phone conversations. Oral communication enables immediate feedback and is most effective when there is an emotional component of the message that would affect the success of the communication.

Written communication

Written communication is more explicit. It can be read over and over again to ensure complete understanding. However, while there is less personality and emotional/visual appeal in a written message, the vocabulary, sentence structure, punctuation and grammar selected by the sender reveals the sincerity and intent of the message.

A business message can be delivered in numerous ways. Each channel has its own rules and standards that can be interpreted by the receiver in specific and diverse ways.

The 10 Cs for writing effectively:

1. *Content*   Are you saying exactly what you want to say?
2. *Completeness*   Have you included all the necessary information your receiver may need?
3. *Correctness*   Have you checked your communication to be sure your facts are accurate?
4. *Clarity*   Have you made your message clear to your receiver?
5. *Coherence*   Does your language contribute to an understandable message?
6. *Conciseness*   Have you eliminated words that might mislead or dissuade a receiver?
7. *Connection*   Have you appealed to the needs of your specific audience?
8. *Creativity*   Have you developed your message in a new and unique manner?
9. *Courtesy*   Have you used a sincere and appropriate tone?
10. *Closure*   Have you asked for the action you want from your receiver?

What you should know is that each message you send will carry a contextual meaning that is as important as the content.

How you say something, and where and when you say it, will carry as much, if not more, weight than what you are actually saying. You must give each message deliberate thought and consideration as to the words, tone, adherence to rules, language style, etc. The receiver will read between the lines, looking for clues into the true meaning and intent of the message.

Types of written business message

Traditional written communications include formal letters, memos and reports. They usually address complex issues that need to be presented in a structured format or used as reference material. Effective written communications are dependent on how well you have thought out your purpose and then how you have structured the message. For example, memos can do the following:

* create a record that can be useful in the future;
* allow for detailed reporting;
* give recipients the opportunity to think about the content and return to it if necessary;
* facilitate a broad distribution (Business Communication, 2003, p. 63).

Types of electronic communication

Technology in the workplace has brought **electronic communication** to the forefront of the business day at all levels of hierarchy, from the CEO to the administrative assistant to the order filler on the production line. Email, faxing, instant messaging, teleconferencing, presentation software, phone messaging options and global visual connections (possibly even more options have been developed since this book was printed) are used to communicate to the person sitting in the office next to you or with thousands of people around the world.

Electronic charts, graphs, budget numbers and annual reports can be recorded, distributed, stored on disks, CDs or flash drives, attached to emails or posted on websites. Pictures, sound, video, graphics, hot links and multimedia effects may be included to add further richness to the message.

Electronic messaging can mean cost savings in paper, printing and postage. Rewrites and revisions are made easily, quickly and inexpensively. Electronic documents use minimal storage space. Instantaneous distribution of electronic documents is feasible across the world to multiple recipients.

Choosing a Channel

The extent of options for sending effective business messages makes choosing the right channel even more complex. When choosing a channel, many factors have to be considered: the intent of the message, the understanding of the receiver and the meaning inherent in the channel itself.

Additionally, a certain expertise is required and expected for using each channel effectively. No longer can you compose an email message and send it off before reviewing it. Spellchecking the document is a necessity, but often this is not enough, as you cannot depend on this limited process to be completely accurate.

You have to reread the email from the perspective of the receiver. Is each word understandable? Will the receiver get what "it" refers to in the first sentence? Is all the necessary information included for a complete understanding of the communication? If any vital element of the message is cloudy or excluded, the communication is ineffective.

Take a look at this internal email memo, sent to 50 people, and see if you can identify some of the communication problems:

TO: Bobby Johnson

SUBJECT: Retirement Party

Hello everyone. As you know Joe Banyon is retiring next month. I've been asked by some of his friends to arrange a little farewell party in his honour.

The date is Friday, 6 p.m. at City Café, and we hope you can make it.

We would like to give him a gift certificate. We are asking everyone to contribute. Let me know ASAP.

See you there.

Bobby

What information was missing? The most glaring, of course, is that there is no date mentioned. What about the address of the restaurant? There is an assumption by the sender that everyone knows where this establishment is located. Details are imperative to good communication.

Bobby wants people to contribute, but, for the people receiving the message, this could be a sensitive issue as it is unclear as to whether their contribution goes to a gift certificate or if it covers the party expenses and the gift. The memo is unclear if the party will include a full-course dinner or just drinks at the bar, nor does it state whether spouses are invited. Finally, ASAP is an unclear directive.

Recipients of this email need more information. Those invited will either send an email asking for more details or place a phone call to get the correct information. Whichever they do, Bobby faces the possibility of 50 email messages or phone calls, all because he didn't take time to read over his memo from an audience-centred perspective.

Accuracy is important no matter which channel you use. Because change is so rapid in the global marketplace, it is imperative that you check and recheck your message for any inaccuracies. Even though senders must file a report quickly, it doesn't mean the message can contain errors. The receivers of messages expect clear, complete and accurate messages. They don't care that you only had an hour to get the report or message out.

The Mechanics of Effective Messaging

In written communication you should take sufficient time to organize your message. Here are some strategies for composing effective messages.

Outlining

Outlining may seem to be a strategy of the past, but, whether it is used in an abbreviated format or a more complex plan, an outline has value. Have you ever composed a communication and, as you pressed "send", remembered something you had wanted to include but forgot? Have you ever thought and thought about all the elements you wanted to cover in a report but, after handing it to the professor, remembered one or two more points you had wanted to include? Have you ever had a conversation with a friend or family member and, after they walked away, realized you had forgotten a crucial point you wanted to make?

An **outline** can be as simple as a few phrases on a piece of paper or as complex as a three-page organizational layout. The key is to refer to your written outline *before* you send the message.

Place your outline, the blueprint of your message, next to the computer as you type your email message or write your report. Look at it during the process and before you finish. For face-to-face meetings, put your main points on an index card and place it in your pocket or briefcase for review.

For complex messages, outlines can be arranged in several organizational patterns as defined below. The goal is to view your information from a receiver's perspective. Which organizational method will make your information easier for your receivers to understand?

You should not choose the one *you* always seem to use, or the one that is easiest for you. Try to think like your receiver and choose the organizational method that will best fit the content of what you have to say.

Organizational patterns for outlines

There are four major types of organizational patterns. Each one has a specific use depending on the nature of the material and audience. Let's look at some organizational patterns:

* chronological pattern
* spatial pattern
* importance pattern
* topical pattern.

Chronological (time) pattern

Chronological material is presented according to a time line. You start at some point in the past and work towards the present or begin at a present moment and move back to the past. This organizational pattern is used for history books and fiction novels. A history text will start at some point in time and chronologically move to the present. A professor teaching the history of war wouldn't begin in 1989, jump back to 1600, move up to 1885 and then back to 1540. It would be too confusing for the reader or listener to follow.

This time-sensitive method is also good for explaining how a project has developed, showing how the past has affected the present, or for relating a message that is best understood with linear exposition. It could be step-by-step directions on how to download software from the Internet. If you were requesting office equipment supplies for the next fiscal year, in your organizational time pattern you might start with initial inventory needs for the first month, show projected uses for each month, followed by monthly restocking amounts, and work your way to the last quarter.

Spatial (space) pattern

A **spatial** outline groups events, facts or problems according to location, such as where it happens, where it will take place, the region of the country, etc. Rather than a time line, it is like a snapshot, and is generally used for descriptions.

For example, if you wanted to request office furniture, you could talk about everything that was needed in the conference room before moving on to the office cubicles and then the lunchroom.

Spatial organization may also be used when talking about geographical regions. For a report on furniture needed by your company in various branch locations, you might arrange the information according to Eastern division needs, Western division needs or the needs of the offices in France, India and Spain.

Importance pattern

The **importance pattern** presents information by starting with the most significant projects or facts and continuing to the least significant. This format can also be reversed as a report goes from the least important to the most important information. Two terms to know here are primacy and recency. **Primacy** means putting first the most important information or the most expensive commodity or the most urgent issue, etc. This works well because readers or listeners may be fresher and more ready to listen at the outset of the report than nearer the end. People tend to remember the first things they hear or read rather than information that comes later in a conversation or is buried in paragraph 3 or 4 of the message.

Recency, on the other hand, means putting the most important information at the end of your message, so it is the most recent point your audience hears or reads before they turn their attention to another matter.

For example, your report on office furniture needs could begin with the most needed items and continue to the least needed items. Or it could start with the less essential things and end with what is really vitally necessary. You could also start with the most expensive items and work to the least expensive.

Topical (relatedness) pattern

The **topical** pattern groups similar topics. In this pattern you would group related facts together to make it easier for the listener or reader to comprehend the information.

Using an office example, you could first talk about desks, chairs and bookcases. Then you could talk about lamps and accessories. Next you could address computers and wiring needs, then forms, business cards and signs. And finally you could discuss furnishings such as artwork and carpet needs.

Remember to choose an organizational pattern that fits your material and audience.

Formal Written Communication Formats

Choosing the appropriate format for **written communication** ensures that the message is delivered with minimal noise or static. A personal letter delivered by the post has a different structure and purpose than email or memos.

Each format has its own "look" and carries certain reader expectations.

Formal business letters

Young executives today have never known a world without email and text messaging. **Formal letters** may seem like something from the Dark Ages; however, there are occasions when formal letters, recommendations, references, letters of credit or letters of introduction are not only appropriate but necessary.

If you have never studied formal letter composition, be aware that there is a prescribed format. This is important because receivers of these communiqués are judging you, your message and your company or organization by the appearance of the letter and its adherence to the rules of style.

Formal business letters have seven main parts:

• heading
• date
• inside address
• salutation
• body
• close
• signature.

Remember, each country has its own variations on formatting a business letter. For example, some individuals are borrowing from a memo format and using a subject line in their formal letters. It is important to access a current model for the country with which you are corresponding to make sure your letter appears correct and respectful.

The **heading** is the return address of the individual or company sending the letter. For most businesses the information contained in its letterhead serves as the heading.

The **date** contains the day, month and year of the correspondence. It is written as "9 October 2006" in most of the world, including the US military. But for other US uses, the date is written "October 9, 2006". The month should always be written out, however, and not used as a number format. The date usually sits two lines below the letterhead or heading, flush left. However in Germany, the correct form is to place the date on the right-hand side of the page.

The **inside address** is the receiver's courtesy title (Dr, Herr, Mme, Mrs, etc.), name, position in the company and address, including the postcode. The information is flush left, usually two lines below the date. Different countries have rules governing acceptable titles that should be used in the address. Under this address you can also include a subject line or a reference line identifying the subject matter of the letter.

The **salutation** is the greeting to the receiver, and varies according to country. Using the proper salutation helps to ensure that your reader will be receptive to your letter. A salutation can be formal or informal depending on how well you know the receiver. It is placed flush left, two lines below the end of the inside address. Increasingly the salutation is being replaced with "Attention: (Name)". Perhaps because we are often writing to people we don't know around the world, the attention line is more acceptable today than in the past.

The body of the letter is where you place your information, and it is single spaced. Paragraphs can be indented or blocked; however, a non-indented style looks more contemporary.

The closing is a phrase that signals the end of the letter. It is double spaced below the last line of the body, and provides space below it for a signature block.

The signature block includes the writer's name written out, either by hand or electronically, and below that the writer's printed name and title. Reference initials for the person formatting the letter, if it is someone other than the person signing the letter, can be included under the signature block. This is also the place where you would include a notice of any enclosures to be sent with the letter or notation of copies sent to other parties.

An example of a formal business letter is shown in Model 5.2, with the parts labelled.

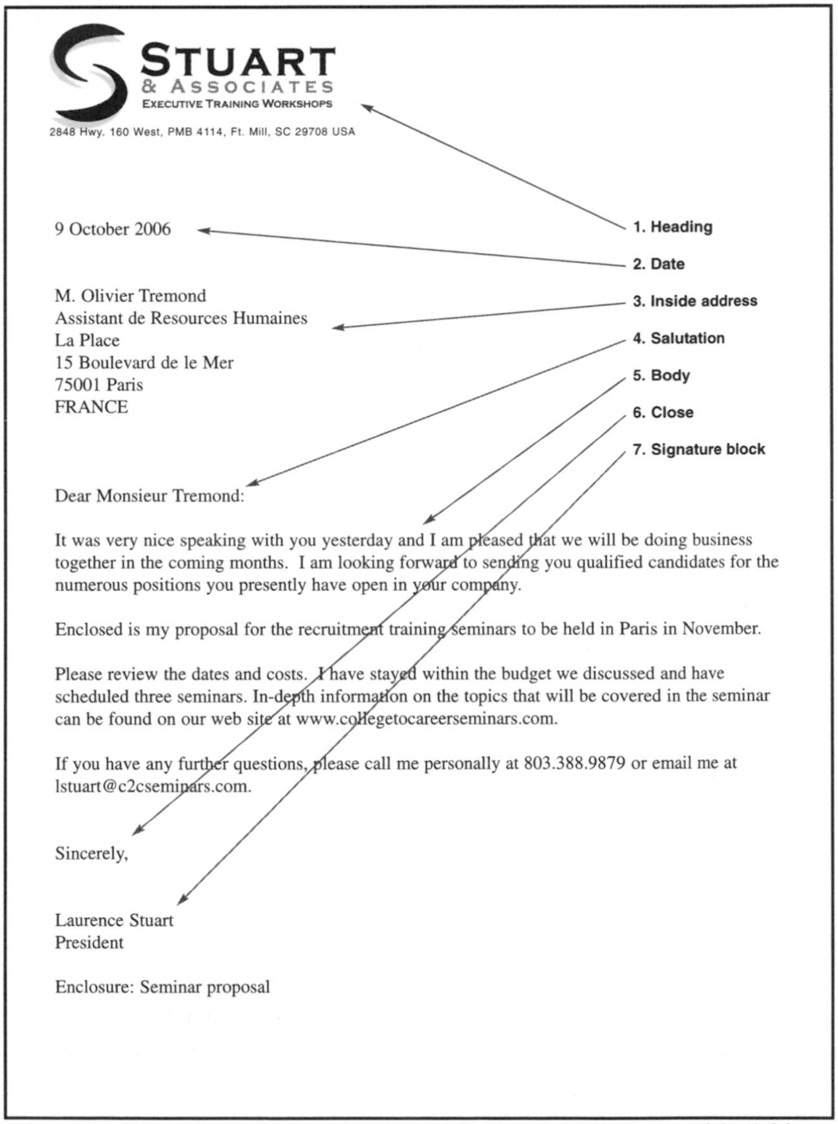

STUART
& ASSOCIATES
EXECUTIVE TRAINING WORKSHOPS
2848 Hwy. 160 West, PMB 4114, Ft. Mill, SC 29708 USA

9 October 2006

M. Olivier Tremond
Assistant de Resources Humaines
La Place
15 Boulevard de le Mer
75001 Paris
FRANCE

Dear Monsieur Tremond:

It was very nice speaking with you yesterday and I am pleased that we will be doing business together in the coming months. I am looking forward to sending you qualified candidates for the numerous positions you presently have open in your company.

Enclosed is my proposal for the recruitment training seminars to be held in Paris in November.

Please review the dates and costs. I have stayed within the budget we discussed and have scheduled three seminars. In-depth information on the topics that will be covered in the seminar can be found on our web site at www.collegetocareerseminars.com.

If you have any further questions, please call me personally at 803.388.9879 or email me at lstuart@c2cseminars.com.

Sincerely,

Laurence Stuart
President

Enclosure: Seminar proposal

designed by D. Stuart

Figure 5.2 Example of a formal business letter.

Office memoranda

The **office memo** (memorandum) is the more common form of a written business message. Memos are usually less formal than a letter and are used for interoffice communication. They announce events, procedures, changes in policy, etc. Today the memo format is being used for emails both internally and externally. Memos include lines designated as "To:", "From:", "Date:", "Subject:" and "Re:" above the body of the memo. Most word processing software provides users with memo templates.

Although memos are usually shorter and simpler than formal letters, they should be approached with seriousness and a commitment to accuracy. Take your time to compose memos that are clear, concise and accurate as they provide a written record of your message.

In summary, written communication in a global workplace requires attention to cultural differences and acceptable etiquette. More than the spoken word, this type of communication can be saved, passed on to others, interpreted from many perspectives and reviewed at will.

Here are some tips:

✓ Study the country with which you are trying to communicate.
✓ Avoid being judgemental or critical of a country's preferences.
✓ Use clear language and define any complex terms.
✓ Be concise and don't cover too much information at one time.
✓ Use summaries or visuals for clarity.
✓ Review your correspondence from the perspective of the receiver.
✓ Revise if necessary to increase readability.

Oral Communication Guidelines

Oral communication is a powerful medium. Your words can entertain, inform and persuade listeners, whether in a public speaking forum (a lecture or award presentation) or a more internal or personal group address (a departmental or regional meeting).

Historians remind us of memorable statements that characterized an era, a nation or its people:

*Never in the field of human conflict was so much owed by so
many to so few!*

Sir Winston Churchill

Anger and intolerance are the twin enemies of correct understanding.
Mahatma Gandhi

*I have a dream that my four children will one day live in a
nation where they will not be judged by the color of their skin
but by the content of their character.*

Martin Luther King, Jr

However, history also captures words that hurt and harm and remain in our memory:

Let them eat cake!

Marie Antoinette
(disputable attribution)

To read too many books is harmful.

Mao Zedong

The media recognize the power of words. A good quote can make or break a story. Reporters know readers like quotes that add authenticity or human interest to a complex or dry issue.

The effectiveness of speech depends on its content and delivery. Aristotle, the acknowledged father of persuasion, said the speaker (ethos) was a crucial component in the equation of communication. Some speakers have charisma or personal charm which makes them appealing and seemingly believable. Other speakers achieve believability through their command of fact and figures. Sometimes it seems people are born with a talent for public speaking, but often becoming a great speaker takes a lifetime of work.

Art/science dichotomy

Effective speaking is more art than science. In a science experiment, if Beth adds solution A to solution B and it bubbles over, the same result will be achieved whether

PMW, Inc.

Office Memo

Date: September 7, 2006

From: Linda Hughes, sales manager

To: Regional sales staff

For the last month, weekly progress reports have been submitted past the deadline of Mondays at 5 p.m.

It is important both for management and the sales staff that these weekly reports are turned in on time so that any necessary actions can be taken in a timely manner

Please make sure you adhere to the weekly progress report deadline in the future.

Thank you.

(a)

Figure 5.3 Examples of memos: (a) PMW (English) – this English–language memo illustrates the relaxed style of internal business communication in the USA; (b) TM Ride (French) – the internal memo from a French company uses formal language and tight construction; (c) personal memo (Marathi) – this personal memo is written in Marathi, the primary language of the state of Maharashta in India, and its traditional style and length reflect the writer's cultural heritage.

L'UNIVERS CULTUREL DE LA MARQUE

NOTE DE SERVICE

TMRIDE \ SERVICE COM \ 01_18.06.2006	**DE :** John Watin, Président Directeur Général
	A : Service communication
OBJET : Remise des rapports d'activité hebdomadaires	**Dossier suivi par :** Charlotte Guibert
DATE DE MISE EN APPLICATION : immédiate	☎ 01 40 59 68 XX
	Réf interne : VZ – 5269

La semaine dernière, le rapport d'activité hebdomadaire du service communication est arrivé en retard au bureau administratif de TM Ride.

Il est rappelé que les rapports d'activité hebdomadaires doivent être impérativement retournés en temps et en heures. Ces documents sont essentiels pour le fonctionnement de notre groupe et la bonne gestion des équipes et des ressources.

Je compte sur chacun d'entre vous pour rendre vos rapports **tous les lundis à 17h au plus tard.**

(b)

Figure 5.3 (*continued*)

she does the experiment at 8 am or noon. The identical result will be achieved if Paul does the same experiment or if the experiment is performed in lab across town. The same result will occur if Beth pours solution A into B the first, the twentieth or the hundredth time.

Art is not repeatable. Artists, musicians, speakers and athletes know that the results of their performances depend on myriad factors. And certainly they know that practice makes perfect.

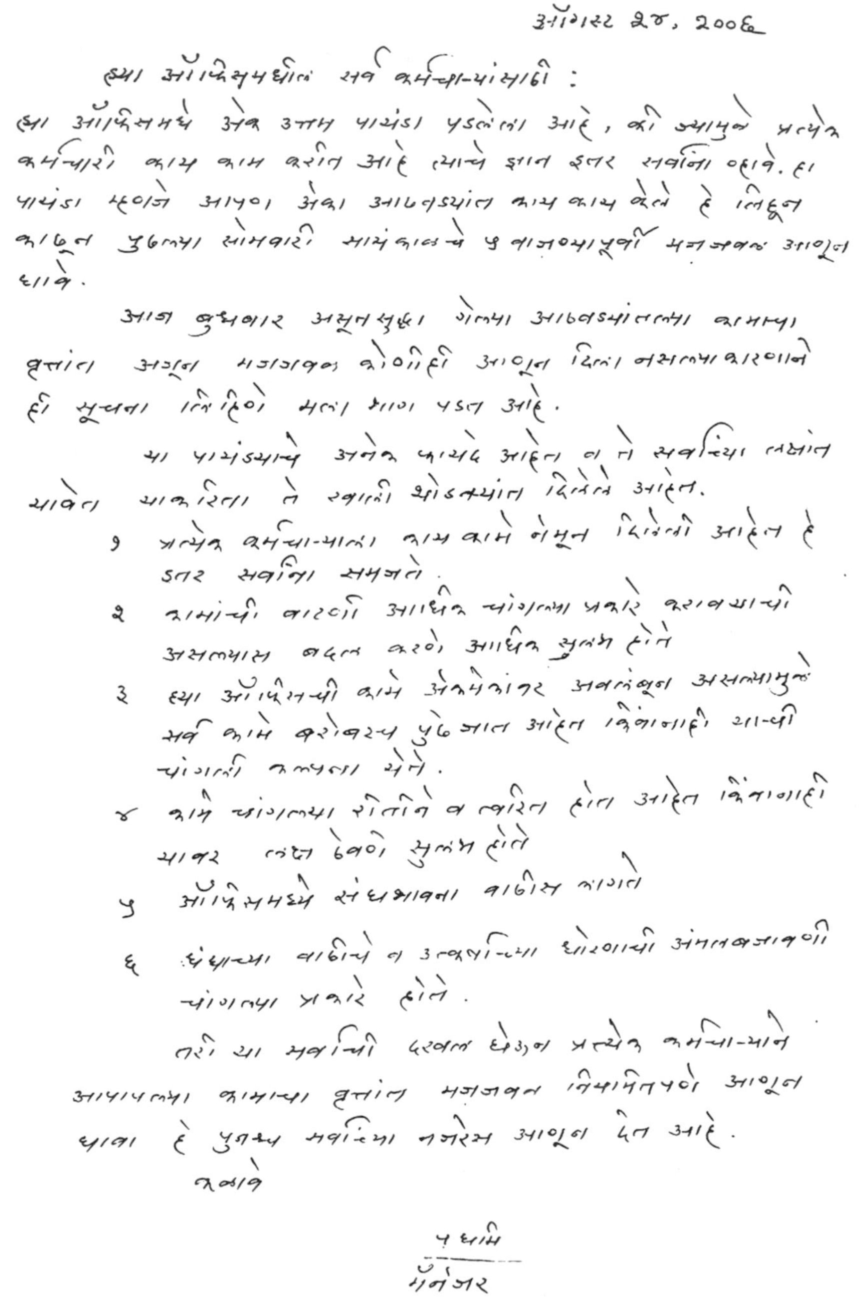

ऑगस्ट २७, २००६

ह्या ऑफिसमधील सर्व कर्मचा-यांसाठी :

ह्या ऑफिसमध्ये अनेक अनेक पायंडा पडलेला आहे, की आमचे प्रत्येक कर्मचारी काम काम करीत आहे त्याचे ज्ञान इतर सर्वांना व्हावे. हा पायंडा म्हणजे आपला अंक आठवड्यात काम काम केले हे लिहून काढून पुढल्या सोमवारी सायंकाळ ५ वाजण्यापूर्वी मॅनेजर आणून द्यावे.

आज गुरुवार असूनसुद्धा गेल्या आठवड्यातल्या कामचा वृत्तांत आजून मॅनेजरकडे कोणीही आणून दिला नसल्याकारणाने ही सूचना लिहिणे मला भाग पडत आहे.

या पायंड्यामुळे अनेक फायदे आहेत व ते सर्वांच्या लक्षात यावेत म्हणून ते खाली नोंदल्यात दिलेत आहेत.

१ प्रत्येक कर्मचा-यांना काम काम नेमून दिलेली आहेत हे इतर सर्वांना समजते.

२ यामांची वाटणी आधिक चांगल्या प्रकारे करावयाची असल्यास बदल करणे आधिक सुलभ होते.

३ ह्या ऑफिसची काम अन्य़ोन्यावर अवलंबून असल्यामुळे सर्व काम करावयाला पुरे ज्ञान आहेत किंवानाही यांची चांगली कल्पना येते.

४ काम चांगल्या रीतीने व त्वरित होत आहेत किंवानाही यावर लक्ष ठेवणे सुलभ होते.

५ ऑफिसमध्ये संवादाला वाहित मागेल.

६ धंधाच्या वाढीचे व उत्पन्नाच्या धोरणाची अंमलबजावणी चांगल्या प्रकारे होते.

तरी या सर्वांनी हरवळ हेऊन प्रत्येक कर्मचा-याने आपापल्या कामाचा वृत्तांत मॅनेजर नियमितपणे आणून द्यावा हे पुन्हा सर्वांना नम्रपणे आणून देत आहे.

धन्य़वाद

प द्या
मॅनेजर

(c)

Figure 5.3 *(continued)*

Like science and art, speaking in public is based on research and practice. Scholars and practitioners have developed scientific models of what seems to work, but, like art, the eventual success of your speech will depend on your talent, skill and expertise. If you were not born to be a public speaker, you can learn to do it effectively. You may not reach the level of Winston Churchill, but you can certainly strive to be effective.

Strategic Thinking

According to Ivy Naistadt in *Speak Without Fear* (Naistadt, 2004), fears of public speaking include:

- fear of criticism
- fear of forgetting
- fear of embarrassment
- fear of success or failure
- fear of the unknown
- fear of past emotional experiences.

What makes you and/or your classmates fearful of public speaking? How can you begin to overcome these concerns? Many experts offer advice for dealing with anxiety. Do some Web research and see what tips you can find.

A quick search of "public speaking" on the Internet will turn up numerous "Dos and Don'ts" to help you with the content and delivery of your speeches. Remember, the art of public speaking depends on you, your ideas, your organization, your presentation, your style and your connection with the audience.

Speech delivery formats

Delivery styles are the ways that speakers can verbally transmit their speech or report and include:

- reading
- memorization
- extemporaneous
- impromptu.

Reading

Reading from a prepared manuscript is not an effective delivery style. Audiences view "readers" as unprepared or uninformed. You risk losing your audience and wasting your time if listeners have tuned out before you even get to the meat of your message.

However, reading is acceptable when you are delivering a message that has been carefully crafted and when any deviation from the written words would risk misinterpretation. For example, suppose you are charged with addressing the media concerning an industrial accident or a personnel action – both of which may have human as well as legal consequences. Reading from a prepared statement would be essential in these instances.

Memorization

Memorizing a speech also is not a recommended delivery format. The audience perceives speakers who memorize their speeches as mechanical and rote, as if speakers are spewing information at them.

Like an actor in a long-running play, if you have memorized your speech, you must work hard to keep your message fresh and interesting. Another problem is that, if you suddenly experience unexpected stress or nervousness on account of internal factors (scratchy throat or a family problem) or external factors (someone sneezes or the microphone doesn't work), you can quickly get thrown off track.

If you have simply memorized your speech and do not "know" it, you will find it difficult to remain composed enough to recite your speech word for word.

The preferred style: extemporaneous

Extemporaneous speaking requires researching, preparing and practising your speech, and, regardless of the number of times you repeat it, delivering it as if it were the first time. This is the preferred delivery style.

Phrases written or typed on note cards remind you of your organization and trigger your memory of the points you want to cover. It is important not to write the speech out word for word on your cards. Choose instead to put your points in key phrases and then connect with minor filler words as you work to establish eye contact with your audience.

Impromptu

Impromptu speeches are common in organizational settings. Your boss asks you to talk at the meeting about your new plan for more product shelving. If you are asked to speak impromptu, consider it a compliment. The person asking you to speak feels that you can do as good a job as anyone else in the room, or they would not have asked you.

Seize the opportunity to be in the spotlight. You never know who may be watching; many a promotion has happened because someone heard a junior executive give an effective presentation. Top employers say that after job skills, they look for employers to exhibit effective communication skills.

Effective presentations

In our world of instant visual media, audiences have seen and heard many memorable speeches and expect professionalism and effective delivery. They want speakers to capture their attention and keep their interest, and they don't want to waste time listening to an ineffective speaker. Whenever possible, consider the use of visual aids to help get your points across and peak audience interest.

Presentation software

Presentation software is universally used to organize and communicate information and utilizes effective visuals for small or large group presentations. In some businesses, presentation software is employed much like memos to convey reports and other data throughout the organization.

Critics of presentation software warn that its powerful capacity to assist the presenter in organizing information often leads to the oversimplification of complex information and also lulls speakers into a false sense of security about their need to prepare. Others suggest that the tendency to overuse special effects and timing devices distracts from the message.

Impromptu speaking tips:

- Take the little time you have to prepare.
- Jot down some notes and organize them.
- Focus on a few main points – three or four is all you can cover in a short time.
- Move through your points deliberately.
- Illustrate your points by using stories, analogies or personal examples.
- Don't feel stressed; you are not expected to give a flawless presentation.
- Don't apologize for your lack of information or knowledge.

Critic Edward Tufte says presentation software "elevates format over content, betraying an attitude of commercialism that turns everything into a sales pitch" (Tufte, 2003).

Perhaps the most significant problem of presentation software is how much or how little the presenter integrates the finished product into the oral presentation process. Text should be used only as a reminder. Abbreviated text gives the presenter the opportunity to elaborate on key points and to tailor a presentation to a particular audience. If the presenter knows the material, the slides become secondary and he or she is able to face the audience and not the slides.

Presentation software is constantly improving; nevertheless, there are other ways to make presentations. For example, an architectural firm presented their designs on brown packaging paper when pitching a project to an environmentally sensitive firm. Innovative presenters think about creative ways to present their ideas.

Dig Deeper

Design presentation tips:

- The choice of background colours is important to the readability of the presentation. Dark colours portray a corporate approach but may be unreadable in a dark room.
- Be consistent with your choice of design templates.
- Avoid the use of special effects, such as objects that fly into the screen or moving type.
- Let graphics or photos tell the story while you provide the words.

Copy presentation tips:

- Use no more than four bullet points and 10–20 words per slide.
- Use 24–48 point type in a readable font.
- Use upper- and lower-case type in body copy.
- Limit the number of slides in your presentation.

Presentation tips:

- Practise, practise, practise.
- Face the audience and not the screen.
- Prepare back-up materials – faulty equipment can ruin an excellent presentation.

Listenability and readability

Above all, it is important to consider **listenability**, defined as the ease of comprehension, when working on your oral presentations. This means carefully analysing your words, phrases and sentences to make sure they will be understandable to your listeners. It will require editing and revising your presentation for content, completeness, correctness, clarity, coherence, conciseness, connection to the audience, creativity, courtesy and closure. The 10 Cs apply to written communication as well.

Scientific measurement tools can evaluate listenability and readability. One such tool is the Flesch reading ease formula which measures text complexity (Flesch, 1951). Originally designed to measure grade levels of written educational materials, it is now used as an effective tool to measure "listenability" in a broadcast context. The Flesch test remains the simplest and most accurate measure of text difficulty for oral materials. The formula takes the average number of syllables per 100 words in a text (word difficulty) and the average number of words per sentence (sentence difficulty) and then combines the two calculations to provide a single index of overall complexity. The Gunning–Fog index measures readability of the written word.

An interesting experiment was undertaken in 2004 as political pundits began to compare the listenability factor in US President George Bush's campaign speeches compared with that of his opponent, Senator John Kerry. According to mediachannel. org, which calls itself "the global network for democratic media", Bush in his first debate used the language of a sixth-grade student. By the second debate he had upped his language to that of a seventh grader, and by the final debate Bush had entered into

Strategic Thinking

Precision listening, defined as in-depth evaluation and processing of the material one is listening to rather than merely engaging in surface listening, has recently attracted much attention.

Managers can gather crucial information through precision listening that will help them evaluate an employee or address the need of a superior. Assessing relevant information and understanding the real meaning behind the words is vital to effective leadership.

For example, a salesperson might use precision listening to ascertain a customer's objections when trying to make a sale. Asking a customer about his particular needs of and uses for a product, and listening for keywords in his response, will help identify possible obstacles to the sale.

the eighth-grade level. Kerry stayed within the seventh-grade level throughout the three debates. The candidates' speaking levels were scored with the Flesch–Kincaid grade level index (Beard, 2004).

Electronic Communication

Scores of articles, websites and public pronouncements discuss how technology is changing the way we communicate. Virtual teams now work from home offices using email, chat rooms and document depositories and lessen the need for permanent offices and conventional office hours.

The cell phone, perhaps the most widely adopted form of new technology, is used around the world. In fact it was accepted so quickly that the rules about usage etiquette are still being written. France, for example, has strict laws regarding driving and using cell phones; such laws are the subject of much legislative debate in the United States, in spite of the fact that accidents involving drivers on cell phones are common. Every third person in the world is reported to have a cell phone, and in the Asia-Pacific market alone over half of the cell phones sold have camera functions and a third play music (`www.Tekrati.com/research/news.asp?id56761`) (Tekrati, 2006).

The media business, in particular, has felt the effects of this technology. Television reporters are now equipped with video phones as well as conventional video cameras. Reporters use video phones to record an event, instantly sending the video and a text message back to their stations. As soon as the station receives the video, it becomes material for Web-based news operations.

Radio stations turn hourly newscasts and local talk shows into podcasts. Newspaper reporters double as reporters on video channels, and then rewrite their newspaper copy for fast-breaking Web coverage.

Technology and communication

Technology offers additional electronic communication forms:

- instant messaging (IM)
- videoconferencing.

Instant messaging

One of the shortfalls of email is the inability to determine whether the receiver to whom you are sending the message is online at that particular moment. The receiver might be out of the office, on vacation or just ignoring email messages.

Socially interactive technologies (SITs) such as **instant messaging** allow the user to create a buddy list or contact list of individuals that he or she might want to contact. The steps to carrying on a virtual conversation with a contact over the Internet are easy with instant messaging (IM).

IM is more popular in the USA than in Europe, where Internet users stay online 5 times longer (Rubens, 2003). Several studies report that 74 % of online adolescents in the United States use instant messaging compared with 44 % of online adults (Lenhart, Rainie & Lewis, 2001), and similar results are reported in the UK (Livingston & Bober, 2005).

Until recently, instant messaging required users to utilize the same software, but the convergence and compatibility of systems have addressed this problem. Some instant messaging vendors also offer such options as videoconferencing, voice conversations and the ability to download photos, pictures and other files.

As with most new innovative technologies, there are issues to address. The popularity of instant messaging among adolescents is of concern to some parents and educators. Some are concerned that the technology might be used as a substitute for social interaction. However, a study by Bryant, Sanders-Jackson & Smallwood found that instant messaging did not result in more social ties for adolescents who used the technology, nor were they likely to create weaker social ties. In fact, individuals who had weak social ties to begin with were less likely to use instant messaging (Bryant, Sanders-Jackson & Smallwood, 2006).

Videoconferencing

For over two decades, videoconferencing technology has existed in the marketplace. The location of, the access to and the expense of the equipment needed tended to restrict videoconferencing to elaborate facilities, but today Web technology and satellites are making access to videoconferencing less expensive and more accessible.

Videoconferencing has practical uses such as holding meetings and conferences when people are located in distant places, or for interviewing job candidates or experts and in training and development. Videoconferencing allows clients to see project drawings and to suggest up–to-the-minute changes in projects that have significant visual components. Precious time, money and energy are saved when managers use videoconferencing instead of tedious and expensive trips to accomplish business objectives.

Videoconferencing has its detractors. A college professor was recently interviewing for a job by videoconference. Unfortunately, the screen on her end of the conversation was experiencing receiver difficulties. She could not see the individuals conducting the interview as their faces were digitized and blurred. She noted that the experience was most disconcerting, as she could not determine how her message was being received.

Some individuals experience problems with stepping on other people's conversation because of the broadcast time delay. Another difficulty cited is that significant rustling of papers may disturb audio transmission.

However, videoconferencing also has its success stories. An Italian-owned company stages amateur golf tournaments all over the world and uses videoconferencing as an amenity to supplement the experience of Chinese business executives. Golfers can attend to their business needs via videoconference and then return to their games (Videoconferencing Insight Newsletter, 2006).

Chapter Summary

This chapter covered the role played by the channel in the transactional communication model. You learned that oral communication is more personal and less formal, and that written communication is more explicit. Choosing the most appropriate channel for your message is crucial to your communication objective.

Forms of oral, written and electronic communication were also explored. Practical tips were presented in this chapter that will enhance your communication skills.

This chapter ends our general discussion of how the communication process works. The next section will begin a discussion of what integrated communication is and how it produces effective messages in a global marketplace.

In future chapters you will learn how to integrate the basic concepts presented in this chapter into a comprehensive integrated business communication strategy. ∎

Learning From Others

Jen Ross identifies herself as a Chilean–Canadian journalist based in Santiago, Chile. She studied at the London School of Economics and Political Science where she earned an MS in International Relations and she received an MA in Political Studies from Queen's University in Ontario, Canada.

Ross has worked at CBC Television as a senior researcher for Newsworld in Ottawa, Canada, and served as reporter and photographer for Politicswatch.com.

Ross specializes in issues affecting women across the Americas. She has written for *The Toronto Star*, the *Christian Science Monitor*, *Women E-News*, *Latin Trade*, *The Globe & Mail*, *The Miami Herald*, *The New Zealand Herald*, *The Washington Times*, BBC World Radio and the *New Internationalist* magazine. She speaks five languages (Ross, 2006).

Ross spoke about the communication style of Michelle Bachelet, Chile's first woman president:

Q: How did Michelle Bachelet rise to power in Chile?
A: Five years ago, nobody knew Bachelet. In 2000 she was appointed Minister of Health, but it was when she became Minister of Defence in 2002 that people began to take notice of her.

Q: Why did she become popular at this time?
A: She was very different from previous ministers who had very militarist styles. Bachelet is said to be "sympatica". People began to suggest she run for the presidency.

Q: What do you mean by she is "sympatica"?
A: This means that Bachelet exudes friendliness. She smiles a lot and expresses her personality in her communication to others. Her style is very different from the institutional military approach everyone was used to.

Q: Do you think being a woman helped her to win the election?
A: Well, during the campaign when everyone was debating whether a woman could run the country, renowned sociologists were theorizing that, because Chile had recently experienced so much upheaval and insecurity during the Pinochet years, the people were looking for a nurturing maternal figure rather than a strict authoritarian leader.

Q: Do you think that was true?
A: They must have been right because Bachelet won. She is a mother herself and embodies motherhood for her people. She makes them feel safe and secure under her leadership.

Q: What do you think is one of her best communication traits?
A: Bachelet has charisma and she is also very real, and that works for her.

Case Study – **Avon**

Avon is a worldwide company of 34 000 employees and 3 million independent sales representatives. It has offices in 135 countries and hosts websites in more than 50 countries. Avon call centres are globally distributed and, according to its website, "serve as Avon's front line of communication with its independent sales reps".

One of Avon's long-time problems is ensuring effective communication between service operators and sales representatives who complain that the operators don't always have current information. It is important that call centre operators have the latest product and inventory figures, sales information and company materials in order to take orders, address questions, handle fulfilment problems, give details on sales incentives and provide promotional product information. Avon says, "…equipping operators with up-to-date information… is a top priority".

To improve operator communication, Avon sent out a request for proposal (RFP) inviting customer relationship management (CRM) software manufacturers to submit solution proposals on how to keep operators up to date. Finalists will present their CRM solution to several hundred senior IT executives.

Avon is hoping to eliminate "the high turnover of its sales reps, which is costly in terms of recruitment, training and missed sales opportunities". The software solution must also interface with Avon's newly developed AvonOrder.com website and eventually offer some method of order-tracking method for representatives. Avon also says: "However, since the vast majority of Avon's order processing is currently done by phone and fax, it's critical that the CRM package support all forms of communication – voice, fax, email, regular mail and the Internet".

This project calls on the three forms of communication – oral, written and electronic – for the presentation to Avon. The traditional oral communication will be used in the presentation before the top executives. Written messages will appear in reports, email communication and on presentation slides. Electronic communication will be used in computer-generated presentations and IT solution demonstrations.

Go to `http://www.informationweek.com/rfp/avon/` or search the words Avon InformationWeek "Functionality and Ease of Use" to read more about the RFP (InformationWeek, 2006).

In small groups, act as one of the software manufacturers and design a sample presentation of a mock idea CRM support (use your own ideas, they don't have to work technically) or to be presented to the senior IT executives of Avon. Follow the guidelines outlined in this chapter for effective oral and written presentations. What buzz words will you use? What "messages" will you convey? What values will you tap into? What will be key concepts to address?

As a class, design an evaluation form that classmates can use to evaluate and judge which group presentation is more effective, based on delivery and presentation techniques.

Class Exercises

1. Pair up with two or three other students in the class. To foster employee morale, you (one student) have chosen to host a luncheon for your department of 20 employees and their spouses (represented by the other two or three students). You have decided that email is the best way to announce the company luncheon. You have three minutes to compose your email message. When you are finished, give the other students the message you have written. They will critique the message and decide if your message is clear or further questions or clarifications are needed. Flush out all the problems or miscommunications that may have occurred via the email message. This exercise can also be done as an actual email assignment, and the in-class critique session can be scheduled for after the communication has actually been received.

2. Write a traditional letter informing store managers of your new plan for keeping grocery shelves well stocked by bringing in additional part-time help in the late evening hours. Give a date when you want your plan implemented and request a report from the local manager stating how your plan will be put into action. Now put the same information about your plan and report request in an email message. What different considerations did you have to make? Now you have decided that you will call the store managers into corporate headquarters and tell them about your plan in person. What types of material will you need for your presentation? Is there a best way? Why do you think so?

3. Go to the *Journal of Computer-Mediated Communication*, `http://jcmc.indiana.edu`, which offers a variety of scholarly articles on emerging technology and its social and cultural effects (JCMC, 2006). Access an article and write an abstract that you can share with the class.

Action Plan

Suppose you are beginning a fund-raising campaign and need to communicate with different levels of potential donors. Consider the following forms of communication:

- email
- billboards
- print advertising
- face-to-face communication
- newsletter, brochures and flyers
- group presentations
- teleconferencing
- handwritten letter
- telephone conversation
- text message
- individual to large group
- fax
- magazine article
- typed letter with personalized greeting
- television advertising
- transit poster.

1. Rank each communication channel in terms of its effectiveness to reach the levels of potential donors for your upcoming fund-raising campaign. What additional forms of communication would you add to the list?
2. At what point in this exercise did you have difficulties with the ranking process?
3. What additional information do you need to help you decide whether a particular form of communication will be effective in reaching a specific donor group?

Websites

For information on global Avon, go to www.avon.com and click on *Company Overview*, then you can explore either *Avon World* or *Corporate Responsibility* tabs (Avon 2006).

For a free index of telecommunications companies and other links to telecommunications sites worldwide, visit www.analysys.com/vlib (Telcoms Virtual Library, 2006)

For information on global Avon, go to www.avon.com and click on *Company Overview*, then you can explore either *Avon World* or *Corporate Responsibility* tabs (Avon 2006).

For a free index of telecommunications companies and other links to telecommunications sites worldwide, visit www.analysys.com/vlib (Telcoms Virtual Library, 2006).

The Pew report on teens and technology offers insight on how American teenagers use technology to communicate. Read all about it at http://www.pewinternet.org/PPF/r/162/report_display.asp (Pewinternet, 2005).

For the office of the future, consult www.groove.net (Groove Virtual Office, 2006) or www.sitescape.com/ (Sitescape, 2006).

References

Agress, L. (2006) "Business writing at its best". Available from: www.business-and-legal-writing.com. [Accessed 5 January 2006].

Avon (2006) Avon.com. Available from: www.avon.com [Accessed 21 August 2006].

Beard, R. (2004) "The final debate: who went down for the word count?" Mediachannel.org. Available from: www.mediachannel.org/views/dissector/affalert280.shtml [Accessed 18 February 2006].

Bryant, J., Sanders-Jackson, A. & Smallwood, A. (2006) "Iming, text messaging, and adolescent social networks". *Journal of Computer-Mediated Communication*, **11**(2). Available from: http://jcmc.indiana.edu/vol11/issue2/Bryant.html [Accessed 26 March 2006].

Business Communication (2003) Boston, MA, Harvard Business School Publishing.

DTI (2006) Department of Trade and Industry website. Available from: www.dti.gov.uk [Accessed 25 August 2006].

Flesch, R. (1951) *How to Test Readability*. New York, Harper and Brothers.

Groove Virtual Office (2006) GrooveNetworks. Available from: www.groove.net [Accessed 25 August 2006].

Hawken, P. (1993) *The Ecology of Commerce*. New York, Harper Business Press: 214.

InformationWeek (2006) "Request for proposal". Available from: http://www.informationweek.com/rfp/avon/ [Accessed 25 August 2006].

JCMC (2006) *Journal of Computer-Mediated Communication*, 2006. Available from: http://jcmc.indiana.edu [Accessed 25 August 2006].

Lenhart, A., Rainie, L. & Lewis, O. (2001) "Teenage life online: the rise of the instant-message generation and the Internet's impact on friendships and family relationships". Available from: www.pewinternet.org/report/toc.asp?report=36 [Accessed 7 September 2006].

Livingston, S. & Bober, M. (2005) "UK children go online: final report of key project findings". London, Economic and Social Research Council.

Naistadt, I. (2004) *Speak Without Fear*. New York, Harper Collins.

Pewinternet (2005) "The Pew report on teens and technology". Available from: http://www.pewinternet.org/PPF/r/162/report_display.asp [Accessed 7 September 2006].

Rhodes (2006) The Rhodes School, Rhodes School District 84.5, River Grove, IL. Technology curriculum. Available from: www.rhodes.k12.il.us/website/tech.html [Accessed 5 January 2006].

Ross, J. (2006) Personal website. Available from: http://jen-ross.tripod.com [Accessed 4 August 2006].

Rubens, P. (2003) "Will instant message be the new texting?" *BBC News*, 30 June 2003. Available from: http://bbc.co.uk/go/pr/fr/-/hi/technology/30311796.stm [Accessed 29 March 2006].

Sitescape (2006) Available from: www.sitescape.com [Accessed 25 August 2006].

Spretnak, C. (1997) *The Resurgence of the Real*. Reading, PA, Addison-Wesley.

Tekrati (2006) "Cell phones and Asia". Available from: www.tekrati.com/research/News.as[?id=6761 [Accessed 2 April 2006].

Telcoms Virtual Library (2006) Analysys.com. Available from: www.analysys.com/vlib [Accessed 23 August 2006].

Tufte, E. (2003) "PowerPoint is evil". *Wired News*, September. Available from: http://www.wired.com/wired/archive/11.09/pp2_pr.html [Accessed 5 August 2006].

Videoconferencing Insight Newsletter (2006) "Videoconferencing for golf fans". Quorum Videoconferencing. Available from: http://rrcs-24-73-183-97.se.biz.rr.com/qvc/modules.php?op=modload&name=News&file=article&sid=540 [Accessed 6 August 2006].

Bibliography

Guerrero, L., DeVito, J. & Hecht, M., eds (1991) *The Nonverbal Communication Reader*, 2nd edn. Prospect Heights, IL, Waveland Press.

PART 2

Towards Integrated Business Communication

CHAPTER 6

Business Communication, Public Relations and Integrated Marketing Communication

Executive Summary

As a communication function of business management, public relations departments act as boundary spanners charged with building relationships, maintaining corporate image, anticipating social change and communicating corporate strategies.

Public relations as a persuasive science can be traced to the time of Aristotle
During the eighteenth century, political leaders in the New World and in England and France used persuasive rhetoric to promote the rights of man over the divine rights of kings. The Industrial Revolution sparked not only big business, but big government as well. Public relations agencies were created out of the need for businesses to cultivate positive public opinion about their activities as well as to communicate with the masses.

The early days of public relations focused more on hype than on truth

By the mid-twentieth century, public relations as a profession was recognized
While there is no standard model for the practice of public relations, the industry trend is towards a two-way symmetrical model that emphasizes the role of publics in shaping organizational communication.

Integrated communication grew out of the recognition that messages to internal and external publics must be unified and coordinated and driven by the need to build diverse relationships

Integrated business communication is conditioned by theory and audience
It employs two-way communication, uses and depends on databases and seeks positive continuous communication. Integrated communication selects the best methods for communicating and uses feedback and assessment to measure success. ■

Business Communication, Public Relations and Integrated Marketing Communication

The greatest problem with communication is the illusion that it has been accomplished.

George Bernard Shaw

Introduction to the Practice of Persuasive Communication

Following the Industrial Revolution at the turn of the twentieth century, businesses recognized the need to inform customers of products and their benefits as well as persuade them to buy. When organizations began to hire professionals to do this job, the field of public relations was born.

This story illustrates how public relations, an outgrowth of early advertising, was used and is still used today. In the early Wild West of the USA, inhabitants of small western towns needed school teachers, store clerks, doctors, attorneys, bankers, women to marry the settlers and other necessary citizens to civilize and grow these communities.

Sometimes advertising was placed in big city newspapers in the East to promote the towns as wonderful places to settle and raise children in a land of opportunity. But this was expensive and promoters found that circulating tall-tales of opportunity through magazine articles and farm bulletins was far more effective. These efforts were labelled "settlement literature."

Many promises could not be kept, but by the time the new settlers realized that the stories were exaggerated, they were not able to turn around and head home.

Today, governments, land consortiums and real estate agents still promote new land settlement with pamphlets extolling the benefits of these areas as recreational paradises, by playing up phrases such as "near or on a lake" or "enjoy country living just 15 minutes from town". Signage for new development seeks to persuade residents of other areas to relocate.

Modern settlement literature is, thankfully, more accurate and less exaggerated. It was deceptive practices such as those found in the settlement literature of the past that contributed to the early negative reputation of public relations, and a public perception the profession is still working hard to shed.

What exactly is the scope of public relations, often called the communication arm of business? How did it evolve? Why is it so important today? How has it changed and adapted to a changing world?

In many ways, the history of public relations mirrors the history of persuasion theory.

Although the term was not used until the twentieth century, evidence of its role in civilization shows that the practice has been around for centuries. Historians point to a farm bulletin, found in Iraq in 1800 BC and describing new ways to sow, irrigate and harvest crops, as one of the earliest examples of a persuasive communication tool.

Rulers of the ancient world were kept abreast of public opinion by spies sent throughout the kingdom who not only championed the king and his laws to the commoners but also spread favourable rumours far and wide.

Early History

By 400 BC the Greeks acknowledged the role public opinion played in establishing laws and running the government. Aristotle (384–322 BCE) developed a study of rhetoric that included effective persuasive techniques. As politicians searched for ways to win public approval for their causes, components such as ethos, pathos and logos were studied and debated in an attempt to determine which element wielded the most persuasive power:

- **Ethos** referred to the power of the speaker and included his credibility, expertise, trustworthiness, sincerity and above all charisma.
- **Pathos** referred to emotional appeals. It became evident that some people were moved first by emotion before considering the credibility of the speaker or the facts.
- **Logos** employed the power of logic.

These elements are still considered the basis of persuasion, but modern persuasion theory has added a fourth dimension, the audience:

- **Audience** refers to the mindset of the public, its culture, educational level, biases, interest in the subject and its power to make a difference.

By 100 BC, the Romans were using the phrase *vox populi, vox Dei* (the voice of the people is the voice of God) to establish the importance of public opinion in their society.

Later in England, the Lords Chancellor were dubbed "Keepers of the King's Conscience" and served to mediate communication between the government and the people. By 1450, Gutenberg's printing press brought communication technology into the mainstream. People of all economic and social levels now had the opportunity to read and learn for themselves what was going on in the world around them. Just as important, writers had the opportunity to employ mass distribution, and the power of the pen became the power of the printed word.

Revolution and persuasion

In the United States, the public relations efforts of early political figures like Thomas Paine and Thomas Jefferson set the stage for the founding of a new nation. The migration of new settlers from many countries around the world meant the need to adapt words and language to new audiences.

In the 1789 French Declaration of the Right of Man and the Citizen, citizens were given the right to express and communicate thoughts freely. Three years later, the National Assembly of France created the first propaganda department as part of the Ministry of the Interior. It was called the "Bureau d'Esprit" and worked to win public support for the **revolution**.

Industrial Revolution

In the early 1900s in Europe, the Dutch began to practise public relations (van Ruler, Vercic & Flodin, 2001). In North America, newer technologies and mass production techniques led to companies distinguishing the uniqueness of their products by advertising certain benefits of their products, and hence the concept of branding of products began.

Businesses across the world recognized that, to prosper, they needed to develop sales methods that would grow their market share. At the same time, government entities discovered that, to stay in power and get their parties re-elected, they needed to cultivate public opinion for their actions and policies. Sigmund Freud and his American nephew, Edward Bernays, the noted father of US modern public relations, later contributed to the formulation of these promotional techniques through their research in the disciplines of sociology and psychology.

Advertising agencies were born to handle the demand for product differentiation, and press agents were hired to protect industrial giants under investigation by conscientious reporters. The war years saw a growth in public relations as nations sought to garner the support of their citizens. When the British government disclosed the decoded contents of a confidential German communiqué (called the Zimmerman telegram) to Mexico suggesting that Germany was about to engage in submarine warfare against the USA, it participated in a planned propaganda strategy designed to influence the USA to enter the war effort.

The public relations industry experienced troubled times in the early years. Press agents and showmen like P. T. Barnum of Barnum and Bailey's Circus were infamous for staging outlandish publicity stunts. These events were organized in detail and held at convenient times of the day to ensure press coverage. Although they were effective at first, the public eventually felt duped and defrauded by these publicity pranks.

The patent medicine industry also cast a shadow over both advertising and public relations. The term "patent medicine" was first used in England in the 1600s when a medicinal formula could be solely owned and distributed after applying for a patent. The concoction did not have to be effective or safe, and by the 1800s the unregulated industry had become blatantly dishonest. The phrase "patent medicines" applied to all remedies whether there was a patent owned or not (Patent Medicine, 2006).

William Swaim, an opportunist of the times, developed Swaim's Panacea, a syrup of sarsaparilla, and promised a cure for any number of ailments. Along with the concoction, he offered a free almanac devoted to health, along with a six-page advertising supplement to promote all cures of the syrup to consumers.

P. T. Barnum was a master at press agentry. His circus featured three arenas and an encircling track where trapeze artists, jugglers, animal acts and clowns performed simultaneously. Barnum capitalized on the freakish and bizarre including a separate tent for the "Specimens of Savage Tribes" featuring "Australian cannibals", and such characters as the midget Tom Thumb, Siamese twins, and Joie Heth, whom he billed as 161 years old and a one-time nurse to the first US President, George Washington.

By the late 1880s, Barnum was able to take his show on the road by railroad. He depended on advance publicity through illustrated newspaper advertisements, promotional publications, posters and billboards to bring in the crowds from areas around the towns where he was staging his shows. Advance teams carried out prepublicity for his shows; some 60 men would fan out in the countryside and distribute or tack up 6 000–10 000 billposters a day (Poignant, 2004).

Barnum and Bailey's innovative contributions to this early form of public relations and advertising formed an important chapter in the USA but a sad example of exploitation of native peoples, the helpless and the handicapped.

Twentieth Century

With the growth of national magazines and radio in the early **twentieth century** and the invention of television a few decades later, messages could be sent to mass audiences instantaneously. This changed the format of advertising forever.

The public relations industry took a firm foothold as an important part of the business process and continued to throw off the stigma of early years and gain a positive reputation in the marketplace. World trade and cultural exchange fostered the need for concentrated communication efforts, and branding became important to a successful sales plan.

The International Public Relations Association (IPRA) was founded when members of the Dutch Public Relations Club and the Institute of Public Relations in Britain met for an informal talk. In March 1950, executives from Britain, France, Norway and the USA met in Holland under the auspices of the Royal Netherlands International Trade Fair and the Public Relations Society of Holland for a foundation meeting. On 1 May 1955 the IPRA was established in London with the mission of promoting the exchange of information and cooperation within the public relations profession in an increasingly international arena (IPA, 2006).

Mergers and acquisitions

The public relations industry grew through the 1950s, 1960s and 1970s, moulding corporate images, building brands, disseminating information and creating awareness. Public relations was recognized as an important adjunct to advertising where the role of the PR professional was to work behind the scene, either trying to get positive press coverage for their clients or serving as image consultants to keep their clients out of the press's spotlight. Sending out media releases and assembling press packets was a daily grind, and event planning was a task to be avoided or assigned to newly recruited employees in this growing industry.

By the 1980s, public relations departments were incorporated into established advertising agencies by astute advertising moguls who wanted to offer full service expertise to their clients in a growing market where public affairs, crisis management and global communication were becoming more and more important.

With demand from corporations to be proactive instead of reactive in handling public opinion, especially in the face of a looming crisis and the public demand for corporate responsibility, public relations soon became an independent function within the advertising agency. The challenge with the agency was to develop the most appropriate plan for a client, whether it be advertising or public relations.

Integrated communication firms or companies specializing in public relations have usurped advertising agencies in the role of communications experts. Fending off unpopular public opinion and addressing negative press and unfounded misconceptions of corporations have provided the public relations agencies the fuel for a new growth spurt.

The public relations profession plays a major role in the marketing mix as it becomes more difficult, and almost cost prohibitive, to reach mass audiences without defining and refining target customers.

As we move further into the twenty-first century, professional codes of ethics and self-monitoring committees are now industry standards.

What's in a name?

In spite of the public relations industry positioning itself as a vital player, the name "public relations" is still problematic in many countries.

According to a study prepared for the 9th International Public Relations Symposium held in Bled, Slovenia, in 2002, many countries prefer other names for this field such as communication, information, mediation, communication management, promotion and corporate communication (van Ruler & Vercic, 2002). Countries also differ on their meaning of the term. The Germans use the word Offentlichkeitsarbeit, translated as "working in public, with the public and for the public", which is different from the US interpretation of public relations as "the management of relationships between an organization and its publics".

The study also notes the strong reaction in many countries against the use of the American expression "public relations", choosing to "rename themselves in their languages into some kind of 'communications' associations", distancing themselves from the concept of public relations as a propaganda tool.

Public relations departments vary from business to business, and functions range from media relations to event planning and from writing internal newsletters to lobbying interests. However, public relations activities are usually part of the marketing mix.

Models of public relations management

Grunig & Hunt identified four models of public relations practice:

- press agentry/publicity model
- public information
- two-way asymmetric
- two-way symmetric.

These patterns correspond to the history of the profession (Grunig & Hunt, 1994).

Press agentry/publicity model

In this model, communication is one-way and the focus is on securing **media publicity**. Today, the film and sports industries try to hype movie openings and sports personalities and often publicity stunts seem to place little value on accuracy and truth.

This one-way communication can, however, serve as a simple way to get publicity. For example, a restaurant chain is opening a new store in an historic town and invites the mayor and other officials to the opening proceedings.

Public information

This model focuses on the source–receiver relationship and the dissemination of accurate, timely **information**. This approach is practised today in government, education and non-profit organizations.

Using the new restaurant again as our example, the restaurant chain will issue a media release with details as to how many people it plans to employ, how much the new facility will cost to build and how it will bring "choice in food services" to the town. A sketch of the new facility will accompany the media release.

Two-way asymmetric

Research is key to the implementation of this model. The model is a source–receiver relationship, but with feedback to the source. This model is unbalanced as the source considers the feedback in the shaping of persuasive communication but does not alter the message to fit the needs of the public. Public relations firms and large competitive organizations practise this model today.

Using the **two-way asymmetric** approach, the restaurant chain would monitor public opinion and media reaction to its proposed facility. It ascertains that there is public concern that the restaurant will detract from the town's charm and flavour. The executives of the chain understand the public feedback and reframe their communications to sidestep the community's concerns.

Two-way symmetric

This balanced model stresses the evaluation of the feedback from publics and then uses two-way communication to resolve conflicts and arrive at mutual understandings. Evaluative research is used to determine if public relations efforts have improved the relationship between the organization and its key publics.

Organizations that practise the **two-way symmetric** approach might use environmental scanning to monitor how strategic management decisions have affected the public by interviewing activists and monitoring websites and media reports.

Using the restaurant chain example again, the organization will consider the feedback gathered from community leaders and the media and change its building design to blend with the architecture of the community. Perhaps it will also offer to contribute a monetary donation to the local historical society and use old photos of the town's history in its dining room.

Organizations often use multiple models in the practice of public relations. But it also should be noted that these models are sometimes criticized for their Western-ethnocentric perspective (Hunt & Grunig, 1994, pp. 8–9).

The Public Relations Industry Today

How strong and effective is the industry today? Worldwide, **the public relations industry** is thriving in every major market from Bangalore to Mexico City.

Major public relations companies are earning up to $500 million in fee income a year and have moved into areas such as entertainment, product placement and civic public relations in response to public demand for accountability and responsibility.

Public relations professionals are part of the corporate team and help determine company strategy. They create corporate buzz, identify and target crucial publics, oversee community outreach projects, deal with the media, handle events and sponsorships and engage in other communication activities.

As a new executive you will quickly have to learn how your company's public relations department operates as it plays a key role in the day-to-day activities of the company.

PR communication activities	Corporate communication activities
	Strategic planning
	Vision statement
White papers	Mission statement
Position papers	Policy handbooks
Media releases	Marketing efforts
Fact sheets	
Brochures/flyers	
Media conferences	Crisis management
Speechwriting	Speechmaking
Website	Website
Feature stories	Internal newsletter
Company profiles	
Special events	Seminars
Sponsorships	Trade/sales shows
	Sales promotions
Promotion of corporate programmes	Training programmes
	Corporate responsibility programmes
	Philanthropy
Blogs/trendwatching	Blogs/visibility
Email announcements	Email, memos, reports

Table 6.1 Organizations will differ as to which department is responsible for what activities. Large companies with multiple departments can divide up various communication functions. Smaller organizations may have one department handling many jobs. Many of the activities listed in this table will overlap at times as traditional roles change and adapt to fit a dynamic marketplace.

Public relations departments are the connection of companies to the outside, particularly to the media. As such they act as **boundary spanners** between an organization and its publics.

Lately, national and worldwide organizations have debated the role of public relations in **strategic management**. This concept is based on the need of managers to balance the mission of the organization with what the environment will allow or support. The public relations role in strategic management, according to Grunig and Grunig, is to build relationships with publics that can impact upon the organization and to design communication programmes that help the organization "manage its interdependence with them" (Grunig & Grunig, 2000, p. 310).

In a complex study of chief executive officers, heads of public relations and an average of 14 employees in each of 323 organizations in the UK, Canada and the United States, researchers found that the role of public relations in strategic management and planning varied widely, but those with more advanced operations (excellence, to use the authors' term) tended to involve communications functions in strategic management.

Significant Publics

Organizations communicate with many entities. Traditionally these audiences have been divided into two separate categories: external publics and internal publics. But some say the lines are blurring. Are stockholders external (outside the company) or internal (part of the company)? Are strategic partners external or internal? Are leased IT support services internal or external? How do organizations include these publics in communication strategy planning? How much information should they share?

Experts are still trying to answer these questions, but it is evident that public relations professionals must be well versed in a variety of activities, from writing speeches and media releases to developing corporate policy regarding potential disaster. See Table 6.1 for a list of PR and corporate communication activities.

External publics

External publics have changed in make-up and expectations. Some publics are expanding beyond traditional audiences. Other publics are retreating into specific and well-defined niches, such as snowboarders, vegetarians or video game players. Still other publics, such as environmental groups, ageing seniors, gay and lesbians and activists are emerging as major players in a consumer-driven world.

External publics are present and potential customers, the local community, suppliers, bankers, media, government agencies, environmental and consumer advocacy

Figure 6.1 An organization and its publics. This is an example of one organization and its multiple publics. The role each public plays varies according to the organization's focus.

groups and any other entity with whom an organization wishes to do business and for whom they want to present their best image.

Most organizations have departments of experts responsible for communicating effectively with various publics: community relations, media relations, government relations or investor relations.

It is important to note that a strong external communication programme is a tool that can preserve the integrity and vision of the company. If effectively and professionally handled, it can enable customer growth, help secure financial backing, keep the corporation in the public consciousness and carry the company through crises.

Without durable, far-reaching and sincere external communications, a company will find it impossible to cultivate and keep its customers. Today's publics are media savvy, wary of big business and its hidden agendas, sceptical of corporate promises and increasingly looking for corporations to support community projects. It is the job of external corporate communication to dispel the negative and enhance the positive public image of a company.

Internal publics

Employee wants, needs and desires of today are not the same as those of only a few years ago. James Houghton, chairman of the board of Corning Glass, Inc., says, "...the age of hierarchy is over". He suggests that management must listen to and address the concerns of employees who are increasingly creative, inquisitive and seeking individual empowerment. They want to make their own decisions and want to be informed of company policy at all levels (Heckscher, 1991). See the case study at the end of the chapter for more on the Corning story and how the company revamped its communication strategy.

Internal publics include employees in the office, in the field or working from home, in corporate headquarters or around the globe; they also include the families of the employees. Effectively communicating with employees builds solid employee–company relationships.

Connecting with today's employees means more relevant and poignant company newsletters and magazines, timely dissemination of information on health and benefits programmes, forms and report templates that decrease time spent on paperwork, the establishment of Intranets that carry company information immediately, email announcements, sales meeting reminders, etc.

When management communicates frequently, regularly and honestly, employees are more satisfied and motivated to work harder for the company. Recognizing that employees are a company's most valuable asset and building a strong internal communication programme can strengthen that asset, encourage excellent work habits, foster pride and esprit de corps and most importantly boost retention.

Communicating with employees is not a luxury but a necessity. Employees want open and honest communications with managers and supervisors and to know that they will have the opportunity to grow and contribute over time.

Why Integrated Communication?

Since the 1970s, the emphasis on communicating with mass populations has declined. Several factors have contributed to the growth of integrated communication.

Population trends in most of Europe and the USA reflect a decrease in birth rates among native populations and an influx of immigrants. These changing demographics are important factors to consider in targeting audiences and shaping messages.

The range of media alternatives available to the public has made the job of targeting a particular audience more complicated. Major changes in media technology opened the doors to "real-time" information while expanding the range of media choices. The BBC and CNN are accessible in almost every corner of the world.

Readership of daily newspapers online and downloading of radio programmes onto iPods are on the increase. Consumers have a variety of media they can use to compare prices, terms of purchase and delivery methods (Schultz & Barnes, 1999).

The development of computer software accessible on PCs enables organizations to store, sort and manipulate data. These databases track what customers buy, how often they buy and how much they buy. Non-profit organizations keep records of donation and membership patterns. For the communication professional, databases provide audience information and track the impact of communication tactics on audience behaviour.

The phenomenal growth of the Internet provides increasing opportunity to reach out to audiences through email, blogs, web pages and Web advertising. Database information helps target and pinpoint customer wants, needs and demands in a cost-effective manner.

Strategic Thinking

How do you ensure your organization's strategy and messages are understood by employees who live in different countries? Jane Sparrow, head of employee communications at Sony Europe, works with local teams across Europe to make certain that the Sony Europe voice is consistent. Sparrow says that developing a broad core message with customized toolkits for each nation allows for differences in local cultures and business practices.

Sparrow says this approach has two key benefits:

1. The overall message is consistent but can be tailored to fit local audiences.
2. The tactics of one team can be replicated in another area (Sparrow, 2006, p. 8).

Sparrow adapts her communication style to fit the workplace culture of the countries in which she works. Common themes in her approach include:

- recognizing the differences in workplace customers;
- appreciating the importance of dialogue and how it is played out in different cultures;
- translating materials and resources;
- identifying key people and hierarchical relationships in each operation (Sparrow, 2006, pp. 8–9).

Impact of globalization

Smart organizations realize that in order to grow they must be players on the global stage. **Globalization** influences how an organization chooses to allocate its fiscal assets, with whom it chooses to do business and how it prepares its employees, investors and other significant stakeholders for organizational change.

Globalization changes communication practices. As companies merge, enter into alliances with foreign firms and build off-shore manufacturing facilities, fewer and fewer companies trade within a single country alone or, for that matter, just in the European Union.

In fact, in both Europe and the USA the ability of companies to invest beyond their borders has resulted in shifting capital investment. For example, Vodafone, a large British telecommunication company, has more than 80 % of its sales and employment outside Britain (Vodafone, 2006). This fact illustrates how Vodafone, among thousands of other companies, has to learn how to communicate with employees across the world.

Global companies must understand the practices of the countries in which they operate and how customs and practices affect the lives of employees. Established in 1865 as The Hong Kong and Shanghai Banking Corporation Limited, HSBC calls itself "the world's local Bank". The London-based bank has over 9 500 offices in 76 countries and its asset allocation tells part of its global story.

In 1985 the bank had 75 % of its assets in Hong Kong. Twenty years later the bank's assets indicate a larger global presence, with 36 % of its assets in the USA, 32 % in Hong Kong, 18 % in the UK and 16 % in other countries. The bank is making serious inroads into India and reportedly is the largest transnational bank operating in the Islamic world (Shameen, 2006).

A worldwide presence obviously means that the company is operating in countries with varying attitudes towards labour management relations, among other functions. In 2004 the company conducted an audit of its employees to gain a better picture of labour management relations throughout its organization by sampling 90 % of its employees (HSBC, 2006).

As organizations become more complex, the tendency to keep information in silos within management structures is no longer practical. In the past, each department within an organization operated as if it was autonomous, and tended not to share information with other departments and their personnel. It was a territorial approach that fostered duplication of effort, wasted resources and frustrated results. Along with this recognition came the acknowledgement that every aspect of an organization's communication process, from signage and telephone screening to logos, memos, newsletters, press relations and promotional activities, are all factors in public perception and should have a unified voice to deliver the message. Integrated business communication recognizes these trends.

Influence of integrated marketing communication (MARCOM)

Integrated business communication is rooted in **integrated marketing communication**. In their 1993 book *Integrated Marketing Communications: Putting it Together and Making It Work*, academicians Don Schultz, Stanley Tannenbaum and Robert Lauterborn considered IMC as "a new way of looking at the whole where once were only parts such as advertising, public relations, sales promotion, publicity, employee communication, and so forth. It's aligning communication to look at the way the customer sees it – as a flow of information from indistinguishable sources" (Schultz, Tannenbaum & Lauterborn, 1993, p. xvi).

In 1995, Ian Linton and Kevin Morley published their take on IMC on behalf of The Chartered Institute of Marketing (UK). They wrote: "Integrated marketing provides an opportunity to improve the effectiveness of programmes by handling all aspects of marketing through a single source" (Linton & Morley, 1995, p. 1).

By 2003, after IMC had been widely practised by industry and its effectiveness studied by academicians and practitioners, the definition of IMC became broader. Schultz and Schultz offer the most comprehensive definition of IMC:

> Integrated marketing communications is a strategic business process used to plan, develop, execute and evaluate coordinated, measurable, persuasive brand communication programs over time with consumers, customers, prospects, and other targeted, relevant external and internal audiences (Schultz & Schultz, 2003, p. 21).

This definition defines IMC as a strategic part of the business process that involves first and foremost customers and consumers but also includes other stakeholders.

Integrated business communication has a focus on the customers but is equally concerned with the power and influence of employees and key publics in the development of stakeholder relationships and the building of brand relationships.

Characteristics of integrated business communication

In this text, **integrated business communication** is defined as the process of planning, executing and evaluating unified messages that create stakeholder relationships and build brand relationships.

As we continue to examine integrated business communication throughout an organization and to various audiences, the following concepts will support our discussion:

1. Business communication should be research based and begin with consideration of the target audiences. Communication programmes are developed to meet audience needs by providing information when and where that audience wants it.

2. Business communication is focused on building relationships. Individual customers or large interest groups that influence how your business is perceived in the marketplace are crucial to building long-term relationships. "Lifetime value" of a customer is used to calculate the worth of that customer to an organization.

3. Two-way communication must be developed. Traditional marketing communication programmes were built on one-way communication activities. Mass media such as television, magazines, newspapers and outdoor advertising spouted clever messages at the consumer but offered little or no opportunity for feedback. Today's consumer demands to be heard. The Internet confirms that the public demands interactivity.

4. Use of databases is a vital component. Well-managed databases, collections of information about relevant publics (such as customers, potential customers, media, competitors, etc.), are at the core of integrated communication strategies. Databases must be shared across organizational lines and are no longer the sole property of one sector of the organization. Databases enable communicators to deliver unique messages to each target group – messages that address individual needs. For example, a large manufacturing plant maintains a database of suppliers – not only for sales and inventory purposes but also to identify how the relationship with a supplier influences economic development in a particular geographic area. This information is vitally important in gaining tax and other political advantages. Most organizations can benefit from a database, but those that do not rely on repeat customers or have small profit margins probably would not benefit from allocating resources to such technology. For example, it's unlikely that a street vendor or a one-man lawn service would find a database helpful or worth the investment.

5. One voice/one message is a primary goal. Organizations have the tendency to send a variety of messages to the public. This occurs if an organization chooses to hire an advertising agency to do its advertising, a different firm to manage its public relations and still another to handle promotions, etc. If the messages do not speak as one voice, the public may become confused. The one voice/one message focus also applies to other forms of communication such as letters and emails sent to customers, the way personnel talk on the phone with clients, the uniform worn by delivery persons or employees, signage and other such communication that may have an unintended effect on consumer perception.

6. The continuous stream of communication must be seamless. Audiences need to receive appropriate communication on a timely basis. Repeated and properly timed messages motivate audiences when many messages compete for their attention.

7. Selecting the best methods for communication needs careful consideration. Organizations that rely on an integrated approach choose the appropriate form of communication to reach a particular consumer. Advertising may be applicable in some cases, whereas public relations or another form of communication may work better in other circumstances. More often it is necessary to use multiple forms of communication to reach a target audience.

8. Feedback and assessment tools should be used to measure performance. Organizations are interested in return on investment (ROI), a ratio of earnings to spending. Communication strategies need to be measured against objectives and modified, if necessary, to achieve those objectives.

Strategic planning

Integrated communication requires a strategic approach to planning based on the above eight points. The planning and execution process succeeds only if creativity and innovation are valued and practised. Strategy development is based on a thorough understanding of organizational goals and a situational analysis of current customers, potential customers and other stakeholders including employees, competitors, suppliers, government regulators and interest groups, among others.

Strategic planning questions include: what are the mission and vision of the organization; what are the IMC objectives; and what are the budgetary

Strategic Thinking

In 2006, Walt Disney Parks and Resorts launched an integrated global marketing theme "Where Dreams Come True" (PROMO, 2006a). The theme is based on two years of research conducted across its five theme parks. Through focus groups and surveys, Disney discovered that park families and other visitors around the world agreed that a Disney park "is a place where dreams come true" (PROMO, 2006a).

Michael Mendenhall, executive vice-president for global marketing for Walt Disney Parks and Resorts, said, "What we are seeing is a market of one. This is a concept that clearly exists in consumers' mindsets. Walt [Disney] 50 years ago branded this idea of this transformational experience ... That message was strong enough and compelling enough it resonated around the world" (PROMO, 2006b).

The company used the theme through various related campaigns including the first anniversary of Hong Kong Disneyland, the 15th anniversary of Disneyland Paris and the "Year of a Million Dreams" celebration in Florida and California in the USA. Ads, contests, sweepstakes and promotional materials will be based on the theme.

Disney says the campaign will be the most expensive campaign it has ever produced and its first worldwide integrated marketing venture.

considerations? The development of messages, and tactics to communicate those messages, comes only after these components of the planning process are complete.

Meeting Public Expectations

To address the rapidly changing world of the receiver, communicators have risen to the challenge. Both internal and external publics not only expect but demand, professional and well-crafted messages. Public relations experts constantly strive to "know" their publics, through research, hard work, trial and error and, sometimes, intuition. Whereas in the early years people were selected to staff public relations departments because of their friendly attitudes and people skills, today's professionals are trained by colleges and universities around the world that pride themselves on turning out knowledgeable and capable graduates.

Chapter Summary

Businesses have embraced and adapted to many changes and have recognized the value and role of communicators as integral to their organizations.

The public relations industry has also transformed itself from its inception as a persuasive tactic used by early Greeks and Romans to the publicity arm of advertising firms seeking to expand their services. Today, public relation consultancies are respectable agents of change in their own right.

Integrated communication became the focus of public relations professionals as companies saw the need to speak with one voice and communicate throughout all levels of their corporate structure. They recognized the need to understand the complexities of integrated communication and concepts such as "lifetime value" of a customer, databasing, branding, feedback and evaluation and the use of measurement tools. Communication programmes target internal audiences such as employees and their families, and external publics such as media, the community and suppliers.

The education and training of communicators are a focus for universities and institutions of higher learning in all corners of the world. ■

Learning From Others

Elizabeth Dougall, assistant professor at the School of Journalism and Mass Communication, University of North Carolina at Chapel Hill, was awarded top honours by the Institute of Public Relations for her research that examines the public opinion environment of organizational populations (Dougall, 2005).

Dougall served as consultant to businesses, non-profit organizations and government agencies on a range of corporate communication and marketing issues in Australia, the UK, Europe and Canada. She has extensive experience in issues management, marketing communication, shareholder relations, strategic planning and crisis communication. Here she examines public opinion as it impacts upon an organization's reputation.

The problematic public opinion environment

Reputation is a critical resource that organizations draw from the public opinion environment, and, while good reputations can take a lifetime to build, they take only a moment to ruin. The court of public opinion is both fickle and brutal; there are no laws of evidence in this court and no burden of proof. And don't forget,

there are now many new media adding their voices to those of activists, advocates, pundits and politicians. The reputation of organizations is made even more vulnerable through interdependence. For example, the pharmaceutical industry, once regarded as a group of virtuous organizations forging new frontiers with important research and life-saving products, now faces accusations of price-gouging, withholding vital drugs to protect patents, deceptive marketing and sloppy research.

The public opinion environment can be defined as the set of issues that concern similar organizations – populations – that share environmental constraints such as size, location and government regulations[1]. Ways to measure, even predict change in the public opinion environments of organizations are still emerging, but some important principles for understanding this critical phenomenon are:

1. The public opinion environment is composed of an overlapping and persistent set of issues that concern similar organizations, that is, issues that emerge for one pharmaceutical company almost always concern them all.
2. The ebb and flow in this environment can be tracked by describing the turnover of issues (*stability*), the number of issues (*complexity*), the volume of media coverage (*intensity*), and the favourability of that coverage (*direction*).
3. What can and does often change dramatically is the intensity and favourability of public attention as new events and topics emerge. The number of issues that can emerge (*complexity*) is not infinite and will reach saturation.
4. Activists and advocates typically have fewer resources than companies and governments, and therefore a more limited voice in the public opinion environment. That voice is more likely to attract attention when used to contend multiple, persistent issues. Groups that can sustain pressure on organizations are themselves institutionalized to some extent, with employees to pay and equipment to lease.
5. The issues that consume most media coverage are those contended most vigorously by influential, resource-rich organizations. The issues attracting attention spasmodically are those contended most vigorously by activists and resisted by organizations.
6. Organizations may try to avoid sustaining an issue by refusing to engage in a public debate. However, this downplaying or buffering strategy often stimulates more conflict which the news media will happily report.

[1]Dougall, E. (2005) "Revelations of an ecological perspective: issues, inertia, and the public opinion environment of organizational populations". *Public Relations Review*, **31**: 534–543.

Case Study – **Dow Corning**

When Barie Carmichael became director of communications for Dow Corning in 1990, she described the internal publications as "… an unwieldy set of company magazines that were unapproachable and untimely". Further, she noted that hard copies of press releases were delivered to employees via interoffice mail after the news had already been published in the newspapers. Employees complained of company forums where they heard lacklustre speeches; many stopped attending the meetings. External communications were no better. Community relations were non-existent and government relations did not seem important. But all that was about to change.

The company's computer network began to post news releases and informational bulletins. The internal newsletter was changed to reflect employees need for news and updates, and the forums were changed to allow discussion and dialogue between management and employees. External publics were addressed and public relations experts consulted. The corporation communicated with the local community and the political front in Washington, DC.

On 15 May 1995, Dow Corning filed for bankruptcy pending litigation in the silicone breast implant controversy. The company survived. Many say it was due to its communications efforts. Carmichael stayed with Dow Corning for 12 years and built a strong corporate communication team that saw the company through its difficulties.

Today, Carmichael is a senior counsellor for APCO Worldwide, a global communication consultancy with offices in Shanghai, Jakarta, Hong Kong, Hanoi, Beijing, Rome, Paris, Geneva, London, Washington, DC, and Brussels (APCO Worldwide, 2006). APCO was named Agency of the Year in 2006 by *PR Week* and was awarded the 2005 Consultancy of the Year by *Public Affairs News*.

Do some research to see how the silicon implant controversy was handled. Take a look at Dow Corning today at www.dowcorning.com (Dow Corning, 2006). Do you see a communication-oriented company? What are your thoughts on its website which invites viewers to receive "instant news release alerts – Dow Corning news – as soon as it is released".

Along with other information, you can access the company's community outreach efforts in various locations and you can also choose which language, Chinese, German, Japanese or Korean, you would like to use. What does this say about the "new" Corning company? A Corning technical information centre recently opened in Germany to provide "rapid responses to technical, regulatory and environmental, health and safety inquiries" to customers in Europe. Do you think this will lead to more positive brand reputation? ■

Class Exercises

1. Some companies staff a full in-house public relations department; others choose to employ one or two executives who manage the major public relations efforts with independent agencies. Do some searching on the Web and make a list of the advantages and disadvantages of both in-house public relations agencies and outside agencies. Look for concepts such as objectivity, freshness in approach, creativity, cost, expertise, knowledge, historical perspective, etc.

2. Databases vary in their usage by organizations. Consider how a clothing store or a lubricant shop/garage might take advantage of a database to reach its preferred customers. Interview some small business owners to find out if they use databases in their companies.

3. (Advanced exercise) The concept of "one voice/one message" is central to integrated business communication. Use your own institution as the source for this exercise. What is the one voice/one message delivered in its recruiting efforts? Is the message consistent? Consider such communication channels as publications, websites, newsletters, campus tours, signage or special events in your analysis. Look for the messages. Interview university officials. Analyse your findings and prepare an oral report with examples to share with your classmates and, if possible, university officials.

Action Plan

In a group of two or three students, choose a visible global corporation that has recently experienced a merger or that has expressed that intent in the near future. Search the media to collect news articles about the companies involved. Can you find evidence of any public relations efforts surrounding the merger? Any attempts to present the company in a good light? Any reputation-building efforts by either company? Any effort to mould public opinion? Does the organization have any outreach programmes to present or potential consumers? Research the company's website to see what news it posts there. Is it different from the messages in the media? If the information is different or more extensive, what accounts for this difference?

Websites

The Public Relations Society of America site offers a wealth of information including a link for PR industry news. A recent story cited the three critical issues shaping the industry today: diversity, ethics and risk. Go to `www.prsa.org`

The International Public Relations Association of more than 1000 professionals may be accessed at `www.ipra.org`. Its website states: "Four years ago IPRA launched a campaign to reduce the incidence of unethical and sometimes illegal practices in the relationships between public relations professionals and the media. The Media Transparency Charter inspired by the campaign which sets international standards of ethical behaviour has now been adopted by public relations practitioners in more than 100 countries" (IPRA, 2006).

Take a minute to view all the universities represented on WorldWideLearn at `www.worldwidelearn.com` (WorldWideLearn, 2006). Click on the "Outside US & Canada?" tab at the top of the page to find a country with which you are familiar and see what degrees, other than public relations and communication, can be obtained online. Discuss your thoughts about online degree programmes in a class discussion.

References

APCO Worldwide (2006) Available from: www.apcoworldwide.com [Accessed 24 March 2006].

Dougall, E. (2005) "Revelations of an ecological perspective: issues, inertia, and the public opinion environment of organizational populations". *Public Relations Review*, **31**: 534–543.

Dow Corning (2006) Available from: www.dowcorning.com [Accessed 24 March 2006].

Grunig, J. & Grunig, L. (2000) "Public relations in strategic management and strategic management of public relations: theory and evidence from the IABC Excellence Project". *Journalism Studies*, **1**(2): 303–321.

Heckscher, C. (1991) "Can business beat bureaucracy?" *The American Prospect*, 21 March 1991: 114–115. Available from: http://www.prospect.org/web/view-print.ww?id=5289 [Accessed 6 November 2006].

HSBC (2006) Available from: www.hsbc.com/'csr/;our-people [Accessed 25 April 2006].

Hughes, A. (2000) *Strategic Databases*, 2nd edn. New York, McGraw-Hill.

Grunig, J. & Hunt, T. (1994) *Public Relations Techniques*. Fort Worth, TX, Harcourt Brace College.

IPA (2006) "History of public relations". Institute of Public Relations. Available from: www.instituteforpr.com [Accessed 4 March 2006].

IPRA (2006) International Public Relations Association. Available from: www.ipra.org [Accessed 8 March 2006].

Linton, I. & Morley, K. (1995) *Integrated Marketing Communications*. Oxford, UK, Butterworth-Heinemann Ltd.

Patent Medicine (2006) Available from: www.discoveriesinmedicine.com [Accessed 8 March 2006].

Poignant, R. (2004) *Professional Savages: Captive Lives and Western Spectacle*. New Haven, CT, Yale University Press.

PROMO (2006a) "In major move, Disney integrates global marketing". Available from: http://www.printthis.clickability.com/pt/cpt?action=cpt&title=In+Major+Move%2C+Disney+... [Accessed 12 June 2006].

PROMO (2006b) "Lengthy research leads Disney to global 'dreams' theme". Available from: http://www.printhis. clickability.com/pt/cpt?action=cpt&title=Lengthy+Research+Leads+... [Accessed 12 June 2006].

Schultz, D. & Schultz, H. (2003) *IMC: the Next Generation*. Boston, McGraw-Hill.

Schultz, D. & Barnes, B. (1999) *Strategic Brand Communication Campaigns*, 5th edn. Lincolnwood, IL, NTC Business Books.

Schultz, D., Tannenbaum, R. & Lauterborn, R. (1993) *Integrated Marketing Communications*. Lincolnwood, IL, NTC Business Books.

Shameen, A. (2006) "The bonding of HSBC". *Chief Executive*, March: 32–35.

Sparrow, J. (2006) "Balancing global and local needs". *Strategic Communication Management*, **10**(2): 8–9.

Vodafone (2006) Available from: www.vodafone.com [Accessed 24 April 2006].

van Ruler, B. & Vercic, D. (2002) "The Bled Manifesto on public relations". Available from: www.bledcom.com/uploads/documents/manifesto.pdf [Accessed 4 March 2006].

van Ruler, B., Vercic, D. & Flodin, B. (2001) "On the definition of public relations: a European view". *Public Relations Review*, **27**: 373–387.

WorldWideLearn (2006) Available from www.worldwidelearn [Accessed 21 April 2006].

Bibliography

Ogden, J. (1998) *Developing a Creative and Innovative Integrated Marketing Communication Plan: a Working Model*. Upper Saddle River, NJ, Prentice-Hall.

CHAPTER 7

External Communication: Messaging to Your Publics

Executive Summary

An organization's primary publics are its customers and employees, but other stakeholders are crucial to the functioning of an organization.

As primary publics, customers are generally the target market, but not all customers are alike

Secondary publics, who do not have a stake in the organization, may be crucial to an organization's reputation and must be considered in the decision-making process

Corporate messages reach targeted publics in many different forms and via many different channels and help to articulate the vision and mission statements of an organization to employees, investors and customers

Communication is the responsibility of all employees in an organization, but several operational departments have primary responsibility

Marketing professionals ensure the customer buys a product or service. Traditionally, marketers considered the product, price, placement (availability of product) and promotions in decision-making. In the integrated approach, the emphasis is on the consumer, cost, convenience and communication.

Public relations is a part of the traditional communication function in the marketing mix, but has the added responsibility for anticipating forces for social change, monitoring institutional policy, and evaluating organizational performance in both the external and internal environment

Advertising is a communication function charged with reaching targeted publics through paid media placement with creative and provocative messages that demand action by the consumer

Other necessary communication functions in a competitive business environment include media relations, investor relations, cause-related marketing and branding

Recognizing the responsibilities of these functions and understanding how and what they contribute to an organization are fundamental to its long-term profitability and success. ■

External Communication: Messaging to Your Publics

> ❝*Your vision will become clear only when you look into your heart ... Who looks outside, dreams. Who looks inside, awakens.*❞
>
> *Carl Jung*

Introduction to Recognizing Publics

The primary focus of integrated communication is the customer, but other groups or individuals – **publics** – also influence an organization's well-being. Organizations attempt to reach their target customers in as many places as possible, from magazine advertising to websites to sample distribution and special events, keeping within budgetary constraints.

Recently a leading cosmetic company decided to launch a fragrance line aimed at a new market – teens, aged 12–18. After researching this market, the company developed a communication plan to reach teens at several points of contact, including mainstream distribution (PROMO, 2006).

This plan included mobile phone messages, an interactive website that asked teens to submit photos of themselves using the fragrance, samples and giveaways distributed at concerts featuring teen artists and personalized bumper stickers. A promotional van distributed scratch-off game cards for prizes, but, in order to get the cards, teens had to provide names and email addresses. The information collected will be used later to measure the success of the company's campaign as well as provide mailing list and database information for future marketing efforts.

These promotions are only one part of this cosmetic company's customer relationship management programme. The long-range communication plan focuses on how to reach customers further, how to establish long-term relationships and how to build brand awareness, recognition and loyalty.

Stakeholders – primary publics

Customers are **stakeholders**, or primary publics, that affect, or are affected by, the actions and reactions of an organization. Consider what would happen if IKEA, one of the world's largest furniture retailers, could no longer ship its goods. To IKEA and other retailers, shipping companies and suppliers are crucial and are primary stakeholders in their success.

The way a company manages its relationship with its stakeholders determines its brand equity – or the value of the brand. A strong brand with greater equity adds to the total value of a company beyond its physical assets used to manufacture and deliver services.

How can you identify stakeholders? Some stakeholders are obvious – for example, informed, contented employees.

To identify stakeholders, the following questions need to be answered:

- Who owns the company? Is it publicly traded? A partnership? A non-profit company?
- How are the products distributed?
- Who are its suppliers?
- Who regulates the company at all levels of government?
- What role does the organization have in the community?
- Who are its competitors?
- What media follow its operations?

Answering these questions will help determine stakeholders; most stakeholders fall into the following categories: employees, investors, interest groups, government, financial, media, scholars and industry leaders, communities, distributors, suppliers, trade and professional organizations and competitors (Gronstedt, 1996, p. 291).

It is impossible in today's environment to operate in a vacuum, given the needs of businesses to create products; secure raw materials; manufacture, produce, distribute and ship; invoice and collect; report and control finances; and make profits. As a result, companies need to develop ongoing productive relationships with the publics that control or influence these resources (Guth & Marsh, 2005). Furthermore, managing relationships between organizations and publics around shared goals results in mutual understanding and benefits for both the organization and the pertinent publics (Ledingham, 2003, p. 190).

Corporate Communications in BMW North America's manufacturing operation targets four primary publics in online newsletters: BMW enthusiasts, manufacturing innovators, educators and environmentalists. The newsletters help the company build ongoing relationships with these key publics while the online tracking helps the company to determine whether the newsletters are read.

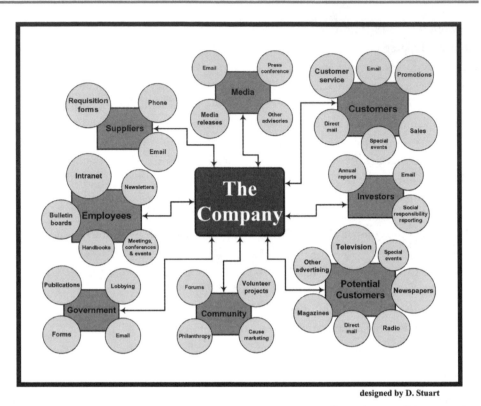

designed by D. Stuart

Figure 7.1 Mapping stakeholder communication channels. This diagram illustrates the complexity of reaching both primary and secondary publics through various channels.

Research suggests customers who feel satisfied with a company's services are less likely to terminate their relationships with that company, even though they were offered financial benefits from other organizations (Bruning & Castle, 2004). This means communication with customers and other stakeholders must be ongoing and symmetrical – or, to use a technology term, "user friendly".

The two most important primary publics and receivers of corporate messages are customers and employees.

Customers

Clearly not all stakeholders are of equal importance. In fact, the order of importance of specific stakeholders varies depending on the circumstances. As a rule, **customers** are generally the most important stakeholders, often called the target market. This includes

Dig Deeper

Revenue assurance is a hot topic in today's uncertain economic times. TMNG Europe, a management consulting firm, advises clients to develop a good communication plan to inform and educate key players in the process. They call it a "Stakeholder Management Plan". Typical stakeholders might include boards of directors, project teams, steering boards, management and staff. Their experts suggest four planning steps:

- create – identify company needs;
- sell – get management to support the plan with resources and personnel;
- implement the plan;
- develop an exit strategy for the project (Sanders, 2005).

individuals or businesses that have purchased goods and/or services or those you want to be your customer in the future.

Marketers talk about the 80/20 rule −20 % of customers buy 80 % of the product. The 20 % is made up of customers who buy the brand and only that brand – those who would rather do without than purchase another brand. Research shows that retaining customers is more profitable than acquiring new ones. Although databases identify current customers, their buying habits, their needs and their profitability, most companies spend approximately 90 % of their marketing budgets to acquire new customers and only 10 % on customer retention (Hughes, 2000, p. 18).

Learning more about customer characteristics, such as their spending habits and motivations, enables the tailoring of messages to fit their individual communication needs. As these groups have greater potential for profit – they have a greater lifetime value – more investment will be needed to communicate with them.

Tom Duncan, an academic leader in integrated marketing communication, believes that consistency in communication, accessibility, responsiveness and commitment are keys to a customer-centred approach to business (Duncan, 2005).

Employees

Loyal **employees** are informed employees and can be public relations ambassadors for organizations. Good internal communications helps employees feel connected to their work and the company's mission. However, if employees believe management is not keeping them informed about company policies or practices, then they are likely to feel disconnected and spread misinformation to other employees or to outsiders.

The two-way symmetrical public relations model illustrates the ideal form of communication management: "Managers need to recognize that, if they provide information to employees and also listen to them, those employees will be excited about their work, connected to the company's vision, and in a position to further the goals of the organization" (Argenti, 2003, p. 127).

Harrah's Entertainment, by nature of its business as the world's largest casino organization, is focused on customer service. But Harrah's does not neglect its 80 000 employees around the globe. "Employee engagement", says a key executive, "is vital to the service-profit chain. We focus on the emotional well-being of our employees and nurture a sense of team membership" (Stuart, 2006, private interview).

Secondary publics

Organizations also need to be concerned about **secondary publics**, groups that are not stakeholders but that may be crucial to a company's reputation.

Consider this example. For decades, an historic home in the heart of a residential district functioned as the administrative offices of a medical institution. The complex needed room for a parking garage. Word surfaced that the medical complex planned to tear down the historic house. Negative neighbourhood and community sentiment surfaced quickly. The hospital board of trustees, realizing they needed the long-term goodwill of the neighbouring community and its leaders, made a wise decision. They agreed to move the house, still keeping it on the property, and build a parking garage next to it. In this case, the neighbourhood association and historical groups were publics that the medical complex needed to include in its decision-making process.

Forms of Corporate Messaging

All communication efforts must work together to deliver a message that is more than just the sum of its many parts. **Corporate messages** reach targeted publics in different forms and via many channels or modes of delivery. Whichever words or channels are selected to communicate the message, it is important that all messages speak clearly with one voice.

For the public to understand a product, service or intent of a company, all messages must reflect a single image conveyed in a sincere and honest way. This interrelatedness of all corporate messages is called integrated communication. If executed correctly, the symbiotic relationship builds strong and valuable corporate images that will connect with the public, help in crisis situations, fulfil the expectations of consumers and most importantly create trust.

Let's examine external communication tools.

Vision statements

An organization's **vision** is a guideline for long-term success, a blueprint for the future. If a company cannot define its vision, it will never reach its potential. When writing a vision statement, management should stretch the boundaries of the ordinary and reach for greatness, but the vision statement should be realistic and achievable. It should be consistent with the company's values and act as a guide for future decision-making. The vision of the company is usually formulated by top management who are privy to company goals and objectives.

DuPont, a global company with 2005 revenues of $26.6 billion and 60 000 employees worldwide in over 70 countries, publishes its corporate vision statement on its website: "Our vision is to be the world's most dynamic science company, creating sustainable solutions essential to a better, safer and healthier life for people everywhere" (DuPont, 2006).

In order to differentiate itself from the parent company, DuPont Australia & New Zealand posts a separate vision statement: "...making growth happen". This example illustrates that a corporate vision statement might be appropriate in one part of the world but needs refining to fit a local culture.

Eurovipp, the European Virtual Institute for Plastics Processing, a consortium of plastic processing experts, publishes its mission statement on its website: "Eurovipp will support the European plastic processing sector to become the most competitive plastic community in the globalized economy and to develop sustainable and environmentally responsible economic growth" (Eurovipp, 2006).

> Corporate mission statements are often posted in multiple languages:
>
> DuPont skall i sin affärsverksamhet uppträda med högt ställda etiska normer och arbeta ihärdigt för att bli en respekterad företagsmedborgare över hela världen.
>
> The DuPont Company will conduct its business affairs with the highest ethical standards and work diligently to be a respected corporate citizen worldwide.

Mission statements

A **mission statement** articulates the goals and objectives of the company and concisely states why the company exists. The development of a mission statement is the responsibility of the entire company, from the CEO and president to the sales force to the employees in the mailroom. Other communications may emanate from specific departments, such as policy manuals from human resources or sales report forms from marketing, but the maintenance of a mission statement and its key concepts requires everyone's attention.

It may make social responsibility commitments to its customers, convey a company's attitude toward clients or state a position on its role in the marketplace.

Patagonia Europe, an environmentally friendly adventure clothing company, posts its mission statement on the company website: "Build the best product, cause no unnecessary harm and use business to inspire and implement solutions to the environmental crisis" (Patagonia Europe, 2006).

The mission statement should reflect the company's vision and the long-range direction of top management. IKEA furniture company states: "Our company vision is to create a better everyday life for many people". The mission statement follows: "We do this by offering a wide range of well-designed, functional home furnishing products at prices so low that as many people as possible will be able to afford them" (IKEA, 2006).

A mission statement is also an affirmation of a company's ideals and ideas and not just a few cleverly worded phrases that read well and look good in the company brochure. When a mission statement is just words, and does not accurately reflect the private or public actions of the company, customers begin to notice this incongruity; they question the company's motives and show their growing distrust by not buying its products or services.

Living up to the promises made in mission statements can be challenging. The spirit of a mission statement must be carried out in all company activities, from customer service to employee treatment. Mission statements also serve as a basis for public relations efforts and establish a yardstick by which to measure success in achieving objectives.

> *If you're trying to persuade people to do something, or buy something, it seems to me you should use their language, the language in which they think.*
>
> *David Ogilvy*

In *Brand Manners*, Pringle & Gordon, British experts on branding, define the mission statement as "the jumping off point for both internal and external communications such as advertising, point-of-sale, direct marketing, public relations, sponsorship and many other channels to market" (Pringle & Gordon, 2003, p. 205).

Marketing and public relations

The communication industry has a history of confusing job functions and position titles. Some of the titles that communicators use include public relations managers, marketing coordinators, public relations coordinators or **marketing/public relations** professionals.

However, in recent years, organizations have realized the all-pervasive function of communication throughout the company. In an effort to centralize and integrate communication messages required by different departments, the name Communications Department is common. Whatever sign on the department's door, the functions of marketing and public relations are interrelated.

Marketing

Marketing is a function that researches and develops strategies to answer the needs, wants and desires of the consuming public and uses these findings to design, package, promote, distribute and sell a product or service. Traditionally, this is called product, price, placement and promotions. Promotions is the communication function within the marketing process.

Marketing involves many types of professionals, from product engineers to accountants, and marketing communicators are vital to the process.

The marketing communication responsibilities are to:

- develop research tools
- carry out research projects
- collect public and consumer opinion
- provide feedback to managers, accountants and salespeople
- coordinate package design
- investigate new markets and distribution points
- influence pricing decisions
- integrate programmes with public relations and advertising campaigns
- support other marketing efforts.

Marketing efforts must be closely monitored because sometimes a clever marketing idea could be a public relations disaster. When the Nestle Corporation, headquartered in Switzerland, had an idea to market its baby formula in developing nations, the plan

> There is only one thing in the world worse than being talked about, and that is not being talked about.
>
> Oscar Wilde

seemed foolproof. Marketers promoted the baby formula as better than mother's milk and gave out free samples to new mothers. They sent sales representatives into hospitals to promote the product directly to new mothers.

As the new mothers wanted to do best for their babies, they decided to use the provided formula rather than breastfeed. But once they got home, they couldn't afford the formula or the purified water with which to mix it. Consequently, many babies went hungry because mothers diluted the formula to make it go further, while others became sick from the contaminated water and died. This promotion became a public relations nightmare for Nestle (Reinhold, 1981). The World Health Organization (WHO) called for a resolution to boycott the baby formula and proposed an international effort to stop the promotion of artificial milk mixes for infants.

The USA entered the lone opposing vote to this resolution, and that action provoked resignations of officials in the United States Agency for International Development who accused the government of "being swayed by the self-interest of the infant formula lobby". These actions spilled over and affected US baby formula companies, Abbott, Bristol-Myers Squibb and American Home Products Corp., who would be financially hit in 1991, as paediatricians questioned their marketing tactics (Siler & Woodruff, 1990).

Marketing also benefits from public relations input, and the key is communication. Could public relations professionals have warned the marketers of the impending disaster surrounding the breast milk versus formula controversy? If they had researched, trendwatched and identified the shift back towards breastfeeding that was occurring in many countries at the time, perhaps they could have averted the disaster.

Public relations

Public relations has four primary functions in a business organization:

- to anticipate social change
- to monitor institutional policy
- to evaluate organizational performance
- to act as the primary communication agent.

The **social change function** requires public relations professionals to be aware of social, economic, cultural and political changes that could affect the livelihood of an organization. For example, a furniture manufacturer knowing that the population is ageing will have to adapt its designs to accommodate the comfort needs of elderly customers.

As **monitor of institutional policies**, it is the responsibility of public relations to ensure that companies do what they say they will do. If they promote literacy as a social cause, they also need to promote literacy among their own employees.

Public relations professionals also **evaluate external organizational performance** by monitoring public perception of company activities. Do stakeholders understand and believe the company's commitment to their customers and their communities? If its mission statement claims it is a steward of the environment, is it? Is this commitment communicated to the public?

Acting as a primary communication agent, public relations communicates information to the public, employees, media and other interest groups to gain publicity and achieve communication goals. Communication functions include lobbying, maintaining customer relationships, promoting corporate strategy, organizing events and media relations.

As the boundary spanner between the organization and its publics, the public relations department provides information to the media. The primary tool of disseminating information is the media release, an **uncontrolled vehicle** over which public relations professionals have little say how the message is used. Media releases are edited, cut, added to and sometimes manipulated by reporters to make news stories for newspapers and magazines appear more interesting. The lack of media message control may mean that a company's name could appear next to that of a competitor at an event or in a media story.

On the upside, however, the appearance of a company's name in uncontrolled media adds what the professionals call "third-party credibility" to your publicity. A medium's reputation for accurate reporting means the public trusts what it says and, by association, trusts the company on which it is reporting. Sponsorship of an event is seen as a goodwill outreach to the community.

Public relations professionals use advertising when they are unhappy with media coverage or want to control the exact meaning and content of their message. For example, Mobil Oil bought space for a series of ads, called advertorials, in the 1970s to promote issues important to the oil industry. Legal experts have said this type of corporate advertising is designed to achieve public relations objectives.

Effective public relations tools benefit many departments, including legal, human resources, sales, special events and others. Here is an example of how a mail order department used a customer questionnaire to increase sales in a unique way. Research showed that mail order returns can climb as high as 30 %. To turn this negative into useful information, Lands End clothing company developed a questionnaire about the product that customers must fill in as part of their return policy. This simple form provides vital customer information that improves customer service, enhances customer relationships and ensures Lands End success as a mail order company.

Advertising

Advertising is information from an identified entity that pays for the media time, space or sponsorship. Advertising as a communication tool has expanded and matured into a billion dollar industry since its rise to importance in the 1930s and 1940s.

Advertising is one of the most useful and common persuasive communication tools. It is a **controlled medium** because a company can determine when and where an ad runs, unchanged and unedited. This is a benefit over an uncontrolled medium like a media release where a company relinquishes control of its story to gatekeepers – reporters and editors.

Some functions of advertising are:

- to introduce a new or sell an existing product or service;
- to build and maintain a brand image;
- to post job openings;
- to fulfil legal notification requirements;
- to announce bond issues or product recalls;
- to offer apologies;
- to state company position on current topics;
- to promote special offers like coupons and sales.

> *Doing business without advertising is like winking at a pretty girl in the dark. You know what you are doing, but nobody else does.*
> *Stuart Henderson Britt, advertising consultant*

Advertising practitioners spend many years learning their craft and pride themselves on a knowledge of the industry. Before advertising messages are created, a thorough knowledge of the target audience is essential. To reach the most appropriate audience, a segmentation strategy is developed to identify those groups that are most likely to respond to a paid message, including customers or potential customers.

Sometimes, **niche markets**, smaller segments of the market that share common interests, are identified, such as a market segment of Hispanics who favour colored contact lenses. Through the use of database research, this audience segment can be further narrowed to a particular target: young Hispanic women between the ages of 18 and 25 who presently wear clear contact lenses but may want to try coloured lenses.

Advertising is also concerned with developing messages for targeted publics. Advertising works better at some levels of persuasion than at others. The levels of persuasion are:

- Raise awareness (advertising is very effective at this level).
- Increase knowledge (advertising also operates well at this level).
- Ensure acceptance of the message (advertising begins to be less effective).
- Change attitudes toward the message (opinion leaders and peers are more effective than advertising at this level).
- Change behaviour (peers and opinion leaders are most effective here).

> *The trade of advertising is now so near to perfection that it is not easy to propose any improvement. But as every art ought to be exercized in due subordination to the public good, I cannot but propose it as a moral question to these masters of the public ear, whether they do not sometimes play too wantonly with our passions.*
>
> Dr Samuel Johnson,
> English author, 1759

The persuasion level chart in Figure 7.2 shows that influencing buying behaviour with advertising can be difficult; nevertheless, advertising is effective in building brand awareness.

When embarking on an advertising campaign, usually a costly endeavour, companies should entrust their image and corporate messages to advertising experts, whether they are part of an in-house advertising department or employees of an outside agency. There are advantages and disadvantages of both, much of which revolve around money, talent, creativity and a thorough understanding of the brand. Before investing in one or the other, considerable research must be completed.

Promotions

Another important tool to the integrated business communication process involves promotional activities. **Consumer sales promotions** seek to encourage customers to try a product they don't currently use or normally purchase. Promotions aimed at building brand images may include coupons, sampling, price deals, sweepstakes and contests.

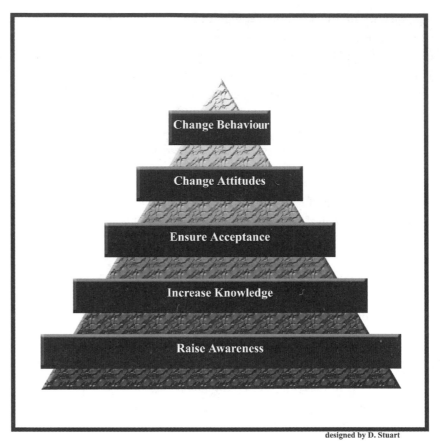

Change Behaviour

Change Attitudes

Ensure Acceptance

Increase Knowledge

Raise Awareness

designed by D. Stuart

Figure 7.2 Levels of persuasion. Advertising is more effective at the awareness and knowledge stages. Changing behaviour, such as persuading customers to buy a product or use a service, is more often influenced by peers and opinion leaders.

Trade promotions offer incentives to retailers, distributors, dealers or salespersons to increase sales or to stimulate excitement. At a trade show, business-to-business marketers show their new products. Automobile trade shows in Germany, fashion shows in Milan, broadcast equipment shows in Nevada, USA, and book dealers shows in various locations draw business people from around the globe. More money is spent on trade shows than on any other single type of sales promotion activity because before you sell it to the end-user (the consumer) you have to first sell it to the distributor or retailer.

A growing phenomenon is the placement of branded products in television shows, movies and store displays. It is more subliminal than overt, but reaches out to a mass audience and contributes to the branding challenges of many companies.

Direct marketing

Direct marketing through print or electronic media enables the customer to order and purchase a product by phone, electronic media or the Internet. Postal regulations in the USA enable consumers to opt out of direct mail or telephone sales. But Internet selling continues to be a growing form of direct marketing. Communication tactics need to be carefully evaluated before any marketing decision is made.

Communicating with special publics

Companies have many target markets such as customers, media, government agencies, investors, etc. Although most executives are not directly involved in the activities of all these interests, it is important to be acquainted with the corporate communication functions that can best spread the word and fulfil communication needs:

- media relations
- investor relations
- public affairs
- community relations
- cause-related marketing.

Media relations

Sending out media releases is not the extent of a company's outreach to the media. **Media relations** involves establishing a symbiotic relationship with media outlets.

For example, knowing reporters at local newspapers helps PR professionals do their job. For science-related industries, for example, knowing the names and interests of science reporters will help target media releases.

Reporters don't want to be bombarded with information that is not valuable to their readers, and media specialists have learned to use a variety of tools to get media coverage:

- ✓ news advisories – small one-paragraph notices of upcoming events, important executive promotions and changes in company policy;
- ✓ photos with stand-alone captions – newspapers like images and will often fill an empty spot on inside pages with a photo rather than text;
- ✓ video news releases or VNRs – video segments that can be worked into the soft news section of news programmes;
- ✓ photo opportunity alerts and photo ops – heads-up announcements to the media that your event will offer great "visual" news, like a hot air balloon race, for example;
- ✓ stand-alone fact sheets – additional information on the subject.

Reporters are always on deadline and often stretched and stressed. In times of crisis, having good relationships with journalists can be very valuable.

Investor relations

Investor relations is a specialized function that works to build and maintain positive relationships with shareholders and the financial community at large, from international stock markets to local trading companies.

Investor relations professionals inform shareholders and build company loyalty. They track market trends, provide financials for annual reports, update financial reports on company websites, and provide information to analysts, among other tasks.

This is a technical field that involves professionals who know corporate finance, industry lingo, national and international business trends, financial reporting requirements and government rules and regulations. Communicating with these professionals requires communicators to be knowledgeable and current with the global financial network.

Annual reports as well as corporate responsibility reports are tools of investor relations operations. Although many predicted that paper annual reports would be replaced by electronic versions, this has not happened. The printing and distribution of annual reports is an expensive but legal responsibility of publicly traded institutions.

Perhaps owing to recent scandals and the need to build and maintain trust with key financial-based publics, hard copy reports are still disseminated to stockowners, investors and financial institutions. However, the reports have changed formats from the large one-size-fits-all annual report to online reports, offline reports, summary reports and multiple corporate reports aimed at specific audiences. For example, Coca Cola sent a letter to its stockholders asking if they would prefer to receive their 2005 report online. If the stockholder agreed to do so, the company promised to plant a tree in his/her name.

Corporate responsibility reports, such as sustainability reports, are a relatively new type of corporate story form, part of the larger picture of corporate accountability information directed towards the public.

Marimekko, a leading textile and clothing company in Finland, posts "Principles of investor relations" on its website: "Marimekko Corporation complies with the principles of equity in its investor communications and publishes all its investor information on its Internet site in Finnish and English" (Marimekko, 2006). Marimekko Corporation's annual report, financial statement bulletin and interim reports are also posted on its site: www.marimekko.com

This access and transparency add to the trust of both customers and the financial community.

Public affairs

Public affairs offices were previously the domain of governmental organizations. Today, many corporations have public or corporate affairs departments to handle lobbying and advocacy efforts. In *Effective Public Relations*, **public affairs** are defined as "efforts related to public policy and corporate citizenship" (Cutlip, Center & Broom, 2000, p. 15).

These specialists "serve as liaisons with governmental units; implement community improvement programs; encourage political activism, campaign contributions, and voting; volunteer their services in charitable and community development organizations" (Cutlip, Center & Broom, 2000, p. 15). They are also involved in grassroots, lobbying and advocacy programmes.

For some organizations, lobbying is an important communication tool. Europa Donna (ED), a Europe-wide coalition of breast cancer groups, develops educational projects and workshops, but it also lobbies governments. ED recounts the culmination of three years of lobbying: "In June 2003 the European Parliament passed a Resolution on Breast Cancer that detailed targets and quality standards on everything from mortality rates to how mammograms are read, and it called on member states to monitor and report back by 2006 on their progress" (Europa Donna, 2006).

Community relations programmes often fall under the public affairs department, and this can include using community forums, town meetings and interviews with community leaders and citizens to gather information on how to communicate better and more effectively with the community at large. It is advantageous to get community input early in the process. Belk Department Stores, the largest family-owned department store group in the USA, seeks community input when it begins to plan for a new store, addressing such concerns as environmental issues, traffic patterns and shopper loyalty.

It is crucial for organizations to interact with the community as well as to understand the wealth of information that can be collected through these efforts. Outreach projects often require a company spokesperson or executive to be on hand to meet citizens, deliver speeches or cut ribbons in opening ceremonies. Readily providing these company contacts can help the community relations department meet its goals and objectives, and it says this is a company that cares.

History of Cause Marketing

The practice of donating a portion of profits to charity is not a new practice in the UK. The Austin Martin Company was involved in cause marketing during World War II when it agreed to donate one shilling to the RNLI for every lifeboat engine built and delivered (Pringle & Thompson, 1999, p. 59).

The first cause–marketing relationship in the USA is believed to be when a physical fitness campaign based on the benefits of walking was developed for Rockport Shoes (Earle, 2000). However, the American Express campaign to support the Restoration of the Statue of Liberty Fund in 1983 is widely mentioned as the first time the term was used.

Cause-related marketing

Organizations know that building healthy relationships with constituencies requires investment in communities. With roots in the ideas of enlightened self-interest of French philosopher Jean-Jacques Rousseau, cause-related marketing relationships involve the business, the organization, the cause it supports and the consumer.

Pringle and Thompson define **cause-related marketing** as "a strategic positioning and marketing tool that links a company or brand to a relevant social cause or issue, for mutual benefit" (Pringle & Thompson, 1999, p. 3). In a typical cause-related marketing campaign, a portion of designated sales is contributed to a non-profit organization. For example, portions of the sales of Avon pink ribbon products go towards fighting breast cancer, and the retail giant Tesco sponsors a computers for schools programme.

Cause marketing works. National surveys indicate that the majority of consumers would be influenced to buy brands, or even switch and pay more for brands, when the product supports a cause, especially when product features and quality are equal (Kotler, Roberto & Lee, 2002, p. 354).

The justification for cause marketing goes beyond the benefits to an organization's revenues. National opinion polls in the USA, conducted after 11 September 2002, and following the disclosure of large corporate scandals, indicated that 89 % of Americans expected corporations to be more socially responsible (Cone, 2002).

Norwegian scholars Brønn and Vrinoi noted that "A firm that is socially responsible acknowledges that it exists and operates in a shared environment, characterized by a mutual impact of a firm's relationships on a broad variety of stakeholders, who are affected by and can eventually affect the achievement of an organization's goals" (Brønn and Vrinoi, 2001, p. 218).

But to be effective, cause–marketing relationships must reflect the core values of both the non-profit organization and its for-profit partner (Lorange & Roos, 1998). Because such relationships may not be immediately profitable, assessment may be difficult.

Dig Deeper

The website for AsthmaUK includes a link outlining the benefits of its cause-related marketing to the organization. According to this website, a cause-related marketing product is bought every second in the UK (AsthmaUK, 2006).

According to the organization, cause-related marketing offers the following advantages to a company:

- unique selling point over the competition;
- increased brand awareness with a cause that affects one in five customers;
- increased sales of associated products;
- boost in staff morale;
- enhanced positioning as a socially responsible company;
- improved reputation among new and potential customers.

AsthmaUK has cause–marketing relationships with a number of companies including Oira Kiely, a textile, accessory and knitwear designer, and Klober, a manufacturer and supplier of asthma-related medical devices.

How do other health-related organizations promote their cause–marketing relationships?

Both organizations, the company and the non-profit organization, need to support the relationship over a period of time. Finally, cause–marketing relationships require consumers to believe the companies they patronize are serious about the cause and that their contributions will be used prudently.

Protecting a brand

A brand name is worth more to an organization than any other physical or financial asset. It's what makes a product different from its competitors. The process of **branding** involves creating a product that resonates with customers. Brand management is a crucial function of integrated communications and involves a continued financial commitment as well as consistent policy efforts.

The common definition of a brand is a registered trademark of goods or services. But a brand is much more than a trademark, it not only includes product advertising but also packaging, point-of-sale images, customer service, price, performance, social causes and a range of other emotional experiences that a customer may have with the particular product. Even the choice of a spokesperson for a brand affects how consumers perceive it. All of these factors help create a brand's personality.

Consider some great brands and their images: Coca-Cola, considered the most valuable brand in the world; L'Oreal, the world's largest cosmetic company; Rolex watches, created by Hans Wilsdorf and known for their quality and reliability; and the Musgrave Group, an Irish-owned grocery distributor with operations in Ireland, Northern Ireland, Britain and Spain.

Scholar Kevin Lane Keller has written extensively about brands and notes that managers must understand what a brand means to consumers. He cites the case of the French company Société Bic, which was very successful making non-refillable ballpoint pens in the 1950s, disposable cigarette lighters in the 1960s and disposable razors in the 1980s, but bombed with inexpensive glass perfume sprayers in 1989. Keller writes that, in spite of the company spending $20 million in advertising and promotion in both the USA and Europe, it failed to grasp how customers viewed the brand image of their perfumes (Keller, 2000, p. 154).

Brands are also about trust. The *Reader's Digest* European trusted brands study, conducted annually since 1999 in 14 different countries, linked attitudes of a brand's responsibility towards the environment and high ethical standards to the issue of trust. In the study, for example, Germans nominated Toyota as their most trusted car because they believed in the ethical standards that the company represented. The most trusted brands were Nivea skin care products and the Nokia phone handset (http://ww.rdtrustedbrands.com/results/results06) (Reader's Digest, 2006).

Brand communication and brand maintenance are tough businesses and subjects of great interest among scholars and marketing professionals. As such, there are many streams of thought about how to leverage brand personalities.

In Chapter 2 we discussed Maslow's hierarchy of needs. Scott Bedbury, former corporate advertising director of Nike and author of *A New Brand World* (Bedbury, 2002), says that businesses that understand Maslow's hierarchy of needs will be successful in leveraging their products to rise above the noise of competing brands. For example, brand messages that stress emotional needs, such as fulfilment or yearning to belong, are more likely to resonate with consumers.

Brand strategy expert John Grant departs from the focus on psychological theories and defines brands as "a cluster of strategic cultural ideas" (Grant, 2006, p. 273). He suggests that successful brands are like molecules that continue to change and grow over time, as do consumer opinions about a brand.

> Brands revitalize themselves by seeking new audiences. Old Spice, the men's aftershave and deodorant product produced by Proctor and Gamble (P&G), was considered a brand for grandfathers. P&G was looking for new audiences (Baker, 2002). Old Spice kept its classic white bottle with the clipper ship on the side for its traditional cologne and aftershave, but added new products such as RedZone body spray for the younger audience. RedZone rapidly became a category leader in the USA and Europe (Neff, 2006).

Chapter Summary

Recognizing the publics that are important to your business and understanding how to communicate with them is vital to an organization's success.

Integrated communication puts the focus on customers who are considered stakeholders and primary publics because they affect, or are affected by, the actions and reactions of an organization.

Other groups or individuals – secondary publics – also influence an organization's well-being and must be addressed as part of the total marketing mix.

Corporate messages must reach these identified targeted publics. They take many different forms and use a variety of channels (modes of delivery). To ensure that your publics understand your product, your service and your company, all messages must speak with one voice. All communication efforts must work together to deliver an integrated message that is more than just the sum of its parts.

Executives may be involved in some of the messages sent to external publics, such as the company vision, the mission statement and the community newsletter. Management must be actively involved in the external communication efforts of the marketing, public relations, advertising and public affairs departments.

External communication efforts help consumers identify with brands. Building a brand requires the expertise and collaboration of management and employees from all departments who work together to communicate with targeted publics with "one voice, one message". ■

Learning From Others

Jean Watin-Augouard is manager of Trademark Ride, a company that promotes the universality and power of brands. He's also the founder and president of the Club des Partenaires de la Marque, whose aim is to study brands and how they can be used as marketing tools.

Watin-Augouard is editor-in-chief of the *Revue des Marques*. He has authored several books on branding: *Le Dictionnaire des Marques* (1997), *Histoires de Marques, Marques de Toujours* (2003), *Markalarin Öküsü* (2004) and *Créateur de Noms, Marcel Botton et l'Aventure Nomen* (2005).

He shares with us his views on using brand history to enrich a company's marketing message.

> *Yesterday is sometimes tomorrow,*
> *Today is often yesterday,*
> *Tomorrow is already here today*

It is often said that history is the past and marketing executives have priorities other than dwelling on the role played by brands in a country's cultural heritage. They must think in terms of costs, consumer reach, market niches and return on investment.

While these concerns are totally justified, it must not be forgotten that many brand managers can often find marketing success by delving into company history. What is it about the product or the company that keeps consumers loyal? Can loyal customers be transformed into ambassadors of the brand?

In the end, it is not so much about "making" history as about "communicating" from an historical perspective. The role of heritage adds intangible value to a brand's assets. Companies often must be convinced that their company's history (*patrimone* in French, from the latin *pater/monium*) has value.

Building a brand is a *chef d'oeuvre*. Some of the more well-known brands that creatively link their past to their future are: Gillette (King Gillette's razor), Renault (Louis Renault's car design), Dunlop (John Dunlop's tyre innovations) and Nestle (Henri Nestlé's baby cereal). The accomplishments of these creators continue to reflect on the companies, and in these histories one can often find the roots of longevity and keys to modernity.

Brand value is found in the men and women who built the brand as well as in those who continue to enhance the brand with their know-how, product knowledge, communication skills, successes and failures.

Enlivening a brand with it own history reinforces its credibility, enriches its imaginative pull, makes the brand unique in a competitive market, keeps consumers loyal and above all adds value to the brand.

Schools that teach commerce/economics must make future brand managers aware of the intrinsic market value of brands with long histories. If yesterday is sometimes tomorrow and tomorrow is already here, then new brands must build the story upon which they will base, for tomorrow, the roots of their legitimacy and the evidence of their staying power.

Case Study – **Eesti Reklaamiagentuuride (ERAL)**

Eesti Reklaamiagentuuride (ERAL), the Estonian Association of Advertising Agencies, was formed in 1998. The group is made up of the most well-known and largest advertising agencies in Estonia. It is funded by the advertising industry and empowered to apply codes and rules regulating advertising content. The Advertising Education Forum (AEF) website says "the purpose of ERAL is to protect common interests and secure the rights of members of the association, regulation of professional ethics, and promotion of advertising-related activity".

In 2000, ERAL commissioned the Estonian Market and Opinion Research Centre (EMOR), "the largest full service marketing research and consulting company in Estonia", to conduct a survey focused on advertising agencies, their services and their relationship to clients.

One of the main goals of the survey was to identify the criteria clients relied upon when selecting an advertising agency. EMOR interviewed 218 clients of the various agencies. Among other findings, clients revealed the "most important criteria for choosing an advertising agency as: competence, accuracy and precision and creativity".

The survey also looked to identify the problems clients had in communicating with advertising agencies.

The Swedish PR consultancy association Foreningen Public Relations Konsultforetag i Sverige (PRECIS) aims to "improve the standards of its members and to enhance the reputation and role of the PR consultant". You can read the bylaws of the Swedish PR industry at `http://www.precis.se/standards.htm`

Why do you think it is important for agencies to self-monitor themselves? Do you think government encourages these organizations? What are some of the benefits of belonging to an association of agencies? Does your country have its own advertising and public relations associations of agencies and consultancies? ■

Class Exercises

1. Students are to choose a global company and make a list of its relevant publics. What communication tools could be used to reach these publics? How difficult will it be to reach these publics?

2. Students are to access the website of the global company they are researching in question 1 and locate its mission statement. In small groups of three or four, students are to discuss the mission statements they have located and decide which one best fits their collective perception of the company. Each group should prepare a brief report to share with the class that discusses why they chose one mission statement over another.

3. (Advanced) The sample survey below was administered to four females, of varying ages and from two countries. Discuss the differences in viewpoints. This limited sample, of course, cannot be used to draw any broad conclusions, but you can conduct a similar or expanded survey on your campus. Expand the survey using your own criteria.

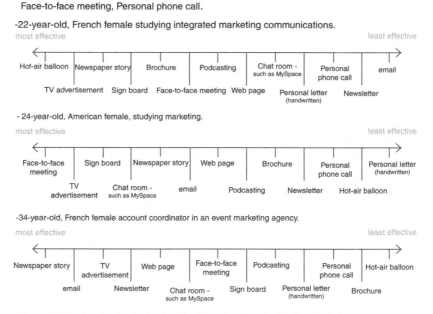
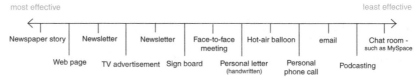

Figure 7. 3 Survey graphic.

Action Plan

Go to the World Advertising Research Centre (WARC, 2006) at www.warc.com and under "Browse the WARC Index" find an article or two that addresses a topic with which you may not be familiar, such as "opt-in" marketing or product placement in the "Other Marketing Communications" section.

What do these wide-ranging topics tell you about the advertising field? Why do organizations like WARC provide this information so readily? How can this information help you to communicate effectively with these professionals?

References

Argenti, P. (2003) *Corporate Communication*, 3rd edn. Boston, MA, McGraw-Hill.

AsthmaUK (2006) "Cause-related marketing". Available from: http://www.asthma.org.uk/corporate_partners/cause_related.html [Accessed 24 March 2006].

Baker, D. (2002) "Reviving a classic: today's Old Spice isn't just for the old guys". *The Cincinnati Post*, 21 August 2002: 7C.

Bedbury, S. (2002) *A New Brand World*. New York, Penguin Books.

Brón, P. & Vrinoi, A. (2001) "Corporate social responsibility and cause-related marketing: an overview". *International Journal of Advertising*, **20**: 207–222.

Bruning, S. & Castle, J. (2004) "Building relationships between organizations and publics: examining the linkage between organization–public relations, evaluations of satisfaction, and behavioral intent. *Communication Studies*, **55**(3): 435–446.

Cone (2002) "Post 9/11 consumer attitudes". Cone Marketing Forum. Available from: www.causemarketingforum.com/page.asp?ID=160 [Accessed 6 May 2006].

Cutlip, S., Center, A. & Broom, G. (2000) *Effective Public Relations*, 8th edn. Upper Saddle River, NJ, Prentice-Hall.

Duncan, T. (2005) *Principles of Advertising and IMC*. Boston, MA, Allyn Bacon.

DuPont (2006) "DuPont vision". Available from: http://www2.dupont.com/Our_Company/en_US/glance/vision/index.html [Accessed 8 April 2006].

Earle, R. (2000) *The Art of Cause Marketing: How to Use Advertising to Change Personal Behavior and Public Policy*. New York, McGraw-Hill.

Europa Donna (2006) Available from: www.cancerworld.org/progetti/cancerworld/ Europadonna/pagine/home/homeframeeudonna.html [Accessed 26 March 2006].

Eurovipp (2006) "Our vision". Available from: http://www.eurovipp.com/opencms/export/euroVIPP/en/about/vision.html [Accessed 8 April 2006].

Grant, J. (2006) *The Brand Innovation Manifesto*. Chichester, UK, John Wiley & Sons, Ltd.

Gronstedt, A. (1996) "A stakeholders' relations model". In *Integrated Communication: Synergy of Persuasive Voices*. Thorson, E. & Moore, J., eds. Mahwah, NJ, Lawrence Erlbaum Associates.

Guth, D. & Marsh, C. (2005) *Public Relations: a Values Driven Approach*. 3rd edn. Boston, MA, Allyn Bacon.

Hughes, A. (2000) *Strategic Databases*, 2nd edn. New York, McGraw-Hill.

IKEA (2006) Available from: www. IKEA.com [Accessed 15 May 2006].

Keller, K. (2000) "The brand report card". *Harvard Business Review*, January–February: 147–157.

Kotler, P., Roberto, N. & Lee, N. (2002) *Social Marketing: Improving the Quality of Life*. Thousand Oaks, CA, Sage.

Ledingham, J. (2003) "Explication relationship management as a general theory of public relations". *Journal of Public Relations Research*, **15**: 191–198.

Lorange, P. & Roos, J. (1998) *Strategic Alliances: Formation, Implementation, and Evolution*. Cambridge, MA, Blackwell Publishers.

Marimekko Corporation (2006) Available from: www.marimekko.com [Accessed 17 August 2006].

Neff, J. (2006) "Axe cuts past competitors: claim market lead". *Advertising Age*, 14 May 2006. Available from: http://adage.com/print?article_id=109174 [Accessed 15 May 2006].

Patagonia Europe (2006) Available from: www.patagonia.com/europe [Accessed 7 November 2006].

Pringle, H. & Gordon, W. (2003) *Brand Manners*. Chichester, UK, John Wiley & Sons, Ltd.

Pringle, H. & Thompson, G. (1999) *Brand Spirit*. Chichester, UK, John Wiley & Sons, Ltd.

PROMO (2006) "Summer push puts new Elizabeth Arden fragrance in teens' hands". *PROMO*, 23 August 2006. Available from: http://promomagazine.com/eventmarketing/news/earden_fair_082306/index.html [Accessed 25 August 2006].

Reader's Digest (2006) "*Reader's Digest* Europe trusted brands, 2006". Available from: http://www.rdtrustedbrands.com. [Accessed 10 May 2006].

Reinhold, R. (1981) "Ideas & trends in summary; furor over baby formulas – where, when and how". *The New York Times, nytimes.com*, 24 May 1981. Available from: http://topics.nytimes.com/top/news/health/diseasesconditionsandhealthtopics/diet/index.html?offset=90&s=oldest& [Accessed 26 August 2006].

Ries, A. & Trout, J. (1994) *The 22 Immutable Laws of Marketing*. New York, Harper Collins.

Sanders, C. (2005) "Revenue assurance – the stakeholder management plan". Available from: www.tmng.com [Accessed 19 September 2005].

Siler, J. & Woodruff, D. (1990) "The furor over formula is coming to a boil". *Business Week*, 9 April 1990: 52.

WARC (2006) World Advertising Research Centre. Available from: www.warc.com [Accessed 16 September 2006].

Bibliography

Aschermann, K. (2002) "The ten commandments of cause-related marketing". Cause Marketing Forum. Available from: www.causemarketingforum.com/page:asp?ID=103 [Accessed 6 May 2003].

Duncan, T. & Moriarty, S. (1997) *Driving Brand Value*. New York, McGraw-Hill.

Marconi, J. (2002) *Cause Marketing*. Dearborn, MI, Trade Publishing.

CHAPTER 8

Internal Communications: Messaging Within Your Company

Executive Summary

Effective communication between and among employees and managers requires constant vigil, and can be accomplished in different formats and through various channels.
Internal communication can be verbal or written.

Verbal messaging, such as face-to-face interaction (in real time and place), or organized formal or informal meetings from small departmental groups to large conferences are examples of internal communication
Teleconferencing adds to the verbal messaging mix. Special events encourage employee involvement and help boost morale.

Written messages include memos, both traditional forms and the modern hybrid formats widely used today, inter- and intradepartmental email, blogs, company newsletters and handbooks containing policy, procedures and codes of conduct and dress

Employee morale relates to feelings of importance and job satisfaction, and depends on communicating frequently and honestly with your workers
Substantive communication establishes a sense of trust in employees and helps them help you protect the company image from within the organization.

A 2003/2004 study showed that a major factor in a company's financial success is the ability to "create internal communication programmes" that effectively reach employees. ∎

Internal Communications: Messaging Withing Your Company

> ❝ *I figured that if I said it enough, I would convince the world that I really was the greatest.* ❞
> *Muhammad Ali*

Introduction to Sending Messages Within the Company

Whether your organization is small, large, virtual or bricks and mortar, communicating effectively with employees is vital and helps bring together employees from various departments.

When new employees join a company, they become a link in the information chain. In order to do their jobs effectively and become part of the team, they must be brought up to speed on the policies and procedures of the company as well as understand the vision of its leaders, its mission and its business objectives. This requires continued and concise messaging delivered with the support of top management.

In most of the world, employees no longer join organizations for life, and thus they may choose to give their time and energy to companies that trust their abilities and recognize their potential. This trust is built on two-way communication.

This chapter begins with a discussion of the theory of organizational communication – the academic discipline that examines management and communication. In the second part of the chapter, the application of organizational communication will be discussed in terms of verbal and written messaging.

Verbal messaging will include interpersonal communication such as face-to-face interaction (in real time and place), formal and informal meetings from small departmental groups to large conferences, teleconferencing and special events. Written internal messaging will include memos, both traditional forms and the modern hybrid format widely used today, inter- and intradepartmental email, blogs, company newsletters and handbooks containing policy, procedures and codes of conduct and dress.

We'll also discuss employee morale and its relationship to job production and satisfaction, and look at protecting the company image and brand from within the organization.

Consider this example of how employees work together to achieve a company goal. Imagine staging a corporate event for 5 000 attendees. A Dutch company hosted an event to mark the three-year anniversary of a landmark merger with a competitor. The event was demanding. Planning and execution needed the input and cooperation of many. An event-planning company contracted for a 70 000 sq. ft heated tent to be erected on the grounds of a local soccer stadium and 40 company banners to be displayed around the facility.

Although these details were important, the ultimate success of the event rested on the creativity and teamwork of employees. The marketing department compiled invitation lists, the advertising department created an event theme and others handled security and set-up.

Because of an effective internal communication programme, the last-minute illness of the major entertainer for the night was an obstacle that was manageable. Coordinators reframed the event from "great success" to "great teamwork" as employees stepped up to provide the evening's entertainment.

Organizations that cultivate the trust and loyalty of their employees thrive both in good and in troubled times.

Organizational Communication

Organizational Communication began under the auspices of the business information/business communication studies of the 1930s and came into its own in the post-war years as scholars began to study large organizations and how they communicated with their members. Researchers were concerned with the effective transmission of messages: how people received messages and how those messages were transmitted.

Early names that fostered growth in organizational communication include: Herbert Simon, who said communication is vital to the success of an organization (Simon, 1993); A. Bavelas and D. Barrett, who wrote "An experimental approach to organizational communication" (Bavelas & Barrett, 1951); Kenneth Boulding, who addressed the ethics of an organization's communication system (Boulding, 1970); and Chris Argyris, who wrote *Personality and Organization*, in which he criticizes the "management knows best" approach to employee communication (Argyris, 1957).

> According to Mark Schumann, global communication practice leader at Towers Perrin Human Resources Services, "Many organizations confuse information with communication. They concentrate on disseminating facts rather than providing the context and business rationale for company decisions and actions. The 'why and how' is critical to understanding the 'what'" (Schumann, 2004).

For more information on organizational communication read:

- *Organizational Communication in an Age of Globalization* (Cheney et al., 2003).
- *International and Multicultural Organizational Communication* (Barnett, 2005).
- *The New Handbook of Organizational Communication* (Jablin & Putnam, 2005).

Today, **organizational communication** is a mature discipline and provides much of the framework for effective management and employee communication. It includes such concepts as formal and informal communication methods, the flow of communication up, down and across all levels of employees and power structures. The "Connecting organizational communication to financial performance: 2003/2004 communication ROI study" by Watson Wyatt Worldwide reported that effective employee communication yields a 26 % total return to shareholders, effectively reducing employee turnover and creating a knowledge base reflected in customer contact (Vogt, 2004).

Dig Deeper

Organizational communication theories

Information systems. Karl Weick says each part of an organization is important for survival; no one part of the organization should consider itself more important than another (Weick, 1996).

Cultural theory. Clifford Geertz and Michael Pacanowsky focus on organizations and the shared meanings of their particular cultures contained in "stories": corporate, personal and collegial. This is an Eastern-influenced theory researched through ethnography (Geertz, 1973; Pacanowsky & O'Donnell-Trujillo, 1983; Eisenberg & Goodall, 1993).

Critical theory. Stanley Deetz takes a humanistic approach and believes that communication dynamically springs from reality rather than statically reflecting reality. He theorizes that an employee's involvement in the company is vital to communication success (Deetz, 1982).

Organization assimilation/socialization. Fred Jablin explains how newcomers use communication to assimilate into an organization. He asserts that individuals succeed according to how well they "fit into" the organization (Jablin & Putnam, 2005).

Workplace relationship theory. Patricia Sias explains that the amount and quality of information employees receive directly impact upon their relationships with co-workers and supervisors. This, she says, points out the importance of effective employee communication for collaboration and satisfaction (Sias, 2001).

Internal Verbal Communication

Managers and employees are rarely satisfied with their **internal communication**. It is an issue that tops the list of organizational problems. Poor communication leads to misunderstood messages, wasted time and low company morale. In fact, there is no "right way" to communicate with employees. Some communication experts say that, because of the complexity of the communication process, it is easy to see why it is so difficult to communicate effectively.

In a perfect world, here's what should happen in the transactional communication model in Figure 8.1:

1. The sender must convey the message clearly with integrity and truthfulness.
2. The receiver must choose to listen and decode the message successfully.
3. The delivery mode must meet the expectations of the receiver and the needs of the message.
4. The content of a message must circumvent any noise, distraction or filter, whether it is internal and external.
5. The message must connect to the receiver in the way that the sender intended.

Let's examine the role of verbal communication in the process, by examining the following verbal channels:

- face-to-face communication
- telephone and voice mail
- meetings
- videoconferencing
- special events.

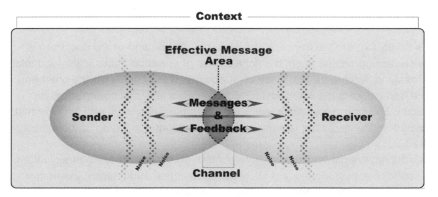

Figure 8.1 Transactional communication model.

Greek playwright Demosthenes practised facial expressions in a mirror, and Japanese Kabuki actors don exaggerated facemasks to display various moods. The Yiddish saying, "The face tells the secret", confirms there is a story to be read in every face. Every culture assigns significance to facial expressions or lack of them.

Skills to interpret a person's face and body language effectively are dependent on the receiver's learning, experience and willingness to see new perspectives.

Face-to-face Communication

Face-to-face interaction is the most personal type of communication in which humans engage. It is also called the "richest" form of communication because it contains cues from many sources that add to the interpretation of the message exchanged by the sender and receiver.

Face-to-face communication includes an infinite amount of non-verbal messages in facial and hand gestures, body language and posture. The depth of understanding of the message is enriched by the speaker's tone, pitch and vocal quality, and the level of feedback of the listener. The experience is further enhanced by information gathered from the occasion, the time of day and the place where the communication occurs.

Much workplace communication is face to face, and therefore it is important for the facial expressions, gestures and body language of the sender to match the content and tone of the message being delivered. It would be inappropriate for a manager to greet an employee with a slap on the back, a cheery smile and a short story about the great weekend he/she had, and then deliver a reprimand for poor performance!

Sending the right messages face to face involves all facets of verbal communication.

Dig Deeper

Let's briefly explore the concept of rich media. At one end of the spectrum is face-to-face communication, the richest form of communication involving facial expressions, voice patterns, body language and word choice. At the other end of the continuum is the flyer (poster), considered a less rich communication medium. This one-dimensional announcement has few words and little contextual information. The message is terse and simple and interpretation of the message is limited.

Media run the gamut from the richest medium, face-to-face communication, to telephone conversations, emails, video messages, audio tapes, interactive websites and classified ads, down to posted notices, the least rich.

Simply stated, you must think before you speak and you must speak with readable non-verbal cues. Choosing a rich medium will more effectively convey a complex message.

Your message delivery method is just as important as the medium you choose. How you say something can be as easily misunderstood as what you say, so giving careful consideration to how a message is communicated is vital. Words exchanged at the coffee machine race through an office; rumours often take on a life of their own, doing irreparable harm to reputation and integrity.

Diversity in the modern workplace exacerbates the difficulty in using readable facial expressions and body language. Each culture has its own rules governing the messages conveyed by non-verbal language, and the meanings of these are culture bound and vary widely.

Facial expressions are perhaps the most visible yet most misinterpreted carriers of meanings. The Japanese "recognize the importance of face perhaps better than people of any culture", explains psychologist D. Matsumoto of the Culture & Emotion Research Laboratory at San Francisco State University (Matsumoto, 2002). But all cultures "read" meanings into various facial expressions; for instance, a yawn can be interpreted as sleepiness or boredom and a grimace can be read as concern or fear, among a variety of other emotions.

Interaction with people of different cultures and ethnicities requires an awareness of what is conveyed in these mannerisms, which may not be what the sender intended. Taking the time and effort to research and learn about the various cultures of fellow workers is the hallmark of an effective communicator and good leader.

Body language and facial expressions convey sincerity and truthfulness, but non-verbal language can undermine a message if it is not congruent with the words spoken.

Telephone and voice mail

A **telephone** call is often a wise communication choice when you have a complex message to deliver, especially if it would take several exchanges using email or another form of communication to accomplish.

The telephone has advanced beyond the dreams of Alexander Graham Bell and his 1900 invention. Today, workplace telephones form intricately connected systems that act as call managers. A sophisticated system routes calls, takes messages, screens callers, relays automatic messages, saves phone numbers, automatically dials numbers and reroutes callers. Mobile or cell phones do all these functions and more, such as display time and date, provide calendars and a world clock, take pictures, send text messages and browse the Internet.

People using mobile phones call people, not places, as traditional landlines do. This brings a new set of contextual cues to a phone conversation. One of the first questions a caller asks is, "Where are you?" This sets the stage for the ensuing conversation. Is the person outside or in a public place? Is the person on the other end able to concentrate, or is he or she engaged in some other activity like driving that might distract his/her attention?

Other considerations, such as is the caller en route and in jeopardy of losing the connection or outside noise, are not necessary when calling a landline but often provide the contextual background for a cell call.

Voice mail helps business people stay connected. As soon as an airplane lands on the runway, business people turn on their cell phones and check for messages. What do you do when your class is dismissed? Check for messages!

Cell phone technology has changed the work habits and accessibility and business/ private time of workers in every corner of the world. Telephone etiquette is expected, and speaking clearly over a phone, whether talking to a person or leaving a message, is good manners. People dislike asking someone to repeat information as if it somehow reflects on their comprehension skills. They would rather pretend they heard and hope they can figure out what is being said. Many voice mail calls are left unreturned because names, numbers and message content are spoken so rapidly or incomprehensively they cannot be deciphered.

Voice mail message guidelines:

1. Be brief.
2. Put the most important information first.
3. Speak slowly.
4. Speak clearly.
5. Repeat any forwarding numbers.
6. Change your message to reflect an extended absence.
7. Be professional.

Meetings

Most employees see meetings as a necessary evil. However, evidence suggests that the number of business meetings and the length of those meetings have grown over the past few years. Psychologist Steven Rogelberg, interviewed on an NPR-affiliated radio station in the USA, believes business meetings have increased because of the "tendency for inclusiveness" on the part of both managers and employees (Rogelberg, 2006).

Researchers gathered information from employees in Australia, the UK and the USA and found that many managers spend as much as 60 % of their workday in meetings. Participants' perceptions of meetings varied from them being considered extremely valuable to them being considered a waste of time.

The study found that perceptions of business meeting also varied with the "type" of worker. People who were focused on task completion goals saw meetings as distractions. But employees who had more social-oriented goals viewed meetings as opportunities to interact with others, while gathering information to help them understand different perspectives.

It also asked employees about how meetings related to their well-being and health. Some individuals reported "meeting burn-out", but many said meetings added to their sense of accomplishment at the end of the workday. Other study participants said meetings helped create a focus for their business-day agenda and most employees wanted at least one meeting per day.

None of the participants wanted no meetings. Bosses liked meetings, while the extent to which employees liked meetings had a direct correlation to how much talking they did and whether they directed the meeting or participated in it. Rogelberg concluded that encouraging participation is crucial to effective meetings (Rogelberg, 2006).

Keeping employees informed may help keep controversial company actions out of the news. Many organizations use employee councils or other such groups to provide input on changes to company policy or practices, such as pensions. Scottish & Newcastle, an international beer-beverage company, consulted with its Employee Council before announcing arrangements for a new pension plan. As a result of this consultation, the company initiated employee briefings, pension workshops and question and answer sessions to address and explain the proposal. This employee communication plan helped the company and its workers cope with changes in the pension programme (Park, 2006).

As meetings have the prospect of conveying both positive and negative messages, preparation and groundwork decrease the possibility of ambiguity.

To plan for a quality meeting, consider these guidelines:

1. Decide if the meeting will be useful, not just for you, but for your employees.
2. Outline what you hope to accomplish.
3. Establish realistic, doable goals.
4. Keep the meeting on focus.
5. Encourage participation.
6. Make sure all needed participants will be present.
7. Distribute any prework, such as data, charts, sales figures or minutes of prior meetings, to employees in advance.

Meetings that make effective use of employees' time create an enthusiasm for future meetings and add to their feelings of accomplishment.

To achieve this objective you should:

- Set a positive tone for the meeting that stimulates a feeling that the meeting will be productive.
- Start with a statement of the meeting's goals. Present the meeting's agenda and expectations.
- Integrate the prework into the meeting. It will set the precedent for reviewing prework information for future meetings.
- Involve attendees in the meeting by soliciting their input; make them feel they have a vested interest in accomplishing the objectives of the meeting.
- Summarize what goals were reached or what actions will be taken because of the meeting.

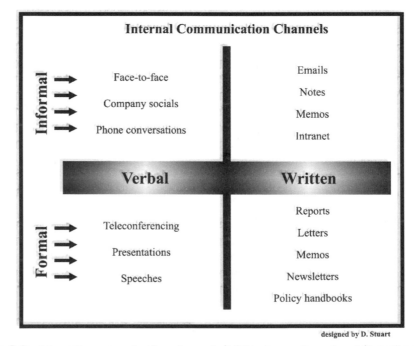

designed by D. Stuart

Figure 8.2 Internal communication channels fall into two categories: informal and formal.

Studies have shown that employees who get follow-up reports on decisions made in meetings feel more committed to company actions and more willing to attend future sessions.

Before the next scheduled meeting you should:

1. Distribute the minutes of the previous meeting within 24 hours.
2. Observe any deadlines set in the previous meeting for further discussion, implement any agreed upon actions and develop a timetable for further action.
3. Establish the precedent for commitment to the plan. Make each employee accountable for his or her portion of the plan. Ask for progress reports that can be presented at the next meeting.
4. Periodically solicit feedback about meetings and their effectiveness. Let employees know you are open to suggestions and sincerely want to improve the meeting quality. Reflect as a group on evaluation information.

Making employees part of the meeting process adds to feelings of inclusiveness.

Videoconferencing

Technology has brought videomessaging into everyday business. The transmission of live conferences via computer cameras or satellite transmission gives messages a sense of interactivity. **Videoconferencing** employs two-way communication by sending both video and audio data in real time over distance. Participants act as both senders and receivers of information.

Technology providers have developed handbooks delineating procedures and protocols for videoconferences. Use this information wisely to ensure videoconference success.

Special events for employees

The idea that employees should and could enjoy going to work is relatively new. Whereas twentieth-century thinking

Advantages of videoconferencing:

- saves money;
- has benefits of face-to-face communication;
- saves time;
- allows for frequent global contact;
- builds relationships;
- keeps participants focused on the meeting.

Videoconferencing Europe is an initiative in which students from schools in six European countries (Spain, France, Sweden, Norway, Belgium and the Netherlands) communicate with each other. They share information via webcams in French, Spanish, English and German (Videoconferencing Europe, 2006).

was, "I pay my employees a salary and they should work and be grateful", workplaces are now designed to accommodate employee convenience, interaction, participation and enthusiasm for the common goals shared by all those within the organization.

Trade fairs, product launches and celebratory dinners are no longer just staged for the benefit of senior executives, customers or investors. Such events are planned and held to boost morale, show appreciation and show strength and profitability. The standard annual retirement dinners and company picnics have been expanded to include family gatherings, special scholarships for the children of employees and outreach programmes for the community, and are all designed to build a sense of belonging. Simple celebrations like monthly employee birthday parties help reduce stress in the workplace.

Organizations with multisites might schedule competitions between teams representing various offices to build cohesion and promote loyalty. For example, a public utility, faced with industry competition for the first time, organized events that featured skits and competitive games fashioned around the need to reorient

Strategic Thinking

What do you need to know to communicate effectively via teleconferencing? The Memorial University of Newfoundland (TETRA, 2006) gives these tips:

1. Introduce all participants at the beginning of the meeting.
2. Be careful with microphone placement. Noise such as paper shuffling or coughing can be distracting.
3. Mute your microphone when you are not speaking to eliminate unnecessary noise.
4. Announce your name and location when you speak.
5. Direct questions to a specific person by name.
6. Be aware of any transmission delay, you may have to wait before responding.
7. Look at the camera as much as possible.
8. Be natural. Minimize your body motion and hand gestures.
9. Wear neutral colours.
10. Set up a simple background, avoid windows and use direct lighting for participants.

How can following each of these tips help the communication process?

Strategic Thinking

An article in *Express Healthcare Management: India's First Newspaper For The Healthcare Business* (Das, Gupta & Toma, 2005) discusses the importance of employee satisfaction. Susan R. Meisinger, president and CEO of the Society for Human Resource Management, says, "For organizations to be successful at competing for new talent and retaining employees, they have to know what workers want, what keeps them happy and what makes them stay". The article's authors suggest that quality communication between employees and management leads to employee satisfaction and long-term success for an organization.

employees to the realities of the marketplace. This helped the utility deal with sensitive issues while at the same time eliciting employee input and ensuring worker commitment.

Special events take creative planning, employee involvement, financial resources and commitment of participation from top management.

Simple spontaneous events take little planning, but most events require attention to detail. Issues to consider in special event planning include:

- Identifying the purpose of the event. Consider whether there is sufficient time, resources, space and staff to stage, publicize and evaluate the event.
- Matching the type of event with its purpose.
- Considering the business culture of the country or area where the event will be scheduled.
- Selecting a committee of employees to help with the planning process.
- Developing a calendar in order to identify dates, duties and responsibilities.
- Writing measurable objectives for the event. Use these objectives in the evaluation process.
- Proposing a budget.
- Planning the publicity. How will employees know about the event? Do special guests need to be invited?
- Considering the logistics. The bigger the event, the greater the number of activities that need to be considered. For example, parking, signage, security and even portable toilets may be necessary for a large event.
- Evaluating your event on the basis of your objectives.

Written Internal Communication

Written internal communication takes a variety of forms depending on the purpose of the communication.

This section explores some of the most common forms used in business today.

* memos
* newsletters
* blogs
* supplemental internal publications.

Memos

Traditionally, the most common form of internal communication was the paper memo, but today the email memo is more popular. In a survey of 400 respondents, when asked if they "had to be without email or phone service for five business days", nearly 75 % said not having email access would trouble them more (Nowak, 2003).

For many, email is the preferred form of inter- and intraoffice messaging. Email programs stay continually opened on some employees' computers. This enables the software to alert the user that a new email has been received. Stories abound of co-workers sending emails to each other even though they sit just a few feet away. Although this may sound impersonal, and perhaps lazy, the sent email provides the sender and receiver with a hard copy record of the message as well as a reminder of any action to be taken, questions to be answered or issues to be addressed at a later date.

As electronic memos have become widely accepted as a form of office messaging, the format of an email memo has been standardized to look much like its paper cousin. However, there has been another transformation. Memos, both paper and email, are now written in a short "high-impact" style, which, according to one study, takes approximately 20 % less time to read and is more clearly understood (Clampitt, 2005, p.110).

Here are examples of a traditional paper memo, a "high-impact" memo and an email "high-impact" memo:

Are you confused by digital etiquette? You are not alone. According to a study conducted on behalf of Telewest Business of more than 1 400 office workers aged 16–64 across the UK, almost half felt it was rude if they had not received a response to an email within a morning, while 5 % felt it rude if they hadn't received a response within five minutes of sending the message.

Fewer than 10 % felt that it was appropriate to discuss human resources issues, financial discussions and meetings with management using instant messaging (IM) or text messaging (TM) (Telewest, 2006).

Traditional memo

TO: All employees of Stuart and Associates
FROM: Executive Training Department

9 October 2006

RE: Teamwork training

Representatives from the Gardner Training Institute will hold a team-building seminar, Thursday, 19 October 2006, for members of the following departments: Sales – 9 a.m., Customer Service – 10 a.m. and Human Resources – 11 a.m. Please mark your calendars with the date and time of your seminar. You will be expected to participate in this interactive seminar where many team building techniques will be discussed and demonstrated.

Coffee and pastries will be available 15 minutes prior to the start of the seminar. Please bring pad and pen with you and expect to spend one hour in the workshop.

The Gardner Training Institute is a leader in the executive training field and their experts in team-building will conduct the seminar. We trust you will find the time well spent as we actively strive to provide you with the most up-to-date training in a variety of areas.

High-impact memo

TO: All employees
FROM: Executive Training

9 October 2006

RE: Teamwork training

Please mark your calendars for a one-hour team-building seminar, Thursday, 19 October 2006, as follows:

• Sales – 9 a.m.
• Customer Service – 10 a.m.
• Human Resources – 11 a.m.

Coffee and pastries will be available 15 minutes prior to the start of the seminar.

Please bring pad and pen with you.

Email memo

From: trainingdept@stuart.net
To: mhelm@stuart.net
Subject: Upcoming team building seminar
Cc:
Date: 9 October 2006

Attached:
To: Michael Helm, Sales

From: Training Department

Re: Teamwork training

Please mark your calendar for a one-hour team-building seminar, Thurs., 19 Oct. 2006, as follows:

- Sales – 9 a.m.
- Customer Service – 10 a.m.
- Human Resources – 11 a.m.

Coffee and pastries available 15 min. before the seminar.

Bring pad and pen with you.

Newsletters

The company newsletter is one of the most useful tools to communicate with employees to foster organizational relationships.

Newsletters vary from a simple single white sheet of paper with black ink in plain text to a high-gloss four-colour magazine with graphics and photos. Some are simple daily, semi-weekly or weekly publications, while others, often of higher production quality, are monthly or quarterly publications.

Whatever the format, newsletters provide top-down (management to employees) communication as well as horizontal (interdepartmental and peer) information. They also provide valuable bottom-up communication by soliciting employee feedback, suggestions or opinions.

Because of advances in desktop publishing software, simple newsletters are relatively easy and inexpensive to produce. They provide timely information targeted to an internal audience and put messages in writing that employees can review at leisure. Newsletters traditionally have been hard copy, but today more and more are published in electronic form called webletters. This electronic format takes advantage of technology and may contain video clips, pictures, links to pertinent websites and a host of other attachments.

An organization often has more than one newsletter targeted at particular audiences. Your college or university may publish various departmental newsletters, a university employee newsletter and an alumni newsletter. Each has a slightly different focus, but all are meant to communicate with and unite a specific audience.

Studies suggest employees want more truthful information from their employers. In an online survey of a 1 000 working Americans, representing a cross-section of companies with at least 1 000 employees, participants were asked how they would rate their companies' communication efforts. Those surveyed felt their employers were more truthful to their shareholders and customers than to them. Almost half of those surveyed indicated they received more credible information from their immediate supervisor than from the CEO (Schumann, 2004, pp. 30–31).

This study, and others like it, point out the need to evaluate newsletter information regularly. What do employees think of its contents? Which stories receive high readership? Is the newsletter readable? Is distribution adequate? Is necessary news left out? What kinds of news do employees want and expect? Is there an easy process to gather feedback and comments?

Getting answers to these questions ensures that the time, effort and money that go into newsletters are not wasted, that the right topics and information are included and that employees recognize they have the opportunity to provide feedback.

Strategic Thinking

Emergency … you have information your employees need to know ASAP. No time to call a meeting … no access to in-house video … and you want them to know the news before they see it on the television. Email? But how do you break through the clutter of messages?

The Australian Tax Office with more than 21 000 employees at 96 sites sends a pdf to each employee's desktop within two hours. Its employees know that this message demands immediate attention (Palframan-Smith, 2004).

This practice may not work for organizations with lots of employees without access to desktops. How about instant messaging?

Blogs

A newcomer to the internal communication roster is the **blog**. "Blog" was the Merriam-Webster dictionary "word of the year in 2004", based on online definition seekers. In 1999, blog was defined as "a website that contains an online personal journal with reflections, comments and often hyperlinks provided by the writer" (Merriam-Webster Online, 2006).

The blogosphere is growing. Technorati, an Internet company that tracks blogs and their links, says there are more than 60 million blogs worldwide. The site posts the following figures of global blogs:

Anglosphere (US/Canada/UK/Australia/NZ)
= 36.2 million blogs
and researchers sense this is a low estimate as some blogs are posted on sites that do not report their figures
Asia (Japan/China/South Korea/Malaysia/Singapore/Thailand/ Philippines/India/ Pakistan)
= 24.35 million blogs
again, this is a suspected low estimate as current reports are difficult to get from some countries
Europe
= 2 million blogs
many European bloggers use Anglosphere sites and are thus included in previous figures
Middle East
= 100 000 blogs
most are probably out of Israel; the Iraqi blog count was 151 as of 25 May 2005
Africa
= 10.000+ blogs
http://www.blogherald.com/2005/05/25/world-wide-blog-count-for-may-now-over-60-million-blogs/

This new medium communicates with present and potential customers, accesses new markets and trends, keeps track of the competition, influences the mainstream media and deals with information and rumours. Marketers are discovering new and different ways to use blogs to enhance communication.

Internally, a blog is an informal way to communicate regularly with your employees. Blogs may be set up either on a commercial website or password protected on a company's website or Intranet. A company blog site is easily maintained, updated by multiple people and shared by all employees or a chosen group. As blogs are more easily updated than web pages, they provide a timely way to disseminate information. Blogs ensure that all employees have access to information at exactly the same time.

The IAOC (International Association of Online Communicators) suggests the purpose of internal blogs should be viewed differently by management: "If a CEO launches a blog to let the company know what he is thinking but doesn't allow – or welcome – comments, then the "so-called" blog will be something different, but not a blog. It is all about openness, transparency and a candid interest for what everybody has to say. It is not about reading CEO's speeches. You have emails for that. Blogs need discussions" (IAOC, 2006).

Supplemental internal publications

An institution's functional messages are presented to employees in any number of handbooks or policy books as well as sent in electronic form. These publications inform employees what the company expects from them and what they can expect from the company.

Information in these publications can be divided into three main types of content: employee information, reference materials and organizational information (Table 8.1).

The newest additions to policy handbooks are computer rules and regulations and Internet use guidelines covering acceptable limits of email sending and receiving, data protection regulations, privacy issues and security parameters. Spelling out what is, and what is not, company policy cuts down on inappropriate behaviour and wasteful use of company resources.

Efficient organizations post this needed information online, but employees often have difficulty locating it. This results in unnecessary time loss and increased requests for help to locate the material. A simple search engine of minimal cost can facilitate employees' search for important documents and forms. Employees who can quickly find forms, related documents and updated calendars have time to be more productive in other areas.

Employee information	Reference materials	Organizational information
Pamphlet welcoming new employees	Folders outlining fringe benefits	Brochure outlining mission statement
Dress code guidelines	Forms for leave time or travel	Fact sheet on company products
Telephone numbers of employees	Brochure on training	Background paper on company"s history

Table 8.1 Internal Communication Types of Content and Material.

Strategic Thinking

US courts have ruled that employee handbooks are considered binding contracts.

In 2002 a university employee, laid off in a mass reduction of positions, sued the organization because the procedure for firing had not been followed as outlined in the employee handbook. The employee won the suit in spite of a disclaimer in the handbook stating that its contents were not a binding contract. Attorneys say using a disclaimer in a handbook is good, but it will not protect against lawsuits. They suggest using flexible language and general terms in handbooks as well as staying clear of specific procedural processes.

Advice to companies: indicate that all situations will be handled on a case-by-case basis, at the discretion of the company and according to the law.

For example, since the 1990s, Cisco Systems, an international systems corporation, has utilized an Intranet called "Cisco Employee Connection" to help employees navigate online resources more efficiently.

Protecting Your Company Image from Within

A company **image** is the aggregate perception people have about the company, its employees and its products or services.

Although this image is often associated with a public viewpoint, it has its roots within the organization. Time, study and resources go into creating an organization's image. Satisfied loyal workers help ensure that a company is well received by the public and the community. A company's image also will be evaluated on seemingly insignificant details such as how a phone is answered or how employees dress.

Any action an employee takes, whether during office hours or over a fence chatting with a neighbour on a Saturday afternoon, reflects on the company's image. Will an employee brag about the company's efforts to set up a better than average pension plan, or will she comment on the lack of her manager's business ethics?

Experts say the surest way to garner the trust of internal publics and establish a reputation as a sincere company is to communicate honestly, openly and frequently with all employees. They are the links to clients, trade partners, suppliers, customers and competitors. Management must work with this influential audience to develop a sense of commitment and loyalty to common goals and objectives.

A study by the Opinion Research Corporation (OCR) reported that 97 % of manager respondents said that company image added to "a significant measure of the successes and failures of their organizations" (Marken, 2005).

Building a successful corporate image requires satisfied employees who can act as ambassadors of goodwill.

Chapter Summary

Communicating with employees is vital to management success. Today there are more ways than ever to disseminate vital information. But it is the wise management team that uses the correct communication channels to distribute this information.

More important than making information available is ensuring that this information is needed and easily accessible to all employees. These communication tasks can be achieved through a variety of formats, including memos, emails, company newsletters, blogs, in-house television and policy handbooks.

Frequent communication with employees builds trust and company commitment. Encouraging employee feedback, sincerely addressed and evaluated, should be a primary goal of any internal communication vehicle. It gives employees a stake in the future success of the organization.

How employees represent a company inside and outside the workplace is crucial to a company's image and reputation. Employees can help reach company goals and objectives or they can work as obstacles thwarting progress.

As a manager, it is your responsibility effectively to utilize multiple communication channels. Knowing what your employees want and need to know, in which way and under what circumstances is a start in the right direction. ■

Learning From Others

Kristi LeBlanc is Managing Partner of Global Consumer, Retail and Hospitality Practice at Nosal Partners, LLC. Her executive placement and management support firm is committed to ensuring that new leaders, executive teams and entire organizations receive the support needed to meet their business objectives together. Winner of the prestigious Excellence in Client Satisfaction Award, LeBlanc has been extensively published and quoted as an expert on leadership, professional development and human capital. She shares her thoughts on corporate culture in this essay.

Pundits have written extensively about corporate culture – a complex and defining set of norms that guide people's decisions, actions and reactions relative to internal and external business issues. Corporate culture reflects collective beliefs, attitudes, values and priorities. But to someone evaluating a prospective employer, what does all of this mean?

As an executive recruiter, I have come to realize that cultural fit is even more critical to an employee's success within an organization than education, experience, skills or intellect. Corporate culture determines the ways in which individuals collaborate as an organization strives towards strategic goals, as well as the values the group upholds. As a result, it affects an employee's sense of belonging in the immediate business environment, chances for success and – ultimately – job satisfaction. A basic understanding of corporate culture is therefore an essential building block of one's career.

What does corporate culture look like? It manifests itself in a variety of ways: hierarchical structure; titles; dress code; expectations around number of hours worked; degree of internal competition; behaviours noticed and encouraged by senior management; attitudes towards risk-taking, innovation and change; conflict resolution styles; modes of sharing information (phone, email, meetings, one-on-one, etc.); physical layout and distribution of offices and cubes; and attitudes towards display of personal items, to name just a few.

While at first glance superficial, such organizational characteristics have a profound collective impact on an employee's ability to thrive. To perform well and feel satisfied, people generally need to feel respected and valued. It is extremely difficult to do either when one is in the wrong environment.

How does one get a fix on a prospective employer's culture? During the interview process, ask as many interviewers as possible about the culture. Observe how employees interact, dress and behave. Are they in groups? Are they laughing? How do they dress?

Cultural fit is no less important to prospective employers. Employees who don't fit into a corporate culture disrupt organizational performance and cohesiveness. Be aware that the employer or search firm overseeing the interview process also will be probing for cultural fit by assessing soft skills – the all-important factors that determine degree of fit with cultural dynamics: propensity for teamwork, assertiveness, creativity, flexibility, etc.

When evaluating a position, don't focus on salary, title or benefits at the expense of corporate culture. Finding the right environment is the first and most important step in your long-term professional success.

Case Study – **Nokia**

Nokia began in 1865 as a pulp mill company in Finland. Boosted by a boom in the lumber industry, the company moved into European markets and won a medal at the World's Fair in Paris in 1867 for its ground wood pulp. The company merged with a rubber company and a cable firm to form the Nokia Corporation.

The company continued to grow but ran into some trouble during the 1970s when environmental issues became hot topics in Finland and forced stringent requirements upon Nokia's manufacturing plants. The company diversified into three areas: the rubber, cable and forestry industry, power generation and electronics (Nokia, 2006).

By the 1980s the company had become a major player in the telecommunications field through acquisitions in Sweden, France, Germany and Switzerland. By the 1990s, Nokia was the largest Scandinavian information technology company. Today, Nokia makes a third of all the phones in the world. Half of its 55 000 employees are Finnish. However, 97 % of all sales are made outside Finland.

The company prides itself on treatment of employees and its responsibility to the community. Its website explains it has taken care of its employees since the early years and continues to do so today; Nokia has received recognition for its "employee career development, lifecycle management, open standards and cooperation, product safety and open communications… It is important that every employee is empowered to promote responsibility in business".

Each new employee receives a booklet outlining the "Nokia Way" and containing this message from the CEO:

> To You from J.O.
>
> Nokia's way of operating –
> Connecting People
>
> Nokia unites people
> In open, honest cooperation.
> It offers equal opportunities
> To develop skills and know-how.
>
> Nokia unites people
> All over the world
> By manufacturing innovative
> Products and solutions.
> Its goal is customer satisfaction.
>
> THE MORE YOU WILL DO FOR NOKIA,
> THE MORE NOKIA CAN DO
> FOR YOU (Nokia, 2006)

The Nokia Way communicates the company's vision. Dan Steinbock, in *The Nokia Revolution*, explains that Nokia's corporate strategy is constantly refined, but is rooted in a "vision which remains steady" (Steinbock, 2001).

Do some further research and see why the Finnish press joke that Nokia's corporate values are taken so seriously they are considered "holy". Find instances where Nokia has lived up to its values in the face of adversity. How and why did the company come up with the slogan "Connecting People"?

Find vision statements of other organizations and look for the common threads that unite them. Here's some that Steinbock included in his book, to get you started (Steinbock, 2001):

Microsoft (1975): "A computer on every desk and in every home".

Apple (1985): "A personal computer to every household".

Nokia (1990): "Putting the Internet into everybody's pocket". ■

Class Exercises

1. Find out how many newsletters your college publishes. Are there various departmental newsletters? Is there a newsletter for the staff, the general faculty or alumni? How about organizations on campus, how many of them publish newsletters? Collect samples you can share with the class. What are the demographics, geographics, psychographics, sociographics and usergraphics of each audience? Compose a statement that explains the prime purpose of each newsletter. Describe how and why they might be alike or different.

2. Your company has completed the development of a new software package. The process has taken more than a year and involves considerable employee overtime. The product will be released to the public in three months. Using the steps for planning a special event, organize a celebration. Include employees and their families. Use your imagination!

3. Divide into groups and discuss how you would go about collecting research to create a baseline or benchmark of how your employees find company information, read/listen to information, act on information and retain information. In what ways could you use this research? What sort of measurement tools could you put in place now to help measure the success of any future efforts to improve employee information access, utilization and retention?

Action Plan

The book *Mainstream Videoconferencing: A Developer's Guide to Distance Multimedia*, written in 1997 by Joe Durran and Charlie Sauer, offers "clear explanations of both 'group' videoconferencing and the emergence of 'desktop' videoconferencing" (Durran & Sauer, 1997). A review of the book says: "For managers leading organizations into the future … (this book) will help you attain a thorough understanding of the underlying technology, evaluate and make use of current and future videoconferencing systems, and create strategies on potential usage".

The review ends by stating that this book offers "an inspiring vision of where the technology is likely to lead in the near future, when videoconferencing truly becomes mainstream".

What do you think about this statement? The book was written almost 10 years ago. Is videoconferencing mainstream now? How long do you think it will take to become outdated?

Does your school library have any books on videoconferencing? Find a book on this subject and share your findings with the class.

Websites

You can download a copy of the "Connecting organizational communication to financial performance: 2003/2004 communication ROI study" by Watson Wyatt Worldwide at www.watsonwyatt.com. The article "Awareness to action: connecting employees to the bottom line" in the March–April 2004 issue of *Communication World* offers insight into many aspects of organizational communication.

An interesting history of videoconference technology is located at http://www.wiredred.com/video-conferencing-history.html (Wiredred, 2006). Read about the major players and innovations responsible for videoconferencing as we know it today.

For more information on weblogs, access *The Blog Herald* at www.blogherald.com (Blog Media, 2006) and a listing of corporate blogs in European countries at http://www.corporateblogging.info/europe/

References

Argyris, C. (1957) *Personality and Organization*. New York, Harper Collins.

Barnett, G., ed. (2005) *International and Multicultural Organizational Communication*. Cresskill, NJ, Hampton Press.

Bavelas, A. & Barrett, D. (1951) "An experimental approach to organizational communication". *Personnel*, **27**(March):367–371.

Blog Media (2006) *The Blog Herald*. Available from: www.blogherald.com [Accessed 31 August 2006].

Boulding, K. (1970) *Beyond Economics: Essays on Society, Religion and Ethics*. Ann Arbor, MI, University of Michigan Press.

Cheney, G., Christensen, L., Zorn, T. & Ganesh, S. (2003) *Organizational Communication in an Age of Globalization*. Prospect Heights, IL, Waveland Press.

Clampitt, P. (2005) *Communicating for Managerial Effectiveness*. 3rd edn. London, Sage Publications.

Das, B., Gupta J. & Tomar, P. (2005) "Employee satisfaction means an efficient healthcare facility". *Express Healthcare Management: India's First Newspaper for the Healthcare Business*, 16 September 2005. Available from: http://www.expresshealthcaremgmt.com/20050930/insight01.shtml [Accessed 31 August 2006].

Deetz, S. (1982) "Critical interpretive research in organizational communication". *Western Journal of Speech Communication*, **46**: 131–149.

Durran, J. & Sauer, C. (1997) *Mainstream Videoconferencing: a Developer's Guide to Distance Multimedia*. Book description. Available from: www.amazon.com [Accessed 7 April 2006].

Eisenberg, E. & Goodall, H. (1993) *Organizational Communication: Balancing Creativity and Constraint*. New York, St Martin's Press.

Geertz, C. (1973) *The Interpretation of Cultures*. New York, Basic Books.

IAOC (2006) International Association of Online Communicators. Available from: http://www.iaocblog.com/blog/Europe/_archives/2005/6/16/947041.html [Accessed 4 April 2006].

Jablin, F. & Putnam, L., eds (2005) *The New Handbook of Organizational Communication*. Thousand Oaks, CA, Sage.

Marken, A. (2005) "Corporate image, we all have one, but few work to protect, project it". Available from: www.markencom.com [Accessed 24 May 2006].

Matsumoto, D. (2002) *The New Japan: Debunking Seven Cultural Stereotypes*. Boston, MA, Intercultural Press.

Merriam-Webster Online (2006) Available from: www.merriam-webster.com [Accessed 24 May 2006].

Nokia (2006) Nokia website available from: www.nokia.com [Accessed 26 May 2006].

Nowak, R. (2003) "E-mail beats the phone in business communication". *Information Week*. Available from: http://www.informationweek.com/news/showArticle.jhtml?articleID=10000052 [Accessed 9 April 2006].

Pacanowsky, M. & O'Donnell-Trujillo, N. (1983) Organizational communication as cultural performance. *Communication Monographs*, **50**: 127–147.

Park, S. (2006) "Smart practice: good ideas and targeted communications". *Business Communicator*, **6**(9): 4–5.

Palframan-Smith, B. (2004) "Employee connection". *Communication World*, March–April: 12–17, 40.

Rogelberg, S. (2006) Interview on *Charlotte Talks,* 27 March 2006, WFAE, Charlotte, NC.

Schumann, M. (2004) "Enhancing corporate credibility". *Communications World*, March–April: 28–32.

Sias, P. & Wyers, T. (2001) "Employee uncertainty and information-seeking in newly formed expansion organizations". *Management Communication Quarterly*, **4**: 549–573.

Simon, H. (1993) "Strategy and organizational evolution". *Strategic Management Journal*, **14**: 131–142.

Steinbock, D. (2001) *The Nokia Revolution*. New York, American Management Association.

TETRA (2006) "Videoconferencing etiquette". Telehealth and Educational Technology Resource Agency. Available from: http://www.med.mun.ca/testopd/tetra/support/Videoconf%20Etiquette%20Quick%20Ref.pdf [Accessed 7 April 2006].

Videoconferencing Europe (2006) Available from: www.novaplein.nl/videoconferencing [Accessed 7 April 2006].

Vogt, P. (2004) "Awareness to action: connecting employees to the bottom line". *Communication World*, March–April: 22–26.

Weick, K. (1996) *Sensemaking in Organizations*. Newbury Park, CA, Sage Publications.

Wiredred (2006) "Video conferencing history". Wiredred.com e/pop. Available from: http://www.wiredred.com/video-conferencing-history.html [Accessed 31 August 2006].

Telewest (2006) "Digital etiquette slowly emerging". *Business Communicator*, **6**(10): 3. www.telewest.co.uk. Available from: http://0-search-epnet.com.library.winthrop.edu:80/login.aspx?direct=true&db=ufh&an=20486064 [Accessed 18 May 2006].

Bibliography

Ho, N. (2002) "Creating an emotional connection with your employees through marketing communications: a new tool for managing your employees as internal 'customers'". *Journal of Integrated Communications*. Available from: http://www.medill.nwu.edu/imc/studentwork/publs/jic/journal/2001/ho.htm [Accessed 8 October 2005].

CHAPTER 9

The Importance of Effective Communication in the Workplace

Executive Summary

The changing face of today's global workplace presents new communication challenges.

Diversity in the workforce extends beyond race and gender issues and includes education level, religion, age, language skills and cultural heritage among other considerations
Diversity contributes to the life blood of an organization, helping to maintain a creative and innovative workforce.

Technology enables organizations to deliver messages to this diverse marketplace in a variety of formats using multiple channels of communication
This demanding environment requires quick and accurate decision-making, often at the expense of meaningful thought and consideration. As a result, stress is prevalent in a workplace where instant access to communication, competition, and constant change are the rule.

Organizations must foster open communication, knowledge-sharing and creativity to build a workforce committed to company values and goals
This requires managers to listen critically, to provide effective training and development opportunities for all employees and to monitor the communication efforts of their organizations.

Strategic planning helps an organization carry out its mission through set goals and objectives
Managers are key stakeholders in formulating and implementing strategic plans. Ultimately the responsibility of management is to train, direct and monitor employees and to build a global workforce that communicates effectively. ■

The Importance of Effective Communication in the Workplace

> ❝ *A lie can travel halfway around the world while the truth is putting on its shoes.*
> *Mark Twain* ❞

Introduction to Effective Workplace Communication

Now that we have looked at some of the specific tools used in communicating with external and internal publics, let's look at some of the current thinking on communicating effectively. We'll discuss why integrated communication strategies work in this demanding environment where creativity and innovation are building blocks to success.

Consider this example of innovation. Facebook.com is a popular form of social media taking US college campuses by storm. Created by Mark Zuckerberg while a student at Harvard University, Facebook is now the seventh most popular site on the Web.

Zuckerberg created the site in his dorm room to rate student attractiveness, but his idea was received with less than enthusiasm by university officials. In response to this criticism, he adapted his site to feature social networking (Lacy & Hempel, 2006).

These humble beginnings created a communication business now worth hundreds of millions of dollars, providing one example of how entrepreneurship and communication make excellent partners. How does this example fit into the bigger picture of the changing workplace?

Remember our communication model showing that effective messaging occurs in the union set when the world of the sender and the world of the receiver overlap? This commonality does not refer to the physical position of the sender and receiver, but rather to the shared understanding of what speakers and receivers think, why, in what manner and under what circumstances.

According to the communication model, a message is made up of words and influenced by an internal context and outside factors that bias a message's interpretation. We will use these parameters to discuss communication strategies from a manager's perspective and explore framing and adapting messages to specific target audiences.

Issues such as diversity, technology, open communication/sharing knowledge, workplace empowerment and diffusion of innovation will also be covered. Finally, we will review strategic planning and goal setting in terms of communication objectives.

The Changing Workplace

Strong communication programmes are the basis of sharing knowledge in an ethnically and culturally diverse employee mix. The increased use of technology, new research findings on employee and management empowerment and the dynamic workings of a demanding information age have necessitated the need for more effective communication management.

Communication management is the deliberate attempt to construct, organize, frame and deliver messages to specific audiences.

Diversity in the workplace

The workplace is much different to how it was just a few years ago. Not only is there a greater diversity among employees in most companies, but these employees have access to and interact with a wider variety of stakeholders, such as customers, vendors, investors, competitors and shareholders across the globe.

This dramatic change in the structure of the workplace forces managers to rethink how they communicate with diverse audiences, both internally and externally, and requires them continually to develop new methods for communicating effectively.

Organizations, whether private, public or government, for profit or not for profit, recognize the need for expert communicators in executive positions to address these new world demands.

In the Commissioner's Advisory Committee on Visible Minorities, the Royal Canadian Mounted Police reports searching for a cultural diversity manager as early as 2002 (RCMP, 2002). The Western Hospital group in Australia also actively recruited a cultural diversity manager to fulfil its mission: "Western Health in partnership with our culturally diverse community will provide excellent clinical and preventative care ..." (Western Health, 2003).

The BBC, McDonald's and Monsanto Corporation use the title "diversity development director", while other organizations use titles such as "diversity programme manager" or "equal employment opportunity manager". Regardless of the name, these people are entrusted with the task of helping employees deal with workplace differences. They disseminate information, hold training sessions, help employees understand complex cultural issues and facilitate relationships within a diverse pool of company employees – all issues important to a global workplace.

A 2004 survey by the Society for Human Resource Management, the world's largest association in this field, representing more than 190 000 members in over 100 countries, cites the role of "EEO/Diversity Manager" as one of the hot positions for 2005, with higher than median compensation (SHRM, 2006).

Diversity efforts in many businesses continue to broaden in scope and reach. Historically, companies looked at diversity from two viewpoints: race and gender. But today other issues have surfaced such as education level, sexual orientation, religion, age, language skills and cultural heritage, to name a few.

Diversity programmes are more than just attempts to influence individual behaviour, they include the implementation of cross-functional teams, training and information sessions and concrete acknowledgement and commitment to diversity in vision and mission statements. In other words, institutions can no longer just give lip-service to diversity, they must show that they mean and do what they say.

Diversity contributes to the effectiveness of an organization as well as fostering a creative and innovative workforce. In a European Union Commission study, 83 % of the 800 businesses surveyed believed that diversity policies made good sense. However, only 42 % thought diversity policies were helpful in resolving labour shortages and retaining high-quality staff. A total of 35 % said positive diversity policies helped the company's reputation in the community, and 26 % said they helped their companies create and innovate (EUROPA, 2005). The survey also revealed that only half of the businesses surveyed were actively engaged in workplace diversity.

Organizations that want to compete in the world's marketplaces need to become engaged in diversity practices or risk failure. The brain drain is a problem that should be of concern to all international organizations. For instance, countries with limited employment opportunities may witness the loss of professionals who are lured away by thriving job markets.

Companies may experience brain drain owing to feelings of insecurity and alienation on the part of employees who have given years of service but suddenly face downsizing, closures and cost-cutting measures.

According to the US National Employee Relationship Report, Americans spend an average of 3.6 years in a company before leaving for another position. While the average number of years

Skandia Corporation, a financial services company based in Sweden, employs people across 20 countries including Latin America and Asia. The company realized that its traditional accounting system measured tangible assets but failed to take into account the value of human capital. Now the company uses such factors as human value, innovation, customer base and process capital to calculate its return oninvestment (ROI) (Vallario, 2006).

is slightly higher in Canada, New Zealand, Australia and some European countries, it is still a cause for concern (Yoshihara & McCarthy, 2006, p. 56).

To stay competitive, organizations must seek employees outside their traditional labour pools, train them and keep them. Educator Tony Zeiss says that, in order to manage the upcoming labour shortage, which is partially due to baby boomer retirements, companies need to have a variety of strategies in place, including compensation and benefit plans based on performance, succession plans, staff development plans and employee recognition plans (Zeiss, 2005, p. 25). Zeiss believes that developing succession plans is an important step, as few organizations take the opportunity to grow great leaders.

Finally, getting the right mix can add measurable value to an organization's performance. Managing diversity enhances good business practices, attracts qualified people, retains workforce talent, helps instil community spirit and fosters a positive perception of a company.

Strategic Thinking

DiversityInc, an online magazine that addresses diversity in the US corporate workplace, announced its sixth "Top 50 Companies for Diversity" list. For the 2006 competition, companies had to show strong diversity management in "human capital, corporate communication, supplier development and CEO commitment" (DiversityInc., 2006).

Effective communication plays a role in all these areas, internally in encouraging and informing human capital and conveying CEO commitment, and externally when dealing with suppliers and planning corporate communication efforts.

Here's an abbreviated list of companies (and their rankings) that have been recognized for their diversity management. Which companies do you recognize? How many do business on a global scale? Which ones conduct business in your country?

- Verizon Communications (1)
- The Coca-Cola Co. (3)
- PricewaterhouseCoopers (6)
- Colgate-Palmolive (16)
- PepsiCo (18)
- Marriott International (22)
- Toyota North America (29)
- American Express (30)
- Hewlett-Packard (31)
- Bausch & Lomb (35)
- Ford Motor Co. (37)
- Kraft Foods (38)
- Daimler Chrysler (43)
- Starbucks Coffee Co. (45).

Increased use of technology

Technological advances continue to alter the workplace, expanding and redefining how employees communicate both vertically and horizontally. How executives and employees communicate on a daily basis runs the gamut from a chance meeting on the elevator in real time to posting an opinion on a company's internal blog half a world away.

Workday activities like solving problems, addressing pressing issues, motivating others and achieving results require the traditional skills of analysis, evaluation, deliberation and intuition; but today, solutions are expected to be made virtually instantaneously in an anywhere, anytime world.

Creating, developing and communicating effective messages involve more options than ever before. **Technology** provides the tools for a high-speed delivery system: digitization, communication infrastructure, mobile phones, videoconferencing, email, etc. Some experts say there can never be too much communication.

What is important to note, however, is that many managers confuse effective communication with more paperwork and thus they shun communicating frequently in an effort to cut down on "busy work". Additionally, many managers equate giving out factual information with keeping employees informed. Merely disseminating information does not necessarily result in effective communication.

Effective communication programmes should be developed to eliminate unnecessary paperwork, repetitive messaging and misleading information, taking into account the sophisticated information needs of today's employees.

Instantaneous messaging

Timing is a crucial factor in effective communication. Today, no one wants, or expects, to wait for essential information. Consider these examples:

Employee: *"The proposal is almost complete, I'll stay late to finish it"*.
Manager: *"Email it to me tonight"*.

Young executive: *"I'll work on the figures today and have them on your desk when you get back in town on Thursday"*.
Supervisor: *"No, fax them to me at my hotel"*.

Salesperson: *"I'm meeting with Mr Jones tonight for dinner and we'll discuss the proposal"*.
Vice-president of sales: *"Call me on my cell when you're done and tell me what he said"*.

A hectic workplace that demands quick response often forces business people to make hurried assessments and decisions, but more than instant messages, receivers want, and demand, accurate and timely information.

Communicating to Employees

Reaching large groups of employees is possible because technology, such as user-friendly desktop publishing software, makes internal publications easy and fast, but that doesn't mean information-gathering, story development or readability considerations need to be hurried.

One of the first steps in the message process should be evaluating your audience. Who are they? What do they know about the situation or problem? Are their perceptions correct?

People approach problems differently depending on considerations such as culture, education, economic status and psychological needs. The communication processes of a 25-year-old single male employee are quite different to those of a 50-year-old female who also may be functioning as a parent or caretaker to ageing parents. The two employees will define problems and approach solutions differently.

Thinking about the needs and expectations of the receivers of messages is of prime consideration in developing employee-centred communication messages and choosing appropriate channels.

Strategic Thinking

Thinking is a good thing. Sitting quietly, staring out of a window or into space while breathing deeply, creates an insulated world that blocks outside distractions and allows individuals time to compose thoughts, work out problems or be creative.

Rick Vogler, manager of advertising and creative services, Entergy Corporation, says, "When I have a specific creative challenge facing me and just can't seem to solve it, I go for a drive. When I get out on the highway, with just the road in front of me and no other distractions, my mind clears and I can focus on the problem. Before I know it, I have a solution".

How do you spark your creativity?

Two ways to reach employees

Two of the most accepted and acceptable ways to reach employees, whether within a specific location or scattered throughout the world, are internal newsletters and internal/Intranet websites:

Internal newsletters

Company newsletters are simple to produce because of easy-to-use software. In the past this ease of production, plus the availability of inside stories about employees, their families and social events, was enough reason to publish a newsletter. But today, in an era where people can retrieve information at the touch of a keystroke, company newsletters must be sure to reach their intended audience with relevant information.

Newsletters must be meaningful to employees as well as management. The "who got promoted", bland executive profiles and superficial articles on company policy need to be replaced with poignant information such as the company's short-term goals, health initiatives, community outreach programmes, the company's new sales incentives, information on industry competition, etc. Insightful newsletter information helps to garner employee support for management's daily problems and concerns.

Internal/Intranet websites

Intranets can serve as connecting links between an organization and its employees. This technological tool helps eliminate misunderstandings by responding promptly to the needs of employees wherever they are located. Offering information in different languages may be a first step in the inclusion process.

Two-way Open Communication

Open communication is key to involving employees in the decision-making process. **Two-way open communication** is a dynamic exchange of information that effectively conveys a message from sender to receiver as it was intended with the expectation that feedback, offered without fear of repercussion, will be considered.

Engaging in open communication is not an easy task for many managers. Business people who like to make decisions find it hard to accept input from others, especially from those lower on the corporate ladder. Others are quick to dismiss feedback or do not consider it valuable input. To build a competent team, a manager must learn to communicate effectively. Open communication ultimately leads to mutual trust, a crucial factor in leadership success.

The website of Adobe Systems, one of the world's largest software manufacturers, describes its open communication policy: "At Adobe, we believe strongly that honest, open communication is the best approach to keeping employees inspired and motivated … [we] provide employees as much information as possible in a timely and frank manner. Respect for confidentiality is critical in such an environment, and we expect all managers and employees to share the responsibility for maintaining that trust. We rely on quarterly company meetings, regular team meetings, the Inside Adobe Intranet site, email and voice mail to share updates and disseminate information throughout the company" (Adobe Systems, 2006).

Dig Deeper

Change is an everyday phenomenon in today's global marketplace. Communication consultants Roger D'Aprix and Cheryl Fields, ROI Communications, Inc., offer these four suggestions for communication professionals involved in organizations undergoing change:

1. Explain to employees specifically why change is necessary.
2. Create a consistent "plot line" for the change story.
3. Understand the motivations, expectations, fears, etc., of those executives, managers and employees involved in the process. Ask them what they are thinking; what drives them; and what concerns them. Then address those concerns.
4. Create situations where employees and leaders can engage in dialogue about the change process (D'Aprix & Fields, 2006).

How do these suggestions relate to the role of managers or executives in the change process of a large organization? Would they work differently in a small company?

Managers must practise the philosophy of open communication if their organization is to succeed. They must encourage everyone within their sphere of influence to speak up, get involved and share their best thinking. This ultimately will ensure a productive environment for a unified and diversified workforce.

Employee and management empowerment

In our transactional communication model, the context, which surrounds and contains the messages of senders and receivers, influences the framing of a message and its understanding and application.

Sociologists explain that employees want to be more involved in the decision-making process, especially in individualistic cultures. James Houghton, chairman of the board of Corning Inc., says, "Today people question the status quo. They want to make their own decisions. They want to share their ideas and enthusiasm and not just be told what to do" (Schaefer, 1993).

Employees, from managers to entry-level personnel, are more involved and accessible to bosses, co-workers and those they oversee than they were in the past. In Germany, which traditionally worked 35-hour weeks, companies have been forced to demand more hours from their workforce just to stay competitive in a global market.

Now when an employee leaves the office, he is on the clock. In high-profile organizations, employees are expected to answer cell phones, check in for messages, return calls and keep pagers active even after the workday ends.

Along with instant access comes increased emphasis on performance and adaptability. Changes in the business climate, such as increased competition, accountability, government oversight, a sagging economy, increased unemployment and health issues, put daily pressure on all employees to engage in productive communication.

Stress is a reality in the workplace. **Stress** can be defined as the uncertainty an individual feels when confronted with a serious opportunity, problem or demand for which the perceived outcome is in question.

Good communicators help turn obstacles, presented by stress and change, into opportunities. To challenge and motivate others, managers must be aware that employees differ in personality and coping style and adjust their communication strategy accordingly. This is called an employee-centred approach.

Strategic Thinking

Communication expert Dr Carter McNamara developed an organizational creed that incorporated his ideas about communication in the workplace:

Key principles to effective internal organizational communications:

Unless management comprehends and fully supports the premise that organizations must have well-developed communication plans, the organization will remain stagnant. Too often, management learns the need for more effective communication by having to respond to the lack of it.

1. Effective internal communication starts with effective skills in communications, including the basic skills of listening, speaking, questioning and sharing feedback. These can be developed with review and practice. Perhaps the most important skill is conveying the idea that you value communicating with, and hearing from, others.
2. Sound meeting management skills go a long way toward facilitating effective communication.
3. A key ingredient to developing effective communication in any organization is ensuring that each person takes responsibility to speak up when he or she doesn't understand a communication, or offers suggestions as to when and how someone could communicate more effectively (McNamara, 2006).

Sharing knowledge

Employees need and often expect to be considered in the decision-making of an organization. The emphasis on quality management, particularly in manufacturing sector initiatives such as Total Quality Management or 6-Sigma, has brought the average worker into the decision-making process.

Employee exclusion leads to alienation and dissatisfaction, negative attitudes and loss of faith in the hierarchy of the company. If employees do not have a stake in the problem, they will not feel part of the solution and will be unwilling to accept any new rules and regulations. This means managers must use the two-way mode of communication to foster open communication.

However, some managers are afraid of sharing information. They hoard knowledge, thinking that "knowing" makes them more powerful, protects their jobs and gives them control over others. Enlightened managers, on the other hand, understand that informed employees are motivated and loyal workers.

Dig Deeper

Research centres around the world enable scholars to study, analyse and evaluate information methods:

- Australia – Centre for Research in Culture & Communication, Murdoch University, Perth, Western Australia;
- Belgium – Studies on Media, Information and Telecommunication, Free University of Brussels;
- France – Ecole National Supérieure des Télécommunications, Paris;
- Japan – Centre for Global Communications (GLOCOM), International University of Japan;
- The Netherlands – ASCoR, Amsterdam School of Communication Research.

Can you find what they are specifically studying?

Encouraging innovation

Innovation is more than just a buzz word in business and industry. The management theorist Peter Drucker defines **innovation** as "the means by which the entrepreneur either creates new wealth-producing resources or endows existing resources with enhanced potential for creating wealth" (Drucker, 2006, p. 33). Drucker believes many factors contribute to innovation, including changes within markets or industries, new knowledge, changing demographics and process needs, among other issues.

Companies that go beyond giving lip service to innovation and creativity and support positive change activities, especially during swings in the economic cycle, are more likely to see new wealth than those who don't. Ideas for innovations most often come from internal sources, but even customers and other outsiders may contribute to the development of new processes or products.

3M, for example, needed growth in its surgical drape business. The company decided to interview practitioners who were leaders in the infection control business (lead users), particularly as it applied to surgical practices. These leaders would, in turn, recommend other leaders to interview, and so on. Ideas came from surprising sources including veterinary surgeons. 3M assembled a team of experts across disciplines to recommend breakthrough ideas and products. Among the ideas that eventually surfaced was a type of antimicrobial coating for medical tubes – a $2 billion market for the new product (von Hippel, Thomke & Sonnack, 2006). The practice of innovation and the encouragement of creativity fall on the shoulders of management.

Communication scholars are interested in the steps in the innovation process and how they are communicated. Everett Rogers defined innovation as "an idea, practice or object that is perceived as new by an individual or other unit of adoption" (Rogers, 1983).

Rogers identifies five steps in the innovation process:

1. Awareness
2. Interest
3. Evaluation
4. Trial
5. Adoption.

Using the 3M example above, let's look at the five steps of the innovation process:

Step 1 – awareness. Awareness involved recognizing that 3M's surgical drape business was no longer competitive and, in fact, was risking being sold off. Awareness in this case was driven by a perceived need.

Step 2 – interest. Interest was aroused by interviewing practitioners and lead users to determine how they perceived the need for new products. At this stage, interpersonal contacts and media outreach in the form of newspaper articles, journals and other communication tools were helpful in identifying contacts.

Step 3 – evaluation. 3M was forced to make a decision as to whether the proposed new products were worth the investment. Would they be accepted by management? Was there a real market demand? Would research and development money be made available for the innovation? In the case of 3M, a team approach was used in developing the breakthrough products.

Step 4 – trial stage. 3M products were tested and the demand was identified.

Step 5 – adoption. Adoption of the new, competitive product developed a $2 billion market and reinforced 3M's reputation as an innovator in the industry.

How quickly a new idea or product is accepted by an organization's employees, a business, an industry or society in general is often difficult to determine. For example, the shift to digital radio, relatively quick in the UK but very slow in the US where availability and cost delayed the process, shows the unpredictability of adoption.

Dig Deeper

One of the steps in the adoption process of a new product or idea is to understand the role of its early adopters and see how they influence others to accept change.

In 2004, Belgium-based Interbrew and Brazilian-owned AmBev combined to form InBev, one of the world's largest beer brewers. According to its vice-president of employee relations and communication, Nigel Miller, "…it would be difficult to imagine two more different companies" (Miller, 2005, p. 30). But the new corporation was determined to forge a workable environment. To help employees understand the newly formed institution's values, how they related to business strategy and the implementation of that strategy, the company employed a global culture network "designed to identify and mobilize 'first adopters'".

The InBev example shows how applying diffusion theory can help organizations facilitate change. Can you think of examples of innovations – products or ideas – that have recently been adopted by your age group. Can you trace which groups used the innovation first? Where did it go next? How long was it before the innovation was mainstreamed?

Effective Communication as a Function of Management

Several tools will help managers communicate better with both superiors and those they manage. We have previously talked about these concepts; let's now apply them to the context of management.

Listening

In "The three 'Ds' in creating a culture of innovation", the *Ivey Business Journal* tells us that innovation "thrives in a culture driven by diversity, dialogue and discipline" (EBSCO, 2006).

One of the most important tasks a manager must master is **listening** effectively. Good listeners make good managers! We have already discussed the differences between hearing and listening and some of the repercussions of ineffective listening. Some of the characteristics of good listeners are shown in Figure 9.1.

How to listen effectively

DO...	DON'T...
Listen carefully.	Interrupt the speaker before the message is delivered.
View the message from multiple perspectives.	Intimidate others with authoritative and intrusive body language.
Understand the message and the sender.	Be close-minded and stoic.
Reflect how answers impact upon the speaker/situation.	Be insensitive to another's problems.
Respond sincerely and empathetically.	Judge or make hasty conclusions.

Figure 9.1 Listening effectively is a learned skill.

Recruitment

Although the **recruitment** and training of employees is still largely a function of the human resource department, managers and other decision-makers are not excluded from the process.

When communicating with job applicants, employers must know what questions to ask of those they are interviewing. Listening to responses will help them determine if the candidate fits the job description and the corporate culture. Privacy laws in many countries restrict the questions that can be asked in an interview, so open-ended questions, such as "Why don't you tell me about yourself", allows the interviewer to learn more about the individual through volunteered information.

Human resource personnel are experts in hiring activities and can provide managers not only with training to conduct successful interviews but also with the tools to evaluate candidate responses and behaviours.

Training

On-the-job **training** for both new and seasoned employees is important. New recruits may come to the job with the knowledge and theoretical perspective of the work they are to undertake, but the real hands-on skills will be learned once they become a part of an organization. What they do bring to the new job is potential. Training new employees to perform their jobs to their potential is absolutely necessary in order to achieve high performance.

Adam Kahane, former head of Social, Political, Economic and Technological Scenarios for Royal Dutch/Shell's London office and author of *Solving Tough Problems: an Open Way of Talking, Listening and Creating New Realities*, offers in-depth insight into problem-solving and conflict resolution. His advice is to talk and listen "openly, reflectively and empathetically" (Kahane, 2004).

Schlumberger, the world's largest oilfield company, with branches in over 80 countries, 80 000 employees and annual revenues of over $12 billion, has an aggressive campus–recruiting programme targeting many degree disciplines. It is estimated they invest up to $100 000 for each new hire during the first year for training and qualifying employees before sending them out into the field. This commitment to quality performance, and the investment the company makes in human capital, has made Schlumberger a sought-after employer.

Retraining or providing new opportunities for skill development for ongoing employees is also in the best interest of the company. Improved machinery, updated computer systems, emerging business practices and new skills have to be shared with employees who are expected to perform at peak efficiency with knowledge and expertise.

Upper-level managers also benefit from training and seminars that expose them to the latest news in their industry. Communication plans need to include necessary training and retraining programmes.

Training sessions need to "connect" with employees. There is nothing more wasteful of time, money and resources than a training session in which employees learn nothing. Managers have the responsibility to review training sessions for effectiveness.

On-the-job training needs to be actively reviewed, analysed, evaluated or adapted on a regular basis. For example, a 2006 study by the Cape Group, a human capital research

Managers must recognize the following needs	Employees must recognize the following needs
Employees want to know their managers support them	Managers want to keep loyal and committed employees
Employees expect frequent communication with management	Managers expect employees to ask questions and seek guidance
Employees value professional development and training programmes	Managers value employees who can adapt and adjust to changing situations
Employees appreciate awards, rewards and individualized evaluation	Managers appreciate employees who step up and accept a challenge
Employees gain confidence from interaction with managers	Managers prefer employees who feel satisfied and in control

Table 9.1 Employee relationship management communication.

Dig Deeper

A **communication audit** is a review of all the company's communication efforts to external target publics and internal audiences. It serves to identify a company's communication strategies and provides the opportunity to evaluate their effectiveness. A communication audit can answer such questions as: Are our communication vehicles receiver-oriented? Do we speak with one voice? Are our messages consistent across departments?

An internal communication audit, usually performed by a neutral, outside organization, analyses and evaluates communication to and from employees, managers and senior-level executives. It may include comments on newsletter content, insight about how employees feel about the company or how customer complaints are addressed.

firm, looking at employee retention in Thailand, said that although most business skills come from training rather than education, many Thai companies do not offer their employees viable training programmes. Some companies have begun to develop training programmes to address this situation (Thapanachai, 2006).

Recruiting and replacing new employees is more expensive than training or retraining existing employees. The more employees feel competent in their jobs, the greater the probability they will stay on that job. Job satisfaction also enables employees to weather changes in the corporate structure, high demands on time and energy, threats to job security, burnout and stress. Despite the proven effectiveness of training programs, most companies do little to retain employees.

The concept of employee relationship management (ERM) is real, and many companies realize the benefits of strengthening employee communication programmes and employee–management relationships. In other words, employees should not be taken for granted. As companies grow larger and more complex, the need for viable employee communication programmes that address various employee segments becomes more necessary (Table 9.1).

Communication Challenges

Communicating with a complex and diverse workforce presents its own set of concerns. In his article "Basics in internal organizational communications", Carter McNamara summarizes some of the causes of internal communication problems (McNamara, 2006):

Ernst & Young, in the top ten of *Working Mother* magazine's "100 Best Companies for Working Mothers", says of its Working Moms Network programme: "We are constantly improving our efforts to retain, develop and advance our women" (Ernst & Young, 2006).

1. Leaders and managers assume that, because they are aware of some piece of information, then everyone else is too.
2. Organizations are often burdened with bureaucratic overhead.
3. Management does not value effective communication or assumes that it just happens.
4. Managers believe they have conveyed information but aren't aware that the receiver has interpreted the message differently to the way intended.
5. When personnel are tired or under stress, it's easy to do what's urgent rather than what's important.
6. Managers often interpret their job to be solving problems, and if there aren't any problems/crises, then nothing needs to be communicated.
7. Management tends to focus on matters of efficiency.
8. Management sees no value in communicating with subordinates, believing they should remain in the dark and just do their jobs.

Companies must communicate with a wide range of employees in many countries and cultures, sharing knowledge, ensuring security and respecting privacy.

Strategic Planning

Traditionally, strategic planning was envisioned as a top-down process that helped executives determine how they could compete better in the marketplace. Today, **strategic planning** is often done in teams representing a variety of skills and disciplines or on various organizational levels. This process is equally important for non-profit organizations who manage people and limited resources to meet particular community needs. Educational institutions, for example, need to think strategically about how they will address such issues as rising costs with less government support and competition from Internet–based organizations, and how they can recruit and educate underserved populations.

Large corporations typically have complex and multilayered planning processes with specific internal groups assigned to the planning process. They often find that engaging employees who represent a broad array of skill sets, expertise and functions encourages creativity and in the end facilitates a "buy-in" from employees. Nokia, for example, credited the development of its smart car telematics, among other innovations, to a strategic planning process that involved several hundred people (Byrne, 2006).

Strategic Thinking

Finland's Nokia Group is exploding in the telecommunications business since it involved 250 employees in a strategic review. Chris Jackson, head of strategy development, says, "We won a high degree of commitment by the process [of involving more employees], and we ended up with lots of options we hadn't looked at in the past".

Nokia managers now have the skills to make strategy an integral part of their jobs. "We've taken strategy away from the yearly cycle that it was in, and we're trying to make it a daily part of a manager's activity", says Jackson (Byrne, 1996).

What do you think about the idea of making strategy "a daily part of a manager's activity"? Is this achievable or a pipe dream?

Small businesses and non-profits may engage consultants, boards of directors or volunteers to help facilitate planning. Some organizations develop yearly strategic plans, while others develop planning documents designed to be implemented over a 2–5 year period. However, long-range strategic plans need to be annually reviewed and revised.

Strategic planning should be guided by the vision and values of an organization and its leaders. Communicating vision and values and helping employees understand how they influence planning are key roles of management.

Marketing and public relations professionals are often considered crucial to the strategic planning team. Strategists should have a thorough understanding of relationships between employees, competitors, supporters and other key groups of publics. These publics must be considered in the planning process, particularly as organizations move to an integrated approach to communication.

Planning for the future

Strategic planning is complex, and most organizations have a standard set of best practices. Most plans include the following steps:

Step 1. Define the problem or opportunity.
Step 2. Conduct a situational analysis – this is the research step in the process and involves primary and secondary research. Primary research includes gathering company history, performance reviews and evaluating mission and value statements along with

both qualitative research (ethnography, in-depth interviews, communication audit, ethnography), quantitative research (questionnaires, polls, etc.) and secondary research (industry data gathered by other research firms, competitive analysis or scholarly articles).

Step 3. Formulate goals and objectives.

Step 4. Formulate a strategy for meeting the goals and objectives.

Step 5. Identify key personnel to take charge of a specific area of the plan.

Step 6. Implement the strategy through a variety of tactics.

Step 7. Evaluate how well the organization has met its goals. The evaluation process occurs at every step along the way, allowing for plans to be modified to fit changing circumstances.

Goals, objectives and tactics

Strategic planning documents include goals and objectives specific to each organizational unit or audience:

- **Goals** are long range in scope and indicate what action or behaviour the organization/ unit ultimately wants to achieve.
- **Objectives** spell out how the unit plans on meeting established goals. As they are short term in scope, they should be audience specific, measurable and date/time specific and designate desired outcome. **Communication objectives** are also

Dig Deeper

How well employees understand company strategy is affected by a variety of factors.

Sinickas Communications, Inc., an international communications consultancy firm, studied communication audits from 27 firms and documented how well their employees reported their understanding of company strategy.

The results showed employees rated their information levels on strategy higher when senior management frequently explained strategy, and when employees had access to the Intranet. Other factors such as access to periodic newsletters, frequency of supervisor's communication about strategy and access to staff meetings also contributed to the knowledge factor (Sinickas, 2006).

developed in this stage to help understand how communication planning can help achieve goals.

• **Tactics** are the specific ways and means of achieving the objectives.

Let's look at two examples.

Example 1

Goal – to communicate the value of safety to all employees;

Objective – to reduce the number of accidents by 50 % during the next six months;

Communication objective – to develop and implement a safety campaign that involves all employees within the next six months;

Tactics – to publicize the safety campaign in the newsletter, to post safety signs throughout the factory and to disperse "I believe in safety" badges to all employees.

Example 2

Goal – to improve the image of Ross Industries in the minority community;

Objective – to sponsor a series of free cultural events during the next year in community centres, schools and churches located in heavily populated minority neighbourhoods;

Communication objective – to promote the events in a timely fashion in the minority community, using a variety of targeted media;

Tactics – to send media releases to local outlets and to deliver invitations to minority organizations and churches.

Goals and objectives are crucial to the planning process for several reasons:

• They give a planning document direction and determine strategic and action activities.
• They provide a tool to measure short-term and long-term success, thus helping to make organizations accountable.
• They help organizations plan and prioritize their activities.
• They influence personnel and financial resource allocations.

The Volvo Communication Group used planning steps to raise employee awareness of its strategic objectives for 2004–2006. A 2002 survey of employees showed 67 % awareness, but the Group's objective was to raise the awareness to 80 % by 2005 and to 90 % by 2007.

The Group determined that managers were key agents in the communication process. They were given access through the company's Intranet system to their unit's part in the implementation of strategic objectives and were expected to communicate and report on how they communicated these strategies to their employees. This process was complemented by focused communications. Units were encouraged to develop their own strategies for communicating the objectives and did so through a variety of written and oral techniques. The results were that 91 % of all responding managers had informed their teams about the strategic objectives (Nordbloom, 2006). Volvo used managers – the opinion leaders – to effect change. Company leaders are entrusted with the task of developing and implementing a company's long-range strategic plan and involving all levels of the company in the process.

Chapter Summary

The obstacles to effective communication are many, but by now you should begin to grasp some of the significant challenges that face managers as communicators in today's marketplace. How you react to these challenges as you move into the world of business will determine your future success and effectiveness as a manager. If you find some of these concepts overwhelming, you are not alone!

Effective communication is as complex as the multinational mix of peoples, places, practices and products that make up the global marketplace.

Embracing diversity must be more than just lip service, it must focus on inclusion. Communication efforts to enhance inclusion include relevant company newsletters and Intranets, open communication, stress reduction, sharing knowledge and encouraging innovation.

Effective managers develop strong listening skills, interact with others, value feedback and encourage retraining workshops and informational seminars. As an integral part of a company's long-term strategic planning process, they are responsible for the everyday communication and implementation of the plan. ∎

Learning From Others

Bill Belchee, Beacon Small Business Solutions, USA, expanded his one-man accounting business in 1996 with a handful of loyal clients and one associate. His story is another example of how entrepreneurship and communication make excellent partners. He shares his thoughts about running a small business "between the steps of the giants":

Communication and the Entrepreneur

When I began, I believed if I networked, ran a few ads, and served my clients well, I would have more business than I could handle.

I was wrong! If I hadn't had my few original clients, Beacon would have become a casualty of statistics ... 90 % of small businesses close their doors within three years.

A first step was to segment my present customers into three areas:

- CAPP (Cooperative, Appreciative, Profitable, Pay on Time) – my best customers;
- undecided – customers who were not CAPP quality yet, but could be;
- NWTE (Not Worth the Effort) – my most difficult customers ... it wasn't until I actually wrote the names that I realized I was beating my head against the wall trying to keep them happy.

To survive, small business owners must focus on CAPP and undecided customers and be personally involved in every transaction, as they are not protected by the layers of accountability and responsibility found in large organizations.

Every customer complaint – founded or unfounded – affects small business owners financially and emotionally.

My next step was to find the right channels of communication to:

- talk to my existing clients;
- network with potential new clients;
- stay on top of the ever-changing tax laws;
- be technologically competent on a limited budget;
- emphasize that I was as good as the larger firms.

Communication, however, takes money. Emails require a computer, letters necessitate stationary, envelopes and stamps and brochures need layout artists, graphic designers and printers.

I listed some affordable communication tools and discovered a wide range of options:

- email (I had a computer);
- face-to-face communication;
- email newsletters;
- handwritten notes sent as traditional mail;
- telephone conversations;
- text messaging;
- faxes;
- writing "tax advice" articles for area and industry publications;
- joining networking groups;
- teaching tax courses at local schools;
- supplying amateur sports teams with uniforms displaying my company's name;
- posting business cards at locations around town;
- volunteering for charity groups.

This was a long list for a small business guy like myself.

Regardless of the channel I used, I focused on communicating one message:

> *Beacon Small Business Solutions is honest, ethical, professionally capable and technically adept to handle your company's accounting and tax needs and without fear of reprisal. We will be here when you need us.*

After 10 years, I have stayed true to my vision. The company is thriving and we recently moved into new, state-of-the-art facilities with additional personnel to handle our growing customer list.

Case Study – Thai Agri Foods Public Company Limited (TAF)

A 2006 article published in the *Financial Times*, the *Global News Wire*, the *Thai Press Reports* and the *Bangkok Post* (Thapanachai, 2006) stated that a major research and consultancy firm, The Cape Group, had reported that 94 % of Thai companies polled cited employee management as a top business priority. However, the report continued, many companies did not implement programmes to retain and motivate employees. This had created a "talent crisis". The research group called for Thai organizations to "manage and retain talent using consistent career development plans in order to perform well".

The study also showed that many companies did not have any criteria in place to identify talented staff, much less programmes to retain and communicate with these workers. The study also called for executives to help human resources by identifying the skills needed for particular jobs and communicating possible solutions for training employees in those skills.

Thai Agri Foods Public Company Limited (TAF), established in 1986, is a successful operation in Thailand. It provides hygienically processed frozen and canned products using fresh seafood, fruits and vegetables. It also produces beverages such as energy drinks and fruit juices, instant foods and ready-to-eat foods like sesame shrimp toast and sweet chilli sauce. In response to consumer demand for these products, Thai Agri exports to over 70 countries around the globe. It became a member of the Stock Exchange of Thailand in 1991.

The human resources page of its website says: "TAF has dynamic and dedicated personnel at all levels, from the factory floor to the top management" (TAF, 2006).

Knowing that the present generation of workers (Generation Y, born 1977–1994) may be technologically savvy and well-educated academically, but lacking in specific job skills, what do you think Thai Agri could do to retain young workers? Discuss such options as training programmes, reward incentives, empowerment, re-education, etc. How would these programmes vary according to the level of employee in the company?

Access the company's website, `www.thaiagri.com,` to see what other information you can find. See if the company's annual report tells you anything about the focus of employee retention and management? ■

Class Exercises

1. A manager's job often involves knowing who needs to know what. Have students list the ways managers could determine what employees want and need to know. What are some of the methods they can use to collect these data? What factors must be taken into consideration? Do you think employees will be forthcoming with the information? What sort of incentives can you suggest that would make employees more willing to express their views?

2. In small groups, discuss possible answers to the following question. In a fast-paced world, what are the most critical challenges for managers and employees concerning communication infrastructure and management style?

3. Do further research on how the workplace will be changed as employees become more empowered through the use of convergent media in an interconnected society? What emerging issues will human resources professionals have to deal with? What new management skills will be required to communicate with this changing workforce?

Action Plan

Topping DiversityInc's list for diverse US companies is Verizon Communications, one of the world's major providers of communication services with an annual revenue of $68 billion. It has operations in Gibraltar and Italy and provides information services outside the USA to 14 countries including Austria, Malaysia, Poland and Slovakia.

Go to the Verizon website at `http://www22.verzion.com/about` and read about its diversity initiatives. You'll see phrases such as "... it is imperative that we have an inclusive workforce" and "... diverse minds, experiences, culture and unique perspectives of our employees are what give us our competitive advantage" (Verizon Communications, 2006). Do some further reading and see if you can discover how Verizon fits DiversityInc's four search criteria, and why it was named the company most committed to diversity in 2006.

Websites

Want market intelligence? Check out the information provided by IDC, a global research company that uses 850 analysts in 50 countries to collect data and consult with experts, at www.idc.com/about/about.jsp (IDC, 2006).

Read the European Union's "The business case for diversity: good practices in the workplace" at http://europa.eu.int/rapid/pressReleasesAction.do?reference=IP/05/1483&format=HTML&aged=0&language=en&guiLanguage=en (EU, 2005).

The British Association of Communicators in Business posts short articles from conventions, reports, etc., about business communication in the UK. Check out www.cib.uk/com (BACB, 2006).

References

Adobe Systems Incorporated (2006) Available from: http://www.adobe.com/aboutadobe/careeropp/communication. html [Accessed 15 April 2006].

BACB (2006) British Association of Communicators in Business. Available from: www.cib.uk/com [Accessed 21 August 2006].

Byrne, J. (1996) "Strategic planning". *Business Week*, 26 August 1996. Available from: www.businessweek. com/1996/35/b34901.htm [Accessed 6 November 2006].

D'Aprix, R. & Tyler, C. (2006) "Four essential ingredients for transforming culture". *Strategic Communication Management*, **10**(3): 22–25.

DiversityInc. (2006) "The DiversityInc top 50 companies for diversity list". Available from: www.diversityinc.com/public/21030.cfm [Accessed 21 April 2006].

Drake, S., Giusto, R., Boggs, R. & Sandler, M. (2005) "Worldwide mobile worker population 2005–2009 forecast and analysis". IDC research report. Available from: http://www.idc.com/getdoc.jsp?containerId=34124 [Accessed 1 September 2006].

Drucker, P. (2006) "The discipline of innovation". *Harvard Business Review OnPoint*, Spring: 33–38.

EBSCO (2006) "The three 'Ds' in creating a culture of innovation". *Ivey Business Journal*, **70**(3): 1. Available from: EBSCO Host Research Databases, Winthrop University-Dacus Library [Accessed 22 May 2006].

Ernst & Young (2006) "Ernst and Young ranked in the top 10 among the "100 Best Companies for Working Mothers". 25 September 2006. Available from: http://www.ey.com/global/Content.nsf/US/Media_-_Release_-_09-25-06DC [Accessed 11 November 2006].

EUROPA (2005) November 28. "83 % of European companies with 'diversity in the workplace policies' see business benefits – commission report". Press release 28 November 2005. Available from: http://europa.eu.int/rapid/pressReleasesAction.do?reference=IP/05/1483&format=HTML&aged=0&language=en&guiLanguage=en [Accessed 3 September 2006].

EU (2005) "The business case for diversity: good practices in the workplace". European Union. Available from: http://europa.edu.int/comm./employment_social/fundamental_rights/pdf/events/business_en.pdf [Accessed 21 August 2006].

Guth, D. & Marsh, C. (2006) *Public Relations: a Values-driven Approach*, 3rd edn. Boston, MA, Pearson.

IDC (2006) "About IDC". Available from: www.idc.com/about/about.jsp [Accessed 21 August 2006].

Kahane, A (2004) *Solving Tough Problems: an Open Way of Talking, Listening and Creating New Realities*. San Francisco, CA, Berrett-Koehler Publishers.

Lacy, S. & Hempel, J. (2006) "Valley boys: Digg.com's Kevin Rose leads a new brat pack of young entrepreneurs". *BusinessWeek*, 14 August 2006: 40–47.

McNamara, C. (2006) "Basics in internal organizational communications". Authenticity Consulting, LLC. Available from: http://managementhelp.org/mrktng/org_cmm.htm [Accessed 21 April 2006].

Miller, N. (2005) "Biggest to best: InBev's journey to a new global culture". *Strategic Communication Management*, **9**(5): 30–32.

Nordbloom, C. (2006) "Involving middle managers in strategy at Volvo Group". *Strategic Communication Management*, **10**(2): 26–29.

RCMP (2002) Commissioner's Advisory Committee on Visible Minorities. The Royal Canadian Mounted Police. Available from: www.grc.gc.ca.library.unl/edu [Accessed 15 April 2006].

Rogers, E. (1983) *Diffusion of Innovations*. New York, Free Press.

Schaefer, M. (1993) "Communication is my job". *IABC Communication World*, June/July: 21–25.

SHRM (2006) "US pay levels for HR professionals continue to strengthen". Society for Human Resource Management. Available from: www.mercerhr.com [Accessed 15 April 2006].

Sinickas, A. (2006) "Improving understanding of strategy". *Strategic Communication Management*, **10**(2): 12–13.

TAF (2006) Thai Agri Foods Public Company Limited. Available from: www.thaiagri.com [Accessed 18 April 2006].

Thapanachai, P. (2006) "Cape Group: manage and retain your talent". *Bangkok Post*, 7 April 2006. Available from: www.thailandoutlook.com [Accessed 19 April 2006].

Vallario, C. (2006) "Creating an environment for global diversity". *Financial Executive*, **22**(3): 50–52.

Verizon Communications (2006) Available from: http://www22.verizon.com [Accessed 21 April 2006].

von Hippel, E., Thomke, S. & Sonnack, M. (2006) "Creating breakthroughs at 3M". *Harvard Business Review OnPoint*, Spring: 66–77.

Western Health (2003) Annual report 2002–2003. Available from: http://www.wh.org.au/about/pdfs/03%20Annual%20Report.pdf [Accessed 27 August 2006].

Yoshihara, H. & McCarthy, P. (2005) *Designed to Win: Strategies for Building a Thriving Global Business*. New York, McGraw-Hill.

Zeiss, T. (2005) *Get'em While They're Hot: How to Attract, Develop, and Retain Peak Performers in the Coming Labor Shortage*. Nashville, TN, Nelson Business Publishers.

Bibliography

Baran, S. & Davis, D. (2000) *Mass Communication Theory: Foundations, Ferment, and Future*, 2nd edn. New York, Longman.

Lovery, S. & DeFleur, M. (1995) *Milestones in Mass Communication Research*, 3rd edn. White Plains, NY, Longman: 115–134.

CHAPTER 10

Issues of Organizational Leadership

Executive Summary

Leadership sets the communication style and culture of an organization. According to Trompenaars and Hampden-Turner (2004), corporate cultures are classified in structure according to two dimensions: person versus task oriented and equalitarian versus hierarchical. A preference for a particular culture varies between types of business and geographical locations and the personalities and leadership traits of the executive management group.

The functions of management and leadership differ: leadership sets the direction for an organization, and management works to achieve the objectives of that direction Leadership theory has a rich history, with scholars and practitioners examining such factors as traits, situations, style and emotional intelligence.

Challenges of leadership include building an atmosphere of trust, connecting with employees in a variety of environments, communicating the values and direction of a company and facilitating innovation and change

Leaders emerge when ethical and legal issues come to the forefront Ethics are values and actions. A teleological approach considers how much pleasure will be produced by a certain ethical action. A deontological approach to ethics judges all actions by whether they are considered right or wrong.

Working in cross-cultural environments requires what ethicist Thomas Donaldson calls respect for human values, respect for local traditions and the belief that context matters when deciding what is right or wrong

Legal issues particularly important to communicators include libel, copyright and trademark protection and advertising regulations The laws governing such actions, and the values supporting them, vary from country to country. ■

Issues of Organizational Leadership

> *"The group will not prosper if the leader grabs the lion's share of the credit for the good work that has been done.*
>
> *Lao Tzu, 6th century philosopher"*

Introduction to the Role of Communication in Management and Leadership

What were the qualities that made you want to do a good job for one boss but not for another? What made you think that a particular place of work was better than another? Were your ideas respected? What tone of voice did your supervisor use in talking to you? Did you feel welcomed by others in the workplace? In most cases, communication between you and your superiors was at the root of the relationship, positive or negative.

International competition, particularly through mergers and acquisitions, forces leadership into uncharted territory and is generally the result of the initiative of an experienced, seasoned veteran who has the vision, foresight and skills to lead the charge.

Let's begin our discussion of leadership with an example. In 2003, PiaggioVespa, the Italian-made scooter company, was in financial trouble. Enter Italian industrialist Roberto Colaninno, known for his ability to turn around companies. Colaninno hired CEO Rocco Sabelli who introduced a new flexible assembly line that could respond quickly and efficiently to consumer demand. Sabelli encouraged product innovation and empowered company workers. In an early move, he gave his email address to every assembly-line employee and told each one to report any problems in production directly to him. He didn't fire a single worker … and he also installed air conditioning in the factory. Productivity continues to increase, and today the company is turning a significant profit (Kahn, 2006).

This chapter views the role of leaders as senders of communication and examines how culture influences communication style. Further, the differences between management and leadership, characteristics of leadership and the communication techniques leaders must develop to build strong organizations will be discussed. The chapter concludes with an introduction to the ethical and legal problems confronting leadership in its communication functions.

Institutional Cultures in International Business

Leadership sets the tone and the structure of an organization's culture. In the past, European, North American and, more recently, Japanese cultures defined the way most of the world did business. Today, developing economies such as Thailand, Korea, Brazil, China, India and other regions of the world are redefining the business market models.

Adapting business culture to fit a particular geographic market is not easy. Cultures have both formal and informal rules and written and unwritten regulations.

Geert Hofstede (1980) used research conducted in 40 independent nations to identify four dimensions of cultures:

1. **Power distance** refers to the range and degree of acceptance of the distribution of power within a culture.
2. **Uncertainty avoidance** describes the willingness of a culture to accept or reject change and take risks.
3. **Individualism–collectivism** relates to whether a society emphasizes individual achievement or group identification.
4. **Masculine versus feminine** describes the emphasis in a society on characteristics such as assertiveness or nurturing.

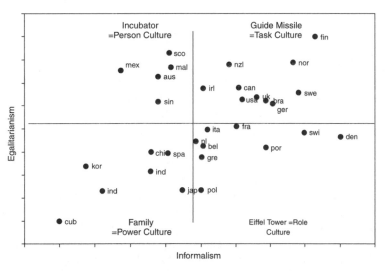

Figure 10.1 Variation of corporate culture across the world. Corporate cultures can be categorized into four quadrants depending on their cultural values. (Permission to reproduce the figure granted by John Wiley & Sons, Ltd on behalf of Capstone press. The chart appears in Trompenaars & Hampden-Turner (2004) *Managing People Across Cultures*. Chichester, UK, Capstone Press, p. 41).

Individual employee recognition is highly valued in North American culture, which is more individualistic and egocentric than others. Praising individuals for their accomplishments would be embarrassing in Asian cultures that are more paternalistic and group oriented. The Japanese teach, "It's the nail that sticks up that gets pounded down".

Hofstede's work revealed that countries held different values to be important – values that may no longer be held by newer generations. Nevertheless, this pivotal research helped fuel other work regarding cultural differences.

In *Culture for Business Series*, Trompenaars and Hampden-Turner use the following definition of culture: "Culture is a pattern by which a group habitually mediates between value differences, such as rules and exceptions, technology and people, conflict and consensus, etc. …" (Tromenaars & Hampden-Turner, 2004, p. 23).

The four models of culture vary in two dimensions, person-centred or task-centred, equalitarian or hierarchical. Most corporate cultures share characteristics from all four models:

- **Incubator organizations** are person centred and equalitarian in nature.
- **Guided missile organizations** are task oriented and equalitarian.
- **Family–centred organizations** are more person centred and hierarchical.
- **Eiffel Tower organizations** are task oriented and also hierarchical in nature.

Good leaders recognize the values of individual cultures. For example, incubator cultures prize individualism and innovation and value creative attempts to communicate

Dig Deeper

Southwest Airlines, a US-based air carrier, is recognized for its fun-loving culture and strong emphasis on its employees as ambassadors of excellent service (incubator organization). In 2004, then executive chairman and co-founder Herb Kelleher noted that the People Department (human resources) seeks to hire employees who are "altruistic, who like to serve and to work with others, and … who have leadership potential".

Kelleher says the Southwest spirit is nurtured through management's engagement in the life and work of its employees. For example, executives are expected to work in line-positions in the field so they can understand and address concerns of customers and employees. Employees are frequently recognized for their service to the company or the community and may be designated as the "Star of the Month" (Cohen, Watkinson & Boone, 2005).

Can you find other companies that engage in communication activities that would represent the other three models?

with employees and the public (as in the Southwest Airlines example). Information released to the media by such organizations will likely stress individual achievement or how the organization has charted new territory with a particular product or service.

Reading institutional culture

Doing background research before a job interview is crucial to learning about a company's **institutional culture**. A mission statement, or the lack of it, implies a business's values but may not explain how the business actually functions. Here are some issues to consider:

- Do employees work in cubicles, offices or share workstations where hotdesking is the norm?
- Do employees share stories or is conversation formal and subdued?
- Ask about the decisional flow chart.
- Find out about the policies and procedures of the organization.
- Look for signs and symbols that reveal company culture.

> **Stories** help people feel connected to an institution and its history and are important to maintaining institutional culture. Universities thrive on the power of stories passed on from generation to generation.
>
> Few universities have such a distinguished history as Trinity College in Dublin, Ireland. Enterprising students, no doubt selected for their wit and enthusiasm, give 30-minute guided tours of the university founded in 1592 by Queen Elizabeth. Along the way, visitors are treated to historical anecdotes, tales of student life and a glimpse of the *Book of Kells*.

Leadership or Management?

The differences between leadership roles and management roles are important to understand. Communication policy is set by leaders and implemented by managers, but they may or may not be the same people. While both leaders and managers are involved in power relationships, their roles in building trust and institutional viability differ. A discussion of leadership will form the basis of the study on how leaders influence the communication context of an organization.

A way to remember the differences between leadership and management is this: **leaders** set goals; **managers** set objectives to accomplish those goals. The distinctions drawn between managers and leaders by Harvard Professor John Kotter are set out in Figure 10.2 (Kotter, 1990).

LEADERSHIP...	MANAGEMENT...
Leadership establishes the direction of the audience.	Management determines how a vision can be accomplished.
Leadership communicates the direction that the organization needs to follow to reach its goals.	Management develops a plan to manage the process.
Leadership motivates management and employees to overcome barriers to reach goals.	Management solves the problems encountered in the process.
Leadership produces change.	Management keeps the organizational processes flowing in a predictable and efficient way while monitoring results.

Figure 10.2 Kotter's theory of leadership versus management differences (adapted from Kotter, 1990, p. 6).

Leadership Theory

The study of leadership is based on a number of theoretical approaches and is studied by scholars in many disciplines. Scholars have constructed leadership paradigms that examine leaders as communicators:

- trait approach
- situational approach
- style approach
- transformational and transactional approaches.

Trait approach

The **trait approach** suggests that for an organization to be effective, its leaders must have certain characteristics. However, this approach tends to be highly selective, focusing primarily on the leader, not on the influence of followers or situations in determining leadership traits.

In 1948, scholar Ralph Stogdill analysed 124 research studies, conducted between 1904 and 1947, on personality characteristics and leadership. From this literature he concluded that there were eight traits of good leaders:

- intelligence
- persistence

- initiative
- self-confidence
- responsibility
- insight
- sociability
- alertness.

Stogdill suggested these traits alone did not determine leadership but rather having these traits allowed leaders to relate to the "characteristics, attributes and goals of the followers" (Stogdill, 1948, p. 64).

In 1974, Stogdill again looked at the research on leadership traits and analysed 163 studies published between 1947 and 1970. He added "tolerance" and "influence" to make a total of 10 psychological traits. Other researchers such as Lord, DeVader and Alliger (1986) and Kirkpatrick and Locke (1991) also analysed the psychological characteristics of leadership.

In his book *Leadership: Theory and Practice*, Peter Northhouse synthesized the literature and identified the following as leadership traits common in studies (Northhouse, 1997):

- intelligence
- self-confidence
- determination
- integrity
- sociability.

Recent scholarship suggests that psychological traits are not in themselves predictors of leadership but, instead, qualities that others perceive as important in leaders (Hackman & Johnson, 1996, p. 58).

Situational approach

The **situational approach**, developed by therapist Fred Fiedler in the 1950s, is based on a self-assessment measurement scale called the least preferred co-worker scale (LPC). Fiedler believed that identifying co-workers with whom one does not like to work provides valuable information on leadership styles. Leaders with high LPC scores (those whom workers have identified as easy to work with) tend

Dig Deeper

The emotional intelligence of a leader is the "hidden driver of performance" according to Goleman, Boyatis and McKee in *Primal Leadership* (2002). Backed by scientific study, the researchers suggest that the most effective leaders match their moods and behaviours to the situation at hand while remaining optimistic about the future.

Read more about emotional intelligence in an interview with Daniel Goleman in the *Ivey Business Journal* (Bernhut, 2002).

to be more relationship oriented, while those with lower LPC scores are more task oriented. These orientations influence leadership and communication style (Fiedler, 1967).

The situational approach identifies three key elements that affect leadership:

1. *The position of power that a leader holds within a group.* In a work situation, leaders could be construed to have more power if they affect promotion decisions.
2. *The nature of the task behaviour.* Some projects are highly structured and involve precise steps that must be followed in order to complete the task; this is particularly true in engineering and manufacturing. Task behaviour is of lesser importance in the arts or entertainment industry where there is more room for individual input and creativity.
3. *The relationship of the leader to the group.* Leaders who developed loyalty and following among group members had higher LPC scores indicating that they were more relationship oriented (Hackman & Johnson, 1996).

Other situational studies have expanded Fiedler's approach over time. The primary tenets of the situational approach, often used in leadership coaching, is to get leaders to evaluate their own leadership style and then learn how to adapt that style to fit a particular situation.

For example, there is a trend in US newspaper newsrooms to move from directing a reporter in writing a story, a low support style of behaviour, to coaching a reporter in the development of a story by suggesting changes in content, etc., a direct but supportive style of leadership behaviour. Today's editors encourage and guide reporters in their writing, and as a result the modern newsroom environment is viewed as more nurturing and productive.

Style approach

The style approach is another way of looking at leadership communication.

Political framework

An analysis of political leadership framed much of the early discussion on characteristics of leadership styles. Lewin, Lippitt and White (1939) analysed the differences in communication styles of authoritarian, democratic and laissez-faire leadership.

Authoritarian leaders believe employees need direct supervision because they feel workers left on their own will be unproductive. An authoritarian approach is evident when a manager orders an employee to follow a certain safety procedure.

Democratic leaders value group participation and are supportive of this process; they believe others have opinions worth considering. A democratic leader would seek input on whether a safety procedure is workable before sending out a directive.

Laissez-faire leaders may offer guidance and support but stay out of the decision-making process. A laissez-faire manager might suggest safety procedures in the belief that employees will follow them or suggest that employees formulate their own safety procedures.

Applied political approach

Phillip Clampitt offers three practical approaches to management decision-making that augment these earlier definitions of political leadership (Clampitt, 2005).

The **"arrow" approach**, grounded in authoritarianism, views communication as primarily a one-way process based on the skills of the sender or leader. Feedback is unnecessary, as the arrow leader believes that he or she is speaking with absolute credibility and authority. Clampitt says arrow managers "assume that receivers are passive information processors" (Clampitt, 2005, p. 8).

The **"circuit" approach** might be called the democratic leadership model. The circuit manager is a networker who stresses feedback over process. Managers who practise this leadership style believe in total openness and that, if employees are satisfied and trusted, effective communication will occur. While such managers have good group organizational skills such as building relationships and seeking feedback, they incorrectly perceive that understanding and empathizing with employees constitute a type of effective leadership.

Strategic Thinking

What are some of the challenges that face great leaders in the business world?

1. *Building an atmosphere of trust where employees feel empowered to make suggestions about company improvement and processes.* Employees who believe they are a part of the broader company community are more likely to be loyal and experience a greater sense of personal accomplishment. Southwest Airlines encourages its employees to be brand ambassadors. Employees are empowered to make decisions about customer service on the spot without asking supervisory management for permission.

2. *Communicating the direction, values and vision of an organization.* Communication consultants Robert Mai and Alan Akerson suggest: "Leaders who drive home the vision of the enterprise help their colleagues connect personal aspirations to those of the larger organization. They work to align individual visions with organizational goals on a level at which people can make common cause" (Mai & Akerson, 2003, p. 53). In other words, leaders who can make their vision resonate with their employees are more likely to see results.

3. *Communicating effectively with employees who work in a variety of environments.* Employees work varying schedules in different time zones and locations. These barriers of space, time and geography require thinking about what communication techniques will be most effective in each situation. Remember how Vespa's Sabelli communicated downwards when he gave employees his email address? This, in turn, encouraged upward communication from his employees. Accenture Ltd, a global consulting firm, sends thousands of employees to more than 100 locations around the world. Most employees in this virtual company have no permanent office space so they use the firm's Intranet, the Internet, telephone, videoconferencing and periodic face-to face meetings to communicate with each other and to accomplish their tasks. During the last economic slowdown, Accenture Ltd's head of financial services held 280 meetings in 18 months with his 12 000 employees (Hymowitz, 2006).

4. *Creating a climate of acceptance where change is part of the vision and corporate culture of an organization.*

5. *Staying true to oneself while understanding the needs of others.* Goffee and Jones (2005) call it "managing one's authenticity". True leadership requires self-disclosure and the willingness to accept feedback from others.

The **"dance" approach** is the most effective management communication style. This leadership style, much like a positive laissez-faire approach, combines the positive quality of direction in the authoritarian approach and the relationship building of the democratic approach. Communication, like dance, involves many patterns and movements, and thus no single approach or movement fits every performance.

Leadership studies

This examination of leadership and communication styles would not be complete without discussing several important research studies that contributed to contemporary thinking.

The Ohio State leadership studies used the leadership behaviour description questionnaire (LBDQ) to examine how subordinates viewed their leaders. These studies identified a two-dimensional view of communication leadership style (Stogdill, 1974). Initiating behaviour was task oriented; leaders told followers what jobs they wanted them to accomplish. On the other extreme was consideration behaviour, which was relationship oriented; leaders expressed concern with employees' problems, asked for their input and worked to maintain a positive work environment. These behaviours were thought of as distinct and independent.

The Michigan leadership studies looked at low- and high-performing groups within organizations and identified a continuum of leadership communication behaviour. "Production-oriented" leaders were task oriented and concerned with finishing work assignments; "employee-oriented" leaders were more interested in training and motivating employees. An initial assumption that leadership was either production oriented or task oriented was later modified. Leaders can manifest both types of behaviour, and those that do are generally considered stronger leaders (Katz, Maccoby & Morse, 1950; Katz *et al.*, 1951).

Test instruments such as the Blake and McCanse's Managerial Grid® are widely used and respected in leadership studies. The grid attempts to identify how managers reach their goals by focusing on two purposes – how to address production concerns and how to address people concerns (Blake & McCanse, 1991).

Transformational and transactional approaches

Transformational leadership involves developing communications that motivate and nurture the values of both leaders and followers (Northhouse, 1997, p. 131) and was first

> Mahatma Gandhi, Desmond Tutu and Martin Luther King, Jr were transformational leaders on the world stage. In business, Richard Branson of Virgin and Bill Gates of Microsoft are considered transformational because they lead with inspiration and are seen as models of ethical leadership.

suggested by political sociologist James McGregor Burns in his book *Leadership* (Burns, 1978). The theory focuses on charismatic leaders who motivate and move followers. Such leaders are master communicators.

Transactional leadership occurs in everyday communication with others. For example, when a supervisor informs an employee about a delay in a shipment of goods or a manager promotes an employee because of her performance on the job, he or she is engaging in transactional leadership.

This type of leadership parallels the work of Maslow and his hierarchy of needs. Transactional leaders are concerned with satisfying physiological, safety and social needs, whereas transformational leaders aim higher in the pyramid and attempt to motivate employees to self-fulfilment and actualization (Hackman & Johnson, 1996).

Both transformational and transactional leadership styles are necessary to move a company forward, but transformational leadership inspires people and ultimately organizations to greatness.

Challenges in Leadership Communication

In international business, ethical decisions involve consideration of cultural differences. Legal issues also present challenges to organizational leaders.

Leaders Emerge when Ethical and Legal Issues Arise

Constantly changing forces within and outside an organization illustrate the need for values and adherence to ethical and legal principles. Leaders emerge when the values of an organization are challenged.

Former Enron CEO Ken Lay's excuse, that he didn't know that unethical accounting practices were going on, didn't wash with the jury or the public at large when he was brought to trial in the spring of 2006 on multiple counts of illegal business behaviour. As CEO he was responsible for setting the ethical standards for the corporation.

Respondents to a leadership survey on business and ethics conducted by *Fast Company* magazine, IMD, a Switzerland-based business school, and Egon Zehnder

International, an executive recruiting firm, reported that 95 % of the 1 665 respondents said "yes" or "absolutely" to the statement that "leadership starts at the top and ethical leadership filters throughout the organization" (Verschoor, 2006, p. 2).

An organization can only be as strong as its weakest link, and in a multinational organization many employees at various levels are responsible for corporate culture.

Definition of ethics

Our communication style has roots in our ethical make-up. Let's briefly discuss a few philosophical approaches to ethics.

The **teleological approach**, advocated by utilitarians, measures how much gratification will be produced by a certain action. Utilitarian philosopher John Steward Mills believed that the quality of the action needed to be weighed against its long-term consequences. A utilitarian would ask: what is the greatest good for the greatest number of people? This approach obviously means some individuals would not benefit from an action. Giving employees time off from work to attend parent–teacher conferences at their children's schools would benefit those with children but not those without. On the other hand, those without children might have long-term benefits from working with employees who feel satisfied on the job because they are meeting their parental obligations.

A **deontological approach** to ethics judges all actions by whether they are morally right or wrong. Immanuel Kant used the deontological approach in his "categorical imperative", saying that, if you can translate your action into acceptable moral law, then your action will be morally acceptable. If a universally accepted moral imperative is "you should treat others as you would like to be treated", then denigrating others for your own aggrandizement will be viewed as unethical.

Ethical standards of practice are often formally and publicly presented as statements of values or codes of conduct by professional organizations.

For example, the Public Relations Society of America (PRSA) and the International Association of Business Communicators (IABC) have ethical codes governing the behaviour of members, and point to the need for honesty and openness in internal and external communications (PRSA, 2006; IABC, 2006).

Business codes of conduct include such issues as "financial reporting, conflicts of interest, supplier relationships, employment practices, product safety and quality issues, protection of the environment, pricing and billing, health and safety issues, personal property and intellectual property issues, and using trading information" (Stanley, 2006, p. 3).

Cross-cultural issues

For multinational companies, practising business across the globe often challenges traditional codes of conduct and value statements. Consider the following approaches to cross-cultural ethics.

Cultural relativism implies that an organization first accepts local values before considering how corporate actions might affect others, its brand or its international reputation. If a country has high standards for the disposal of toxic chemicals, an organization may make sure its good waste management practices are communicated to stakeholders before addressing other issues such as recruitment policies or green office design.

On the other extreme, **ethical imperialism** says that organizations follow their home customs in conducting business. This precept fails to recognize different cultural beliefs or to acknowledge that there is a global standard for ethical behaviour. A US company that mandates a course in sexual harassment in a Saudi Arabian facility fails to understand the strict rules regarding male–female contact in that nation's workplace.

Ethicist Thomas Donaldson says companies should be guided by three principles when shaping their ethical behaviour internationally (Donaldson, 1996, pp. 3–4):

- respect for human values, including respect for human dignity, basic rights and good citizenship;
- respect for local traditions;
- the belief that context matters when deciding what is right or wrong.

In spite of these recommendations, making ethical decisions is rarely clear-cut. For example, the practice of giving gifts is common in the business culture in Japan. But receiving gifts is often seen as a form of bribery in Western cultures. How does one reconcile the differences? As Donaldson notes, gift giving does have some limitations in the Japanese culture. Going beyond the accepted limit – in fact trying to bribe public officials – would be considered unethical. International companies doing business in Japan need to understand this custom.

In the 1990s, Levi Strauss dealt with the problems of using child labour with two of its Bangladesh suppliers by agreeing to pay wages to children while they attended school and then offering them a job at the age of 14. It also agreed to pay tuition and books. This enabled their families, dependent on their children's wages, to sustain an income while their children received an education. This creative move reconciled the company's core values with the culture while providing long-term benefits to the Bangladesh people (Donaldson, 1996, p. 8).

The reconciliation of cultural differences means that organizations need to be committed to their own values while considering the impact of those values on the countries and populations in which they do business.

Legal issues

This section addresses three legal areas particularly important to communication:

- intellectual property
- copyright
- libel
- advertising.

Laws and regulations regarding communication activities and the organizations that enforce them differ from nation to nation. What's acceptable advertising in Denmark may be totally unacceptable in Canada; furthermore, what may be legal in one region of the world may also be perceived as offensive or culturally unacceptable in another.

> Good taste? VW in a series of edgy ads targeted at Hispanic consumers in the USA found that what was considered amusing to some was interpreted by others as rude or inappropriate. The company pulled the billboards from both its Speedy Gonzales and Turbo-Conjones campaigns after objections from the Hispanic community. "Conjones" means testicles in Spanish but is often used in English to mean guts or willingness to take risks.
>
> The replacement for the campaign was "Here today, gone tamale" and "Kick a little gracias".

Intellectual property

Buying a knock-off (a cheap imitation of an established brand) purse from a vendor on the street, downloading a song illegally to an iPOD, copying the design of a brochure or ad to use as an assignment, using recorded material as background music for a presentation or failing to cite sources on a paper – all are abuses of intellectual property.

Intellectual property rights involve ownership of intellectual activity in the literary, artistic, industrial or scientific arenas. The protection of intellectual property is a crucial issue in the global marketplace and, fortunately, international treaties administered by the World Intellectual Properties Organization (WIPO) provide protection against global piracy. However, such protection is costly to monitor and sometimes difficult to enforce, and the misuse of patents, artistic performances, trademarks, etc., is on the rise, costing artists, scientists, businesses and their stockholders billions of pounds, euros and dollars a year.

What constitutes intellectual property?

- inventions
- scientific discoveries
- artistic, literary and scientific works
- performances of artists, broadcasts and recordings
- industrial designs
- protection against unfair competition
- trademarks, designations and business names.

Trademark abuse that might have been ignored in the past in developing nations is less and less tolerated on the global stage. As a document from the US State Department noted, "robust intellectual property protection ... spurs economic expansion and the growth of new technologies" (Salmon, 2006).

Copyright

The purpose of **copyright** laws is to reward and protect creativity. In sixteenth-century England, printers were rewarded with government protection in return for their loyalty in reporting antigovernment writers. Copyright protection for individual authors was not acknowledged until the eighteenth century when the British Parliament recognized the legal rights of those who created a work or those who acquired the work.

In 1886, the Berne Convention for the Protection of Literary and Artistic Work developed the first international copyright standards.

Dig Deeper

A single international standard for the protection of intellectual property was created as part of the Uruguay Conference on General Agreement on Tariffs and Trade (GATT) negotiations in 1994. This agreement on trade-related aspects of intellectual property rights (TRIPS) is administered by the World Intellectual Property Organization (WIPO) and requires member countries of the World Trade Organization (ratified by 114 countries) to adhere to the treaty, and ensure their domestic laws comply with all aspects of the treaty.

It establishes minimum standards of protection for several forms of intellectual property, mandates judicial and legal enforcement and requires participants to submit to binding, enforceable dispute settlement. Since the ratification of TRIPS in 1994, the WIPO has negotiated new treaties dealing with biotechnology, information technology and patents and trademarks.

What organization(s) are responsible for governing the use of intellectual property in your country?

The USA considers copyright law as conferring economic rights, while international standards view it as both an economic and a moral right. Although the USA had adopted a similar protective statute to that of the British in 1790, significant differences between its copyright laws and that of the Berne Convention prevented the USA from signing the Berne agreement.

Consequently, the USA found it necessary to enter into agreements with individual countries around the world and in 1989 finally signed the Berne agreement.

Today, under the Berne agreement, works are protected for the life of the creator plus 70 years; works created by more than one person are protected for 70 years after the death of the last living creator. Works for hire are protected for 95 years after publication, and this protection applies to printed materials including books, maps and charts, musical compositions, photography, sound recordings, pantomimes, works of art, translations and other creative works.

But there are often grey areas in the law. While many countries debate the legal implications of copyright as it applies to such platforms as podcasting, it seems clear that activities such as downloading copyrighted material and posting it without the author's permission is an abuse of copyright law.

Individual countries have their own regulations regarding how copyright is recognized and the extent of fair use. For example, issues such as the purpose and nature of the use must be considered (Pember & Calvert, 2007/2008, p. 593).

Trademarks/service marks

A **trademark** differentiates a company's product or services from another's. Luftansa is a trademark, as is the Coca-Cola bottle shape and the shade of pink of Owens-Corning's fibreglass insulation. Service marks identify particular services, as opposed to goods, but both trademarks and service marks are protected under international law and subject to the regulatory registration rules of individual countries. Such protection is particularly crucial for companies and individuals seeking to expand trade into other countries.

Advertising regulations

What is considered legal television advertising in the Netherlands may be illegal in India. Knowledge of cultural norms and mores, sensitivity to stereotyping and an understanding of government rules and regulations are paramount for countries wishing to advertise beyond their borders.

Many **regulations** are based on cultural, social and religious traditions and dogma. For example, in France, alcohol and tobacco advertising is prohibited. In some South American countries, most forms of nudity are banned from the public airwaves. In the USA, nudity that may be allowed to run on a cable channel is restricted from the major networks.

In some countries, comparative advertising is generally considered libellous, whereas in other countries, comparing one's products to those of a competitor's may be legal. Australia requires all broadcast advertising to be produced by Australian crews. In Canada, all text has to be in both French and English. If this sounds confusing, it is.

Most business executives will have little interaction with the production of advertising messages; however, they should appreciate the complexities of producing commercials and buying media in the international arena. To shape a consistent coherent brand message, advertising executives need to participate at the highest level of the marketing strategy process.

Chapter Summary

This chapter should leave you with the question: what kind of leader am I now, and what kind of leader do I want to be in the future?

The first step in developing a leadership style is to know yourself. Understanding and translating theory into practice will enhance your leadership skills.

Communication forms the basis of effective leadership which in the global marketplace requires a sophisticated knowledge base and sensitive application of principles to business situations.

Business messages are communicated around the world in different formats and for various reasons. To be effective, leaders have to be aware of governmental rules and regulations and sensitive to an organization's cultural differences. Leaders must consider how ethical challenges affect an organization's various publics, from employees to the community to consumers.

What constitutes good leadership remains a question of great debate among academics and the popular business press. It is up to each executive responsible for a company's vision to take advantage of opportunities to build leadership behaviour. ∎

Learning From Others

The Shaw Group, based 80 miles north of New Orleans, is a US multidimensional global engineering, construction, pipe fabrication and disaster relief and recovery company. It was one of a handful of prequalified disaster relief companies called in by local, state and federal agencies to meet emergency needs when Hurricane Katrina turned towards the Louisiana coastline and the city of New Orleans in late summer 2005.

Chairman and CEO James Bernhard, Jr started the Shaw Group in the late 1980s and directed its growth and diversification to become a Fortune 500 company with nearly $5 billion in annual revenues. Through technological innovations that made it the global leader in pipe fabrication, and with acquisitions of brand companies such as Stone & Webster, a leader in nuclear and power construction and engineering, Shaw emerged as a one-of-a-kind designer for providing solutions to some of the world's most complicated problems.

Bernhard explains how the Katrina crisis altered, adapted and enhanced the company's new branding and communications campaign:

> Just as Shaw began introducing its branding and communications campaign "A World of Solutions", Hurricane Katrina blew on shore, and within hours Shaw was at work pumping water from the streets and providing temporary roofing to houses throughout the Gulf Coast area. Shaw workers – with their identifiable orange working shirts – were seen everywhere there was need. The news media were calling Shaw for answers more than they were calling government agencies. "A World of Solutions" was a reality, not just a branding slogan.

"This was tactically quite taxing," Bernhard said. "We wanted to be everywhere, but we also wanted to work with local, state and federal agencies seamlessly and coordinate breaking issues responsibly and in a timely fashion".

As part of "A World of Solutions", Shaw created a communications centre for local, state and federal agencies to work with emergency contractors. Walls were lined with aerial photographs and maps of the region, and emergency communications lines were set up to keep track of contracts and contractors. Two daily reporting sessions brought all project directors together to keep track of performance; results of these meetings were relayed publicly.

"We needed to send signals that action was being taken", Bernhard said. Shaw's community relations staff worked with non-profit companies to meet needs in shelters, to coordinate with other agencies in directing dollars toward need and to provide assistance in a timely fashion to those whose needs seemed to be falling through the cracks.

Shaw's first ever television advertising campaigns, one directed at Louisiana audiences who needed to know problems were being solved and that the state could be "bigger, better, stronger", and the second outlining Shaw's commitment to hiring Louisiana workers first and towards spending dollars in-state, were launched, giving viewers a better sense of "who Shaw is" in addition to what it did. These advertisements were welcomed by political and community leaders facing questions about who was being hired and how much money would be spent towards rebuilding the state.

"Ultimately, our crisis communications reactions, like our recovery and relief reactions, reflected more about our company than most audiences would see in years of paid advertising", Bernhard said. "It's not the way I would have rolled out a branding and advertising campaign if my only concern had been Shaw favourability". In any case, Shaw was able to control its own destiny and not be publicly defined by others, as often happens in a crisis. It earned its timely "World of Solutions" image.

Case Study – **Toyota**

Toyota opened its first plant on the continent near Valenciennes, France, in 2001. The plant builds the petrol/diesel engine for Yaris, a top-selling car in the European Union. The melding of French customs with Japanese practices required both workers and management to accept cultural differences.

One of the greatest cultural challenges was the need for Toyota to incorporate France's mandatory 35-hour work week into its production schedule. Japanese workers are accustomed to working much longer hours, often into the evening. Shiegefumi Goto, director of Toyota Motor Europe, said the company "feels a responsibility to comply with prevailing legislation in every country in which we operate".

Since the beginning of the operation, Japanese management has learned to work with strong French unions and has been required to learn French, not a common second language for the Japanese.

French plant workers also have adjustments to make. Each morning, employees participate in physical exercises, and cafeteria food includes typical Japanese entrees. Workers are also offered free company attire. Acceptance of the clothing was reportedly a slow process, as the French value individuality.

Administrative functions also challenge traditional French industry practices. Company executives have no private offices or dining rooms. Toyota values company training and seeks unskilled workers, unlike the typical French company that values diplomas and previous training. In addition, administrative meetings are scheduled when necessary rather than every morning, the usual industrial practice in France.

Perhaps the largest sacrifice for the French employers was giving up wine in the company dining room. In justification of Toyota's ban, an official told a *New York Times* reporter that the company cited "health and working conditions" as grounds for prohibiting a traditional French custom.

Communications at the specially designed plant are facilitated by the open configuration of the work space (investinfrance, 2004; Tagliabue, 2001).

Questions to consider:

What other cultural accommodations do you think the French and Japanese made in this new organization? What accommodations were not made?

What type of communication practices should leadership employ in a start-up company in a new country of operation versus one that has been acquired by another organization?

Investigate the issues surrounding the acquisition of Ford/Volvo. What were the cultural issues involved and how were they addressed? ■

Class Exercises

1. As a class, brainstorm and make a list of social or political leaders that exhibit "transformational" leadership styles. What makes these leaders "great?" Now, in groups of four or five, research a particular industry (retail, banking, health, education, etc.) and identify the names of 10 well-known leaders in their fields. How did you come up with the list? Who identified these people as leaders? Why? Do they possess any of the characteristics mentioned in the section on leadership approaches? What are their leadership styles?

2. Access the article "Managing in an Anywhere, Anytime World", an Ernst & Young white paper for the Governor's Meeting at the 2006 World Economic Forum in Davos, Switzerland, at http://www.ey.com/global/download.nsf/International/ TCE-AnywhereAnytime-2006/$file/EY _ TCE _ AnywhereAnytime _ 032206. pdf (Ernst & Young, 2006). Individually, list and justify the five key points you feel the paper makes. Now, in groups of five or six students, discuss what you and your classmates listed and why you did so. Your group task is to come up with the two most important points in the article. The caveat is that the success of this project will depend on whether or not your two points match what your professor thinks are the two most important points. [The professor should put this information on a piece of paper on the desk before you reveal your group decisions.] Was it difficult to decide which points to choose? Why or why not? At what point in the process did a leader emerge?

3. Think about a boss or professor you've had to work with. Using the leadership versus management chart (Figure 10.2), try to pinpoint specific examples of why you would categorize that person as a leader or a manager. Do you think all managers need to be leaders? Give reasons for your answer.

Action Plan

Empirical evidence points to a high rate of failure for corporate mergers and acquisitions (M&A) across borders. How do cultural differences impact the success of these business decisions? In his book *Managing Cultural Differences*, Piero Morosini points out that cultural differences are usually not the primary obstacle in M&A activity (Morosini, 1998). He notes: "… it is not any particular or 'given' environmental factor which can make or break such a partnership, but rather the company manager's commitment, patience and ability to work and adapt to difficult conditions and different cultures overseas, as well as to build critical 'local' knowledge and networks of relationships in these countries" (Morosini, 1998, p. 37).

Adaptability appears to be the key. What is the role of communication in that process? How can a company determine the cultural differences of an organization they are considering acquiring? Look into recent mergers in your community – how did they resolve cultural differences?

Websites

Compare how two megacorporations highlight their values.

Johnson & Johnson, long revered for the handling of the Tylenol poisoning case in 1982, posts its credo and statement at http://www.jnj.com/careers/global/shared _ values/our _ credo/index.html;je ssionid5SJQN02TQNNP51CQPCCEGU3AKB21lWTT! (Johnson & Johnson, 2006). On this site, you can also assess the company's value-based leadership statement.

Unilever, one of the world's largest corporations, posts its code of business principles at http://www. unilever.com/ourvalues/purposeandprinciples/ourprinciples/ (Unilever, 2006).

Job hunting? Consider the "100 best workplaces in Europe" published by the *Financial Times* on 18 May 2006, and compiled by the Great Place to Work® Institute. Available from: http://www. greatplacetowork-europe.com/best/list-eu.php (GPWI, 2006).

The Center for Creative Leadership is a non-profit organization offering leadership training in the US, Europe and Asia. Read about the current issues in leadership training at http://www.ccl.org/leadership/ index.aspx (CCL, 2006).

References

Bernhut, S. (2002) "Leader's edge". *Ivey Business Journal*, May–June. Available from: http:wwwiveybusinessjournal.com/article.asp?intARticle_ID362 [Accessed 23 June 2006].

Blake, R. & McCanse, A. (1991) *Leadership dilemmas – grid solutions*. Houston, TX, Houston Gulf Publishing.

Burns, J. (1978) *Leadership*. New York, Harper & Row.

CCL (2006) Center for Creative Leadership. Available from: http://www.ccl.org/leadership/index.aspx [Accessed 23 June 2006].

Clampitt, P. (2005) *Communicating for Managerial Effectiveness*, 3rd edn. Thousand Oaks, CA, Sage.

Cohen, A., Watkinson, J. & Boone, J. (2005) "Southwest Airlines CEO grounded in real world". *Babson Insight*, 28 March 2004. Available from: http//searchcio.techtarget.com/originalContent/0,289142,sid19_gci1071837,00html [Accessed 14 June 2006].

Donaldson, T. (1996) "Values in tension: ethics away from home". *Harvard Business Review*, **74**(5). Available from: Business Source Review, 00178012 [Accessed 23 June 2006].

Goffee, R. & Jones, G. (2005) "Managing authenticity: the paradox of great leadership". *Harvard Business Review*, December: 87–94.

Goleman, D., Boyatzis, R. & McKee, A. (2001) Primal leadership. *Harvard Business Review*, December: 43–51.

GPWI (2006) Great Place to Work® Institute. Available from: http://www.greatplacetowork-europe.com/best/list-eu.php [Accessed 14 June 2006].

Ernst & Young (2006) "Managing in an anywhere, anytime world". Available from: http://www.ey.com/global/download.nsf/International/TCE-AnywhereAnytime-2006/$file/EY_TCE_AnywhereAnytime_032206.pdf [Accessed 23 June 2006].

Fiedler, F. (1967) *A Theory of Leadership Effectiveness*. New York, McGraw-Hill.

Hackman, M. & Johnson, C. (1996). *Leadership: a Communication Perspective*, 2nd edn. Prospect, IL, Waveland Press.

Hofstede, G. (1980) "Motivation, leadership, and organization: do American theories apply abroad?" *Organizational Dynamics*, **9**(1): 42–63.

Hymowitz, C. (2006) 5 June. "Have advice, will travel". *The Wall Street Journal*, 5 June 2006: B1, B3.

IABC (2006) "Code of ethics". International Association of Business Communicators. Available from: http://www.iabc.com/about/code.htm [Accessed 26 June 2006].

investinfrance (2004) "An interview with Shigefumi Goto". *France Now*, 24 February 2004. Available from: http:www.investinfrance.org/France/Newsroom/Newsletter/Attractiveness/en/nws002/suc [Accessed 8 June 2006].

Johnson & Johnson (2006) "Our credo". Available from: http://www.jnj.com/careers/global/shared_values/our_credo/index.html;jessionid=SJQN02TQNNP5lCQPCCEGU3AKB2llWTT!/ [Accessed 20 June 2006].

Kahn, G. (2006) "Vespa's builder scoots back to profitability". *The Wall Street Journal*, 5 June 2006: B-1, B-8.

Katz, D., Maccoby, N. & Morse, N. (1950) *Productivity, Supervision and Morale in an Office Situation*. Ann Arbor, University of Michigan, Institute for Social Research.

Katz, D., Maccoby, N., Gurin, G. & Floor, L. (1951) *Productivity, supervision and morale among railroad workers*. Ann Arbor: University of Michigan, Institute for Social Research.

Kirkpatrick, S. & Locke, E. (1991) "Leadership: do traits matter?" *The Executive*, **5**: 48–60.

Kotter, J. (1990) *A Force for Change: How Leadership Differs from Management*. New York, Free Press.

Lewin, K., Lipitt, R. & White, R. (1939) "Patterns of aggressive behavior in experimentally created 'social climates'". *Journal of Social Psychology*, **10**: 271–299.

Lord, R., Devader, C. & Alliger, G. (1986) "A meta-analysis of the relation between personality traits and leadership perceptions: an application of validity generalization procedures". *Journal of Applied Psychology*, **71**: 402–410.

Mai, R. & Akerson, A. (2003) *The Leader as Communicator*. New York, American Management Association.

Morosini, P. (1998) *Managing Cultural Differences: Effective Strategy and Execution Across Cultures in Global Corporate Alliances*. Oxford, UK, Pergamon.

Northhouse, P. (1997) *Leadership: Theory and Practice*. Thousand Oaks, CA, Sage Publications.

Pember, D., Calvert, C., 2007/2008. *Mass media law*. New York: McGraw-Hill.

PRSA (2006) "Code of ethics". Public Relations Society of America. Available from: www.prsa.org/_About/ethics [Accessed 28 June 2006].

Salmon, C. (2006) "US State Dept: guide to international IPR treaties". *US Fed News*, 2 January 2006. Available from Lexis-Nexis [Accessed 24 May 2006].

Stanley, T. (2006) "The ethical manager". *Supervision*, **67**(5): 10–12. Available from: Business Source Preview, 20838247 [Accessed 23 June 2006].

Stogdill, R. (1948) "Personal factors associated with leadership: a survey of the literature". *Journal of Psychology*, **25**: 25–71.

Stogdill, R. (1974) *Handbook of Leadership: a Survey of Theory and Research*. New York, Free Press.

Tagliabue, J. (2001) "At a French factory, culture is a two-way street". *New York Times*, 25 February 2001: BU4. Available from: Thomson Gale A70872235 [Accessed 8 June 2006].

Trompenaars, F. & Hampden-Turner, C. (2004) *Managing People Across Cultures*. Chichester, UK, Capstone Publishing.

Unilever (2006) "Business principles". Available from: http://www.unilver.com/ourvalues/purposeandprinciples/ourprinciples [Accessed 20 June 2006].

Verschoor, C. (2006) "Strong ethics is a critical quality of leadership". *Strategic Finance*, **87**(7): 19–20. Available from: Business Source Preview, 19737528 [Accessed 23 June 2006].

Bibliography

Ket de Vries, M. & Florent-Treacy, E. (1999) *The New Global Leaders: Richard Branson, Percy Barnevik, and David Simon*. San Francisco, CA, Jossey-Bass.

Overbeck, W. (2005) *Major Principles of Media Law*. Belmont, CA, Thomson Wadsworth.

Seidenberg, R. (2004) *Ethics in Action. Building Trust. Leading CEOS Speak Out: How They Create it, Strengthen it, and Sustain it*. New York, Arthur W. Page Society: 96–105.

Sieb, P. & Kilpatrick, K. (1995) *Public Relations Ethics*. Ft Worth, TX, Harcourt Brace.

Trompenaars, F. & Woolliams, P. (2003) *Business Across Cultures*. Chichester, UK, Capstone Publishing.

Yoshihara, H. & McCarthy, M. (2006) *Designed to Win: Strategies for Building a Thriving Global Business*. New York: McGraw-Hill.

PART 3

INTEGRATED BUSINESS COMMUNICATION

CHAPTER 11

Global Communication Expands

Executive Summary

People connect with people around the globe as electronic communication services become more readily available and wireless capabilities expand. This all-pervasive interconnectedness has led to a flat world where companies must create a communication infrastructure that supports and encourages global relationships.

Technology is a major force in the global communication revolution
Innovation and adaptation play key roles in the communication process as traditional channels for connecting with one another change to fit the new world order.

Businesses must recognize the inevitability of change and accept the role they play in helping internal and external publics respond to those changes
Dispelling stereotypes and embracing the diversity of today's workplaces are ways that companies can think globally and act locally.

Websites become important communication tools to communicate with consumers across the globe
Social media, such as blogs, MySpace sites and Wikis, are making inroads in content-driven media, impacting communication and restricting the ability of organizations to control the image of their brands.

Communicasting allows interest groups to use electronic media to develop their own messages and then distribute them via the Web
Datacasting extends programming possibilities to electronic media.

Technology can support organizations as they compete in the global marketplace
Knowledge of how to make best use of these new tools is basic to effective communication strategy. ■

Global Communication Expands

Introduction to Global Communication as Everyday Communication

Communicating on a global scale reaches many of the world's citizens on a personal level and, as computers become necessities rather than luxuries, individuals and businesses have seen a fundamental shift in how they organize and interact with one another.

This global integration of everyday experiences has spilled over to both large and small businesses. Organizations see the need, more than ever before, for a communication infrastructure that supports and encourages global relationships with various publics, from customers to suppliers. What has emerged as researchers try to make sense of the "new ways" of doing things is a trend towards complete integration of business communication throughout an organization, from top to bottom, across all levels and within and among all departments.

Economic forces such as the rise of the European Union and the emergence of markets in Brazil, China, India and other parts of Asia continue to influence the need for dialogue and multilateralism among nations. These forces challenge traditional political, social and economic systems and require leadership that can analyse, synthesize and adapt to change.

Technology drives the global communication revolution, and even those in remote corners of the world, with limited access to the latest innovations, are able to integrate new technology with old in creative ways.

In Unalaska/Dutch Harbor, an Aleutian Island off the coast of Alaska, the nearest hospital is 800 miles away on the mainland. Most of the island's inhabitants are engaged in the crabbing industry, considered one of the world's deadliest industries. Medical treatment is provided by a group of physician assistants and nurses who communicate to medical specialists via the Internet and other forms of technology.

Jessica Ambrose, PA-C, tells the story of an 11-year-old boy who came to her clinic one day with a displaced fracture through the growth plate in his leg. Ambrose consulted with an orthopaedist (bone specialist) in Anchorage, the nearest major medical centre. The physician asked to view the X-ray to see if the dislocation could be set "blindly", without the assistance of continuous X-rays viewed in real time, the standard medical practice. The medical team at the clinic took a digital photograph of the "wet" film hanging on the fluorescent lamp and emailed the image to the orthopaedist waiting in Anchorage.

The doctor reviewed the X-ray and, over the telephone, told Ambrose to proceed with the blind bone-setting process. When she had manoeuvred the bone into alignment, a new X-ray was taken, digitally photographed and emailed to the physician. Based on the new X-ray, the orthopaedist instructed Ambrose, again by phone, to adjust the bone to a slightly different angle. Again, the X-ray/digital photo/email process was followed. Ultimately, the boy's bone was successfully set without complications, and the cost of a long, arduous and expensive trip to the mainland was avoided (Ambrose, 2006, personal communication).

Innovation and adapted technology will be key factors as countries like the United States, the United Kingdom, Germany and other older industrialized countries work to find their place in the new world order. This chapter works from the premise popularized by author Tom Friedman that the "world is flat" and that the growth of digital technology has played a major role in shifting the economic, political and social ways business is conducted (Friedman, 2005).

The World Is Indeed Flat

Thomas L. Friedman, Pulitzer Prize-winning author, noted that, when conducting interviews for his book *The World is Flat*: "I kept hearing the same phrase from different business executives. It was strange; they all used it, as if they had all been talking to each other. The phrase was, 'Just in the last couple of years...'" (Friedman, 2005, p. 339).

Friedman's book explores the levelling power of the global marketplace. Globalization has, in effect, flattened the world by giving small companies, entrepreneurs and individuals unprecedented business opportunities. He continues to point out that businesses have recognized the inevitability of this change and that companies that want to survive and thrive are responding to the many changes they see around them.

Embracing change in the business environment can propel companies forward as they begin to increase their dependency on viable communication strategies. How will companies communicate in the future? With whom? Where? Many organizations realize that, in the "flat world" Friedman describes, they will be communicating with employees, consumers, suppliers, governments, environmental groups and other stakeholders from various countries, socio-economic levels, cultural backgrounds, education, religions and business orientations.

Overriding stereotypes

The effort to dispel stereotypes is one of the major changes occurring throughout the world. Stereotyping is not necessarily negative in concept. How do people who have never been to a rain forest know how it looks? They may have read books or seen a television documentary or talked to someone who has been there, but what they have gathered, via the media and personal relationships, are stereotypical second-hand images.

A person cannot be everywhere, go everyplace or meet every type of person, and so individuals depend on stereotype imaging to understand a place or a group of people. What do Eskimos look like and how do they live? You could probably build a good description of their facial features and the landscape they live in.

Stereotypes are short cuts for identifying people, places and things. They are often a compilation of information we have received from what we consider reliable sources such as books, newspaper articles or friends. In this manner they are neutral storehouses from which we can "know" the world without having to experience everything first-hand, a logistical impossibility. Many times, however, rigid and unrealistic stereotypes are conceived from unreliable sources such as rumour, bigotry, folklore or impersonalized media portrayals.

Stereotyping, however, can become a negative tool for "knowing" when we believe that everywhere or everyone must fit into a stereotypical image. They will not. Just as in our own world, where people are one-of-a-kind individuals and places are diverse and unique, a continuum stretches from one extreme to the other.

Take a small town with which you might be familiar. Does everyone fit the small town image? What about the writer who has left the big city for a quiet workplace? What about the wealthy widow who travels the world collecting art treasures? Does every place have only small town features? What about the new coffee shop or the science museum that brings visitors from neighbouring towns? Although everyone holds stereotypes of people, places and things they have not yet experienced, they must be insightful enough to realize that these collective descriptives do not apply to all, or even most, of the group's members. The characteristics of any group are varied and complex and stereotypes concerning them should be constantly readjusted as new information is considered and evaluated.

Organizations must overcome stereotypes as part of their operational process, in order to compete for employees and customers. Diversity management is one way of addressing this issue.

Diversity management

When companies embark on diversity management, they often meet with the barriers of existing stereotypes. Even diversity training sessions can lead to categorizing groups of people, as well as individuals, as to what and how they think, react, work and live. While this risk raises pertinent questions about confronting differences, management should not be deterred from addressing diversity issues. Education and discussion of inter- and intragroup similarities and differences are crucial to building success in a global marketplace.

Diversity training needs to be based on reliable research and conducted by capable experts. For example, addressing the research-based information that Chinese and Japanese workers, stereotypically, are more reserved and tend to avoid face-to-face confrontation is not implying that they are inferior to Western workers, but rather are different when studied as a whole.

On the stereotype continuum of a company, a Chinese employee who works in the corporate cafeteria may not be nearly as reserved as Jacques Arquette in Accounting, and the Dutch employee in the mail room may avoid confrontation much more than the Japanese employee in sales.

The above statement exhibits how pervasive stereotyping is – did you assume Jacques Arquette was French? Do only Frenchmen have "French" names? Are all accountants reserved? Of course not, but certain traits are manifested in certain groups.

It is important to note that every individual deviates in some respect from the norms of their stereotypical group. Researcher Sujova Basu in a report for the Indian Institute of Management Calcutta says, "One way to counter inaccurate gender stereotyping is by increasing gender diversity in the

Negative stereotyping

- is based on false assumptions or inaccurate information;
- assigns negative traits to individuals within a group;
- assumes all members of a group are alike.

Neutral stereotyping

- uses mediated information to help "know" a particular group;
- assigns traits that are neither good nor bad, neither inferior nor superior, to group members;
- knows each group member is inherently different from all other members.

workplace". She suggests that "improvement in stereotypes occurs if the quality of intergroup contact is increased" (Basu, 2006).

Diversity management calls on all company employees to address and understand the complex interplay of stereotypical group traits, which are neither good nor bad, and adapt and refine those traits to include the unique characteristics of each individual group member.

Think Globally, Act Locally

In the early stages of multinational marketing, a company's first step to "go global" was often to manufacture goods in greater quantities, to meet expected demand and to ship these products to distribution points around the world. When this proved to be costly and inefficient, they began to set up extensions of their home base operation in partner markets.

Employees were sent to other countries to set up plants and satellite offices. Sometimes a local manager was hired to communicate with and direct local workers, but control of the operation remained based in the home country. However, as markets across the globe began to reject the generic products being offered to them, business practices changed dramatically.

Think globally, act locally refers to the concept that, to succeed in the modern marketplace, companies must expand beyond national borders yet act responsibly by considering the wants and needs of the countries into which they move. The phrase "think globally, act locally" was first used in 1972 by Rene Dubois, advisor to the United Nations Conference on the Human Environment, who called for "a rich system of communications to achieve this sustainable interactivity" (Eblen & Eblen, 1994, p. 702).

Today's consumers tend to refuse generic goods, opting for products that fulfil their specific requirements. Companies must think about global products designed for local needs, and two-way communication plays an important role at both ends of the equation.

Companies must communicate their willingness to solicit information and attend to consumer needs. In addition, consumers must be forthcoming in communicating their wants and needs so that companies can understand and utilize this information.

To ascertain global needs effectively, new communication techniques are necessary. When Eastman Kodak created its DC20 pocket-sized digital camera in less than a year, eschewing the normal three-year development process, it was due in large part to a unique communication process in which development teams around the world worked around the clock, handing off results to others along the chain as the workday progressed (Pinto, 2004).

Thinking locally also means protecting the interests and resources of local environments. Pharmaceutical giant GlaxoSmithKline (GSK) has committed its resources to thinking globally and acting locally. In an interview in *The Warsaw* (Poland) *Voice*, Beata Golebiewska, the head of the Polish division of GSK, noted: "... GSK worldwide acts according to the strategy 'think globally, act locally'; therefore our ultimate vision is long-term investment in local economies in order to bring benefits to the country" (Loughran, 2003).

Golebiewska works to make sure that Poland benefits from GSK expansion. For example, he said, "We plan to start production of a new, innovative medicine, which will be exported to markets worldwide ... this will involve up to 100 new workplaces internally. It will also mean additional work for external customers" (Loughran, 2003).

In 2003, GSK Poland won the Supportive Employer award which highlighted its HR management standards. The parent corporation, along with 100 other companies, received the Human Rights Campaign Foundation's perfect score for corporate equality in 2006, and a Swiss company, Covalence, awarded GSK first place in its 2006 ethical ranking of the world's largest companies, among 250 multinational companies in major sectors (Covalence, 2006).

Covalence, a Geneva-based group that tracks and rates multinational companies in the area of ethical behaviour, ranks the following companies:

Best ethical score	Best ethical progress
1. GlaxoSmithKline	1. Unilever
2. Merck	2. HSBC
3. Bristol Myers Squibb	3. Alcoa
4. Unilever	4. Starbucks
5. Starbucks	5. BP
6. Toyota	6. Toyota
7. Hewlett-Packard	7. Ford
8. Alcoa	8. Intel
9. Boehringer Ingelheim	9. Citigroup
10. HSBC	10. Procter & Gamble

Changing Markets

As companies expand into new markets, communication challenges increase. Let's explore how two approaches to market expansion change the way businesses approach communication strategy:

- building traditional markets
- reaching emerging markets.

Traditional markets

Communicating with **traditional markets** does not mean using traditional communication methods. Quite the contrary, many traditional markets and loyal customers demand the use of new and innovative ways to reach them. Newspaper readers of yesterday are today's Internet news-gatherers, and radio listeners have morphed into iPod enthusiasts. Promotional efforts, including advertising, must communicate in new and unique ways to break through the daily bombardment of messages striving to entertain, inform and persuade traditional target markets.

While a continued presence in traditional media is important, the use of new forms and formats is essential to grow market share, and the ultimate media mix is a result of marketing needs assessment. Effective communication means reaching the consumer where he or she wants to be found and in a format that is acceptable and welcomed. This presents new marketing challenges and forces industry specialists to rely more on databases and outside research organizations that offer innovative and creative ways of data collecting such as ethnography.

Strategic Thinking

Among the challenges for a company operating internationally is the identification of practices that can be standardized across borders. For example, the practice of employee recognition in many Western cultures is well received but is full of potential problems in societies where group work is prized over individual accomplishment.

In recognition of a company milestone, an American pharmaceutical company gave all 44 000 employees a company watch. Each employee received the special watch on the same day in meetings around the world. Many employees wore the watch with pride. Hispanic employees, however, felt the watch was indicative of the US obsession with time. Watches given to Taiwanese were associated with death – and possible termination. Even reward programmes need to be culturally sensitive (Odell, 2005).

Emerging markets

As the world gets flatter, new markets emerge. From niche marketing to global expansion, companies are finding consumers in places they had never explored before. As we have previously discussed, an understanding of local culture is key to entering emerging markets. Whirlpool Corporation introduced a large washing machine into the

Chinese market. But the machine lost out to the "Little Prince" model manufactured by a Chinese company, Haier Group. Why?

The smaller washing machine model fitted better the Chinese lifestyle – it could handle many wash loads without consuming too much electricity. No doubt Haier Group chose the name because it directly communicated the Chinese "one child" policy and resonated with the cultural preference for male children. During the hot summer months, multiple loads of clothes could be run inexpensively, including loads of nappies for the precious Chinese child (Williamson, 2004).

Communicating with **emerging markets** will take a concentrated effort on the part of those responsible for establishing communication channels, including selecting the correct content and format. Being open minded is a first step; listening to experts also is key. To be successful in reaching these markets, companies must tap into the nuances of local cultures and acceptable practices for doing business. Public relations strategies, such as investing in a local community cause, might be one of the relevant ways an organization can build relationships with various publics.

Dig Deeper

Bob Nelson, author of *1001 Ways to Reward Employees*, says there are five ways to motivate employees even in cross-cultural settings:

1. Support employees in their work and involve them in decision-making.
2. Give employees autonomy in decision-making and authority to carry out that decision.
3. Consider flexible scheduling.
4. Support and encourage skills development and training.
5. Be accessible and open to employees' questions and concerns (Odell, 2005).

Communication Technology in the Global Marketplace

Social psychologists argue that computer-mediated communication has the power to promote or discourage social identification, conformity to group norms and stereotypical behaviour by individuals or groups.

Some theorists suggest that the Web has the power to "release" individuals from the restraints imposed by significant others and groups, enabling an individual to assume any identify he or she wants. Witness, for instance, the increase in the number of stories about individuals who establish relationships with others online on the basis of false information.

The debate is ongoing: does Web-based communication free users from the influence of others, thus facilitating open communication and promoting democracy and diversity activities? (Lea, Watt & Spears, 2000).

Let's explore some of the challenges of technology in the global arena.

Websites

Marketing goods and services online requires more than designing a colourful website! Effective **websites** must be able to accept and process orders; enable efficient and reasonable shipping; provide knowledge of import–export laws and regulations; include sensitivity to cultural practices and mores; and implement efficient payment practices.

Website managers also have to "think globally and act locally." *Transform* magazine's Michael Voelker says, "Effective global content management is a challenging process of providing localized content, maintaining corporate branding and enabling cooperation between corporate and regional staff" (Voelker, 2004). He adds that success in the globalization process means customizing a Web experience that is local to the markets it is targeting, while maintaining a controlled brand identity.

> Website design priorities involve simple solutions according to Jakob Nielsen, a leading researcher and expert on Web design (Nielsen, 2006). He asserts that business is lost when websites:
>
> - don't communicate clearly;
> - fail to provide information that users want (like telephone numbers);
> - use complicated designs with awkward navigation.

Language translations by automated services do not always communicate the proper tone and nuances of the message. Some companies translate certain content but leave other content, such as product specifications, in the language in which it was created.

For example, the Whirlpool appliance website is in English, but there are regional and local levels of personalization within its global framework. Some long-life, static information is translated into six languages, while other fast-changing content is kept only in English. Headers and links are in various languages, as are local stories. A large part of the content of the website is often locally driven because what is important to one country may be insignificant to another. Whirlpool's Gil Urban points out, "We wouldn't want an article on Whirlpool's

100th anniversary in the United States populated in the global news" (Voelker, 2004). Relevance and language (slang and jargon) are important in posting Web content.

Localizing a website also refers to the look and design of its pages. Such factors as how the average customer would view the site and the use of platforms and search engines must be considered. Chinese viewers expect to see a busy site, packed with information, while Germans expect a well-ordered page. Such colours as black, red and purple should be avoided as background colours to avoid cultural conflicts. Nevertheless, Mexican viewers like lots of bright colours and emotion-laden words (Radosevich, 1999). However, changing the look of web pages to fit a particular country or culture runs the risk of brand blur. Communicating a strong corporate image that speaks with one voice and one message, while trying to fulfil diverse viewer expectations, is a major challenge to thinking globally and acting locally.

Social media

Social media is a term applied to digital media that enable customers to control content. iPod users choose the music they want to listen to and the news they want to hear. Teenagers and young adults flock to MySpace, YouTube and other commercial sites to establish their own communication links and spaces. Every search engine

---

Dig Deeper

Developing multiple-language websites is an expensive but important issue to consider. A study of 362 non-Japanese companies listed on the Fortune Global 500 found that businesses targeting consumers were more likely to have Japanese sites than those sites targeting business-to-business customers (B-to-B).

Financial markets and retail companies were less likely to offer Japanese language sites. Only 35 % of the companies that had Japanese offices offered websites in Japanese, while Anglo firms were as likely to offer Japanese sites as non-Anglo firms.

The study findings suggest that "international marketing decisions were more strongly associated with the decision to localize websites". However, the author noted that these influences work in concert with "the degree to which firms have access to the market of interest" (Tiessen, 2004).

inquiry illustrates how consumers direct media content. Online discussion groups and Wiki sites designed for collaboration are further examples of social media. In previous sections of this book we discussed the power of blogs, and alluded to other forms of social media, but this phenomenon, also called "Web 2.0", is yet another source for tapping into customer behaviour.

David Friedman, a Seattle-based executive in the interactive business, identifies four realities of social media (Friedman, 2006):

1. New consumer perspectives are likely to emerge.
2. Social media amplify what consumers are thinking about and acting upon.
3. Social media offer marketers new product and service insights and opportunities, but they will have to dig for them.
4. Consumers are in control, and as a result organizations have less control over their brands.

Corporate communication professionals must keep vigilant guard over what is appearing in blogs. Angry customers, dissatisfied with products and services, and disgruntled employees can now publicly express their opinions online. Organizations turn to "blog monitors" to learn what the online public is saying about them. On the positive side, monitoring blogs may help organizations track weaknesses of competitors as well as detect industry rumours (Economist, 2006).

Private individuals, particularly young people, have discovered the hard way that material on personal websites may come back to haunt them if future employees discover online information detrimental to their hiring. US companies are routinely tapping into social media sites to gather more information on prospective hires.

On the other hand, companies have set up their own internal weblogs. IBM boasts 2 800 active bloggers and 20 000 registered users who share ideas across countries and continents to solve problems. IBM says the internal weblogs save travel time and money and build networks between employees and departments (Coleman, 2006).

The pervasiveness of social media has created a new industry. Syndication services offer a blog-powered newswire service in the USA that accesses more than 1 000 blog sources including blogs hosted by traditional and new media.

Communicasting

Communicasting refers to the merging of media and community for the purpose of empowerment and engagement. The concept was pioneered by Donald Mains, at Johns

Hopkins University, and has broadened to include using media to cast public views and opinions to, and through, a community of people with like interests.

Likewise, citizens are encouraged to use the new media to create their own media messages and then post them in social media outlets. At the heart of this new communication tactic is, of course, the Internet, which creates a sense of belonging and involvement within communities by uniting groups through technology.

Communities by definition are the gathering places of people from all ideologies and ethnicities, from the smallest town to booming megacities. In fact, the people who make up these communities often find they have more in common with people thousands of miles away than they do with those living next door. Chess players, for example, can connect with each other and "cast" communications about competitions, books and even play tips. They may know no one in their immediate vicinity or family with whom they could communicate about these interests, but online they find a community that allows their voices to be heard.

Groups have been empowered by this sense of belonging to help their larger communities. Mains explains that communicasting is a tool with which "anyone with an idea has a chance to send that message out to get likeminded people to join with them" (Schuster, 1996).

Knowing how to reach people is important to business communicators, and knowing where they want to be reached is even more important. Through the power of communicasting, online communities may hold a key for communicating with niche markets that are getting narrower in definition yet diluted by overexpanded boundaries.

Dig Deeper

The US government first used the term "communicasting" two decades ago to refer to "two-way television for community use" in its Institute for Research and Development in Occupational Education. It alluded to the "intent on the part of several communities to undertake projects using communicasting technology" (Cohen, 1979). The concept has since morphed into new paradigms.

Hanyang University in Korea defines communicasting as "communication + broadcasting = communicasting". The university also uses a new term, "compunicasting", defined as "computing + communication + broadcasting = compunicasting". How does this new concept relate to what is happening in social media? (Hanyang, 2006).

Datacasting

Examples of datacasting services:

- Australia – Datacasting service is using the DVB-T system in a three-year trial in Sydney, offering news, sport and weather (Channel 41), Expo home shopping (Channel 49) and federal parliamentary broadcasts.
- Malaysia – MiTV Corporation Sdn Bhd began service in 2005 to deliver multicast streaming and datacasting.
- United States – MovieBeam delivers high-definition movies to subscribers using the PBS national datacast (NDI) network.
- Finland – Digita, MTV, Nelonen, Nokia, Elisa Oyi, TeliaSonera Finland and YLE, supported by Finnish authorities, are trying out IP datacasting (IPDC) to bring TV-like content to mobile users.

Datacasting is the transmission of data as a secondary service on digital broadcasting networks (Quinion, 2000). Datacasting efficiently and effectively communicates with large audiences, using Internet protocol to distribute digital content.

This would include the transmission of transcripts, pictures or additional information concerning a televised programme to your television or computer. Additional types of material that can be datacast include biographies, statistics, music, weather reports, etc.

New technology and improved digital television quality have increased the availability of, and the demand for, more datacasting. Governmental regulation plays a role in datacasting services and charges. For example, in Australia, The Datacasting Charge (Imposition) Act of 1998 governs the service, and a transmitter license must be obtained from datacasting service providers (Jackson, 2002).

On 12 September 2001, one day after the deadly terrorist attack on New York City and the US Pentagon, the US Department of Defense asked digital broadcasting companies to create an emergency data communications system that would help with rescue and relief efforts.

Within days, vital information could be transmitted from the WNYE-TV station in one part of New York to mobile laptop computers throughout the city. Information transmitted included emergency Web content, satellite imagery and live streaming news. It is called the "digital emergency datacasting system".

WorldSpace Corp. provides datacasting service via satellite to Africa, the Middle East, Asia and Latin America. It helps Internet users receive content they could not get with sluggish connection speeds and congested bandwidth traffic and offers education, health and entertainment content.

Datacasting is a revolutionary way to communicate with global consumers who are mobile, in a hurry and ready and willing to receive messages in new and different ways. A major benefit to datacasting is that it is a flexible medium. The multidimensional information transmission may be saved to a hard drive, copied or manipulated by spreadsheet and/or photo software.

The technology is so in demand that expanded applications for providing programming services for hand-held devices, including cell phones, have been developed. News, weather and other timely information can be sent directly to consumer communication appliances as free or for-charge information.

Applied Global Communication

As established and innovative forms of communication reach, formally and informally, both traditional and emerging audiences, senders must be aware of how their messages will be interpreted.

Here are some tips for communicating with a global audience:

1. Consider the receiver's perspective. Reading your message from the viewpoint of someone who is not familiar with your country or culture is key to the understanding of your message. Edit out any idioms, adages, colloquiums, double entendres or misleading language. Think about using universal measurements, times and dates. Be sure to give complete location information, and don't assume the reader will know the village, county, province or region of the world to which you are referring.
2. Research and explore cultural differences and preferences. Humour in one country may not be so funny in another country. Colours have different meanings in different cultures. In China and Vietnam the colour red symbolizes good luck. In the US, red neckwear, worn by political candidates who want to be seen as in control, has earned the title "power tie". Avoid stereotype generalizations. Consult regional experts before composing your message, to ensure cultural sensitivity and protocol.
3. Strive to make the message clear and readable. Use simple sentence structure. Avoid difficult words, abbreviations and complex sentence structure. Explain acronyms and jargon. Use universal icons, pictures, charts, tables and graphs to put what you want to say in graphic form. Remember, a picture says a thousand words. This is particularly true when you are communicating in multiple languages.

Chapter Summary

The power of digital communications opens doors for businesses to rethink the way they communicate with customers, employees and other stakeholders. Opportunities for international commerce are available to both large and small businesses if they learn to communicate to customers on a one-to-one basis.

In a flat world it is not enough to rely solely on technological expertise. Managers need to develop a deeper appreciation of, and broader perspective for, the social and human dimensions influenced by technology.

Global business must make an effort to reach those parts of the world that are technologically poor and undeveloped. Public accessible gateways to computers and the Internet, such as public libraries, cyber cafes, information kiosks and community networks, are possible steps in the inclusion process.

Websites, social media, communicasting and datacasting are a few of the emerging technologies available to those involved in the global communication expansion. ■

Learning From Others

Dr Padmini Patwardhan spent a decade as creative consultant and copywriter for international advertising agencies in India before coming to the USA. Her scholarship on international communication is widely published. She presently teaches advertising at Winthrop University, Rock Hill, SC. Patwardhan's work on advertising, culture and change has been presented at various national conferences. She shares with us some of her research.

The Dragon and the Elephant

Q. Both China and India are ancient cultures with booming economies. Why are these markets so attractive to international businesses?

A. Both countries are attractive to international business because of their vast populations and the rise of the consumptive classes. In 2006, China had a 10% annual growth rate and India had a 6–8% annual growth rate.

Q. What makes business environments different in India and China?

A. India has a history of democracy and free media. The country's primary languages are Hindi and English, but there are also many regional languages. Its Aryan/ Dravidian roots and Hindu and Islam religious heritage influence its culture. China, on the other hand, is a communist country with state-controlled media. The primary culture is Han, although there are many other ethnic groups in China. Like India, the country is an Eastern culture, but with religious roots in Buddhism and Daoism. The primary language is Mandarin but there are multiple dialects spoken throughout the country. English is a language learned in school but is not widely spoken.

Q. How would you compare the cultural values of East and West?

A. In general terms, Eastern culture values conformity, oneness with nature, security, spiritualism and the importance of virtue and collectiveness, while Western culture values freedom, conquering nature, success, individualism and hedonism. You can see these values portrayed in TV advertising.

Q. How were values portrayed in Indian and Chinese advertising?

A. We studied 723 commercials – 515 Chinese and 208 Indian – during a one-week period in June 2005, and found interesting similarities and differences among the values emphasized. The value of modernity was more frequently portrayed than tradition in both Indian and Chinese commercials – particularly in the case of products of foreign origin. Indian commercials tended to reflect a more Western orientation, with a greater emphasis on information or utilitarian uses, while collectivism, veneration of the elderly and patriotism received more emphasis in Chinese commercials.

Q. What does this mean for companies seeking to promote their products in these countries?

A. International advertisers should be cognizant of the cultural context of advertising. Symbols, artefacts, signs and images of a particular culture must be accompanied with an understanding of the interpretive context. For example, in China, Nippon Paint (a Japanese paint company) used images of traditional Chinese dragons on pillars coated with Nippon paint in an ad. One of the dragons was shown sliding down the pillar, emphasizing the company's product claim of "a smooth paint finish". The ad offended Chinese audiences. Symbolically it presented a venerated Chinese symbol – the dragon – paying homage to a Japanese product, a sensitive reminder of both history (the Japanese aggression during World War II) and modern-day Chinese patriotism. These identified cultural value patterns – in terms of Eastern versus Western values and symbolic versus utilitarian values – indicate that international advertisers have to treat markets like China and India differently in their advertising strategies.

Dr Elnora Stuart has been writing about and teaching integrated marketing communication for over two decades. Stuart, professor of marketing at the American University in Cairo, has taught IMC courses in the USA and Spain. Her observations about media use in Egypt illustrate the need to understand local communication customs and practices. She is the co-author of *Marketing: Real People, Real Choices*. She shares her observations about the practice of communication in Egypt with us.

Land of the Sphinx

On personal communication. Computers are an important source of information and the Internet and blogs have an important role in personal communication. The government provides free dial-up numbers for the public to use.

On mass communication. Owing to the economic conditions of the country and the low media involvement of much of the population, signage plays an important role in reaching the average Egyptian. Merchandising is also influential. For example, one marketing challenge for Unilever is how to connect with the owners of very small grocery stores. Newspapers in a variety of languages, including Arabic and English, are widely available and read by the country's citizens. Moreover, among a certain portion of the population, local society magazines are particularly popular.

On advertising. Advertising is practised without the assistance of media research. Large multinational advertising companies, such as J. Walter Thompson and Satchi and Satchi, have an important presence in the country. These firms, staffed primarily by locals, practise integrated marketing communication and are setting the standard for the business of advertising.

On public relations. Public relations as a communication process is not well developed. The media release is a popular tool, and a company that wants its release printed often pays for its publication or supports a large advertising budget. However, professionals who belong to international public relations organizations are working hard to improve the profession.

Case Study – **Grapedistrict**

Wine is a traditional drink in many countries. However, with over 5 000 varieties of grape from scores of regions around the world, choosing just the right bottle can be difficult. Couple the extensive selection list with the overwhelming volume of wine facts describing blending, ageing processes and sparkling and fortified varieties, and it is easy to see how young, inexperienced wine enthusiasts may feel bewildered. But one new company is trying a new communication method to reach a mass market.

Grapedistrict has a sleek, modern storefront in Amsterdam that has discarded the oak-panelled, stodgy décor of most wine shops. It combines wide open spaces with simply arranged product to communicate a modern, unencumbered spirit to its customers.

Grapedistrict categorizes its wine by flavour, rather than by region, type or price. The wines are arranged in colour-coded sections of the store: yellow for light wines, soft gold for honey wines, purple for hearty reds, plus several levels of colours in between. To tap into personal feelings evoked by a good wine,

Grapedistrict focuses on consumers' sensual experiences. Time for a summer picnic in the park? Try a rosé wine. Having lamb for an intimate dinner? Choose a smooth wine (Springwise, 2006). Grapedistrict's innovative approach communicates a new message to consumers, one that is earning a good deal of customer loyalty.

Contrast Grapedistrict's website at www.grapedistrict.com with that of Berry Brothers & Rudd (BBR), Britain's oldest wine and spirit merchant, which has traded from the same store for more than 300 years, at www.bbbr.com. What do the websites say about the companies? What messages are being sent to consumers? What elements seem traditional? What seems modern?

Find concrete examples to support your profile of each company. Look at the colours used on the websites as well as the language. What image does each company project? Do you think it is consistent with their communication messages? BBR has initiated a new, at-home, wine-tasting experience service, for a price, that includes advice from the sommelier. It also offers online purchasing and a wine club.

Experts on how to build and protect a brand say many companies portray one image in the digital realm but another in their workplace or storefront. What do you think this statement means in relation to the two wine sellers, Grapedistrict and Berry Brothers & Rudd?" ■

Class Exercises

1. In a group of three, make a list of the stereotypical groups that each member belongs to, such as ethnicity, economic strata, profession, leisure activities (who's a skier, a gardener, a techie, an Irish soccer club fan, …?), etc. Discuss the positive and negative connotations of these stereotypical labels. Now think about a group of which you have only second-hand information, for example, farmers or snowboarders. Compile a list of attributes of this group. Ask your class members if they have any first-hand information of this group and see how your image compares with this new information. Was your stereotype accurate or inaccurate? Discuss how stereotypes limit or enhance understanding.

2. Discuss the effects of social media on conventional media. How are conventional media using social media to reach segments of the population that they previously didn't reach? How is this changing the face of conventional journalism?

3. Do your own research on how companies headquartered in your country, but operating in the global marketplace, use their websites to reach a diverse audience. In your analysis, consider such factors as use of multiple languages, photographs, colours and symbols. Develop a rating scale and share your results with your classmates.

Action Plan

Continuing to focus on the beverage industry, let's look at a new product, co created by Heineken and Groupe SEB (Krup, Rowneta, Moulinex and Tefal brands).

The BeerTender is an at-home draught beer system first tested in Switzerland. This refrigerated unit holds special kegs of Heineken beer fresh for three weeks (Springwise, 2004). Go first to the Heineken website at `http://cheers.heineken.ch/`. What message is Heineken sending to its targeted market? Look at its use of colour, language, images and sense of humour.

Now go to the BeerTender website at `http://www.beertender.ch/beertender/index-en.asp`. Look again at colour, language, images and humour. Are the messages the same or different? Is Heineken targeting different age groups or economic levels? Click on some of the links, finishing with the Beer Club link. Does the page that this link takes you to seem incongruent with the BeerTender homepage? Why or why not?

Go to the Stella Artois website at `http://www.stellaartois.com` (Stella Artois, 2006). What does this website "say" through colour, language, images and tone?

Websites

An informative article on stereotyping, "The malleability of automatic stereotypes and prejudice" by Irene V. Blair can be found at `www.apa.org/ppo/blair.pdf` (Blair, 2002).

"Inaccurate gender stereotypes: research implications from a contact hypothesis perspective" by Sujova Basu for the Indian Institute of Management Calcutta explains why female managers are treated differently to male managers and can be accessed from `http://www.iimcal.ac.in/res/upd%5CWPS%20581.pdf` (Basu, 2006).

For a more extensive discussion of datacasting, see "What is datacasting?" at `www.lawfont.com/2006/03/07/what-is-datacasting/` (LawFont, 2006a) and "LawFont.com, an analysis of law, technology, economics and policy" at `http://www.lawfont.com/2006/03/07/what-is-datacasting/#more-238` (LawFont, 2006b). Skystream provides an insight into the growing datacasting field. You can search the term at `http://www.skystream.com/corp/cussuccess _ eas.pdf` (SkyStream, 2002).

References

Blair, I. (2002) "The malleability of automatic stereotypes and prejudice". *Personality and Social Psychology Review*, **6**(3): 242–261. Available from: www.apa.org/ppo/blair.pdf [Accessed 25 April 2006].

Basu, S. (2006) "Inaccurate gender stereotypes: research implications from a contact hypothesis perspective". Working paper, January 2006. Indian Institute of Management Calcutta. Available from: http://www.iimcal.ac.in/res/upd%5CWPS%20581.pdf [Accessed 25 April 2006].

Cohen, L. (1979) Abstract of annual report No. 8, Institute for Research and Development in Occupational Education, 1 July 1978–30 September 1979. Available from: http://eric.ed.gov/ERICWebPortal/Home.portal?-nfpb=true&_pageLabel=RecordDetails&ERICExt [Accessed 28 April 2006].

Coleman, A. (2006) "Analysis: information industry pushes Web 2.0". BBC Worldwide Publishing, 18 May 2006. Available from: http://0-web.lexis-nexis.com.library.winthrop.edu/universe/document?_m=5568ac5a0fel [Accessed 24 June 2006].

Covalence (2006) "Covalence ethical ranking 2005" Available from: http://www.covalence.ch [Accessed 25 April 2006].

Eblen, R.A. & Eblen, W. R. (1994) *The Encyclopedia of the Environment*. Boston, Houghton Mifflin Company.

Economist (2006) "The blog in the corporate machine; corporate reputations". *The Economist*, 11 February 2006. Available from: http://0-web.lexis-nexis.com.library.winthrop.edu/universe/document?_m=flaed400ea92d [Accessed 24 June 2006].

Friedman, D. (2006) "Social media: out of control, on target, and changing the rules". *Chief Marketer*. Available from: http://chiefmarketer.com/social_media-05212006 [Accessed 23 May 2006].

Friedman, T. (2005) *The World Is Flat*. New York, Farrar, Straus & Giroux.

Hanyang (2006) "Digital convergence". Hangyang University. Available from: http://gsim.hanyang.ac.kr/about/05-chang.PDF++communicasting+compunication&hl=en&gl=us&ct=clnk&cd=1 [Accessed 28 April 2006].

Jackson, K. (2002) "Digital television and datacasting". Available from: http://www.apa.gov.au/library/inguide/sp/digdata.htm [18 April 2006].

LawFont (2006a) "What is datacasting?" Available from: www.lawfont.com/2006/03/07/what-is-datacasting/ [Accessed 26 April 2006].

Lawfont (2006b) "LawFont.com, an analysis of law, technology, economics and policy". Available from: http://www.lawfont.com/2006/03/07/what-is-datacasting/#more-238 [Accessed 8 November, 2006].

Lea, M., Watt, S. & Spears, R. (2000) "How social is the Internet? A social psychological analysis of computer-mediated group interactions". *Virtual Society? Get Real? Conference*, Ashridge House, Herfordshire, UK, 4–5 May 2000. Available from: http://64.233.16729.104/search?q=cache:LWBVeiDly_kJ:virtualsociety.sbs.ox.ac.uk/events/GetREal.htm+% [Accessed 12 June 2006].

Loughran, M. (2003) "Think globally, act locally". *The Warsaw Voice*, 16 October 2003. Available from: http://www.warsawvoice.pl/printArticle.php?a=3827 [Accessed 25 April 2006].

Nielsen, J. (2006) "Growing a business website: fix the basics first". Jakob Nielsen's Alertbox, 20 March 2006. Available from: http://www.useit.com/alertbox/design_priorities.html [Accessed 20 March 2006].

Odell (2005) "Motivating employees on a global scale: author Bob Nelson". *Promo P & I*, 5 November 2005. Available from: http://promomagazine.com/incentives/motivating_empolyees_110905/ [Accessed 8 November 2006].

Pinto, J. (2004) "Think globally, act locally". *Automation World*, February 2004. Available from: http://www.jimpinto.com/writings/global1.html [Assessed 25 April 2006].

Quinion, M. (2000) "Worldwide words: datacasting". Available from: http://www.Worldwidewords.org/turnsofphrase/tp-dat3.htm [Accessed 18 April 2006].

Radosevich, L. (1999) "Going global overnight". *Infoworld*, **21**(16). Available from: http://o-find.galegroup.com.library.winthrop.edu/itx/retrieve.do?subjectParam=Locale%252... [Accessed 8 June 2006]

Schuster, E. (1996) "Election'96 produces Action: Vote advertisements". Newsletter, 1 November 1996. Available from: http://www.jhu.edu/~newslett/11-01-96/Features/Election_'96_produces_Action._Vote_advertisements.html [Accessed 28 April 2006].

SkyStream (2002) "Digital emergency datacasting system case study". SkyStream Networks, Inc. Available from: http://www.skystream.com/corp/cussuccess_eas.pdf [Accessed 26 April 2006].

Springwise (2004) "Stella Artois takes on the BeerTender/Home sweet Heineken". Available from: www.springwise.com [Accessed 26 April 2006].

Springwise (2006) "Simplicity and selling wine". Available from: www.springwise.com [Accessed 26 April 2006].

Stella Artois (2006) http://www.stellaartois.com [Accessed 25 April 2006].

Tiessen, J. H. (2004) "Multinational multilingualism on the Internet: the use of Japanese on corporate websites". *Canadian Journal of Administrative Sciences*, June: 1–21. Available from: http://findarticles.com/p/articles/mi_qa3981/is_200406/ai_n9446381 [Assessed 29 June 2006].

Voelker, M. (2004) "Web content management: think globally, act locally". *Transform*, May 2004. Available from: http://transformmag.com/showArticle.jhtml?articleID=19200187 [Accessed 25 April 2006].

Williamson, P. & Zeng, M. (2004) "Strategies for competing in a changed China". *Sloan Management Review*, **45**(4): 85–92. Available from: http:0-web103.epnet.com.library.winthrop.edu:80/citation.asp?tb?tb=...B1+%2Dinternatioal++businesss+st%580+%2Dweb+6557&cf=1&fn=11&rn=17 [Accessed 5 June 2006]

CHAPTER 12

Communication in the New Management World

Executive Summary

Communication in the new management world faces extensive challenges as leaders will be expected to promote and encourage strategic communications at all levels. Leaders must strive for greater visibility by connecting with employees in the workplace through one-on-one conversations, group meetings, email and other appropriate means of communication to ensure their message is understood.

They will also need to connect with external publics by developing positions on key points of community concern and addressing these issues in public forums
Through a public presence, leaders gain insight into the concerns of employees and the perceptions customers, stockholders and other external stakeholders have of the company.

Effective leadership must build management teams responsible for ensuring that organizational goals are accomplished and adapt their leadership styles to individual team members to motivate them as well as to prompt them to do their best

Today's leaders must be effective mediators and negotiators
Both roles require expert communication skills that address specific audiences and their particular needs. And most of all they have to know when to "listen" and learn from employees.

Accountability is at the crux of ethical decision-making, and transparency ensures that company actions are above board and available for public inspection

Pressures from investors and competitors will force leaders to measure their communication effectiveness, foster learning at all levels, encourage collaboration, communicate change through various channels, advocate inclusiveness and support creativity, innovation and skill building. ■

Communication in the New Management World

One point of view gives a one-dimensional world.
Liz Murray, homeless teen who won a scholarship to
Harvard University

Introduction to Communication Challenges

Access to marketplace information and consumer research was once restricted to only large, elite organizations, but relatively inexpensive technology and software makes such information accessible to small businesses in remote areas of the world.

Today's employees are more educated, sophisticated and technically skilled than in the past, but face competition from the growing number of educated professionals in emerging economies. In addition, consumers have access to greater choices and are more willing to seek out and accept goods from organizations located around the world.

The danger of information overload requires employees and executives to draw critical distinctions between what information they will process and what information they will ignore.

Corporate leadership continues to be under fire. Scandals involving leadership from TYCO, WorldCom and Enron, as well as other international companies, have placed CEOs under increased public scrutiny. As James Houghton, CEO of Corning, noted: "30 % of my day is devoted to creating the appropriate organizational environment and value system which stimulates the morale and productivity of the workforce and leadership" (Lucansky, Burke & Potapchuk, 2006).

Consider this example. A men's clothing manufacturer faces a financial and human resource dilemma. It is losing market share and can no longer compete by selling its products at the same price points as overseas manufacturers. Company executives struggle to chart the best long-range goals for the organization. Should they attempt to lower employee wages, lay off some employees and further mechanize its manufacturing operation or move all manufacturing operations overseas?

The decisions the company ultimately makes will be based on many factors, and explaining the company's position to employees, customers, opinion leaders, stockholders and suppliers will require serious consideration.

Obviously, face-to-face communication will be essential to garner employee support and community acceptance. Other communication strategies such as helping people cope with economic uncertainty while simultaneously working to build community trust will require diplomacy, altruism and skill. If the leadership has a history of credibility and is trusted to make ethical business decisions, then its communication will be more successful.

It is clear that, at the core of these business challenges, for all types of organization (large or small, local or global, service oriented or manufacturing), is the need for effective communication. As research indicates, effective communication significantly correlates with profitability.

This chapter builds upon previous discussion of the characteristics of leadership, highlighting some of the latest research and its practical application to the role of leaders as communicators.

Strategic Communication Management

Executives are the "face of the organization" and must represent the company through effective and strategic internal and external communication. Regardless of the size of the communication department, company principals are the foundation behind any communication effort, from addressing employees and other internal audiences to executing external programmes such as advertising or community outreach.

Trust and credibility are integral to relationship building and communication strategy development. How can leadership build long-term relationships that foster effective communication?

Visibility of the executive

Global markets make communication and executive visibility challenging. Leaders responsible for companies in geographically dispersed locations find it difficult physically to connect with employees, a phenomenon that Pringle and Gordon call "corporate distancing" (Pringle & Gordon, 2003).

Strategic Thinking

How does the size of an operation affect its communication effectiveness?

Robin Dunbar, a British anthropologist, studied the relationship of the brain to social arrangements and concluded that 150 individuals is the maximum number with whom an individual can carry on a social relationship. Beyond that number, the ability to relate to those individuals diminishes.

In his bestseller *The Tipping Point*, Malcolm Gladwell says the power of the number 150 continues to surface in the history of organizations. As an example, he cites the Hutterites, self-sufficient agricultural communities in Europe and the USA, who require the formation of a new colony when the population of that colony exceeds 150 people (Gladwell, 2000).

Some successful industries follow the same pattern. Gore Associates, a privately held company in Newark, DE, manufactures Gore-Tex fabric and other industrial products. Company leaders have a policy that no operation can have more than 150 employees. Once that level is reached, employees are reorganized into a new facility – even if this means moving to a plant next door. Gore's leadership discovered that, beyond 150 employees, efficiency decreases and innovation suffers.

Think about this number. How could you apply the rule of 150 to your education, work or social situation? Have you ever been in a class of 200–300 students? How did you feel? How did the size of the class affect your connection with the professor?

Nigel Nicholson, London Business School, notes that 40 % of the world's workforce is employed in companies with less than 150 people, but many international companies such as the Forbes 500 have an average of 373 000 people (Pringle & Gordon, 2003, p. 110).

The ability to communicate ideas to others within an organization depends on how the receivers of the message perceive the senders. Connecting to others, whether in the elevator, on the assembly line floor, during meetings, in the lunchroom or while attending employee recognition programmes, allows employees access to decision-makers.

When two-way communication occurs, employees and executives build relationships that work towards achieving common goals.

As communication scholar Philip Clampitt says, face-to-face communication is a rich channel: "No other channel permits communicators to send and receive messages of such an interpersonal nature, on the one hand, and objective complexity on the other. Lean media such as emails and web pages are effective tools for sharing *information* but they are poorly suited for sharing *knowledge*" (Clampitt, 2005, p. 107).

However, corporate executives often find it time consuming to meet with employees in the field. Pringle and Gordon (2003) offer this suggestion: organize and implement a mandatory cycle of annual experiences for company executives that would require them to work on the factory floor, in store retail establishments or in the service delivery process.

For example, Family Dollar, a US retail discount chain, requires company executives to work in its retail stores during the holiday season. This gives company leadership access to employees and customers.

Being visible to an organization's external audiences does not require running for public office or delivering speeches. It means developing a position on a few key points of community concern and speaking out on these issues in minimal risk situations such as interviews, speeches and in media interviews.

> Successful executives reflect the essence of their companies both internally and externally.
>
> Rebecca Fannin, writing for *Chief Executive*, explains how Steve Jobs of Apple Computers earned his first-place ranking among top US CEO brand leaders. She quotes one respondent to the annual CEO survey: "… in the notably bland consumer electronics market … he (Steve Jobs) is the brand" (Fannin, 2005).

Executives might designate others to speak for them in public meetings or use publications, company-sanctioned blogs or institutional advertising to reinforce the company's position. The point to remember is that position statements should be restricted to a few succinct and relevant points communicated repeatedly in various places by a number of people.

The bottom line to this discussion is that executives must be visible, accessible and, most importantly, available to spend quality time in two-way communication. The long-range effects of connecting with others will influence how they are perceived and how their opinions are accepted.

The executive as team builder

A primary function of leadership is to build management **teams** responsible for ensuring that the goals of an organization are accomplished. Corporate culture may dictate how teams are used in an organization; however, the use of cross-cultural or cross-functional teams is the norm in successful businesses today.

In the classroom setting, students are no doubt challenged by being required to participate in teamwork. The litany of problems of working in teams on the collegiate level differs little from those encountered in the workplace.

Teams are often selected by instructors or by students without knowing the talents and personalities of the membership. In other words, students are assigned to a team with little orientation or skill building. The choice of leadership is generally painful – sometimes a member of the group willingly agrees to lead the team while at other times the leader is selected by default. The same arrangement frequently occurs in the workplace.

Consider this example. Boeing stepped up its commitment to teamwork and partnering when it announced that its 777 jetliner would be produced by more than 200 teams from engineering, finance and production. Team meetings often included suppliers and possible customers such as United Airlines, British Airways and Japan Airlines. Boeing teams engaged in intensive dialogues with customers concerning options and equipment. Aerospace companies in Europe, Russia, Japan and other countries provided parts for the 777 (Boeing, 2006).

Teamwork did not end once the aircraft was completed. A Boeing-led team of engineers, technicians and research and development personnel are still working on making the jet quieter. Today, the 777 enjoys better than a 99 % dispatch reliability rate, the highest in the industry (Burnett, 2006).

As discussed in Chapter 10, the leadership style of the leader is fundamental to the effectiveness of a team. Good leaders adapt their style to any situation. Authoritarian or arrow-style leaders may be more effective in groups where members are reluctant participants or when only one member understands what is to be accomplished. But the authoritarian leader is unlikely to be popular or to spark creativity within the group.

If group members are committed to their assignment and all agree to share equally in the work, the democratic leader or circuit model will more likely be effective. On the other hand, if team members are highly motivated and share the knowledge and expertise to complete the task, a laissez-faire or dance approach, where leadership delegates the work to members of the group and allows them to complete the task with limited leadership or simply guided leadership, might be appropriate.

Trust is at the core of team building. Two types of trust have been identified: ethical trust and practical trust:

- **Ethical trust** centres on integrity, honesty and fair play.
- **Practical trust** develops because of competency and successful behaviour over time.

Leaders communicate these values through such activities as greeting co-workers, listening to other's opinions, using open body language during face-to-face

Dig Deeper

Here are some tips to encourage group participation:

- Remind team members of the purpose of your group. What is the common goal?
- Ask for people's opinions. Make sure all members of the team are given an opportunity to voice their opinions.
- Connect the task at hand to the talents or responsibilities of those in the group. For example, a leader might ask: "Mary, you have been talking to customers recently, what are they saying?" or "John, you are our Web expert, how can we use this vehicle to get more customer feedback?"
- Synthesize comments from group members, and then ask for feedback.
- Share information with group members. Report feedback from management: "I reported on our plan at the last managers' meeting and received an excellent response".
- Communicate the group's efforts to others in the organization.
- Use the opportunity to gather information that might be helpful in other forums.

Adapted from Mai and Akerson (2003, p. 151.)

conversation or employing positive language in emails. Everything leaders say and do, as well as how they say or do it, will contribute to the level of trust others have in them and their action plans.

The executive as mediator

Effective communication in times of conflict is crucial to maintaining the integrity of the workplace. Conflict derives not only from problems in interpersonal relationships but in institutional structures, systems and processes.

Communication is a key component in determining how to reach those involved in a conflict on a mutually comfortable level. **Mediation** involves a host of delicate issues such as cultural expertise, participant satisfaction, fairness, motivation, listening and other management skills. There are, of course, effectiveness and efficiency concerns: how can the matter be resolved in the most productive and long-lasting way while at the same time making the best use of company time, effort and resources.

The executive as negotiator

Leaders must constantly negotiate from both inside and outside an organization, from chairing a committee or managing a new division to dealing with suppliers or board members. Learning how to communicate appropriately in various situations helps garner necessary support and facilitate resolution.

In the **negotiation** process, leaders must consider what is of most value to the organization and then capture that value for themselves and for the company; others will follow when they believe that it is in their best interest to do so (Watkins, 2002). For leadership, understanding the motivation of followers is the primary step in the negotiation process. When followers' needs are understood, leaders are better able to shape the appropriate messages to achieve goals.

Suppose one of the members of a team represents the organization's financial operations. If the team wants a buy-in from that individual and the interests that he/she represents, they must address how a particular action will impact upon the bottom line. Relationships in any organization need to be cultivated and nurtured.

In the role of negotiator, leaders must work to build strong coalitions among individuals or groups who have separate interests. Finding common values or goals will help that building process.

Strategic Thinking

In the late 1980s, Coca-Cola's division chairman for Eastern Europe, E. Neville Isdell, proposed a restructuring of its bottlers into a single entity in Germany. Isdell got approval from the company headquarters to negotiate an equity buy-out from the 116 bottlers affected.

On the first day of the negotiation process, a deal was sealed with a bottler. However, later that evening, Isdell and his team were told by corporate headquarters to "take this offer off the table". Bottlers all over the world were calling the company to express concern about what the equity buy-out would mean for them.

Isdell, now chairman and CEO of Coca-Cola, said he had failed to anticipate the multiple constituencies that needed to be addressed before he began the negotiation process: "The lesson I learned is you have to look outside the narrow view you have of where the areas of influence exist. Be sure that you have them all covered" (McGregor, 2006, p. 50).

Effective negotiations are based on trust; in a negotiation situation, it is beneficial if followers believe the following (Salacuse, 2006):

- the leader is capable of performing the function;
- the leader will seek input from members of the group;
- the leader will keep commitments;
- the leader will appreciate the contributions of others.

In the negotiation process, leaders need to choose the best medium to communicate their message. Rich media will generally be the most effective; a phone call or a personal visit to an opinion leader will be more persuasive than an email message which can be ignored or deleted.

The executive as educator

Effective leaders understand their roles as collaborators and educators and seek opportunities to communicate with their employees about the goals of the company and the roles employees have in achieving these goals. They insist on the use of applied research to study the attitudes and opinions of employees on a variety of topics, and create platforms for feedback for those voices seldom heard in the organization. Leaders recognize that new ideas and practices should come from those most knowledgeable about a company, its products and its stakeholders – its employees.

Leaders as teachers encourage the development of mentoring or support programmes for the development of new leaders within the company, particularly among those sectors of the population underrepresented in the organization.

Leaders as **educators** encourage and support training and development while insisting on accountability and the sharing of new ideas and practices. For example, a small business may be able to budget only one outside training experience per employee per year, but requires that employee to share the ideas learned from the training activities in open forums and employee meetings.

The executive as facilitator of creativity and innovation

Creativity and innovation go hand–in–hand. Creative ideas with investment potential may come from employees within an organization or entrepreneurs outside the organization. Leaders open to innovation strive to create a workplace climate where new ideas are encouraged and rewarded.

For example, Rite-Solutions, a software company that builds advanced and highly classified command and control systems for the US Navy, encourages innovation from all its employees. Employees develop proposals for new businesses or efficiency improvements. These proposals become stocks traded on the company's internal market, Mutual Fun. Each employee receives $10 000 in "opinion money" to invest in the stock offering, or they may volunteer to work on the project development. Volunteers share in the proceeds of the project if it becomes a product or delivers savings. Mutual Fun encourages creativity and innovation in the organization and has led to new business opportunities for Rite-Solutions (Taylor, 2006).

Organizations such as Rite-Solutions will survive competition from the creative talent now emerging in developing nations. Traditional professions such as engineers, programmers, physicians, etc., whose creative ideas, skills and expertise shaped the economies of North America and much of the European Union in the past, may no longer be competitive in the workplace of the future. But encouraging creativity and innovation may be the distinguishing factor that separates those who succeed in the new world order from those who fail (Devine, 2006).

Accountability and Decision-making

Accountability means owning up to one's actions in activities involving both internal and external publics. Perhaps because of recent corporate scandals, today's managers are taking more pains to act ethically and make sounder judgements. But being accountable is not enough. Executives must ensure that honest, positive information concerning an organization's activities is communicated to important stakeholders.

One of the reasons why communications concerning ethics and company reputation do not receive the serious allocation of funds to operate effectively is that these intangible concepts cannot be explicitly accounted for in the bottom line. Professor Paul Argenti of Dartmouth's Tuck School of Business believes corporate intangibles are not valued enough, but, he says, "… some 80 % of the value of a corporation is based on intangibles". He urges executives to find ways to quantify the impact of effective corporate communication in the realm of ethics and sound business practices, just as they do for other profit-reflecting variables (Prince, 2005).

The new global definition of **accountability** is communicating to others that you have been responsible in everyday tasks, both large and small.

Internally, executives address accountability issues on many levels. For example, management might ban employees from receiving gifts over a certain minimal amount from suppliers in an effort to support their fairness ethic, or executives may be asked to identify their outside activities such as consulting with firms that may be bidding on upcoming projects to make sure the company is seen as free of hidden agendas.

Personnel accountability is addressed when human resources managers hold face-to-face meetings with new employees to outline what is expected of them and the consequences of non-compliance.

In whatever form or format, executives today are expected not only to document their actions and adhere to accountability requirements but also to ensure they are communicating these actions to others in the company.

Today's managers must also be accountable to the public. **Transparency** is a new buzz word that means everything done in the company's name is above board and, when appropriate, open for public inspection. It has become a means of garnering public trust, a vital component of doing business in an increasingly scrutinized world.

A large community foundation that manages millions of dollars from donors and then distributes these funds to various non-profit service organizations reinforces its commitment to transparency by using glass partitions between offices.

Jessica Bishop, director of Donor Services, explains: "When donors tour our offices, we want them to see concrete proof that we mean it when we say we can be trusted with their money. We want everything we do to be open and fully visible. This way they trust that we will objectively direct their monies to worthy organizations. No one can hide here; no one can build their own private empire" (Bishop, 2006, personal interview).

Investors, in particular, are more eager to hold company executives accountable not only for sound business practices but also for facilitating the rise in stock value. They know effective communication with various publics reflects positively on their returns, while negative communication may send stock prices plummeting.

Accountability in business requires ethical **decision-making**. A recent study by Opinion Research Corp. (OPC) found that "Less than half of all retail investors have confidence that CEOs of public companies are engaged in ethical business practices". The move to more accountability has been noted, but communication experts say the word has to get out to the public. Jeffrey T. Resnick, in charge of OPC's corporate management division, points out, "There is a trust chasm between where executives probably believe they are and where the public believes they are" (Prince, 2005).

Communicating accountability to the public takes many forms, from posting mission statements online to using recycled water for manufacturing. All communication that tells the public a company is acting responsibly will add to the accountability factor.

Argenti calls for executives to "keep corporate communications on the cutting edge." He explains that doing this will help companies compete in a new business world. He says, "Since few managers recognize the importance of the communication function, they are reluctant to hire the quality staff necessary to succeed in today's environment. As a result, they tend to keep the communication people 'out of the loop'" (Argenti, 1998, p. 13).

Let's examine how business people work within the structure of their company to facilitate existing communication efforts, and then examine what they can initiate on their own to take on more executive responsibility and power.

Leading the Way for Effective Communication for the Future

An effective leader must look ahead, knowing that what he or she does today will impact upon others tomorrow. Communication takes many forms and, while ideally it is centralized, generally it is carried out in several departments by individuals with varying degrees of expertise. Most of their efforts are aimed at the present or the immediate future: what ads will be placed, what sales will be run, what letters need to be sent or what reports are due?

> Websites must communicate what consumers want and need to know, whether they are customers, financial investors, employees or recruits.
>
> "If you can identify a very clear consumer proposition for your site and have a clear understanding of the demographics and webographics of those consumers, then a site promotion strategy will logically flow from this" (Pincott, 1999).

Measuring communication effectiveness

Business students are accustomed to thinking about return on investment (ROI). The insistence upon a measurement process should extend to employees, suppliers and other stakeholders across the board. Measuring the effects of all integrated business communication efforts, from marketing and advertising to employee communication and community relations, is equally necessary.

Customer-centred marketing communication may be measured in several ways. Databases appropriately integrated across an organizational structure assist in determining with whom to build strong relationships as well as the effectiveness of promotional activities on customer activity, particularly sales.

Traditionally, marketing communication efforts have used "soft" measurement techniques, primarily qualitative research techniques such as focus groups, interviews and ethnographic studies, to measure such factors as customer awareness, motivation, expectations, preferences, perceptions and attitudes and values. "Hard" measurement tools will help communication professionals within an organization generate data to measure product trials, purchases and repurchase behaviour, as well as other marketing efforts.

For example, the 3M Corporation developed a four-step process to determine the effectiveness of its marketing communication efforts:

1. Data from sales, marketing communication and point-of-sale are gathered.
2. Data are analysed using a variety of statistical techniques including regression and analysis of variance. This analysis allows patterns and trends in the sales process to be assessed.
3. A review of marketing communication spending and allocation patterns and trends over a given period of time is undertaken. Using similar statistical tools, such questions as why was advertising increased during this period or why did promotions receive more money than public relations are addressed.
4. The results are analysed with consideration for time lags in communication effects factored into the model (Jung & Robinson, 2005).

Reading, researching, learning

A wealth of information in books, on CDs, on websites and through organizations focuses on improving business leadership. Keeping track of new ideas and new concepts in business management is the responsibility of every present or future leader.

Appreciative inquiry (AI) is a new concept. This burgeoning field has expanded into the business world and attempts to "give life" to organizations by concentrating on what the company is doing right, rather than, as some consultants suggest, what is going wrong.

AI attempts to build constructive and collaborative relationships that lead to positive business practices (Cox, 2004). This new concept is being used to help organizations forge meaningful connections among employees.

An online search of the term "appreciative inquiry" yields over 1.3 million hits. The movement is the subject of numerous books such as Cooperrider's *Appreciative Inquiry: A positive revolution in change* and Elliot's *Locating the Energy for Change: An Introduction to Appreciative Inquiry.* Newsletters (www.aipractitioner.com), informative journals (*Organisations & People* at www.amed.org.uk) and multiple websites (http://ai.cwru.edu; www.appreciative-inquiry.org; www. taosinstiture.net; and http://www.gervasebushe.ca) focus on this social construction.

Sound decision-making

Most of the content of this book has been devoted to giving historically based and up-to-the-minute information on factors governing effective communication. Making good decisions, armed with this information, is the communicator's task. Using the information learned and putting theories into practice will help executives formulate and implement good decisions.

Opening new communication channels

Executives with an understanding of communication look for new and innovative ways to facilitate effective messaging, from implementing more relevant reporting to holding team-building sessions.

Mike Eskew of UPS, a top CEO in *Chief Executive*'s survey of brand leaders, recently expanded his company's communication arm. He created a new senior vice-president for communications and brand management position and included this executive on his management committee. These bold moves are being taken in many successful companies across the globe.

Communicating changes to others

Preparing others for inevitable change is central to ensuring satisfied workers. Developing a communication plan that will address the concerns of those involved in any significant changes in the company is crucial before, during and after the event. We will talk more about change in the final chapter of this book.

Dig Deeper

More and more companies are faced with succession planning. According to Tom Neff, co-author of *You're in Charge – Now What?*, a CEO today can expect to replace the company's CFO twice, the CIO twice and the CMO three times during his tenure with a company (Curry, 2005). But all levels of executives are keepers of important knowledge, and maintaining detailed reports of activity can mean the difference between crippling a business and facilitating an easy transition. Leaders must insist that all key executives document their business functions and industry knowledge in a written format. This is a vital component of a working communication plan.

In "Getting Your Bench Right", Sheree R. Curry for *CEO Magazine* points out this problem: "… much of the debate over formal succession planning remains focused on grooming a successor for the CEO's position, and far less so on planning for the exit of his or her direct reports, let alone deeper into the organization" (Curry, 2005).

Human capital management experts say lack of transition plans erodes employee confidence in management and results in low morale and decreased productivity. A British study found that immediately naming a successor to a vacated position can mitigate damage from an unexpected turnover in top-level positions.

Communicating inclusive strategies

In the past, high-level executives who sat in ivory towers with little input from the rank and file formulated corporate strategy. Information was communicated to the rest of the organization in a "cascade" method, "which was also flawed because it was too slow; the message was diluted and distorted as it moved down the pyramid; it was a passive 'tell or sell' process resulting in low levels of commitment; and there was no feedback loop to provide for organizational learning" (Cox, 2004).

Today, strategy is often formulated by a more representative cross-section of company executives with varying agendas and a wide range of concerns. Including more voices in strategic planning takes into account not only the various needs of a diverse workplace but also the concerns of other important stakeholders, such as suppliers, customers and the community.

Inclusive strategy requires "continuous organizational learning and the open sharing of knowledge" (Cox, 2004). It necessitates giving as many people as possible a

Strategic Thinking

Have you thought about what kind of executive you want to be? Leadership comes in many forms and embraces many styles. What talents do you have that you can develop into top-notch leadership skills?

Burson-Marsteller, a worldwide public relations and public affairs firm, conducted its fifth annual CEO and corporate reputation study of 600 business influentials in 65 countries. Here are the top 15 CEOs with the best corporate reputation in the world in 2005 (Norton, 2005):

Bill Gates	Microsoft	USA
Steve Jobs	Apple	USA
Warren Buffett	Berkshire Hathaway	USA
Michael Dell	Dell	USA
Richard Branson	Virgin Group	UK
John Browne	BP	UK
Carlos Ghosn	Nissan Motor & Renault	Japan/France
N. R. Narayana Murthy	Infosys Technologies	India
Jeffrey Immelt	General Electric	USA
Rupert Murdoch	News Corporation	Australia
John Bond	HSBC Holdings	UK
John Chambers	Cisco Systems	USA
Jorma Ollila	Nokia	Finland
Terry Leahy	Tesco	UK
Lakshmi Mittal	Mittal Steel	The Netherlands

part in the decision-making process. For this to happen, strong communication plans must be in place and must function effectively.

Inclusive strategies also require reaching out to, and including, diverse groups of people in daily business practices. Discrimination on the basis of gender, age, religion or ethnicity ultimately hurts organizations in the global arena.

Dig Deeper

Here are some words of wisdom from global CEOs. Find a quote by someone you admire in the business world and add it to this list. You might want to tape it to your bathroom mirror so you can reflect on the inspiration every day.

Ray Vallee, Avnet: "We place great value on human capital. When you have the right person in the right job it not only makes for their own personal success, but the company's as well".

Dorothy Cann Hamilton, The French Culinary Institute: "To be a good leader you must surround yourself with good people. Believe in them. Let them show you what they can do".

Joseph Deitch, Commonwealth Financial Network: "For the conscious leader, every act is an opportunity to learn – and improve. We try to facilitate the sharing of expertise as much as possible".

Niranjan Ajwani, Ajwani Group: "A leader should not only harmonize his different needs but also be an enabling and empowering factor in harmonizing the different needs of his teammates so that they enjoy work, play, love, relationships and spiritual growth so very essential for a sustained joy".

Strategic partnering

Cooperation between businesses is not new, but it has consisted primarily of complementary efforts (companies working on different aspects of a project), as opposed to the trend today of collaboration. Some organizations, such as the Airbus consortium of European aircraft manufacturers, already engage in the process of strategic partnering. Some companies have found that joining forces, even with competitors, helps achieve common goals.

Other examples of the collaboration between competing companies is the work by General Motors and DaimlerChrysler on a hybrid engine powertrain and Ford and Nissan's use of Toyota technology in their 2006 hybrid cars. This collaboration between car manufacturers is estimated to save billions of dollars.

Concerned companies are "rethinking the compete/collaborate ratio" as a way to "avoid redundant expenditures and capitalize on economics of scale and shared expertise", says Adrian Slywotsky, author of *How to Grow When Markets Don't* (Slywotsky, 2005).

Any collaboration requires communicating clear and understandable messages to the many stakeholders involved. Communication skills are at the core of making these collaborative efforts work as managers shift from a competitive mindset to a collaborative mindset. Slywotzky says, "Given the harsh realities of business today, managers should move toward a more productive balance between competing and collaborating – before it's too late" (Slywotzky, 2005).

Communicating strategically is a real challenge. Steven S. Little, writing for ASAE & The Center for Association Leadership, says communicators need to "stop focusing on the process of creating pretty language that means nothing" and begin to take a real, strategic look at how they can convey their core messages to constituencies (Little, 2005).

Improving Two-way Communication

Two-way communication is imperative in today's business culture. Information gaps are dangerous for organizations as they disrupt morale, productivity and, ultimately, a company's competitive edge (Dulye, 1992, p. 210).

Consumers want to send their comments and complaints via email to customer service departments, media need to talk to executives about ongoing stories and employees like to feel their feedback is important.

Because of the speed of change both within and outside an organization and the sheer quantity of information to be disseminated, communication lines cannot depend solely on the one-way information flow of employee newsletters, annual reports or company press releases. These channels are geared to mass audiences, carry general information and are limited to fixed transmission schedules.

Employees, action groups and financial analysts want to know not just what is happening but how it will impact them, the community and investors, on a frequent, and often immediate, basis. This means choosing rich, two-way media that are fast, interactive, personalized, accessible and understandable.

Managers and executives are a vital part of this information loop. They must act as primary information sources, internally and externally, and function as feedback conduits to upper management to foster and sustain a successful two-way communication process.

Chapter Summary

Our discussion of the communicator as a leader in the twenty-first century reflects our transactional communication model and insists that leaders act as active senders and receivers of messages.

Executive leaders must be sensitive to the advantages and disadvantages of various communication channels in message delivery. Strategic practices such as visibility, negotiation and mediation help counter noise and interference in the global marketplace.

Leaders are collaborators with their various publics in the learning process. They must seek feedback from both internal and external audiences to carry out their responsibilities effectively. Furthermore, they must be sensitive to the context of their communication at all times.

Understanding how others perceive the organization and its leadership and addressing any areas of concern enhances accountability and builds credibility and trust in an organization. ■

Learning From Others

Geof Cox heads New Directions Ltd in Bristol, UK. He specializes in individual, management and organization development and works with multinational companies and family firms across Western, Central and Eastern Europe, Africa and the Middle East.

Cox is on the faculty of the Institute of Management, a member of the Learning Consortium and author of several books. He is editor of *Cuttings*, the New Directions newsletter and contributed this essay on appreciative inquiry (AI).

Strength or deficit based communication?

There is a bias towards weaknesses, deficits and problems in our communication patterns – just think of what your parents noticed on your report card – the F or the As and Bs? What did your coach do – try to fix your weaknesses or build on your strengths? In organizational communications the discussion is often about risk, problem solving, cause and effect analysis and what is going wrong.

Paradoxically, even while we improve, we continue to find problems and weaknesses. As we tend to get more of what we focus on, the questions we ask and our mindset affect what we hear and see, and therefore we get conditioned into deficit thinking.

In an experiment with a bowling team, half the team was coached only on correcting their mistakes, the other half only on enhancing what they were doing right. At the end of the season, both halves of the team had improved, but the success-coached half, the players who were conditioned to focus on what they were doing right, had improved 100 % more than their colleagues.

Recognizing this phenomenon led David Copperrider and others at Case Western Reserve University to use different conversations with people engaged in organizational change. Instead of asking "What's wrong?" they asked "What's working here?" and then built futures based on the outcomes.

This is the practice of appreciative inquiry – the process of looking for and enhancing the root causes of success rather than trying to fix the causes of failure.

Appreciative inquiry is based on dialogue. The first step is collecting opinions and observations through stories of peak experiences. These observations are then shared to identify common themes. Finally, selecting the most important themes forms the basis for a series of provocative propositions that describe how the organization will be.

This groundbreaking philosophy is now central to the communication and organizational development of companies as diverse as BP, ANZ Bank and Roadway Express; community development and aid projects like Imagine Chicago; and global initiatives such as United Religions and the Dalai Lama's conferences.

In one company, AI was used to conduct an analysis of the total system, which was completed in less than two weeks by the employees themselves. In another, a summit meeting brought together all 750 employees, the company's leadership and 100 customers to create the business model for their new-century organization – a year later, profits were up over 200 % and absenteeism down 300 %. These are real success stories.

Case Study – **Dundee Council of Scotland**

Because of a national shortage of qualified social workers, local councils in the UK had recruitment problems. As more and more positions remained vacant, organizations began offering unparalleled incentive plans to attract new staff. Rather than fix the problem, this practice presented a new obstacle: retention. Organizations saw many of their staff leave to take advantage of the benefits offered by other groups.

Dundee Council of Scotland found itself in this predicament. But rather than follow the flawed pattern of enticing employees away from other organizations, it sought to change the system.

Dundee Council brought in an organizational team from a management consultancy firm, New Directions, to find a workable solution to their staffing problems.

Think out of the box. Before reading further, can you suggest one way for Dundee Council to improve its recruitment and retention?

Here's what happened at Dundee Council.

New Directions, committed to appreciative inquiry (AI), saw the immediate possibility of offering employees more job satisfaction through flexible working practices.

Nine teams of employees were chosen to participate in the initial research phase: four investigated flexible working locations, four looked at flexible working hours and one addressed organizational issues.

At facilitated workshops using an AI methodology, team members identified problems on the job and shared success stories with each other. Freedom of expression permeated the workshops and the staff felt empowered and trusted. Managers of the pilot teams were involved in the dialogues, but it was left to the staff to design manageable systems.

As news spread of how excited employees were about their new flexible working conditions, other staffers demanded similar freedom and flexibility.

Did the experiment work? How would you evaluate the success of this programme? What do you see as some of the pitfalls of such a plan?

At a six-month evaluation, the new flexible programme showed improved operational performance: more reports completed on time, more cases closed and no backlogs. One success story: "a community care team offering home support at specified times of the day had no backlog of client requests for the first time ever".

Employee absences were reduced and staff reported less job-related stress. Team members were able to work from home during minor illnesses or emergency childcare situations. One staffer said she felt more trusted and less guilty when she had to rearrange her schedule because of a personal emergency.

Flexible working did not solve the understaffing needs of the organization, but it helped keep employees who were now better able to cope with the pressure of high workloads. A fear that some would abuse the flexibility system did not materialize, and quality communication was enhanced by mobile phones and remote access systems (Cox, 2005).

Do you see "flexibility" as enhancing worker satisfaction in other industries in the new world of management? What are some of the positive and negatives of allowing employees the freedom to design their own working conditions? ■

Class Exercises

1. In teams, identify principles that you all agree are important to the functioning of your team. After you have agreed upon some basic principles, write a contract covering the workings of your team. Be sure you cover such issues as absenteeism, responsibility, respect for other's ideas and meeting behaviour, among other issues. Sign the contract and give it to your professor. If feasible, use the contract in your next team project. After the project is completed, evaluate the contract. How did it address your team's needs? If not, how would you modify it?

2. Formulate your own opinion on accountability. Using examples from politics, business and non-profit organizations, discuss how accountability has become more or less transparent in today's global marketplace and why.

3. Review one of the many popular press books on how to be successful in business. What does the book say about the role of communications in that process? Write a one-page review of the book. Be prepared to discuss your review in class.

Action Plan

During troubling times, AEB, a division of a Fortune 100 firm, instituted a "communications cascade". The company had approximately 2 500 employees, four management layers between the vice-president and employees and two facilities, 15 miles apart. In the cascade, information flowed from management and then filtered through each management level below until it reached employees. AEB also adopted a "48-hour rule" during which key messages covered in manager's staff meetings reached employees in 48 hours (Dulye, 1992, p. 214).

See if you can draw a model of the cascade process on the basis of the above description – make sure that the model illustrates how employee feedback might be communicated to management. Share the model with other members of your class and discuss its strengths and weaknesses.

Websites

Timing is central to the success of any negotiation effort. Social scientists often refer to the "ripeness" or the ripe moment to begin the negotiation process, particularly in labour relations or international relations. Read more about the concept of timing and international conflict negotiations from the website of the Conflict Resolution Consortium at the University of Colorado, USA at `http://www.colorado.edu/conflict/peace/treatment/idripe.htm` (CRC, 2006).

For insight on how executives can communicate professionally on many levels, go to the ASAE and The Center for Association Leadership site at `http://www.asaecenter.org/` (ASAE & CAL, 2006).

To learn more about leadership, consult *BusinessWeek*'s Special Report on Leadership at `www.businessweek.com/go/06leadership/` (Business Week, 2006). The site is especially designed for junior executives.

References

Argenti, P. (1998) *Corporate Communication*. New York, McGraw-Hill.

ASAE & CAL (2006) ASAE and The Center for Association Leadership. Available from: http://www.asaecenter.org/ [Accessed 5 July 2006].

Boeing (2006) "The Boeing 777 family: the most technologically advanced airplane in the world". Available from: www.boeing.com/commercial/ 777family/pf/pf_background.html [Accessed 10 July 2006].

Burnett, B. (2006) "A Boeing-led team is working to make quiet jetliners even quieter". *Boeing Frontiers*, **4**(8). Available from: www.boeing.com/news/frontiers/archive/2005/december/ts_sf07.html [Accessed 10 July 2006].

BusinessWeek (2006) "Special report on leadership". Available from: www.businessweek.com/go/06leadership/ [Accessed 5 July 2006].

Clampitt, P. (2005) *Communicating for Managerial Effectiveness*, 3rd edn. Thousand Oaks, CA, Sage.

Cox, G. (2004) "Developing inclusive strategies". *Strategy Magazine*, November: 12–13.

Cox, G. (2005) "Discovering the benefits of flexible working with social workers in the UK". *AI Practitioner*, November: 32–34. Available from: http://www.newdirections.uk.com/Flexible%20working%20AiP.pdf [Accessed 3 September 2006].

CRC (2006) Conflict Research Consortium at the University of Colorado, USA. Available from: http://www.colorado.edu/conflict/peace/treatment/idripe.htm [Accessed 5 July 2006].

Curry, S. (2005) "Getting your bench right". *CEO Magazine*, October: 30–32.

Devine, M. (2006) "Creativity in the world of work". *Peer Review*, Spring. Available from: www.aacu.org/peerreview/ pr-sp06/pr-sp06_analysis2.cfm - 40k [Accessed 5 July 2006].

Dulye, L. (1992) "Toward better two-way". In *Corporate Communications for Executives*. Goodman, M., ed. Albany, State University of New York Press: 210–217.

Fannin, R. (2005) "2005 brand leaders". *The Chief Executive*, October: 24–32.

Gladwell, M. (2000) *The Tipping Point.* New York, Little, Brown & Co.

Jung, K. & Robinson, B. (2005) "Measuring the return on your communication investment". *Journal of Integrated Marketing Communications*: 32–26.

Little, S. (2005) "Unwrap your growth strategy". *Associations Now*, October. Available from: http://www.asaecenter. org/ [Accessed 20 April 2006].

Lucansky, P., Burke, R. & Potapchuk, L. (2006) "The lean perspective". Vipgroup. Available from: www.vipgroup. us/Lean-Leadership.pdf [Accessed 3 September 2006].

Mai, R. & Akerson, A. (2003) *The Leader as Communicator.* New York, American Management Association.

McGregor, J. (2006) "How failure breeds success". *BusinessWeek*, 10 July 2006: 42–52.

Norton, J. (2005) "The world's most admired leaders of 2005". Burson-Marsteller, 14 December 2005. Available from: www.burson-marsteller [Accessed 8 June 2006].

Pincott, G. (1999) October. "Website promotion strategy". *Conference on Performance Measurement for Web Marketing*, October 1999. Available from: http://www.intelliquest.com/resources/reports/mbi_report09.asp [Accessed 9 June 2006].

Prince, C. (2005) "Investors doubt CEO ethic". *Chief Executive*, May: 12.

Pringle, H. & Gordon, W. (2003) *Brand Manners.* Chichester, UK, John Wiley & Sons, Ltd.

Salacuse, J. (2006) "Real leaders negotiate". *Negotiation*, May: 3–5. Available from: http://search.epnet.com/login. aspx?direct=true&db=buh&an=20673498 [Accessed 5 July 2006].

Slywotzky, A. (2005) "When bitter rivals should team up". *Chief Executive*, October: 12.

Taylor, W. (2006) "Here's an idea: let everyone have ideas". *The New York Times*, 26 March 2006: BU-3.

Watkins, M. (2002) *Breakthrough Business Negotiation: A Toolbox for Managers.* San Francisco, CA, Jossey-Bass.

Bibliography

Goodman, M. (1998) *Corporate Communications for Executives.* Albany, State University of New York Press.

Guttman, H. (2005) "Conflict management: a core leadership competency". *Training*, November. Available from: http://0web12.epnet.com.library.winthrop.edu/citation.asp?tb=1&_ug=sid+38921186%2D3 [Assessed 5 July 2006].

Kolb, D. (2005) "Negotiate for what you need to succeed". *Harvard Management Update*, **10**(9): 1–4. Available from: http://search.epnet.com/login.aspx?direct=true&db=buh&an=18236671 [Accessed 5 July 2006].

Schultz, D. & Schultz, H. (2003) *IMC: the Next Generation.* Boston, McGraw-Hill.

Yaverbaum, E. (2004) *Leadership Secrets of the World's Most Successful CEOs.* Dearborn, MI, Dearborn Trade Publishing.

CHAPTER 13

Emerging Issues Affecting Communication Strategy

Executive Summary

Well-developed communication plans prepare organizations for unpredictable events that can severely affect operations, safety, the reputation of employees and the company and the bottom line.

Management must ensure that employees understand the importance of engaging in productive customer relations, as well as listen to the information that employees are learning from customers concerning company practices, product quality and services Insight into what customers want in products or how customers view specific brands is valuable information for all company employees, not just marketers.

Issues management fortifies organizations against potential legal disputes, criticisms of environmental procedures, community awareness issues, product recalls, labour actions, natural disasters and anything in between

Crisis management sets strategic plans and procedures for addressing accidents, natural disasters, labour unrest and ethical dilemmas among other issues Trendwatching tracks new ideas and practices that promise or threaten the competitive edge of an organization. Strategic partnering, increased emphasis on customer relations and mass customization (product differentiation) offer exciting collaborative solutions to a competitive global marketplace. Cocooning and timewarping help explain consumer behaviour.

Given the unique, and often intense, communication that issues management, crisis planning and trendwatching require, it is vital that personnel, led by communication professionals across the organization, are active in the process. ■

Emerging Issues Affecting Communication Strategy

As a rule, the most successful people in life are those who have the best information.

Disraeli, former British Prime Minister

Introduction to New Approaches to Communication Strategy

Planning strategies are covered extensively in marketing, management and business courses. In this chapter we will examine some of the emerging issues that call specifically for well-developed communication plans and that depend on the communication expertise of the individuals who develop these plans.

The planning of communication strategies no longer takes place at boardroom tables behind the closed doors of sacrosanct executive suites, where top-level managers nod their heads in agreement with everything the CEO proposes.

Today, most companies embrace the concept of inclusiveness and reach out to many "company voices" throughout the organization to understand and address emerging issues. The success of a company depends on how well it can formulate effective strategy, both short and long range, based on the best information it is able to gather.

Consider this case. A multinational company spends millions of dollars in environmental safeguard standards for waste disposal in anticipation of pending laws requiring such action. The company learns there is a movement among certain government bureaucrats to delay the enactment of these standards. A delay will have long-term public health implications and give a competitive advantage to companies that have yet to invest in improving their waste disposal (Eppes, 1998).

What should the organization in question do? Support the delay but risk long-term public safety and goodwill? Seek help from opinion leaders to oppose the delay? Seek assistance from other organizations that have already complied with the environmental standards and attack government bureaucrats through the media? These options are possible communication solutions to a complex and expensive crisis. But what is the best solution?

Integrated communication is particularly adept at addressing situations where company reputations are at risk. Understanding the value of addressing the needs of all affected stakeholders and protecting the corporate reputation and its brand should be at the core of a strategic communication plan.

Bridging the Communication Gap between Executives and Employees

Most executives spend the majority of their days multitasking a number of projects and putting out fires. They execute, as the word "executive" implies. How well they execute their duties determines their performance rating.

Strategic Thinking

The article "Global perspectives: how can communicators bridge the gap between executives and employees?", published in *Communication World*, a publication of the International Association of Business Communicators, gives advice from global experts around the world who urge executives to listen, gather opinions and communicate (IABC, 2004, pp. 6–7).

- Executives need to learn "how to verbalize messages that reflect the company's real objectives, how to pick the right channel and media to communicate, how to present themselves so that people will listen, how to anticipate the outcomes of communication and how to gather feedback" (*Madrid, Spain*).
- Our executives "walk around departments and visit employees at the coalface, one on one. They sit with them, talk about projects they are working on and demonstrate real interest ... this fosters a culture that encourages innovation, respects ideas from all levels and removes hierarchical barriers" (*Melbourne, Australia*).
- Effective corporate communicators turn "the broad, high-level vision of the CEO and management team into day-to-day realities for staff". They "facilitate easy, effective ways for employees to share their ideas and perspectives with management, identifying links to corporate goals and vision" (*Edmonton, Alberta, Canada*).
- "To bridge the gap between executives and employees, it is necessary to create a feeling of friendship and cooperation through timely and clear communication (in) meetings, building sessions, orientation/training manuals and other vital media" (*Lagos, Nigeria*).

Although executives may know is it important to communicate with their co-workers and employees, they often fall short in this practice, focusing more on execution than on developing interpersonal and business relationships.

Executives need to recognize the value of timely and effective communication, which means accepting advice from experienced and professional communicators.

Bridging the Communication Gap between Employees and Customers

Customer experiences and perceptions often differ from the promises a company makes in its advertising, on its website or in other company communications. Understanding the needs of its customers requires organizations constantly to monitor present customer, potential customer and supplier satisfaction with products and services rendered. This information can be collected through multiple sources, from toll-free complaint lines and surveys to product return records.

Asking employees on the front line is one of least expensive and most effective ways of monitoring customer satisfaction. A clerk at an international discount chain complained that her company monitored returns that were subject to national recall but failed to record those brands that were returned on a regular basis by customers who found them inadequate or of poor quality. "We have had dozens of these chair cushions returned", she lamented. "Customers have told me that they are all too small for the average dining room chair … and yet we keep selling them".

Woolworths, UK, initiated an 18-month campaign called "Making Families Smile" to help improve employee–customer communication. Former head of Internal Communications at Woolworths, Fergal McDonnell, said the campaign was designed to build employee engagement. "Eighty-four per cent of Britain's working population is not fully engaged, yet engaged people are more powerful to an organization than passive wage earners and can add value to the bottom line", he noted (CIB, 2006).

The campaign to build better relationships between customers and employees utilized multiple techniques to reach employees at various sites, including face-to-face training, employee meetings, leadership workshops, peer-to-peer communication techniques and other vehicles.

Customer insight contributes to better marketing communication and more effective customer service. Advertising expert Lisa Fortini-Campbell calls the process of gaining insight into customer needs and motivation "hitting the sweet spot" (Fortini-Campbell,

2001). Executives should encourage their communication teams scientifically to study what motivates customers to buy their product, and then communicate that information to company management and employees.

Let's now explore how an organization can anticipate and plan for issues that may affect its long-term viability.

Issues Management Strategy

Issues management is the process organizations use to anticipate, analyse, respond to, evaluate and take control of complex issues that affect their business. It can involve legal disputes, environmental concerns, community awareness issues, product recalls, labour actions, natural disasters and other developments.

The term was first used in 1976, by Howard Chase, founding member of the Public Relations Society of America (PRSA), to define the process of dealing long term and proactively, with increased outside forces affecting companies. He suggested a network of company leaders, including senior management, should be in place to sound an early alert regarding emerging issues. Issues management should not be allocated to a single department but should involve areas, such as public relations, community relations, human resources, the legal department, financial areas and even research and development.

Strategic Thinking

An issues management plan consists of five steps (Issue Management Council, 2006c):

1. Issue identification
2. Issue analysis
3. Issue change strategy options
4. Issue action programme
5. Evaluation of results.

What audience do you think is at the core of each step? What role do organizations, citizens and government play in this model? In which steps would interaction be important?

> The world press has questioned the objectivity of medical spokespeople, particularly if their research has been funded by the organizations for which they are acting as spokespeople. The trend of increased media scrutiny leads some companies to shy away from communicating to the public at all, but it is precisely at this transparency-demanding time that an organization's communication efforts should be clear, consistent and frequent.

Conducting a vulnerabilities audit is a first step in getting serious about issues management. This involves meeting with people in every department of the company and identifying key issues that could possibly affect the company.

These threats can be both internal (Joe Young from accounting says he thinks certain financial information should be stored in more protected files because a friend at another company said dissatisfied employees had leaked some confidential information to the media) and external (Suzie Jones from personnel says she heard that enrolment in local technical schools is on the decrease and this might affect the company's supply of workers).

Astute leaders recognize that a gap often exists between what the organization thinks it's doing right and what stakeholders' perceptions of these efforts are. Audiences' expectations of the organization often are not met and consequently create negative attitudes, leaving inattentive companies to wonder what went wrong.

Sometimes things go right. For example, Heinz, a food consortium, hired the issues management team at a global public relations firm to promote Starkist tuna as "dolphin-safe tuna" when videos of fishermen trapping dolphins in tuna nets went public. This quick management response and control of the situation prevented the public from viewing the company as an uncaring, passive giant (Edelman, 2006).

The Issue Management Council, composed of representatives from 200 companies worldwide, believes issue management is the business tool to help organizations meet public expectations. It defines nine "best practices" for effective issue management under the broad headings of structure, implementation and integration (Issue Management Council, 2006b):

Structure

1. Develop a process to identify current issues.
2. Establish a formal process for addressing any identified issues.
3. Assign responsibility for managing issues to specific individuals.

Implementation

4. "Ownership" of major issues is linked to accountability.
5. Progress is monitored at high management levels.
6. Management has power to intervene if an issue is not being handled properly.

Integration

7. Formal channels allow managers to integrate issue concerns into strategic planning.

8. Managers of issues are part of the strategic planning unit.

9. Issue management is positioned as "a core management function" and not confined to any one department.

Managers must be ready to address emerging issues before they escalate into problems. Risk assessment will help determine a company's future planning and communication strategy that will optimize management decisions, ensure effective messaging, establish alliances with various publics and develop monitoring and evaluation procedures.

Consumers demand committed, interactive, accurate and credible communication. This means managers must develop global viewpoints based on expertise, knowledge, understanding and insight, and bring these perspectives to the strategy planning table.

The Commonwealth Bank of Australia, recognizing the importance of education to its community, initiated an issues management approach to provide information on the bank's education programs, particularly financial literacy. The bank hosts a DollarsandSense website that explains e-learning grants available to primary schools (Issue Management Council, 2006a).

**The Issues Management Council defines what
issues management is and is not**

Issues management is ...	Issues management is not...
A formal process that anticipates and manages emerging issues.	A form of damage control.
An "outside-in cultural mindset" that considers stake-holder wants and needs.	Defensive behaviours that alienate stake-holders.
A long-term commitment to two-way, inclusive public social responsibility.	One way communication to control public perception.
An ethical approach that focuses on connectivity rather than the control of others.	A display of superficial values orchestrated to deceive the public.

(IMC, 2006c)

Figure 13.1 The Issues Management Council has addressed the role of issue management in business.

When an organization addresses emerging issues and prepares a plan of action and communication, it is more in control of the situation. The benefits of an effective issues management process are consumer acceptance, positive coverage by the media, employee pride and investor confidence.

Internal issues management

Besides managing the outside forces that might impact upon a company, managers must also tackle internal issues that threaten the inner stability of the workplace.

Exit strategy

Employees will leave companies, some on good terms and others under undesirable circumstances. Monster Intelligence, in a 2005 study involving 600 HR managers from various US industry sectors and representing businesses of all sizes, found that 40 % of

---

Strategic Thinking

Here are some benefits of issues management from the Issue Management Council website www.issuemanagement.org/documents.im_details.html

External benefits:

- good stakeholder relationships
- early product introduction
- reduction in "communication noise" which can hamper messaging
- corporate stewardship enhancement
- real-world knowledge of emerging issues.

Internal benefits:

- boundary-spanning communication efforts
- relevant messaging
- improved teamwork
- issue accountability
- uncertainty reduction and crisis avoidance.

Can you think of any other benefits?

the companies reported an increase in employee turnover during the 18-month research period.

The study further revealed that about half of the HR managers used exit interviews to survey exiting employees. However, only a third of these managers said that personnel and workplace changes were made as a result of feedback from exit interviews (Monster Intelligence, 2005, pp. 1–8).

Exit surveys are valuable sources of relevant information, and, as competition for talent gets tighter, companies are increasingly trying to discern what makes employees leave.

Unicru, a $38 million employment services firm, uses a two-person team to interview employees who are leaving the company. Each 90-minute exit interview consists of a set list of 15 questions. The team is friendly, but getting relevant answers to their questions is a priority.

HR analyses the results of exit interviews, focusing on the broad scope of findings to eliminate taking one disgruntled employee's viewpoint as an indication of overall opinion, to see if any trends emerge. Such was the case when Unicru discovered that many employees left because they didn't feel the company offered enough opportunity for professional development.

HR vice-president Elaine Lees says that most departing employees are willing to share their reasons for leaving in the interviews. She explains, "For the most part, even dissatisfied employees who are leaving the company have a connection with most of their co-workers and genuinely want to see the company improve and succeed" (Westcott, 2006, pp. 40–42).

Databasing information, gathered from exit interviews, has helped a US call centre, with 2 000 employees at seven locations, reduce employee turnover to less than half the industry rate. The company used the information to design profiles of the type of people who will or will not stay with the company for an extended period of time. The information also has led to "changes in supervisor training, incentive programmes and pay packages" (Westcott, 2006, pp. 40–42).

Upgrading exit interviews from a perfunctory rite of passage to a real opportunity to communicate with those who can offer constructive criticism is one way to address employee retention. Mining this information provides valuable insight into an organization's culture.

Consulting firms encourage a comprehensive and analytical exit interview strategy. Richard Harding of Kenexa explains, "It used to be the main point of an exit interview was to find out why people were leaving. The new thinking is to turn it around and figure out why good people want to stay" (Westcott, 2006, pp. 40–42).

Crisis management and risk assessment

All organizations, from manufacturing to municipalities, are vulnerable to crisis situations. How they manage these crises is crucial to their reputation and long-term health.

The components of risk

Risk assessment experts agree that all crises have certain characteristics in common – suddenness, uncertainty and time compression (Lerbinger, 1997).

Bombings in New York, London and Madrid were unexpected – in spite of the fact that counterterrorist organizations expected an eventual outbreak in major American and European cities.

In business, product liability cases are often brought before the public by watchdog groups or the media. For example, concerns about the efficacy of the drug Vioxx surfaced in the media before Merck pulled it off the market in September 2004. The drug had $2.5 billion in sales in 2003, but soon after the announcement, Merck's stock fell more than 25 % (DeNoon, 2004). By July 2006, the manufacturer was faced with over 16 000 lawsuits and the company's reputation was seriously threatened in the court of public opinion (Johnson, 2006).

Even though management may conduct statistical assessments about the risk of a particular crisis occurring, they often engage in wishful thinking – "Oh, that situation will never happen". The news media is full of stories of lawsuits and reports of government investigations where companies failed to acknowledge they had a problem. As Lerbinger notes: "Only when a crisis occurs does management learn the hard way that low-probability, high impact events must be taken seriously" (Lerbinger, 1997, p. 8).

Time compression further aggravates decision-making in a crisis. Managers, who are already under stress, are forced to make quick decisions. Without appropriate training, they may react in a confrontational or reactive manner rather than trying to address the situation positively or proactively.

Warning! Social media may be dangerous to the reputation of companies.

On a social networking site, one employee wrote about Blockbuster, the movie and game rental giant with 7 700 stores throughout Europe, Asia, North America and Australia: "'im [sic] angry at the fact that the corporate idiots cant [sic] find ways to make money without screwing the employees".

The company's comment: "We don't believe many of the comments are an accurate reflection of Blockbuster or of our thousands of high-quality employees".

While the grammar and language of this blog may be offensive to some, the emotional charge it contained could potentially damage the company's reputation. Because these comments are so dangerous, many companies have issued rules preventing interns and employees from blogging in the workplace (BusinessWeek, 2006).

Assessing vulnerabilities

Certain organizations are more vulnerable to risk, and thus to crises. Managers need to think about their organizational potential for crisis exposure. In his book *Crisis in Organizations*, Laurence Barton suggests asking the following questions as "litmus tests" to possible risk (Barton, 1992, pp. 59–71):

- Is the organization publicly owned? Shareholders are likely to react negatively to a crisis by selling their stock.
- How large is the company, and how well is it insured? Larger companies produce more products and have more exposure in the marketplace.
- Is the organization under current public scrutiny?
- Has the organization established open communication both internally and externally?
- Do employees know what they are supposed to do during a crisis?
- Does the company have good media and community relations?
- Are the company's products and services naturally more vulnerable to risk? Chemical manufacturing plants, amusement parks and public transportation are more susceptible to crises than small neighbourhood businesses or clothing stores.
- How well known is the company? Companies whose names appear frequently in the media – through advertising or news – are more likely to catch the attention of the public, concerned interest groups and the media.

Dig Deeper

In August 2003, England, Wales, France, Italy and Portugal recorded 22 080 deaths attributed to the severe temperatures of a record-breaking heat wave. The heat wave led to forest fires in Portugal and to air quality and ground-level ozone problems in England, Wales and France.

In France, meanwhile, the highest recorded temperatures in 53 years contributed to 14 800 deaths due to extreme temperatures during the first two weeks of August. However, a systematic analysis found that the city of Marseille had developed a plan of action and public communication strategy to address the needs of the elderly and lower-income groups in heat-wave conditions. This action plan was developed in response to a previous heat-wave crisis the city had experienced. Owing to the timely implementation of this plan, Marseille recorded fewer deaths than other cities. As a result of this analysis, the French government developed a national heat health watch warning system. Its objectives are to protect vulnerable groups from the effects of heat waves and to alert authorities in time to set up plans of action (Kosatsky, 2005; Pirard *et al.*, 2005).

Steps in crisis communication planning

Crisis communication planning needs input from all levels of an organization. A crisis management team should include personnel from areas such as communication, human resources, security and legal. In some countries, hospitals are required by accreditation agencies to have detailed plans spelling out the roles of each department in a crisis situation.

Crisis plans have five essential steps:

1. Assess the possible risk to the organization. What can happen? How and why? What is the potential for injury?
2. Identify all levels of vulnerability. How would a crisis affect the day-to-day operations of the organization? How will various stakeholders react to the information?
3. Determine the most urgent and likely vulnerabilities and develop plans of action to address these issues. Meeting with the key publics, the media, interest groups and governmental leaders might be strategies to use in this step. This step should assess how to handle risks efficiently and costs effectively.
4. Implement the plan of action. Failure to communicate or unwillingness to be honest and open often further exacerbates an already tense situation. A team of experts should be charged with delivering the company's messages to key audiences with one person acting as chief spokesperson.
5. Evaluate the effectiveness of the action. Modify the master-planning document to reflect what was learned from the experience.

Much of the success of crisis management depends on the preplanning process. Communication plays a central role in this. The World Bank, with 115 sites and some 10 000 employees, has developed crisis management teams (CMTs) responsible for individual country offices and staffs around the world. In addition, the Bank has established separate HR crisis teams to develop messages and receive feedback. An outbreak of avian flu influenza in Asia mobilized World Bank CMTs across the globe using multiple media formats to communicate to staff the plans in place for their safety. The media included online interviews with those leading the work, a website, meetings and a hotline. After using CMTs in several crisis situations, a lesson was learned from their expertise – "Leave the communication to communication professionals" – they are the most familiar with communication tools and practices (Morier & Eagan, 2006, p. 25).

Strategic Thinking

Here are 10 lessons designed to help an organization's communication team get a negative story out of the news as quickly and effectively as possible:

1. Be prepared for a possible crisis by simulating a team response. Make sure the roles of all departments/players are clearly articulated.
2. Let employees know about a situation before discussing it with the media.
3. Use a prepared statement and Q&A so that a single message is communicated to the public.
4. Select spokespeople who can articulate the organization's position in a knowledgeable, understandable and non-defensive manner.
5. Never lie to the media. Likewise, avoid the phrase "no comment". This suggests hidden information.
6. CEOs may be called upon to give a statement and/or visit the site of a crisis. Time is always an issue in such cases. If the wait is too long, the CEO may appear to be out of touch or uncaring.
7. Never speculate about the cause of an accident or situation. If the spokesperson is not clear about details, he/she should get back to the media when details become available.
8. Identify a place, away from the scene of the crisis, to house the media. Tell them when the company spokesperson will communicate with them, and how.
9. If appropriate, enlist the help of government or other appropriate experts to help tell the story.
10. Don't ignore customers. Build into the crisis plan how company representatives will handle customer relations during a crisis.

An organization that practises integrated communication will be less likely to have long-term negative effects following a crisis.

Public affairs takes new directions

Global economics are intertwined with government on many levels and in many sectors. **Public affairs** is a public relations function that works with and communicates to governmental bodies. To be successful, multinational companies must develop positive working associations with government representatives in all consumer markets.

In Germany, a public affairs campaign was successful in repealing government retail regulations that limited discounts and free gifts. Various industries came together, from telecommunications to restaurants and wine growers, to develop a three-prong strategy: face-to-face meetings with decision-makers, coalition development and an informational media relations plan.

In a new model of lobbying, the group used websites and information kits to assemble and disseminate its persuasive arguments to government bodies and the public in order to garner their support for change. The two-year effort was successful (Tydecks, 2004).

As less developed countries become markets for global companies, public affairs will become a more crucial element in communication planning strategy. Because markets become saturated, new untapped areas must be targeted. Many companies are looking at China, a country of 1.3 billion people, but the sea of legalities and regulations that need to be addressed requires a diligent public affairs focus. (For more information on marketing to the Chinese, see McEwen *et al.*, 2006.)

Trendwatching: What's on the Horizon?

Issues management is identifying, monitoring and managing issues that affect or will affect your company or your stakeholders, whereas **trendwatching** offers a telescopic view that can detect emerging issues. Trendwatching requires awareness, insight and thinking out of the box. It is not the realm of staid managers, uncomfortable with supposition or prediction.

> "Strategic Issues Management argues that issue management is not just one of the many communication functions, but a management function that can entail the use of public policy resources to achieve harmony with key publics".
> Robert L. Heath, author of *Strategic Issues Management: Organizations and Public Policy Challenges* (Heath, 1997).

It is hard to predict what trends will surface in the coming years, but indications of emerging trends are everywhere, if you are astute enough to pick up on them. Years ago, the lure of e-commerce was just a novel idea, but those who began early to embrace e-commerce profited by being forerunners of a now mainstream market.

After the first round of managerial incompetence scandals (Enron and WorldCom, for example), the role of the trendwatcher would have been to suggest that his or her company should implement more accountability and

Dig Deeper

In *The International Herald Tribune*, 2 October 2005, Doreen Carvajal reported: "In a nation where school cafeterias routinely offer five-course meals ... France is preparing to become the first country to impose mandatory health messages on all television and radio advertisements that promote processed food". Other countries are following this lead, especially with regard to food advertising aimed at children.

What implications will this regulation have on advertising? Do you think it will help or hinder the food industry? Should governments interfere in private enterprise in this area? Access the full article "Processed foods? Read this, France says" at `www.iht.com/articles/2005/10/02/business/food03`.php, or get it from your library database.

transparency policies. Companies had ample time to clean house before media and government agencies stepped up investigations, but many of the offenders remained unaware and unprepared.

Database mining and data warehousing concepts were once innovative ideas that are now standard procedures. Even the subject of this book, integrated business communication, once viewed as a new trend in business strategy, is now being taught at universities around the world.

Trendwatching can be reactive or proactive.

- **Reactive trendwatching** is picking up on trends that have already entered the outer fringes of an industry.
- **Proactive trendwatching** is picking up on early trends in unrelated industries and adapting them to your industry.

Reactive responses to trends

Current trends that companies may address reactively are:

- cocooning
- mass customization
- maximizing customer service.

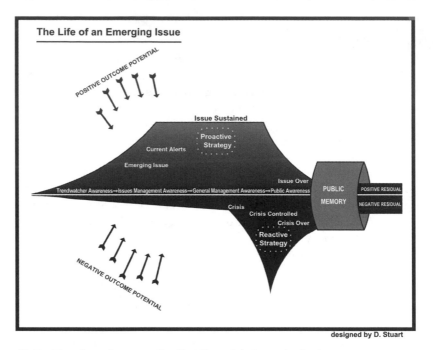

The Life of an Emerging Issue

POSITIVE OUTCOME POTENTIAL

Issue Sustained

Proactive Strategy

Current Alerts

Emerging Issue

Trendwatcher Awareness→Issues Management Awareness→General Management Awareness→Public Awareness

Issue Over

PUBLIC MEMORY

POSITIVE RESIDUAL

NEGATIVE RESIDUAL

Crisis

Crisis Controlled

Crisis Over

Reactive Strategy

NEGATIVE OUTCOME POTENTIAL

designed by D. Stuart

Figure 13.2 Trendwatchers are the first line of defence in the issues management process. When an emerging issue is detected early, a proactive strategic plan facilitates a positive outcome. Lack of early detection jettisons the company into a crisis mode. Reactive strategies often go awry, resonating negatively with consumers long after the issue has dissipated.

Emerging trends that companies may address proactively are:

- company loyalty
- timewarping
- tryvertising.

Cocooning

In 2004, American futurist Faith Popcorn coined the word **cocooning** to describe the phenomenon whereby, when busy people get home in the evening after a hectic and stressful day, they retreat into their homes, or cocoon. This trend continues to characterize American culture.

Strategic Thinking

Trendwatching has its critics. In his book *The Brand Innovation Manifesto*, Englishman John Grant is critical of trendwatching as a predictor of consumer behaviour. He says, "Real trends are those ideas or artefacts that people *agree* are growing in acceptance" (Grant, 2006, p. 64). For example, he notes that cocooning was accepted by the marketing community and the media but was proven untrue – Americans now spend less time at home and more time in their office or cars.

Grant views trend thinking as narrow and linear – not helpful in brand innovation or strategy. Do you agree? Have companies like Starbucks capitalized on the need to have a home away from home? What about the consumption of DVDs, especially through online programs where movie watchers can get their selections delivered directly to their homes, and is this same trend contributing to the fall in movie attendance?

So how can a trendwatcher adapt this trend to his or her industry? Manufacturers of elaborate home sound systems will want to reach cocooners, as will already prepared food brands, hot tub designers, home-shopping distributors and furniture makers. These are obvious. But how might the insurance business use this information? Could the insurance industry use this trend to develop business telemarketing plans or help their company's employees relax during lunchtime by tapping into their cocooning activities?

Mass customization

Forecasting consumer demand is tough in the ever-changing marketplace. **Mass customization** is a marketing trend that manufactures for the masses but offers individual product customization to its customers.

This concept has been taken to the extreme by Starbuck's, where coffee lovers in any city worldwide can get the exact concoction they want, in the exact way they want. Mocha decaf grande with low-fat milk and no sugar will taste the same in Milan, Paris or an out-of-the-way village in southern Spain.

The Italian-based clothing manufacturer and retailer Benetton uses the practice of delayed differentiation to overcome problems in trying to predict what colour or style its worldwide customers prefer. While most companies first dye yarn for material, weave it and then cut and sew garments, Benetton makes some items in an undyed state called "greige". It sends test batches of dyed clothes in the season's colours to select stores to gauge consumer demand, and then, using that feedback, quickly dyes the greige garments and sends them to its retailers. The process is more expensive but reduces the cost of overstocking and lost revenue from discount sales (Sheffi, 2005, p. 63).

Mass customization is used in many industries and is successful if carried out close to the end-customer. Customers can build their own Dell computers or design their own athletic shoes online. They can choose the ending of a book or design messages for T-shirts. The Austrian manufacturer Frenkenburger makes custom-made flavours for its hemp milk, Trinkhanf, already in mango/ginger, cocoa/vanilla/maple and coffee-flavoured varieties; the company asks customers to submit possible new names.

Yossi Sheffi, director of the Massachusetts Institute of Technology, suggests "mass customization and delayed differentiation could have a huge impact on the outsourcing debate by developing into a large-scale industry that then employs many of the workers displaced by offshore outsourcing" (Sheffi, 2005).

Customer service and more customer service

Customer service is a growing trend in many industries, including retail, banking and computer technology. Increased customer service means stepping up communication outreach to stakeholder groups. Treating customers right means keeping customers, a more economical endeavour than looking for new customers. For example, Lexus not only rushed a letter of apology out to customers when it discovered minor problems with a new vehicle, but had company representatives pick up the cars and bring them to the dealership for repairs.

Consumers get frustrated when they are constantly rerouted by the multilayered automated message systems of large companies. One consumer posted short cuts to reach a human representative instead of a machine. To help others, he listed the direct phone numbers of representatives in 200 businesses on his website. The site receives over 1 000 hits daily (Inc. Magazine, 2006).

Proactive trendwatching

Forward-looking innovators look for emerging **trends** in every industry, in any country, no matter what the product or service. They then try to envision how that trend could affect their specific industry or company. Communicating these new and unique ideas to top-level management is not an easy task; it often means persuading linear thinkers to open their minds to endless connections and possibilities.

Trendwatching.com is an excellent site to catch a glimpse of some of the latest trends. Read about "kitchenless restaurants" and "frozen food bistros" or learn about "vanchising" and "urban farming" (Springwise, 2006). What are some of the newest trends that communicators will be using to reach consumers in the next few years? Here are a few.

Company loyalty

Company loyalty has been declining since the 1980s and employees expect to change jobs every few years, but there is a growing trend of employee loyalty in smaller companies. Is the cycle of employee loyalty coming full circle? Will employees of today look forward to the reward of a gold watch or other such symbol that decades ago signified 20 loyal years to one company? No one can really predict the future for sure, but this information might be helpful in developing new employee loyalty programmes.

Timewarping

People want things faster than ever before, faster than thought possible. This demand for speed is called **timewarping** and is witnessed in new products such as "super fast pizza" and quick khao gaeng style meals from Thai Mango Chili. Emerging fast-food chains in traditional markets like MTR Foods in India hope to become the "McDonald's of Indian food" (Springwise, 2006).

Knowing people want their food fast is not new, but realizing that they want it even faster than ever before is an insight that can be applied to other areas such as the benefit of timely customer communication, the length of training seminars or the importance of keeping office supplies handy for busy employees.

Tryvertising

The term **tryvertising**, coined by trendwatching.com, means offering customers the ability to try various products at minimal cost and effort. The Swedish company Vinotek encourages customers to buy a smart card that allows them to access and taste dozens of bottles of wine. Customers are happy to pay for small samples of wine before they invest in particular bottles. Ralph Lauren, Benjamin Moore, Farrow and Ball and other paint companies sell 2–4 oz sample cans of paint to fill the customer need to see paint on the wall before making a decision. Will this trend of tryvertising continue? Can it be adapted to an unrelated business? Think out of the box on this one.

No one knows whether any new trend will become more than a passing fad, but being aware of the endless possibilities for communicating with stakeholders can help keep companies dynamic and responsive to consumer needs and wants.

Chapter Summary

Advanced technology promises the ability to carry on new types of conversation with our employees and customers – blogs, podcasting and time-shifted media, among others, provide new communication possibilities for business. Learning to use this new technology to address current issues and reach targeted stakeholders is a necessity.

Proactive issues management and crisis planning are survival tools that are rooted in communication functions. The availability of instant communication makes these planning functions even more critical. Such trends as mass customization and delayed differentiation are changing the way we conduct business and talk to customers. An increased emphasis on customer service, at the heart of an integrated marketing strategy, requires using a variety of media to satisfy customer needs.

As innovative ideas fuelled by new technology gain hold in the marketplace, businesses must prepare for a more competitive environment than ever existed in modern society. ■

Learning From Others

Alan Stine is Manager of Technology Integration for Eaton Corporation's Heavy-Duty Transmission Division. Eaton, the world's leading producer of heavy-duty and synchromesh medium truck transmissions, has manufacturing plants in the USA, the UK, Brazil, China, Poland and Mexico and sales staff all over the world.

Stine assesses the feasibility, cost and applicability of new technology in product development. He has been with Eaton for 25 years in various engineering management and supervisory positions. He discusses international business, communication and leadership qualities.

Q. Eaton has sales forces and plants in many countries. How does Eaton prepare its employees to address cultural differences?

A. When we seek to develop a relationship with a particular overseas operation, we frequently bring in language tutors and circulate books and other educational materials. Most importantly, we try to hire local people to run these businesses. This is particularly difficult in the hot spots for industrial development, such as China, where the competition for talent is fierce. It's hard to keep someone excited about a business that may be in the incubator stage, and for which the rewards may not seem to be immediate.

Q. How important is communication to the success of your business both in the USA and abroad?

A. Communication is important in many areas. Eaton is known for customer service. Our expertise is such that several non-competing truck companies have contracted with us to serve as field marketing and service representatives nationally.

Continual communication with customers is paramount to our success. Certain markets, such as Japan and most of the European Union, are saturated; like many other industries, we are developing relationships with China and India. It takes long-term commitments to build products in developing markets and to find people and companies that are excited about your product and the growth opportunities. Leadership has to build trust between the company and the new market.

Internally, Eaton continually works to improve internal communication processes. For example, senior executives are concerned that general managers, who have primary responsibility for interacting with employees, often become swamped with reviews and other paperwork preventing them from that valuable "face time".

We use a variety of tools to communicate internally – emails, small group sessions, training videos and companywide meetings, among other tools.

We have standardized some work processes to improve communication and save employee time. In the past, employees spent a lot of their time putting together presentations and progress reports – in each case, trying to be unique. Using standardized formats allows employees to spend time in more efficient ways.

Q. What advice would you give students who aspire to leadership in industry?

A. Communication skills are crucial in any position. Leaders have to be able to relate to people at all levels in the organization. This requires learning how to read people and being approachable. And humility – it's important to acknowledge that you don't know everything.

Leaders need to know how to work efficiently and cross-functionally. When we hire new employees, we look for people who have a strong self-identify and dare to be different. It's easy to be a clone – another engineer – but that doesn't make you stand out.

Case Study – **Chiron**

Carefully read the following timeline (FDA, 2004) in the Chiron flu vaccine case and see if you can identify any points along the way when the company or the governmental bodies involved could have used various communication tools to save reputations, avoid negative publicity or bolster public confidence:

25 August 2004	Routine testing by the US Food and Drug Administration finds bacterial contamination in a limited number of lots of flu vaccine at the Chiron Liverpool, UK manufacturing plant.
	Chiron quarantines its entire flu vaccine supply and begins an internal investigation.
September 2004	Chiron informs the FDA and the CDC (Center for Disease Control) that its investigation points to a limited number of contaminated lots of the vaccine. Chiron says it will submit its final report during the week of 4–8 October and announces it is still on track to provide the US market with 46–48 million doses of the vaccine in October.
28 September 2004	The UK Medicines and Healthcare Products Regulatory Agency (MHRA) inspects the Chiron facility but does not notify the FDA of this action.
5 October 2004	The FDA learns that, after its inspection on 28 September, MHRA had subsequently (on 4 October) suspended the company's license for three months. A team is organized to meet with the MHRA and Chiron.
7 October 2004	At the scheduled meeting, MHRA discloses to the FDA its concerns that led to Chiron's license suspension.
8 October 2004	The FDA team meets with Chiron which discloses the results of its investigation: contamination to only a limited number of flu vaccine lots.
9 October 2004	The FDA inspection team travels to Liverpool and is joined by two MHRA inspectors.
10 October 2004	FDA inspection begins.

15 October 2004	In a meeting with Chiron management, FDA inspectors report that they have found "significant deficiencies in quality control and concerns regarding the test results". The FDA ends the meeting with this disclosure: "Although Chiron's retesting of the unaffected lots of vaccine has been negative for contamination, the FDA has determined that it cannot adequately assure the sterility of these lots to our safety standards".
March 2005	Chiron gets the go-ahead from MHRA to resume production. The suspension resulted in a $304 million dollar reduction in sales figures, a write-off of existing supplies amounting to $91 million and a drop in shareholder earnings (Taylor, 2005).
April 2006	Chiron announces its merger with Novartis.

Some other considerations in the case:

On 5 October 2004, a "Statement from the Department of Health and Human Services regarding Chiron flu vaccine" was issued by the HHS Press Office. It stated, "Clearly the loss of the Chiron flu vaccine poses a serious challenge to our vaccine supply for the upcoming flu season" and went on, "Our immediate focus will be on making sure that the supply we do have reaches those who are most vulnerable".

The release explained the situation this way: "We are in the process of learning more detailed information about why the UK regulatory authority suspended Chiron's license for three months … [US agencies are] working with their counterparts in the British government as well as Chiron regarding this situation".

On 17 June 2005, *Inpharma* posted this headline: "Chiron will not meet 2005 flu vaccine targets". The article explained that, although Chiron had said in April that it would be able to deliver the needed amount of vaccine, it was now behind "because it has been unable to get production back up to speed at its manufacturing facility in Liverpool, UK, as quickly as hoped". The company had been given the green light in March 2005 to resume production.

The report gave some additional information: "Last year, the US Food and Drug Administration cited violations of bacterial contamination of vaccine batches; inadequate cleaning procedures; microbial growths on equipment used to fill vaccine vials; unacceptable levels of bacterial toxins in some vaccine preparations; and contamination in some viral seed cultures used to produce the vaccine".

On 12 October 2005, *USA Today* carried this report: "Just over a year after its license was suspended, the nation's second-biggest supplier of flu shots got the Food and Drug Administration's approval on Wednesday to start shipping ...". That's the good news.

But did Chiron's reputation survive the turmoil of 2004? The report ends with a grim quote from a clinic that ordered the vaccine and that "worries that the Chiron shipment may not arrive until December, which may be too late, leaving the clinic stuck with unused vaccine".

By 2006 Chiron had lost much of its market share in the USA. GlaxoSmithKline supplied a million vaccine doses to the USA under emergency procedures, and MedImmune, Inc.'s nasal flu mist received a US order of three million doses.

What can other pharmaceutical companies learn from this case about communication with suppliers, customers, government agencies and the public? What should Chiron do now to rebuild its credibility in the marketplace? What are some of the key messages it needs to get out to its stakeholders? Access `www. naccho.org/topics/infectious/ documents/FLUVIRIN _ PreBook _ Letter.pdf` to find one of Chiron's efforts to communicate with its customers. ∎

Class Exercises

1. Consider this question: is it unethical for organizations to ignore crisis planning? Develop a 3–5 page paper on this topic and include in your answer examples from a crisis that you may have read about. You might consider such historical cases as the famous Alaskan oil spill of the Exxon Valdez in 1989, the Tylenol (Johnson & Johnson) bottle tampering cases in 1982 and 1986, the 2002 Taiwanese-manufactured Fruit Poppers choking crisis in Canada or the bombing in the City of London in 2005. What about the anti-McDonald's campaigns in England and France in the late 1990s or the crisis regarding its use of beef-flavoured frying oil in India in 2001?

2. Tryvertising is about customers trying a product or service in a relevant setting for a minimal price. The Springwise newsletter (springwise.com) offers examples of this emerging trend, including the case of a British fireplace company opening a London restaurant where customers can have drinks and dinner in front of one of the company's designer fireplaces to see how they like it. Identify other cutting-edge companies using this technique and share your results with the class.

3. In small groups, discuss Chiron's merger with Novartis. Consider the possible benefits and problems for both companies and their publics. Do some research to support your assumptions. It might be interesting to look up the price of Chiron shares immediately before and after the 2004 debacle and the price of shares by the time of the merger. Go to `http://www.quote.com/qc/stocks/charts.aspx` and enter Nasdaq: CHIR for a chart of the company's stock rise and fall over the past few years.

Action Plan

Ogilvy Public Relations Worldwide believes "issues management is an ongoing process of aligning corporate behaviour with stakeholder expectations. Issues become issues when this alignment is missing" (Ogilvy, 2006).

Use Ogilvy's eight-step programme (Ogilvy, 2006) to analyse and develop solutions to the decreasing number of technical school graduates mentioned earlier in the chapter. Apply the same procedure to the accounting issue or any other issues you think are relevant:

1. Identification – what issues could emerge?
2. Prioritization – what damage could occur?
3. Monitoring – how is this issue evolving?
4. Preparation – can action plans be developed?
5. Action to influence – what steps can be taken to ensure a positive outcome?
6. Issue response –what would happen if the issue took a negative turn?
7. Evaluation – what was the effect of the response?
8. Reclassification – has the issue lessened or escalated?

Websites

Find past and present stock prices at `http://www.quote.com/qc/stocks/charts.aspx`. Choose a company that has recently handled a scandal or media exposé and see if that action has affected the price of its stock.

The International Association of Business Communicators website offers information on many communication issues. Its bookstore features *Issues Management: Anticipation and Influence* by George B. McGrath. Go to `http://iabcstore.stores.yahoo.net/isman.html` (IABC, 2006) and skim chapter titles to find a topic to read more about.

Developing marketing messages that tap into trends can benefit innovative companies. Interesting trend patterns can emerge in specific demographic groups. Find out what women are thinking at `http://www.ivillage.com/?vty=women.com/` (iVillage, 2006) and Hispanics at www.hispaniconline.com (Hispaniconline, 2006) and see if you can identify any future trends of these two groups.

References

Barton, L. (1992) *Crisis in Organizations: Managing and Communicating in the Heat of Chaos*. Cincinnati, OH, South-Western Publishing.

BusinessWeek (2006) "The young and the vicious". *Business Week*, 31 July 2006: 34.

Carvajal, D. (2005) "Processed foods? Read this, France says". *The International Herald Tribune*, 2 October 2005. Available from: www.iht.com/articles/2005/10/02/business/food03.php [Accessed 14 June 2006].

CIB (2006) "Fergal McDonnell: art, science or alchemy?" CIB Conference 2006. Available from: http://cib.uk.com/artman/publish/printer_590.shtml [Accessed 29 May 2006].

DeNoon, D. (2004) "Arthritis drug Vioxx pulled off market". 30 September 2004. Available from: http://www.webmd.com/content/article/94/102995.htm [Accessed 31 July 2006].

Edelman (2006) "Crisis & issues management". Available from: http://www.edelman.com/expertise/practices/crisis/ [Accessed 13 June 2006].

Eppes, T. (1998) "Integrated marketing is crisis management". *IMP*, September–October: 10–11.

FDA (2004) "2004 Chiron flu vaccine chronology". US Food and Drug Administration. Available from: www.fda.gov/oc/opacom/hottopics/chronology1016.html [Accessed 13 June, 2006].

Fortini-Campbell, L. (2002) *Hitting the Sweet Spot*. Chicago, The Copy Workshop.

Grandmaison, P. (2004) "Corporate social responsibility: a real challenge for companies or not?" *The Public Affairs Newsletter*, February.

Grant, J. (2006) *The Brand Innovation Manifesto*. Chichester, UK, John Wiley & Sons, Ltd.

Heath, R. (1997) *Strategic Issues Management*. Thousand Oaks, CA, Sage Publications, Inc.

Hispaniconline (2006) Available from: www.hispanicsonline.com [Accessed 2 September 2006].

IABC (2004) "Global perspectives: how can communicators bridge the gap between executives and employees?" *Communication World*, March/April: 6–7.

IABC (2006) IABC store. Available from: http://iabcstore.stores.yahoo.net/isman.html [Accessed 2 September 2006].

Inc. Magazine (2006) "The man who wanted a live operator". *Inc. Magazine*, February: 30.

Issue Management Council (2006a) "IMC board of directors". Available from: www.issuemanagement.org/documents/bios/jill_lester.html [Accessed 12 June 2006].

Issue Management Council (2006b) "Nine issue management best practice indicators". Available from: www.issuemanagement.org/documents/best_practices.htm [Accessed 12 June 2006].

Issue Management Council (2006c) "What is issue management?" Available from: www.issuemanagement.org [Accessed 12 June 2006].

iVillage (2006) Available from: http://www.ivillage.com/?vty = women.com [Accessed 1 September 2006].

Johnson, L. (2006) "Latest Vioxx win justifies Merck strategy". *The Mercury News*, 14 July 2006. Available from: http://www.mercurynews.com/mid/mercurynews/business/financial_markets/15042161.htm [Accessed 17 July 2006].

Kosatsky, T. (2005) "The 2003 European heat waves". *Eurosurveillance*, July. Available from: http://www.eurosurveillance.org/em/v10n07/1007-222.asp [Accessed 16 July 2006].

Lerbinger, O. (1997) *The Crisis Manager: Facing Risk and Responsibility*. Mahwah, NJ, Lawrence Erlbaum.

McEwen, W., Fang, X., Zhang, C. & Burkholder, R. (2006) "Inside the mind of the Chinese consumer". *Harvard Business Review*, March: 68–76.

Morier, R. & Egan, M. (2006) "Preparing for crisis at the world bank". *Strategic Communication Management* **10**(2): 22–25. Available from: http://0-web11.epnet.com.library.winthrop.edu:80/citation.asp?tb=1...B1+%2Dcommunicat ions+st%5BO+%2Dstrategic++planning + BB11&fn=1&rn=5 [Accessed 22 May 2006].

Monster Intelligence (2005) "Retention strategies for 2006 and beyond". Available from: http://media.monster.com/a/ i/intelligence/pdf/Monster_Research_Retention_Strategies_for_2006.pdf [Accessed 31 July 2006].

Ogilvy (2006) "Expertise: issues management". Ogilvy Public Relations Worldwide. Available from: www. alexanderogilvy.com/expertise/issues-management.cfm [Accessed 12 June 2006].

Pirard, P., Vandentorren, S., Pascal, M. *et al.* (2005) "Summary of the mortality impact assessment of the 2003 heat wave in France". *Eurosurveillance*, July. Available from: http://www.eurosurveillance.org/em/v10n07/1007-224.asp [Accessed 16 July 2006].

Quote.com (2006) Nastaq. Available from: http://www.quote.com/qc/stocks/charts.aspx [Accessed 2 September 2006].

Sheffi, Y. (2005) "Maxing the gain". *Chief Executive*, August–September: 62–64.

Springwise (2006) "Food and beverage ideas". Available from: http://www.springwise.com/food_beverage/index. php?page = 5 [Accessed 4 September 2006].

Taylor, P. (2005) "Chiron will not meet 2005 flu vaccine targets". *Inpharma*, 17 June 2005. Available from: http://www. drugresearcher.com/news/ng.asp?n = 60700-chiron-will-not [Accessed 13 June 2006].

Tydecks, M. (2004) "New type of lobbying: issue-specific business alliances beyond all industry brands". *The Public Affairs Newsletter*, September. Available from: http://www.apcoworldwide.com/content/Newsroom/Staff_Insight/ index.cfm [Accessed 14 June 2006].

Westcott, S. (2006) "Goodbye and good luck". *Inc. Magazine*, April: 40–42.

Bibliography

Clow, K. & Baack, D. (2004) *Integrated Advertising, Promotion, and Marketing Communications*. New Jersey, Pearson Prentice Hall.

Gillin, P. (2006) "New technology, new media, new paradigm". *B to B Interactive Marketing Guide 2006*:38.

CHAPTER 14

New Focus on Responsible Communication

Executive Summary

New research and the wisdom of experts can help companies formulate viable communication programmes.

Integrated marketing communication (IMC) came into practice over 15 years ago when technology enabled marketers to understand their customers and the value of speaking with "one voice" to consumers
Identifying the six steps of an integrated marketing communication plan helps clarify the process.

Today, integrated business communication (IBC) extends marketing efforts beyond the traditional model and recognizes the benefits to the entire company when line employees to top-level executives speak with "one voice" to various stakeholders
This process requires more in-depth analysis of the communication process and greater understanding of internal and external stakeholder behaviour.

Brand building uses long-term strategies to acquire customers and ensure product loyalty, and includes guerrilla marketing and permission marketing. Corporations, dependent on consumer opinion, have discovered the advantages of supporting environmental causes
The public expects this involvement, not only of big business but also of small local companies.

Customer communication management involves customer relationship management (CRM), the process of gathering information and feedback and using that information to achieve customer satisfaction and loyalty

Employee communication management means providing employees with clear and pertinent information in a timely manner, as well as empowering employees as ambassadors of company goodwill

Adaptations of traditional communication processes, such as guerrilla marketing, buzz marketing, word-of-mouth marketing and other forms, continue to add complexity to the communication mix. ■

New Focus on Responsible Communication

"You must work; we must all work, to make the world worthy of its children.
Pablo Casals, Spanish Cellist"

Introduction to New Communication Directions

Not all communication is good communication, nor is all communication necessary or justified. But by now you should realize that effective communication is vital to the success of any business, especially to those in the global marketplace. In this chapter we will discuss integrated marketing communication (IMC) and how integrated business communication (IBC) emerged out of this growing movement. We will also explore the new concept of civic public relations, an extension of civic journalism efforts in which community newspapers partner local governments and social institutions.

We'll take a look at how making informed and workable decisions impacts upon a company's communication efforts. Let's start with a real-life scenario. In a beverage retail company, district managers found that account managers (salespeople meeting with large accounts at client headquarters) and sales managers (salespeople meeting with accounts in the field) were bogged down with daily emails coming from managers who were not their direct bosses. They ranged from "favour asking" and FYIs to urgent messages. One manager was getting up to 50 emails a day, not from corporate personnel, her boss or her customers, but from her counterparts.

District managers, feeling that account and sales managers were spending too much time reading and answering daily emails, directed that all email messages should go through them. District managers would decide which emails were important enough to be redirected to lower-level managers.

Now, while this may have seemed a good plan, it was not. District managers could not redirect the important emails quickly enough for managers to take immediate and necessary actions, and the "not so important" delayed messages that the district managers did not send immediately, soon became "urgent" messages from customers.

The district managers called the managers together to discuss how the problem of email overload could be solved efficiently. The managers came up with this solution: all managers were issued company cell phones. If a problem required immediate attention (within two days), a cell phone call would be placed, but if the message was not so important or an FYI, an email would be sent. This solution allowed managers in the field or on business trips at least two days to access email before worrying that they were missing messages that needed immediate attention.

Effective messaging requires the total integration of communication into all aspects of business, every day and in every department.

Integrated Marketing Communication

Organizations that practise integrated marketing communication tailor their messages to specifically identified target customers. Schultz and Schultz call such organizations "customer-centric" because they work "to provide the best customer products, services and solutions" (Schultz & Schultz, 2003, p. 51). IMC works; in fact, successful companies such as Apple, Dell, IKEA, Proctor and Gamble and Wal-Mart, among others, use this approach.

Customers are multidimensional and, over time, adjust their buying patterns as their lifestyles and needs change. Knowing the influences on customer buying behaviour provides valuable insight to companies and helps shape the message and choice of communication tools.

Integrated marketing communication operates under the premise that "all points of brand contact" (Schultz & Schultz, 2003) must be planned and controlled. IMC recognizes that just buying media is not an effective way to reach consumers. In fact, there are many contact points or touchpoints with a brand – points where the consumer interacts with the brand, talks to other consumers (viral marketing) or reads the instructions on a package (Calder & Malthouse, 2003). Multiple forms of communication options must be considered and strategically selected to reach consumers in a world where there is considerable product parity, an overload of messages from a variety of sources and a limited time to make purchase decisions.

As Rudolph Magnani, president and founder of Magnani Continuum Marketing, notes: "In the costly world of marketing, diluting or forfeiting any morsel of the message is unsound, but it happens all the time" (Magnani, 2006, p. 12). Corporations that practise IMC integrate their marketing communication operations and align them internally to serve the needs of their organizations.

Steps in integrated marketing communication planning

The six steps in developing an integrated marketing communication plan (adapted from Schultz and Schultz, 2003) include:

1. Identifying customers and potential customers. Through the use of databases and demographic, psychographic, geographic and behavioural data, knowledge of customers and what motivates them is gained. Note that customers and potential customers are considered different groups.
2. Determining the value of both customers and potential customers. How much income flows to the company through current customers? What is their lifetime value to the company?.
3. Developing communication messages that reach both customers and targeted potential customers.
4. Developing and implementing communication strategies to reach both groups.
5. Determining the return on investment (ROI) by reaching both groups.
6. Evaluating results.

Steps 1–3 have been discussed throughout this book. Step 4 deserves more attention.

Developing and Implementing Communication Strategies

Let's examine more thoroughly communication strategies, from choosing the best communication channel to making branding decisions.

Choosing communication channels

What criteria govern which communication tool should be used? And how can we ensure that messages are integrated across media? Kevin Lane Keller identified six dimensions for evaluating the selection of media in an IMC programme (Keller, 2001, pp. 832–839). These criteria work equally well in integrated business communication:

1. *Coverage.* How much of the target market is reached by each communication vehicle. How much of the market is duplicated?

2. *Contribution.* Will the particular medium create the desired response from the targeted audience?

3. *Commonality.* How is the concept of one voice, one message reinforced? Keller suggests that certain media have more power to reinforce a common meaning than others.

4. *Complementarity.* How are different associations and linkages stressed across media? Public relations tactics are good at introducing a new brand into a market. Promotional tactics, such as coupons, generate quicker sales but do not reinforce brand loyalty.

5. *Robustness.* How effective are the communication vehicles in reaching those who already know about a brand versus those who are just being introduced to a brand? The Internet is a robust medium that can effectively reach both types of potential customer.

6. *Cost.* How cost effective is a particular vehicle? There are many acceptable systems for measuring cost effectiveness.

As Keller indicates, the choice of communication vehicle often means trade-offs. For example, striving for robustness in vehicle selection may mean that complementarity must be sacrificed.

Implementing mass media vehicles

The selection of multiple tactics to reach an identified target audience requires media planners and buyers. Here are some general points to remember about media usage:

• Print media (newspapers, magazines and brochures), interactive media and sales promotions are effective at conveying product information. Consumers engage with an active medium that requires their participation in the message.

• Television is effective in eliciting emotional responses from audiences, whereas print media and sponsorships are less so.

• Interactive media and sales promotions are less effective in provoking an emotional response.

• Corporate advertising or public relations activities are effective in the development of a brand name.

• Sponsorships (sponsoring a sporting or charity event) are effective, credibility-building tools.

Communication tools such as face-to-face meetings, newsletters, brochures, Intranets, special events, community outreach programs, etc. can be used alone or in conjunction with mass media.

The business of branding

Brands emerged at the turn of the twentieth century, but their value was amplified in the 1980s. Schultz and Barnes suggest that branding became a topic of interest when corporate raiders purchased organizations for their brands and brand values alone (Schultz & Barnes, 1999, pp. 39–40). To enhance brand worth, marketing executives, particularly in the USA, began to place more emphasis on short-term promotional techniques (couponing, price promotions, etc.) to produce short-term value. In the end, short-term promotional tactics did nothing to enhance brand equity and, in many cases, started the brands on a downward spiral of profit margin erosion as companies couldn't withdraw from using coupons to stimulate sales.

Today, however, the issue of branding is reflected in long-term strategy and is a foremost concern in the business communication process.

Experts compare the process of branding to the cycle of evolution – **brands** are created, live and die, and, in some cases, are revived. Often the brand name survives longer than the product (Ries & Ries, 2004; Ryder, 2004). Opportunities for companies to build new brands, argue Ries and Ries, frequently mean creating new categories rather than going after established competitors. In the world of brands, being first in a product category can be an advantage. Why was the success of iPod so astonishing? It was a new category.

Whether you are creating a new brand or promoting an old one, the rules of branding are changing. Simon Williams (Parry, 2005) from Sterling Branding makes the following suggestions about the future of branding:

> The value of brands to organizations is measured by Interbrand, an international brand valuation company. Coca-Cola leads the list of international brands, followed by Microsoft, IBM, General Electric, Intel, Nokia, Toyota, McDonald's and Mercedes Benz (Interbrand, 2006).

- Brands that influence the way we behave and live – our culture – will sell more. Google, for example, is changing the way we track and receive information.
- Brands must have a point of view. Today's customers are smart and expect to be involved in the buying process. Starbucks, for example, presents a strong point of view about letting customers decide on product specifications.

- Today's customers are intolerant of mistakes in the communication process. A poorly designed website, a public relations blunder or a production error that results in a recall have serious long-term effects on how consumers view a brand.
- Social responsibility from a branded company is expected.
- Mass customization is important to the future of brands.
- Packaging and display of a brand affect consumer purchases.

Specialized marketing techniques

Marketing practices have evolved to meet the demands of a dynamic marketplace. Small business owners, in particular, should be aware of some of the latest trends in marketing communication. Three of the more popular techniques are:

- guerrilla marketing
- permission marketing
- word-of-mouth marketing.

Guerrilla marketing

Guerrilla marketing focuses on the use of low-cost alternative media to reach targeted small groups of consumers. It is based on the premise that all organizations, no matter their size, can and should develop marketing programmes. As in the practice of IMC, guerrilla marketing encourages small businesses to use databases to build long-term relationships with customers and to use a variety of grass-roots communication vehicles to reach target audiences.

Jay Conrad Levinson, widely quoted in the field, says a guerrilla marketing programme for a small business might include the following tactics: an ad in a phone directory, a website, signage, a direct mail campaign consisting of a business card and a brochure and follow-up calls to those targeted by the literature (Levinson, 1998, pp. 22–23).

Small businesses have the advantage of making personal contact with potential customers. Guerrilla marketing concentrates on building long-term relationships with customers who will, in turn, communicate to others through word of mouth the value of that relationship.

Permission marketing

Customer agreement to accept promotional material from a company is called **permission marketing**. A customer, contacted by a telephone caller or responding to a website or direct mail piece, often agrees to accept information from a company. For example, a furnace filter company includes a postcard in a package of filters that offers to send a "friendly reminder" to the customer notifying her when it is time to change the filter. The customer merely returns the postcard or sends her email address to the company accepting the offer. This furnace filter company is attempting to build life-long relationships, over time, with customers by offering them incentives to remain loyal.

Jim Stengel, global marketing officer for Proctor & Gamble, believes permission marketing is "a state of mind across all aspects of marketing rather than a tactic". He told an audience of the American Association of Advertising Agencies that the goal for marketers should be to "create messages across all elements of the marketing mix that are so compelling that consumers invite marketers into their homes" (Mislowski, 2005).

Permission marketing programmes have definite advantages: they reduce noise from the marketplace, boost the effectiveness of direct mail and other tools and help overcome product parity issues.

Word-of-mouth marketing

The value of **word-of-mouth communication**, strategic efforts to encourage customers and employees to recommend products to other consumers, has been "rediscovered" by marketing professionals.

Although people always have recommended products to friends and family, the idea that companies can manage such communications is new. Some companies strive to get their product into the hands of the innovators, connectors and mavens that Malcolm Gladwell described in *The Tipping Point* (Gladwell, 2002).

The concept is catching on. The Word-of-Mouth Marketing Association (WOMMA) has over 300 member groups worldwide, and the rapidly growing list includes Coca-Cola, Drum Finland, Dell, Eu Yan Sang and Lucent Technologies. On its website, WOMMA says its members "are the leading companies pioneering WOM techniques" and that they are "working together to grow the business from a natural phenomenon to a core part of the marketing mix" (WOMMA, 2006).

A Glasgow neighbourhood group used word of mouth to garner support for its grassroots clean-up campaign, Proud of Pollokshields. Volunteers met with local civic groups and encouraged everyone with whom they spoke to "tell their friends and family about it as well". The effort was so successful that the campaign has become an annual event (BBC, 2006).

The buzz in the marketing world is that word of mouth is able to infiltrate the no-marketing shields people build around themselves, and that informal, unmediated communications, such as social media, are alternative ways to communicate with certain publics.

That is, of course, as long as the medium is trusted. Some experts predict that cynical consumers will continue to view advertising as nothing more than persuasive sales pitches and will be eager to question the authenticity of a blogger's remarks. Recommendations from these channels may be more vulnerable to criticism than those from family and friends.

Other marketing techniques

Marketers have found some success using the following techniques:

- *Buzz marketing.* Focusing consumer attention on your product by getting celebrities to use or display it or by giving the product celebrity status by making it fascinating or entertaining. One inherent danger with using celebrities as "walking billboards" is that, if they should fall into disfavour, the products receive negative publicity.
- *Product placement.* Paying for your product to be featured in a movie, song or television show. This field, which pulls advertising dollars in its direction, is becoming overcrowded and ineffective. Some companies have opted to pull out of product placement.
- *Stealth marketing.* Marketing surreptitiously to an unaware public through covert and sneaky persuasive arguments aimed at consumer vulnerabilities. Some consider this practice as having ethical limitations.
- *Viral marketing.* Getting word of a product or service out to the public through the networking capability of the Internet. Messages can snowball rapidly.

> A survey of 100 UK brands conducted by buzz marketing specialists CommentUK reported that 87 % of the companies polled were "confident of generating live buzz PR around campaigns at a trade and mainstream level". Another 65 % said they would use buzz marketing in their 2007 communications plans (Donohue, 2006).

Integrated Business Communication

The foundations of integrated business communication were built on the principles of integrated marketing communication. Corporate leaders quickly realized the benefits of integrating communication in and throughout the organization, not just from the marketing department. In addition, they reasoned, external messages, particularly those sent word of mouth by employees, needed to speak with one voice.

The foundations of integrated business communication (IBC)

In the global marketplace, companies talk to suppliers, customers and business partners around the world with computers that interface with other computers in various locations with 24/7/365 access.

These information floodgates opened in the late 1990s when Web-based standards of operation were established. This technical innovation enabled digitized data (images, words, music) to be shaped, manipulated, transmitted and stored readily without concern as to geography or computing device.

Communication management became a prime focus for all types and sizes of organizations. The *Manager's Guide to Excellence in Public Relations and Communication Management* reported in its survey of 321 organizations in Canada, the UK and the USA that effective communication constructs are the same in all types of organization. The report said "communication excellence is universal … it is the same for corporations, not-for-profit organizations, government agencies, and trade or professional associations".

IBC is now necessary throughout an organization, in all areas, both internal and external, for all levels of employees, from structural maintenance personnel to top-level executives, and with and within all departments, from accounting to sales.

The integrated business communication model

Let's look at how IBC fits within our transactional communication framework.

The IBC model shows the organization communicating with both internal and external publics. **External publics** are customers and potential customers reached through marketing efforts and those reached through other communication efforts, such

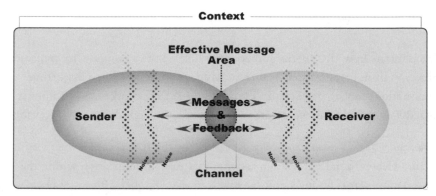

Figure 14.1 Transactional communication model.

as suppliers and governmental agencies. The **internal oval** includes boards of directors, executives, managers, employees and their families.

Noise also affects an organization's communication with its publics, from information overload to poor reception. Situational context is subject to distortion by noise. The interpretation of an advertising message may be different if you receive that message at home, sitting in an easy chair while watching your favourite television sitcom, as against receiving the ad in a less receptive and more noise-laden context (getting children bathed or during a late-night news segment just as you are heading to bed).

Even when all components are working together, effective communication is difficult to achieve. One of the key determinants is structuring the organization to facilitate the integration of communication.

Figure 14.2 Compare this model with the transactional communication model in Figure 14.1. Notice how the transactional communication elements are adapted to the integrated business communication model to illustrate internal and external publics, their messaging and feedback.

Making IBC work

Models illustrate how IBC works in theory but tell us little about how to implement the processes in an organization. The pioneering works of integrated marketing communication scholars (see Schulz, Tannenbaum & Lauterborn, 1994; Schultz & Schultz, 2003) provide starting points in this discussion. Consider these suggestions:

1. *Organizations need to plan strategically.* As a study by the American Productivity and Quality Center found, integration requires intense communication within the organization, across business units and with outside suppliers. It cannot be driven by plans and programmes alone (Schultz & Schultz, 2003). In the IBC model, groups such as the media, interest groups, government and other publics are important stakeholders that must be integrated into the communication strategy.

2. *Points of contact with stakeholders need to be identified and evaluated as to importance.* This requires organizations to have a thorough knowledge of their customers and prospective customers. It necessitates benchmark procedures, such as internal audits of organizational infrastructure and communication processes, to ensure both are optimally aligned to serve the company's IBC mission. Audits should include areas such as human resources, IT, product development, customer service and the traditional communication functions of public relations, marketing, advertising, sales, special events and public affairs.

   As Magnani (2006) and others have noted, organizations are often not internally aligned – that is, the structure of the communication process within an organization is fragmented. Part of the problem in integrating communication platforms stems from the silo mindset within organizations: public relations believes it is being usurped by marketing communications; sales refuses to share data with marketing; advertising feels affronted by e-commerce; human resources thinks it should be the sole voice for communicating with employees – each unit creates its own silo of information.

   Of course, individuals responsible for developing advertising, public relations, special events, etc., should have specific expertise, but achieving organizational goals requires that all communication functions work together. The IBC model illustrates the strength of organization–stakeholder relationships.

   Organizations must be properly restructured to facilitate integration, and even successful businesses may not have yet addressed the inherent problems in making systemic changes.

   A telecommunications marketing executive at a regional operation of a global company explained that public relations in his company functions only as a source for community relations and government affairs. Marketing efforts are independent of the public relations department, and sales managers implement their own promotional campaigns. While this gives each department hierarchal power, it negates any collaborative effort to speak with one voice and could lead to multiple messages being sent to the public.

A problem in implementing IBC plans is the traditional education and training of communication professionals in the often rigid silos of higher education. Business students often know little about communication theory and communication students are naïve about the way business functions.

3. *Reporting structures must allow for communication to flow effectively in a timely fashion between cross-functional units and teams.* Individuals who lead such communication efforts must be able to see beyond traditional silos, value collaboration and work towards implementing a total communication effort in their organizations.

4. *Databases need to be utilized at all appropriate points in the communication process to store information about customers and potential customers and to track the effectiveness of communication strategies.* Considerable capital is spent annually on the collection of data, while much of that data goes unused. The key to effective databasing is using it as a basis for more effective decision-making. Data analysis can be difficult and resource-consuming. Organizations need to specify which decisions they are interested in guiding before they fall under the "lure of the data sirens" (Hopkins, Duhachek & Iacobucci, 2002, p. 213).

5. *Evaluation of the effectiveness of a strategic plan must be an ongoing process.* Successful global companies evaluate and analyse their communication efforts in order to adjust and refine procedures and processes.

Dig Deeper

As part of an effort to improve communication during and following devastating earthquakes in South Asia, an Earthquake Relief & Rehabilitation Communication Plan "for a systematic and coordinated health education and communication response to the earthquake" was formulated.

The Communication Plan brought together the Ministries of Health, Environment and Social Welfare as well as UNICEF and WHO and other partners to address three programme areas: Health, Water & Sanitation and Child Protection. Its objectives are "to create awareness and motivation in order to prevent further sufferings, diseases and disabilities and to encourage information sharing/coordination amongst concerned ministries, agencies and other partners" (Pakquakecommunication, 2005).

The plan is called an "integrated communication plan" and includes such key concepts as communication objectives, communication strategies and communication outcomes. A copy of the integrated communication plan can be found by following the link at http://www.pakquakecommunication.org/site/content/blogcategory/19/63/ (Pakquakecommunication, 2005).

Issues in IBC Planning

Communication, both internal and external, reflect the company's reputation, brand image and customer relationship. Today, consumer demand for involvement, transparency and accountability must be addressed.

The corporate social responsibility movement

Corporations realize stakeholders expect them to help support social causes and ecological initiatives and understand that doing so enhances their visibility and credibility. Acting responsibly, for example allocating areas around manufacturing facilities as wildlife habitats or as recreational areas for employees, is not only good for image building, it is good for business.

Consider this example. ITC, a private agricultural company in India, began its e-choupal program which provided computers and gathering places to rural farming villages so farmers could get together to discuss current market information and check buying prices for their crops. ITC helped catalyse rural improvement, alleviating isolation and price gouging. By 2003, e-choupal services were being accessed by nearly 1 million farmers in 11 000 villages. ITC gained more than just goodwill, it benefited from developing a loyal and trusted network that serves as a distribution channel for its products (Annamalai & Rao, 2003).

"Doing well by doing good" is a well-worn phrase; but it is widely recognized that a company can do well financially when the public is aware that it is doing good (Murphy, 2004).

Social responsibility reports have evolved from cursory retrospectives to vehicles that provide stakeholders with information on strategy, partnering and outreach efforts. They function to bring awareness to a company's transparent efforts to be more socially

Dig Deeper

The International Organization for Standardization (IOS) is a global movement interested in establishing voluntary guideline standards that will encourage social responsibility. The organization plans to develop common benchmarks for evaluation and issue a report by 2008. Leading the effort to develop the guidelines are the Swedish Standards Institute and the Brazilian Association of Technical Standards. Read more about the IOS at its website: http: www.iso.org (IOS, 2006).

responsible. These reports are often bundled with other related publications such as health and sustainability reports, philanthropic reports and annual business reports (Williams, 2005).

Not all organizations have an interest in promoting themselves as socially responsible. Corporations in France have not been very vocal about their corporate social responsibility (CSR) affairs, according to an article in *The Public Affairs Newsletter*, because their business culture does not highly rank the image-maintaining tactics of companies in other countries. French corporations usually leave social concerns to the state and operate under a high level of social protection regulation. Medef, the French Business Federation, began a campaign to raise the awareness of CSR among companies in 2001.

Research conducted by Maignan and Ralston (2002) compared how CSR was discussed on the websites of 50 companies in France, the Netherlands, the UK and the USA. They found that the French and the Dutch were more likely to mention practices that were linked to the production process (such as environmental policies) and traditional promotion activities (sponsorships, etc.); US businesses were more likely to mention activities beyond conventional corporate venues such as philanthropy and volunteerism; while the UK took a more intermediate approach by talking about traditional production and promotional activities and also citing efforts that exceeded conventional practices. For those who see CSR as a misplaced function of private enterprise, for those who believe CSR is an organization's "key source of innovation

Strategic Thinking

The Business Case for Corporate Citizenship, developed by Arthur D. Little for the Global Corporate Citizenship Initiative, cites eight areas in which a company can benefit from good corporate citizenship (Roberts, Keeble & Brown, 2003):

- reputation management
- risk profile and risk management
- employee recruitment, motivation and retention
- investor relations and access to capital
- learning and innovation
- competitiveness and market positioning
- operational efficiency
- license to operate.

Why are these areas important to corporate citizenship?

and partnership for growth" and for all those organizations in between, the debate on the role corporate social responsibility should play, continues (Grandmaison, 2004, p. 29).

Civic public relations

Civic public relations focuses on community issues, locally, regionally and globally. Organizations add to their positive image when they show concern for issues that affect not just their customers, but humanity.

This relationship-building work goes beyond supporting a local soccer team or donating to a cancer fund. It means being involved in various civic activities, from issuing position papers on new governmental regulations to sponsoring town hall meetings to addressing neighbourhood concerns. Civic public relations calls for company programmes that are integrated into everyday practices, and empowers employees to become involved in community projects.

Corporations are aware that the financial world is influenced by the role businesses play as good global citizens. Rating systems evaluate companies from an environmental perspective, and these findings are used by stockbrokers and fund managers when making investment decisions.

Arthur Wiese, vice-president of corporate communications at Entergy, a global electrical utility, explains the company's communication programme to make various publics aware of Entergy's environmental stewardship:

> In 'free' media, executive speeches and employee communications, we emphasize how Entergy is an atypical utility company that emphasizes sustainable development, concern for its poorest customers and environmental protection (especially our unconventional support for federal limits on greenhouse gas emissions as a means of controlling global warming). This has been favourably received by investment funds that stress responsible, sustainable corporate behaviour (Wiese, 2006).

Customer communication management

The customer is a key stakeholder in the IBC model, and choosing the right way to reach that customer with an effective message requires knowledge and expertise.

Customer relationship management

Customer relationship management (CRM) is the process of gathering information and feedback and using that information to achieve customer satisfaction and loyalty. At the core of this process is a variety of communication tools, from direct mail to electronic billing to call centre services. Many CRM programmes are using an integrated teamwork approach that combines virtual communication tools such as blogs and threaded discussions with real-world information sources such as databasing and lifetime value assessment. Time is no longer a prime factor in the 7/24/365 world of email and website access.

Datastream Systems, a software company, spends most of its marketing dollars on building "relationships with specific groups – most importantly, existing customers". While their competition funds splashy ad campaigns and attends popular trade shows, Greg Sutter, Datastream vice-president of marketing, says, "To defend our position, we don't go wide, we go deep" (Neuborne, 2006).

Using effective customer communication as everyday business practice in all departments and across all levels of management is what integrated business communication is all about.

Citizen relationship management

Taking its cue from business, government has begun developing positive relationships with its constituents using a process called **citizen relationship management** (ZRM). Customer relationship marketing (CRM) is primarily a customer-centred

Dig Deeper

John H. Roberts, Australian Graduate School of Management and London Business School professor, says, "In times of turbulence, relationships and behaviours are loosened up and the glue that holds customers to one's product is weakest".

He suggests companies can use customer relationship management as a core business strategy, especially when competition emerges surreptitiously as technology and globalization lower barriers to entry. Roberts believes building customer relationships and guarding a market niche are crucial.

Read more about Roberts' research on defensive business tactics at www2.agsm.edu.au (Roberts, 2006).

marketing tool that uses the long-term value of a relationship to optimize selling techniques. ZRM involves servicing rather than selling, but uses the CRM concepts of identification, differentiation, interaction and personalization to develop citizen–institution relationships (Barquin, 2004).

Customers as opinion leaders

Historically, experts have cited the diffusion theory (early innovators pass down messages to the masses) to explain the dissemination of news and information, but this theory has its critics. Experts say customers who have access to information sources, traditionally reserved for innovators, form their own opinions in real time.

When Monsanto began to garner public support for using biotechnology in crop production, it tried a new tactic. Instead of relying on scientists and other experts to disseminate the information, it talked directly to the people through advertising, face-to-face meetings and other media resources. Consumers felt they were part of the information loop.

This dramatic shift in communicating with various publics emphasizes the two-way integrated business communication model. Organizations need to present messages that are personalized and credible and at the same time provide interactive opportunities for customer response and feedback.

Strategic Thinking

Instant information, easily accessible by various levels of stakeholders, requires organizations to be vigilant in their communication efforts and to connect with relevant publics where, when and how they want to be reached.

Non-government organizations (NGOs) are seen as powerful brands trusted by people around the world. Communicating a company's cooperation with organizations such as Greenpeace or Amnesty International can enhance a company's image and help encourage public acceptance of ecological, environmental or humanitarian-related issues.

Communication relating to mergers and acquisitions must flow not only to the financial sector and government regulators but also to concerned communities, consumers and customers.

Your company, a mega grocery store chain, plans to buy a small neighbourhood store. What key messages would you send and which media would you use to reach your relevant publics and continue customer loyalty?

Employee communication management

Satisfied and loyal employees enable management to achieve objectives; dissatisfied employees stymie organizational growth. All employees influence public opinion about a company, its leadership and its products or services. As Ursula Stroh at the University of Technology in Sydney, Australia, says, "The attitudes and loyalty of employees are directly influenced by their participation in communication efforts" (Gillis, 2004).

A 2005 IABC Research Foundation report, *Best Practices in Employee Communication: A Study of Global Challenges and Approaches*, indicated that management in 48 % of the

Strategic Thinking

After survey findings revealed that managers and employees felt they weren't getting the company information they needed, the Australian Tax Office faced implementing a communication programme for its 21 000 employees at 96 locations across 8 million square kilometres. Problems: (1) the agency's distribution of information on the Intranet was not regular; (2) the content of the agency's electronic magazine was mainly employee contributions; (3) no one was regulating which messages were sent (or not sent) and to whom.

Belinda Flint, internal communication director, decided on a push–pull communication approach. She said, "Our communication approach is to engage our employees wherever possible and not force information upon them constantly". Only crucial information is pushed; optional information is available in many media channels for pulling by the consumer (Palframan-Smith, 2004).

Here's a list of the communication tools that were developed. Which ones would you label as push tools?

- electronic employee magazine
- priority message delivery system
- subscribe message delivery system
- Internet
- Intranet
- email
- satellite television
- videoconferencing
- advertising
- notice board screens.

472 companies surveyed worldwide failed "to effectively explain to employees the purpose of their jobs and the mission and strategy of their businesses". Perhaps owing to this statistic, the report also revealed that only 37 % of organizations felt that employees "are effectively aligned to the missions and visions of their businesses" (IABC, 2005).

IABC's Paul Sanchez cautions: "Management often sends inconsistent messages to employees, and isn't as visible as it should be … managers, including senior-level leaders, lack the necessary skills to effectively engage employees, or don't understand the roles they need to play" (IABC, 2005).

Laying the foundation

Five key concepts that serve as the foundation for viable and effective communication programmes are:

1. All communication to, from and within the company is seen as having value.
2. Communication feedback from all levels is valued by management.
3. Communication is an important component of strategic planning.
4. Communication efforts are supported by the company and integrated into everyday practices.
5. Positive communication is nurtured by the company.

Management plays a crucial role in formulating successful communication programs, but it requires feedback from all interested groups.

Chapter Summary

The practice of integrated business communication requires organizations to think about how an organization is structured, how it relates to its stakeholders, how its brands are perceived by the public and how its actions are translated in the civic arena.

Databases are important sources of information that can assist in decision-making. Silos within the organizational structure work against the integration of communication and prevent the creative, insightful decision-making required in the competitive, global marketplace.

Communicators play many roles, both formal and informal. Excellent communicators are a high-demand resource as communication becomes totally integrated throughout a company, enabling it to speak with one voice to its essential publics. As a result, IBC is gaining momentum. ■

Learning From Others

Stephen Salyer serves as president and CEO of the Salzburg Seminar, a global centre that brings together emerging leaders from all parts of the world to address, define and come up with creative solutions to global problems.

In his Washington, DC, office, Salyer works across the Atlantic to create a common language for the world's problem solvers – current and future. He copes with national boundaries, professional jargon and international cultural sensitivities.

Addressing the World's Problems

Launched in 1947 by three men studying at Harvard University, the Salzburg Seminar has been operating for almost 60 years on the family estate donated by the widow of Austrian theatre impresario Max Rheinhardt.

The first class of 92 Europeans – many of whom had been combatants on opposing sides of World War II – came together under the leadership of famed anthropologist Margaret Mead.

That first seminar attempted to jump start European intellectual exchange, as the Marshall Plan of that period sought to spearhead the physical reconstruction of Europe.

Salyer says, "By definition, each of our seminars brings people from business, from government, from academe, from NGOs (non-governmental organizations), all of the other philanthropies … media … around a common issue, a common idea, a common strategy".

The biggest communication challenge at the Seminar, Salyer says, is to speak in plain language and in understandable terms to people who bring specialized language from their professional and academic disciplines.

He also manages the language and cultural priorities of Seminar staffers located in Salzburg and the USA, along with a governing board comprised of members located around the world.

"We bring people from all parts of the world and from all cultures together, as well as all sectors. That, too, is a challenge, from the food we serve to the way we think about their customs and their needs, to the way we are mindful that issues must be framed in terms that allow people to come to the table and make progress in their discussion", he says.

"We are of the mind that the world needs a place that reflects global perspectives, not merely the perspective of a single culture or a single nationality".

Salyer encourages college students who are interested in careers in diplomacy or international business to make a sincere investment in learning the details of another national culture.

"Some of the best advice I ever got was to pay attention to the literature, thinking, history and language of the place that one is seeking to understand and do business with", Salyer commented.

Although Salyer acknowledges English as a common language in business and diplomacy, he encourages young professionals to learn how to express themselves plainly and simply.

"Often I find that people who are native English speakers can get very carried away. They speak too fast, use long sentences and choose words that even a very good English speaker won't readily understand.

In an American allusion, more Hemingway and less Henry James is very, very useful".

Case Study – **Patagonia Europe**

From its start in the USA in 1973, Patagonia staunchly protected environmental resources and developed innovative environment-friendly fabrics such as a polyester fleece made from recycled soda bottles that to date has kept over 86 million bottles from landfill sites. The company is also committed to sustainable architecture, using green design for all of its facilities.

The company's mission is to "Build the best product, cause no unnecessary harm and use business to inspire and implement solutions to the environmental crisis". In 1984, Patagonia pledged to allocate 1 % of its sales or 10 % of pretax profits, whichever was the greater, to the protection and restoration of the natural environment. In 2005, the company donated $2.1 million to support environmental groups.

Patagonia Europe was started in 1987 (Patagonia, 2006).

Before you read further, how do you think Patagonia Europe integrated the parent company's mandate to help protect the environment? Did it emulate Patagonia, USA?

Patagonia Europe decided to focus on environmental causes close to home. It works with outside groups to reduce truck pollution in the Alps and helps replenish fishing areas in the Loire and other rivers.

But there is expense involved in being environment friendly. The building materials that Patagonia uses cost 10 % more than conventional ones, and installation and construction can take up to 20 % longer, raising labour costs. In 1991, Patagonia, Inc. was in financial trouble owing to an economic recession and a reduction in credit by the troubled Security Pacific Bank.

Do you think the company compromised its commitment to green design or lowered its donations to environmental groups in an effort to save the company from ruin?

Here's what Patagonia did. The company laid off 120 of its 620 employees and restructured its internal organization. But Patagonia did not cut expenses or its commitments in the two areas on which it had built its reputation. The Research and Development department continued exploring new ways to protect the environment and the grants were sustained.

Do some web research and see how experts are touting Patagonia as a model of green sensibility. *Built to Last: Successful Habits of Visionary Companies* (1994) says "Patagonia's environmental mission lies at the heart of the company's enduring success" (Hildebrand, 1999). ■

Class Exercises

1. British Petroleum has been advertising its environmentally responsible plans to spend $350 million in the next few years to develop energy-efficient products. Starbucks offers coffees that encourage environmentally responsible cultivation and recently announced a programme that will contribute $10 million from the sale of its Ethos bottled water to clean drinking water initiatives. In Belgium, Manpower Unlimited developed a recruitment plan for the disabled to help surmount the barriers to employment of people with disabilities. A 2006 TNS study reported that, among global automotive corporations, BMW (Spain and Italy), Honda (the USA, the UK and Indonesia), Toyota (Japan, Korea and Thailand) and Volvo trucks (Sweden and the Netherlands) ranked highest for social responsibility in two or more markets. Do some web research and see what these companies did to earn this recognition. What are their future plans?

2. Select a small business in your community. After completing an analysis of the business's customers or potential customers through interviews with the owner and present customers, develop a single message for the business. Then, using the examples in the guerrilla marketing section, suggest four or five communication tactics that the owner can use to boost his/her business in a cost-effective and efficient manner.

3. Find out more about the best global brands according to Interbrand. Consult its website at `http://www.interbrand.com` (Interbrand, 2006). Analyse the top 50 brands. What product categories do they represent? What countries are represented in this list? Choose several of the companies and research their new brand categories for the last two years. Report to the class on your findings.

Action Plan

Vitro Sociedad Anonima, a Mexican glassmaker with $3.5 billion in sales, entered into a joint venture with US Corning Glass Works in 1991. The two companies looked forward to sharing industry technology, licensing, research and development and marketing their products together in the US and Mexican markets.

The companies seemed to have a lot in common. They had been founded by innovative individuals more than 100 years earlier and were presently run by management teams that included members of the founding families. They were global companies with many product offerings and both had previously engaged in successful alliances and joint ventures with foreign companies.

When the two companies merged, the cultural differences were evident from the beginning. Vitro's sales approach was less aggressive than Corning's style, and Vitro employees felt the Americans were too direct. Decisions at Vitro meant considering hierarchal traditions and consulting with family members. Corning middle managers typically made their own decisions based on situation analyses and assessment without consultation with top executives.

There were other problems, such as US decentralized management versus Mexican centralized decision-making, differences in customer needs and expectations and distribution methods and, not to be overlooked, the US standard for short lunches as opposed to the Mexican penchant for long, leisurely meals.

Do you think these corporate and cultural problems were resolved? What communication tools would you use to reconcile the two management styles as well as the differences in culture? Do some research on the Web and see how this joint venture turned out.

Websites

Ursula Stroh researched the effects of employee participation in times of organizational change. Her research study can be found at http://www.iabc.com/rf/pdf/Stroh _ paper2002.pdf.

Read all about the success story of e-choupals in India and how they brought a lagging agricultural industry into the twenty-first century at http://www.digitaldividend.org/case/case _ echoupal.htm. You can also visit the e-choupla website at http://www.echoupal.com.

The Ernst & Young Entrepreneur of the Year programme recognizes entrepreneur leadership in several general and industry categories in 25 countries of the world. The programme, now in its twentieth year, works from a base of regional programme winners who then proceed to the national level. How does this programme dovetail with the goals of the company? For more information visit its website at http://ww.ey.com/global/content/nsf/International/EGC _ - _ Eemts _ - _ EoY (Ernst & Young, 2006).

References

Annamalai, K. & Rao, S. (2003) "What works: ITC's e-choupal and profitable rural transformation". World Resources Institute Digital Divide. Available from: http://www.digitaldividend.org/case/case_echoupal.htm [Accessed 8 June 2006].

Barquin, R. (2004) Citizen relationship management (ZRM) – the challenge and the promise. Office of Citizen Services and Communications [newsletter], January: 20–21. Available from: www.gsa.gov/gsa/cm_attachments/ GSA_DOCUMENT/ 14-ZRM-Barquin-Intl_R2OA3-r_0Z5RDZ-i34K-pR.doc [Accessed 7 July, 2006].

BBC (2006) "Residents tackle litter problem". BBC News, 2 July 2006. Available from: http://news.bbc.co.uk/2/hi/ uk_news/scotland/glasgow_and_west/5134386.stm [Accessed 8 August 2006].

Calder, B. & Malthouse, E. (2003) "What is integrated marketing?", in *Kellogg on Integrated Marketing*, ed. by Iacobucci, D. & Calder, B. Hoboken, NJ, John Wiley & Sons, Inc.

Donohue, A. (2006) "Use of buzz marketing on the increase". *IncentiveBulletin*, 30 June 2006. Available from: http:// www.brandrepublic.com/bulletins/incentive/article/566537/use-buzz-marketing-increase/ [Accessed 8 August 2006].

Ernst & Young (2006) "Ernst & Young Entrepreneur of the Year". Available from: http://ww.ey.com/global/content/ nsf/International/EGC_-_Eemts_-_EoY [Accessed 1 August 2006].

Gillis, T. (2004) "In times of change, employee communication is vital to successful organizations". *Communication World*: 8–9.

Gladwell, M. (2002) *Tipping Point*. Boston, Little, Brown & Company.

Grandmaison, P. (2004) "Corporate social responsibility". *Public Affairs Newletter*, February.

Hildebrand, C. (1999) "Turn green". *CIO Magazine*, 15 August 1999. Available from: http://www.cio.com/ archive/081599_green.html [Accessed 25 March 2006].

IABC (2005) "Management failing to connect with employees at almost half of companies, says survey". IABC News Centre – press releases. Available from: http://news.iabc.com/index.php?s=press_releases&item=17 [Accessed 7 July 2006].

Hopkins, N., Duhachek, A. & Iacobucci, D. (2002) "Decision-guidance systems", in *Kellogg on Integrated Marketing*, ed. by Iacobucci, D. & Calder, B. Hoboken, NJ, John Wiley & Sons, Inc.: 208–226.

Interbrand (2006) "Best global brands". Available from: http://www.interbrand.com [Accessed 1 August 2006].

ISO (2006) "Social responsibility". International Standards Organization. Available from: http:// www.iso.org [Accessed 1 August 2006].

Keller, K. (2001) "Mastering the marketing communications mix: micro and macro perspectives on integrated marketing communication programs". *Journal of Marketing Management*, **17**: 819–147.

Levinson, J. (1998) *Guerilla Marketing*, 3rd edn. Boston, Houghton Mifflin.

Magnani, R. (2006) "The blur age: effective communications in today's changing environment". *Journal of Integrated Marketing Communications*: 10–15.

Maignan, I. & Ralston, D. (2002) "Corporate social responsibility in Europe and the U.S.: insights from businesses' self-presentations". *Journal of International Business Studies*, **33**(3): 497–514.

Mislowski, W. (2005) "Marketing neo-renaissance: an opportunity for tomorrow's multi-channel integrated marketer." *Journal of Integrated Marketing Communications*: 17–25.

Murphy, N. (2004) "Corporate social responsibility: a communicator's challenge". *Leading Perspectives*, Fall: 14.

Neuborne, E. (2006) "Playing defense". *Inc. Magazine*, March: 31.

Pakquakecommunication (2005) Pakistan Earthquake Relief & Rehabilitation Communication, 2005–06. Ministry of Environment, Government of Pakistan. Available from: http://www.pakquakecommunication.org/site/content/blogcategory/19/63/ [Accessed 8 August 2006].

Palframan-Smith, B. (2004) "Employee connection". *Communication World*, March–April: 12–16.

Parry, T. (2005) "Simon Williams: the 10 new rules of branding". *Chief Executive*. Available from: http://www.printthis.clickability/com/pt/cpt?action=cpt&title=Simon+...ort%2F10_New_Rules_of_Branding_11152005%2Findex.html&partnerID=80947 [Accessed 17 November 2005].

Patagonia (2006) 25 March. "About us". Available from: http://europe.patagonia.com/europe/about_us.shtml [Accessed 25 March 2006].

Ries, A. & Ries, L. (2004) *The Origin of Brands*. New York, Collins.

Roberts, J. (2006) Personal website. Available from: www2.agsm.edu.au [Accessed 2 September 2006].

Roberts, S., Keeble, J. & Brown, D. (2003) The business case for corporate citizenship. Available from: www.adlittle.com/insights/ studies/pdf/corporate_citizenship.pdf [Accessed 7 July 2006].

Ryder, I. (2004) "Opinion piece: anthropology and the brand". Unisys, Bakers Court, UK. Abstract from the book *Beyond Branding*. Available from: http://www.beyond-branding.com/chapters/anthropology.htm [Accessed 9 August 2006].

Schultz, D. & Barnes, B. (1999) *Strategic Brand Communication Campaigns*. Lincolnwood, IL, NTC Business.

Schultz, D. & Schultz, H. (2003) *IMC: the Next Generation*. Boston, MA, McGraw-Hill.

Schultz, D., Tannenbaum, S. & Lauterborn, R. (1994) *Integrated Marketing Communication: Putting It Together and Making It Work*. Lincolnwood, IL, NTC Business Books.

Wiese, A. (2006) IBC questionnaire.

Williams, P. (2005) "Annual reports and the new corporate strategic agenda". *Communication Arts*, **47**(4): 212–216.

WOMMA (2006) "About WOMMA". Available from: http://www.womma.org/about.htm [Accessed 13 November 2006].

CHAPTER 15

Looking Ahead

Executive Summary

The new world order change will influence both large and small businesses and require leadership that engages employees and communicates the need to conduct business in innovative ways.

Change will involve people, place, time, information and technology
Time shifts will require businesses to adapt to new ways of working. The need for continuous information mandates that every employee have the ability to access and share data, whether telecommunicating or in a conventional setting. Management will be forced to work harder to build employee engagement and trust.

The range of channels driven by technological development offers innovative ways to communicate
However, technology brings challenges, from cutting through the clutter of messages to considering issues of privacy and the influence of consumers on public opinion. Changes in conventional media will contribute to concerns about accuracy, balance and accountability.

As the Internet flattens the marketplace, organizations are forced to examine a range of social responsibility issues, from the environment to health and wellness
Security of information promises to be an even greater problem in the post-9/11 era.

Strong communication skills are expected of senior management
Improving your communication skills will be a life-long task of continuing education as you look towards a future of exciting, creative challenges. ∎

Looking Ahead

> ❝ *It is not the strongest of the species that survives, nor the most intelligent that survives, it is the one that is the most adaptable to change.*
>
> *Charles Darwin* ❞

Introduction to Communicating in the Future

Who will be the communicators of tomorrow? What issues will they have to face and why? In a virtual world, will "when" be a factor? Where do we go from here and, of course, how? The agent influencing the answers to all of these questions will most assuredly involve change, from the smallest adaptation to the most dramatic alteration.

Change is the theme in this final chapter on communication. As the world flattens, change is necessary. Describing the discussions at a 2006 IBM meeting in Bangalore, India, market analyst Cindy Shaw said, "There was widespread agreement at IBM's meeting that the world is flattening. In our opinion, the rapid pace of change as the world flattens creates great opportunity – and risk" (Digman, 2006, p. 30).

We often think that change is addressed more quickly in large conglomerates that have huge revenues, the need for the latest technology, stockholders who demand higher returns and a management group who must bear the responsibility for the well-being of hundreds of thousands of employees and customers.

But small businesses are gaining in importance in the global marketplace as established blue-chip companies wrestle with new business issues.

Scott Peterson for *eWeek* says technology conglomerates may have tapped out growth potential with the large global companies and "… are putting on their reading glasses to find new customers among smaller companies" (Petersen, 2006, p. 5).

Stan Gibson, executive editor of *eWeek*, reports, "With the high-end enterprise market growing at a snail's pace, and big vendors desperate for new revenue, industry heavyweights … have been turning their attention to small-enterprise customers" (Gibson, 2006, p. 21). This means small companies will have to face making changes to meet the opportunities ahead.

In *Leading Change* (1996), John Kotter outlined the primary errors made by leadership in organizations undergoing change. He noted that the biggest mistake organizations make is the failure to communicate the necessity or urgency for change to managers and employees. "Too much success, a lack of visible crises, low performance standards, insufficient feedback from external constituencies, and more all add up to: 'Yes, we have our problems, but they aren't that terrible and I'm doing my job just fine …'" (Kotter, 1996, p. 5).

He called for leaders to communicate their vision in credible ways that will convince management and employees that change may require sacrifice.

Look at this example of a small business owner who must make some changes or risk damaging her successful operation.

Sally McIntyre owns a growing architectural and design business in a large metropolitan area. She has developed a niche for her restaurant design business. McIntyre's business has grown from five employees to 25. But she still runs the business as if she has only five employees. She makes most of the day-to-day decisions with minimal input from a few trusted managers.

Last week, McIntyre left the country for a vacation in the South Pacific. Unfortunately, she left the country without signing the payroll checks – and she has never gotten around to giving any manager the power to co-sign checks. Her employees are faced with a payless weekend while her managers try frantically to track her down so they can arrange to have checks sent to a remote island and then returned as quickly as possible. Meanwhile, the rumours in the small company begin to spread – the company is bankrupt, the boss has fled with the company's money and so on. The managers, who were delegated little power in the organization, are confronted with angry employees. Their frustration is passed on to clients, and problems escalate.

Aside from the problems of the payroll checks, McIntyre faces another dilemma. As her company grew, she failed to adapt to the change brought about by that growth, nor had she created an environment where her employees were empowered to make decisions on their own.

This chapter will look towards the future. We'll talk about what's happening right now and take a look at what's on the horizon. Eric Lundquist in *eweek* describes a new world where executives "need to be up front with their staff, use open standards and replace the traditional walls built of technobabble with transparent information that business mangers can understand" (Lundquist, 2006, p. 10).

We'll discuss "futurists" and their thoughts on the new world ahead. We'll also look at your role as future business leaders in the global marketplace. Whether you see yourself as an innovative entrepreneur, a corporate executive, an agency director or a defender of a worthy cause, your communication skills are of prime importance for your success.

The simple truths about change:

1. Change is inevitable.
2. Few people really like change.
3. Individuals usually don't want to be changed.
4. Change is seldom easy.
5. Change affects everyone, everywhere.
6. Change has the power to shape lives.

Organizational and Technological Changes

To communicate effectively with shifting target markets, managers seek out innovative strategic alternatives to traditional communication tools. Various publics such as customers, environmental groups and the media will scrutinize the words and behaviours of managers and employees in the new marketplace. Companies that accept their social responsibility role and follow ethical codes of conduct are more likely to gain customer acceptance. Communicating these activities to the public requires leaders to hone their skills, increase their knowledge and, above all, embrace a new mindset.

Strategic Thinking

Frustrated by the system of health care in South Africa, Veronica Khosa started Tateni Home Health Care Nursing, thus initiating the practice of home health care in her country. Starting with virtually nothing, she and her team of health care practitioners took to the streets to provide health care to people in their homes. The idea eventually took root and was adopted by the government.

Veronica Khosa is a social entrepreneur, and there are many thousands of such individuals attempting to change social systems in their countries. She is also an Ashoka fellow, a member of a global non-profit organization that supports global innovation and social entrepreneurship.

The Ashoka programme was founded in 1980 by Bill Drayton who believes that anyone was capable of making changes in society. This organization helps innovators develop and market their ideas, which have a high rate of adoption (Drayton, 2006).

The organization places special emphasis on building leadership and teamwork. As Drayton notes, "... we perpetuate a world in which only 2–3 % are so called 'natural leaders'. What a difference it would make for this society if we went from 2–3 % to 50 % in the next generation" (Drayton, 2005).

For more information, visit www.ashoka.org/home/innovators.pdf

Organizational changes

Organizational changes will result from shifts in:

- time
- place
- people
- power
- information.

Organizational change requires the commitment of leaders and resources to effect positive outcomes. Alterations, adoptions and adaptations must be approached strategically and must be communicated across all levels of the organization.

Bill Quirke, managing director of Synopsis Communication Consulting, UK, notes that:

> Integrated communication will become a key issue, whether that's outside, within or across an organization. A blurring of organizational boundaries means "internal" communication is a distinction, which will increasingly disappear. Outsourced partners, offshored call centres, joint ventures, supply chain partnerships will all fall into the remit of internal communication, in an attempt to harmonize the different voices customers hear from an organization (Strategic Communication Management, 2006).

Strategic Thinking

Geof Cox of New Directions, Ltd, an international consultancy specializing in management and organization development, suggests a holistic approach to organizational change in which:

- The rate of learning is faster than the rate of change.
- Internal flexibility is greater than external turbulence.
- Internal collaboration is greater than internal conflict.
- Clarity of vision rises above the information explosion.
- Corporate mission is stronger than disintegrative forces.
- Innovative proactivity predominates over conservative tendencies.
- Quality supersedes quantity as the basis of achievement.
- A wide sense of the complex takes precedence over narrow perception.
- We think global, act local; think local, act global.

Time shifts

Companies of the new millennium are no longer insulated entities; they are part of a global network that operates across time zones. This time-shift paradigm requires new communication forms and formats that effectively connect with traditional and emerging stakeholders.

Wal-Mart, one of the world's dominant retailers, has learned to use information technology to its advantage, whether communicating with suppliers or tracking deliveries using radio frequency identification (RFID). Tracking systems are also used by relief organizations to follow rescue operations. ABN AMRO Bank of the Netherlands employs a mobile service that gives employees anytime, anywhere access to a wireless network of critical business applications heretofore only available on desktop computers (Jordan, 2005).

Experts are predicting that companies "hamstrung by a 40-year archeology of computer systems, built piece by piece and siloed by division" will not be able to communicate effectively in the new environment. Companies need "a digital nervous system that seamlessly, and securely, connects to customers, suppliers and employees around the globe" (Jordan, 2005).

Place shifts

Technology has provided the impetus for a dramatic shift from traditional, brick and mortar, location-based workplaces to a location-free, anywhere company network. With the proper equipment, employees can function from any place on the globe, from branch offices, satellite locations or coffee shops. Bank of America has shifted employees out of its corporate offices and into their homes, but has found it necessary to provide "how to" training for those employees.

People shifts

Consumers are marketplace savvy. Companies have found it challenging to adjust to this new customer, realizing that operational processes must be secondary to a consideration of consumer wants, needs and desires. When US retailer Sears continued to do things as it had in the past – self-branded merchandise, vertical leadership and antiquated catalogue processes – it failed to anticipate the changing demographics, geographics, psychographics and sociographics of its customers. It did not consider such recent analytical tools as webographics or usergraphics. Consequently, it failed to communicate with its publics on many levels and lost market share. As a result it was forced to close its catalogue division, allowing new competitors to take over the market niche it once dominated.

Appealing to global customers means managers must learn to function in an **open system**, a system that affects and is affected by various stakeholders and subject to change from a wide range of external factors. Communicating with these entities requires synergy, efficiency and expertise.

Power shifts

Computer technology has shifted the balance of power from the elite to the masses. The ability of the public to access deep and detailed information instantaneously as well as to use Internet resources to tell their own stories means the power of effective communication is no longer in the hands of a few. Even those with limited education can take advantage of imagery, graphics and audio facilities to acquire information. As a result, information dissemination is no longer unidirectional; it is multidirectional, cuts across national and political boundaries and can be transmitted rapidly to diverse publics.

The Internet empowers the vocal public. Protests, once confined to a geographical area, now take place in the streets as well as via the computer, and, because news is delivered in real time, the public may view, assess and react within minutes to an event halfway around the world. Online participation is easy, and, because it is often anonymous, previously inactive protestors are raising their voices. For example, activists in the UK began a protest campaign, Reclaim the Streets, to contest a criminal justice law. Activists used the Internet to mobilize participants and create a space to exchange information and protest tactics (Sassen, 2004).

In the consumer world, sites like BzzAgent solicit opinions from first users of products. After signing up to try and spread opinions via various real and virtual activities, agents are provided with free products to try out. When a coffee maker was criticized by several agents, the buzz was out. A member of the network pointed out that at first "it seemed like an awful lot of excitement over a few people sharing their opinions about the product. Then again, the power of people sharing their opinions is exactly the point" (Hofman, 2006).

> Check on the latest protest activity around the world at www.Protest.net. The site lists upcoming protests by area and date. You may also search events by issue, for example, animal rights, religion and spirituality and the environment.
> The site describes the organization as activists who are "standing up and showing that serious activism is alive and well" (Protest.net, 2006).

Strategic Thinking

Bloggers in Spain are being hailed as "an emerging class of opinion leaders". Nokia released its new model phone to bloggers with an "open blogging policy" that allowed bloggers to post whatever they thought about the product. The unprecedented power shift caused an industry buzz, with hundreds of comments and posts. Nokia also launched an advertising campaign for the new phone on one of the Spanish gadget blogs (Rojas, 2005).

Do you think launching product releases to bloggers with an open policy is a good idea? Can traditional products be marketed on new media?

Editorial Planets, a leading publishing house in Spain, Portugal and Latin America, has tried to get bloggers to write about its books, but the plan doesn't seem to be working. Why do you think the book publisher is having trouble using the blogosphere as an advertising medium? Are traditional books not seen as "hot" items?

Information shifts

An organization that taps into these new people-powered, word-of-mouth sites gains valuable insight and feedback into what it is doing right… or wrong.

On the consumer side, the two-way communication capability of the Internet signifies that customers, as well as media, no longer have to wait to get information from the source – the company or agency. Reporters have the resources to access thousands of documents to find details for their stories; consumers use search engines to compare products or services and prices; concerned activists connect environmental neglect or abuse to unresponsive organizations. Verifying unattributed information that appears on the Web is crucial for both reporters and consumers.

A blook is a printed book based on a blog. Two well-known blooks are *Salam Pax: The Clandestine Diary of an Ordinary Iraqi* (Grove Press) and *Belle de Jour: The Intimate Adventures of a London Call Girl* by Anon (Phoenix). Both authors received real-world book deals.

The 2006 Lulu Blooker Prize non-fiction winner is *Julie & Julia*. Author Julie Powell writes about preparing all 524 recipes in Julia Child's cookbook while trying to find herself.

Blogs have also facilitated the **information shift** as more and more individuals and corporate personnel join the ranks of bloggers. Newspapers are concerned about the power of blogs to erode their business of providing the news. *The Atlanta Journal-Constitution*, a large regional paper in the USA, jumped at the chance to integrate this new communication tool with traditional information-gathering methods and now has 60 bloggers who provide valuable information to the paper's readers.

Blogs offer management an innovative opportunity to impact positively upon their public perception by fostering open dialogue within and without the organization. Official weblogs may be utilized in many departments where two-way communication is valuable: marketing, communications, public relations, research and development, human resources and investment.

Blogs give anyone with access to the Web a venue for speaking out as well as a source from which to gather information, but this may not be good news. In an online interview, the public relations director of Mitsubishi Motors in North America said he worries blogs make everyone's opinion equal. We are "losing our sense of accountability", he said (Schwartzman, 2006).

This lack of accountability should be a concern of every organization looking for information from media outlets that appear to provide information in a fair and balanced manner. How should you judge if the information is accurate or believable? Where can organizations turn to obtain unbiased reliable information? These questions will be the subject of much debate as consumer usage of technology unfolds.

> Based on online look-ups, Merriam-Webster named "blog" as its "word of the year" in 2004. The 2005 "word of the year" was integrity (Merriam-Webster, 2005a; Merriam-Webster, 2005b).
>
> Oxford University Press chose "podcast" as its 2005 word of the year and defines podcast as "a digital recording of a radio broadcast or similar programme, made available on the Internet for downloading to a personal audio player" (Podcasting, 2005).
>
> Will "splog", a new word in the making, be found on a future list?

Dig Deeper

News seems to be a commodity in oversupply. While the culture of newspaper journalism differs around the world, the shift from print to online will have a significant impact on the way information is viewed and processed (Rosenstiel, 2006).

In a study of 3 204 adults conducted by the Pew Research Center for the People and the Press (Pew, 2006), 29 % of respondents between the ages of 18 and 24 reported they regularly received news online. An equal number of 50–64-year-olds reported they relied on online information, but young people reported less interest in any type of news.

The report found that those who use the Web for news still spend more time getting news from other sources – primarily TV – than they do getting news online. Online editions are helping newspapers stem the tide of audience decline, "but even the highest estimates of daily newspaper readership – 43 % of both print and online readers – is still well below the number reading a print newspaper on a typical day 10 years ago (50 %)" (Pew, 2006).

Can the newspaper industry rebrand itself as the best newsgathering and news-providing business?

Technological changes

By the time you read this information, technology will already have brought about new change in the business world. But let's look at some innovations currently working their way into the marketplace.

Database of intentions

Technologist and founder of *Wired* magazine John Battelle expanded the idea that the Internet had made it possible for computers to predict the future. He reasoned that, when people logged on to search engines looking for products or information, they were disclosing their intentions. A person searching "ski resorts" was thinking about going skiing; a person entering "coffee makers" was in need of a new coffee maker. He further considered that, if all the information from these search engines could be categorized, a good indication of human wants, needs and desires as well as thoughts, language use and concepts would emerge. Analysts could formulate a composite picture of where the world was headed and who was getting there first. Batelle called this prognosticating ability of the digital world "**the database of intentions**".

Microformatting

The traditional structure of the media release, the workhorse of public relations practitioners, is undergoing intense examination by those who think it should serve new media more appropriately. Social media experts, such as Chris Heuer, Tom Foremski, Jen McClure, Tantek Celik and Todd Defren, are attempting to create a new media release **microformat**. Their hope is that the traditional media release will not die, as some have predicted, but rather change and adapt in such a way as "to improve the quality of journalism across the entire spectrum of media production" (Heuer, 2006).

New Communication Challenges Emerge

Communication forms will evolve as the electronic age matures. New markets bring ethical dilemmas, higher consumer expectations and increased demands. Effective communicators will be entrusted to manage corporate image, build brand strength and ensure positive public perception of all business activities.

Strategic Thinking

Organizational change is a popular topic in management self-help books. Such books help managers validate their decision-making in times of turbulent institutional change.

How do such books discuss the role of communication in the change process? Four communication scholars selected 25 books that had appeared in the top 100 management bestsellers from Amazon.com (Lewis *et al.*, 2006). They used content analysis to determine the trends in communication advice offered in these popular bestsellers.

The scholars discovered that the books emphasized the need for broad participation of various stakeholders in the change process. A major task of the change agent was gaining and facilitating that participation, as change agents were encouraged to empower others and to "take ownership of the change process" (Lewis *et al.*, 2006, p. 129). The books also encouraged the use of various communication channels for providing information and feedback about this process.

However, the scholars noted the books provided little theory to back up their advice and were often short on specifics. Communication advice was often boiled down to "sound bites and general philosophy" (Lewis *et al.*, 2006, p. 132).

Ethical uncertainties

The age-old question of what is considered ethical in business will continue to be a subject of debate, particularly in the global arena.

The Business of Truth: A Guide to Ethical Communication, a 2006 study involving more than 1 800 communication professionals around the globe by the International Association of Business Communicators (IABC) Research Foundation, reports that only 46 % of the companies surveyed encourage discussion of moral questions among their employees.

Most respondents, however, reported that their companies maintained a healthy ethical climate, and 70 % reported that the lines between ethical and unethical behaviour at their organization were clear (IABC, 2006).

Privacy

Access to information through databases and tracking of Internet usage raises significant questions concerning consumer privacy. For example, large hotel chains now keep records of customer preferences from room service orders to the kind of liquor consumed from the room's bar. Hilton Hotels Corp. is pioneering a radio-frequency identification system that will enable hotel employees immediately to identify not only their guests' identity but their preferences for services while staying at the hotel, by way of a microchip card. Guests who opt in for this service are provided with the cards.

While the industry has the ability to track all kinds of information about its guests, it must also balance the problem of privacy. Hotels build their brand reputation on being discrete. Knowing customers' tastes may be comfortable for some travellers but could be decidedly awkward for others (Johnson, 2006).

Privacy issues are at the heart of data collection. Consumers who use reward cards to receive discounts on retail items may or may not understand that their purchase behaviour is being tracked for marketing purposes. Others may resent the fact that, in order to take advantage of sale items, particularly in US grocery stores, customers must sign up for reward cards which in turn allows the store to track purchases. The question becomes when does convenience and service invade privacy.

The ability of Internet providers, advertisers and others to track Web usage patterns raises ethical concerns about individual privacy. For example, Google Trends allows a user to check the history of any search term, how it has evolved and in which cities it is most popular. This tool appeals to marketers who can track activity following ad campaigns or special events. "Already more than a million analyses are being done on Google Trends", said Marissa Mayer, Google Search vice-president (Leonhardt, 2006).

Issues of privacy will force change on many fronts such as legal systems, corporate–consumer relationships, organizational infrastructure and Internet services.

Social responsibility

What is the responsibility of business to growing social problems and issues? Although there is considerable room for improvement, we have grown accustomed to making manufacturing operations live up to environmental standards and practices. Consumer and food safety issues receive support from interest groups and are often subject to government regulations. Issues concerning discrimination of customers and employees can quickly alter the reputation of an organization, damage its brand and destroy its profits. These issues, among others, promise to remain on the radar screen as global businesses expand and new markets open.

The fast-food industry is currently the subject of public, governmental and media scrutiny for its role in contributing to obesity. Fast-food consumption, high-sugared soft drinks and large portion sizes have been linked to the increase in weight gain and the diseases associated with it, including diabetes, heart disease and some forms of cancer. Movies such as "Super Size Me" and the bestselling book *Fast Food Nation* have done much to raise the public consciousness.

McDonald's is the subject of much of the criticism, although it is not the only fast-food enterprise to be targeted by public concern. In response to this criticism, it has initiated healthier meal choices and packaging with more nutritional information, and includes an exercise DVD in some of its products. Concerned about international pressure to cut fats and sugars, the company recently organized a Global Mom's Panel to seek advice on the well-being of families (Case, 2006; Astrup, 2005).

The McDonald's example points to the responsibility of all businesses to respond to customer feedback concerning social issues.

Security issues

Humans were once dependent on face-to-face communication and facial expressions that carried weighted messages. As technological advances provide faster and better communication options, the problems of security continue to require attention.

Today, face recognition software means that computer users, dependent on electronic communication for basic messaging, can rely on their facial expressions to initiate the communication connection. This new tool will eliminate the need to remember passwords, memorize codes or worry about identity breaches.

Organizations spend billions each year to establish layers of security to protect them against fraud and other security breaches. In July 2006, an administrative assistant at Coca-Cola and two accomplices were arrested after trying to sell trade secrets concerning a new soft drink to a rival manufacturer. The employee tried to lure Pepsi into paying for a secret formula, but Pepsi officials turned over the information to US officials. A Pepsi official was quoted as saying, "We only did what any responsible company would do. Competition can sometimes be fierce, but it always must be fair and legal" (Wilbert, 2006).

Nonetheless, Coca-Cola's CEO was forced to reassure stockholders and the public that its formulas were officially locked away in bank vaults, while telling his employees that security within the company was under review.

Security concerns plague the promotions business as well. Misguided individuals often create hundreds of email addresses and then automatically submit multiple contest entry forms. As a result, anti-thief programs, as well as tracking systems to monitor where entries originate, must be built into contest designs (Scott, 2006). Promotional activities are popular in the marketing business but must be planned and supervised to protect them from fraud.

Creativity Rules the New Global Marketplace

Creativity will be highly demanded of managers in the future. The ability to create and implement new ideas will lead to invigoration of organizations in the new marketplace. In *The Gower Handbook of Management*, Geof Cox says, "The real need for organizations is **innovation** – the process of applying creative ideas in a practical way to improve the organization" (Cox, 1998).

Examples of companies with an above-average track record for innovation are Sony (1 000 new products a year), Toyota (its suggestion programme implemented 580 000 ideas in 2003 in Japan alone) and 3M (it grants funds for new ideas even before they are sanctioned by management).

Creativity and innovation will lead to new alliances, such as businesses partnering with universities, subsidizing of inventors and inventions and research support for start-up companies.

Training Communicators for the New Global Marketplace

Good communication, in a flat world, is an economic issue. Ineffective communicators cost companies money, resources, time and reputation. By now you should be more aware and knowledgeable about the communication process and understand the power of effective communication. But there is more to learn, of course, as you enter the real world. Skills training is an ongoing process, and as you complete this book you have the knowledge to begin the process.

Educational training

Business schools around the world are beginning to look at the integrated business communication concept of planning, executing and evaluating unified messages that create stakeholder relationships and *build brands* as a standard for business.

The University of Wisconsin–Madison School of Business alumni newsletter says, "Good communication matters because business organizations are made up of people. As Robert Kent, former dean of Harvard Business School has said, 'In business, communication is everything'" (Blalock, 2005).

A Columbia University School of Business study reported that "successful executives must have multi-environment and multinational experience to become CEOs in the twenty-first century" (Blalock, 2005) where organizations will take part in an array of activities including negotiating, selling around the world and forming cross-cultural partnerships. All of these will require in-depth and effective communication skills.

> "The importance of working to improve communication skills cannot be overestimated and should be a top priority for supervisors, managers and employees committed to developing positive and productive relationships with employees and consumers.
>
> The top-down management model of the past is increasingly being replaced by collaborative teams that depend on effective business communications to build trust, promote understanding, share information and motivate others" (University of Arizona (UA) Center for Computer & Professional Education, 2006).

Futurists See the World from a Different Perspective

Futurists are a specialized breed of thinkers who analyse past and present patterns of change to predict the future. By the mid-twentieth century, future studies became an academic discipline (Slaughter, 2000). Several authors are recognized as futurists, such as Alvin Toffler (*Future Shock*, 1971), John McHale (*Give Us Your Best and Brightest*, 2005), Nicholas Negroponte (*Being Digital*) and John Naisbitt (*Mind Set*, 2006). International business futurist Frank Feather is credited with creating the phrase "thinking globally, acting locally" in 1979.

Research centres known for their forward thinking provide insights into the needs of a future world. Some of the most prestigious include Australia's Foresight Institute, the Futures Studies Department at Budapest's Corvinus University, the Finland Futures Research Centre at the Turku School of Economics and Business Administration, the Institute for the Future in the USA, the Futures Academy in Ireland and SUBITO! Research & Futures in Norway.

Business futurists across the globe are trying to predict what consumers and the marketplace will look like in the near and distant future. They are interested in areas such as what motivates consumers and why, emerging communication channels, language and discourse alterations and adaptations, the role of increased technology and trend analyses.

Before moving into the real world, take some time to investigate the futurist thinking on the changes that will affect global industries, and ultimately your career. Whatever path you take, communication will play an ever-increasing role in business relationships.

Chapter Summary

Integrated business communication will enable organizations to deal with technological breakthroughs and the consequences of dramatic changes in time, place, people, power and information.

Integrated business communication affords companies the ability to deal with change, at the same time satisfying consumer demands while delivering a seamless and continuous flow of information to multiple stakeholders.

Integrated business communication demands that people work cross-functionally from a base of common understanding, increased knowledge and shared values.

Integrated business communication requires professionals to be innovative as they unlearn as well as learn, adapt old ways of thinking and create new ways for doing business.

Integrated business communication in a global environment challenges organizations to be socially responsible, ethically sound and acutely sensitive to cultural differences and practices.

Integrated business communication will restructure business communication in the global marketplace. ■

Learning From Others

Arthur E. F. Wiese, Jr is vice-president, corporate communications, at Entergy Corporation, a company with 14 000 employees worldwide and annual revenues of over $10 billion.

Wiese is responsible for all external and internal communication, including media relations, community relations, public relations, advertising, websites, radio and television production, communication with employees and other stakeholders, event planning and public opinion research. He helps develop and shape communication policies and procedures and, indirectly, enforces them.

Wiese splits his time between Washington, DC, and New Orleans, LA. Previously he was vice-president, public affairs, for the American Petroleum Institute and before that he was a journalist for 17 years covering the White House under Presidents Nixon, Ford, Carter and Reagan.

Wiese talks about his career and offers advice to young people beginning their careers.

Q. What personal qualities do you feel contributed to your professional success?
A. I have a broad perspective shaped by my education, my experience and my reading, especially in the liberal arts area like history, political science and literature; and analytical and leadership skills honed over a 40-year career.

Q. How would you rank effective communication skills in your leadership profile?
A. Communication is an important component of leadership and breeds confidence in both the communicator and his/her audience. It is key to employees understanding their roles, their goals and how they will be evaluated.

Q. Is effective listening a necessary skill in today's business world?
A. One of the greatest attributes of any manager is being a "good listener" with the perceptiveness and patience to let employees communicate with him/her. You build team trust not by talking, but by listening.

Q. What form of communication do you use in your organization?
A. For internal audiences, email has become the dominant method of communication inside Entergy Corporation both because of its immediacy and the geographic spread of our employees. The largest verbal means of communication is face-to-face meetings, although their proportion of the total is shrinking fast. Our third method of communication would be telephone conversations. We also post a newsletter (available both online and in printed form), with emails to alert employees to fresh, important news.

Q. How do you know if your customer communication is effective?
A. We do customer surveys quarterly that measure, among other things, their understanding of our communication messages (which are sent via advertising, bill inserts, occasional letters and the news media).

Q. Can you describe a communication problem?
A. We had a problem scheduling personal visits by the CEO to major work sites since they were in so many widely dispersed locations. We solved it by interspersing face-to-face meetings with interactive webcasts where the CEO accepts questions from employees in any physical location.

Q. What are the challenging issues when communicating with the global community?
A. There are many issues. Because modern audiences are bombarded with communication messages every day, it is a challenge to break through to them with a

relatively moderate advertising budget. Another obstacle is that the quickened pace of life, especially in industrialized nations, means less time and less attention paid to conventional communication outlets like newspapers, news magazines and even television.

Q. Would you recommend that students learn a second language before entering the workforce?
A. A second language is vital. For persons whose first language is anything except English, I would suggest it as a second language since it now totally dominates international commerce. For those whose first language is English, I would recommend as a second either Spanish, the fastest-growing Western Hemisphere language, or Chinese, since it is coming into its own as a global business language.

Q. Which values are important for students to develop to become effective leaders and communicators in their career choice?
A. I would suggest three values to carry throughout a career and, more importantly, in life:

1. A strong sense of honour and responsibility.
2. Enthusiasm, even passion, for your work.
3. Intellectual curiosity.

I would like to encourage you young people reading this to broaden your mind, exercise your curiosity and never stop learning!

Case Study – **Dove Soap, an Integrated Campaign**

"Wrinkled? Wonderful?" That's what a 96-year-old London grandmother asked in a billboard for Dove soap. The billboard featured the grandmother and five other real women in a campaign designed by Uniliver's Lever-Faberge group.

In 2004, Dove introduced its real women campaign themed a "Campaign for Real Beauty". First released in the UK for Dove firming lotion, the campaign was expanded a year later to the USA.

Global brand director Silvia Lagnado said the campaign was designed to "make women feel beautiful every day" (Prior, 2004).

The campaign grew out of research. Ogilvy & Mather and Unilever commissioned a study to determine women's attitudes about beauty. The study sampled 3 200 women in 10 countries and found that only 13 % were very satisfied with their body weight and shape. Only 2 % described themselves as beautiful and only 9 % were comfortable describing themselves as attractive (Prior, 2004). Three-quarters of those surveyed wished the media portrayed beauty in more terms than physical attractiveness (Gardner, 2005).

The campaign used the real women in print ads, TV advertising, Web advertising and outdoor advertising. Billboards invited viewers to discuss their opinions about the advertising message, and their comments were displayed on an electronic billboard in Times Square in New York City. A website offered interactive activities including a self-esteem quiz, a workbook with activities designed to raise self-esteem, a T-shirt, an opportunity to join a Real Beauty Entertainment Club and an interactive calendar for mothers and daughters (http://www.campaignforrealbeauty.com/dsef/) (Unilever, 2006). The campaign also featured workshops and discussions with advertising and media leaders in several US cities.

Some critics say the campaign theme was a "gimmick or novelty" rather than a trend in the tone and content of advertising for beauty products. Others saw the campaign as a social responsibility effort.

Was the campaign effective? Sales of the firming lotion in the UK reportedly doubled during the first month of the billboard campaign (Prior, 2004).

What is your response to this campaign? Is it socially responsible or merely a new way to gain customers? How does the ad campaign appeal to the emotional side of women? Consider how the campaign integrates various media to communicate its theme? What would you expect from Dove advertising in the future? ■

Class Exercises

1. In a small group, formulate a definition of creativity in the workplace. Then answer these questions: How can you recognize creativity? Do all creative ideas lead to innovation? Are all creative ideas beneficial to the organization? How can creative ideas be evaluated? Should creative ideas be rewarded? How?

2. According to futurists, portable communication devices will be put to increasing use in the near future as we move towards more mobile socialization. Other predictions are in the works. Do some Web surfing and gather a list of the top five business trend predictions. Hint: one is "simplicity-led" design (Glasner, 2005). Now find four more and report on them to the class.

3. Privacy issues continue to plague companies seeking more information about customers and their buying habits. Conduct library research on the topic and then

consider organizing several focus groups of college students, senior citizens and other groups to gather their reactions to the issue. Finally, invite two or three of the business leaders in your community to talk about the privacy issue to your class.

Action Plan

When Corning's TV glass business was in trouble owing to poor quality, management tried talking with employees, informing them of the need for better quality in the products they were working on. Messages were even sent out that jobs were on the line if quality didn't improve. But nothing worked. Poor quality continued as a main concern to Corning executives.

Assuming that the quality controls of the company are sufficient and in place, what steps would you take to make employees more concerned about the quality of your product? If you were to write a business report on how to approach this problem, what information would you need? What tone would you take? Come up with one traditional method and one creative method to solve the problem.

Hint. Using customer feedback is valuable to a successful business. What did Ken Freeman, former head of the division, do? Access "Putting your angriest customers to work: CEOs benefit by getting fed-up customers to tell it like it is" in *The Chief Executive*, May 2005, by Joe Queenan, available from `http://findarticles.com/p/articles/mi _ m4070/is _ 208/ai _ n13788093` (Queenan, 2005).

Websites

Take a look at what's new at the Copenhagen Institute for Futures Studies at `http:// www.cifs.dk/en` (CIFS, 2006) or go to Principia Cybernetica at `http://pespmc1.vub.ac.be` (Principia Cybernetica, 2006) and search "business" in the search box.

CEOs have a blog site just for them, started by a Frenchman in September 2004, at `http://prplanet.typepad.com/ceobloggers` (CEO Blogger's Club, 2006). The international club, with more than 100 members worldwide, posts its purpose on its website: "to gather CEOs who believe in the blogosphere and its extraordinary potential and to offer them a place to share with other companies' leaders the experimentation they are conducting thanks to weblogs" (CEO Blogger's Club, 2006). Go to the site and find its list of members. See what industries the CEOs represent.

Find out about the influences of new media on conventional media. Go to `www.ipressroom.com` (ipressroom, 2006).

References

Astrup, A. (2005) "Super-sized and diabetic by frequent fast-food consumption? [comment]". *The Lancet*, 1 January 2005. Available from: Thomson Gale Health Reference Center Academic, ref. 365.9453, Winthrop University Dacus Library [Accessed 7 August 2006].

Blalock, M. (2005) "Listen up". *Wisconsin Business Alumni Update* [newsletter]. Available from: http://www.bus.wisc.edu/update/winter05/business_communication.asp [Accessed 9 July 2006].

Case, T. (2006) "Fast food". *Brandweek*, 1 May 2006, **47**: 18. Available from: Business Source Premier (Info-Trac-Gale), ref. 100644318, Winthrop University Dacus Library [Accessed 7 August 2006].

CEO Blogger's Club (2006) Available from: http://prplanet.typepad.com/ceobloggers [Accessed 3 September 2006].

CIFS (2006) Copenhagen Institute for Futures Studies. Available from: http://www.cifs.dk/en [Accessed 6 September 2006].

Cox, G. (1998) "The creative organization". *The Gower Handbook of Management*, 5th edn. Aldershot, UK, Gower Publishing.

Digman, L. (2006) "The buzz". *eWeek*, 19 June 2006: 30

Drayton, B. (2005) "Working convergences: liberal education, creativity, and the entrepreneurial spirit [speech]". Annual Meeting of the Association of American Colleges and Universities.

Drayton, B. (2006) "Everyone a changemaker: social entrepreneurship's ultimate goal". *Innovations*, Winter. MIT Press. Available from: www.ashoka.org/home/innovators.pdf [Accessed 30 July 2006].

Gardner, M. (2005) 12 January. "Ageless beauty, touched by time." *The Christian Science Monitor*, 12 January 2005: 15. Available from: Thomson Gale InfoTrac Custom Newspapers, Winthrop University Dacus Library [Accessed 26 June 2006].

Gibson, S. (2006) "The big deal". *eweek*, 5 June 2006: 21–24.

Glasner, J. (2005) "Futurists pick top tech trends". *Wired News*, 25 October 2005. Available from: www.wired.com/news/business/1,69138-0.html [Accessed 7 July 2006].

Heuer, C. (2006) "Chris Heuer's idea engine [blog archive]". Available from: www.chrisheuer.com/project/new-media-release/ [Accessed 8 July 2006].

Hofman, M. (2006) "Priority". *Inc. Magazine*, April: 25–27.

IABC (2006) "Less than half of companies encourage discussion of ethical issues at the workplace". IABC News Centre [press release]. Available from: http://news.iabc.com/index.php?s=press_releases&item=97 [Accessed 7 July 2006].

ipressroom (2006) Available from: www.//ipressroom.com [Accessed 5 September 2006].

Johnson, A. (2006) "We know who you are and we know what you want". *The Charlotte Observer*, 12 February 2006: 4D.

Jordan, M. (2005) "Leapfrogging past today's IT mess". *Chief Executive*, May: 20.

Kotter, J. (1996) *Leading Change*. Boston, Harvard University Press.

Leonhardt, D. (2006) "The Internet knows what you'll do next". *The New York Times*, July. Available from: http://www.nytimes.com/2006/07/05/business/05leonhardt.html?ex=1309752000&en=8be0be92819a6f8f&ei=5088&partner=rssnyt&emc=rss [Accessed 9 July 2006].

Lewis, L., Schmisseur, A., Stephens, K. and Weir, K. (2006) "Advice on communicating during organizational change: the content of popular press books". *Journal of Business Communication*, **43**(2): 113–137.

Lundquist, E. (2006) "Welcome to CIO Version 2.0". *eWeek*, 2 June 2006: 10.

Merriam-Webster (2005a) "Merriam-Webster words of the year 2004". Merriam-Webster online. Available from http://www.m-w.com/info/04words.htm [Accessed 8 July 2006].

Merriam-Webster (2005b) "Merriam-Webster words of the year 2005". Merriam-Webster online. Available from: http://www.m-w.com/info/05words.htm [Accessed 8 July 2006].

Peterson, S. (2006) "This eWeek". *eWeek*, 5 June 2006, p. 5.

Pew (2006) "Online paper modestly boosts newspaper readership". Pew Research Center for the People and the Press, 30 July 2006. Available from: http://pewresearch.org/reports/?ReportD=38 [Accessed 7 July 2006].

Podcasting (2005) "The 2005 word of the year is … podcast!" *Podcasting News*, December. Available from: http://www.podcastingnews.com/archives/2005/12/the_2005_word_o.html [Accessed 8 July 2006].

Principia Cybernetica (2006) Available from: http://pespmc1.vub.ac.be [Accessed 5 September 2006].

Prior, M. (2004) "Dove ad campaign aims to redefine beauty". *Women's Wear Daily Friday*, 8 October 2004. Available from: www.wwd.com [Accessed 26 June 2006].

Protest.net (2006) Available from: www.protest.net [Accessed 11 August 2006].

Queenan, J. (2005) "Putting your angriest customers to work: CEOs benefit by getting fed-up customers to tell it like it is". *Chief Executive*, May. Available from: http://findarticles.com/p/articles/mi_m4070/is_208/ai_n13788093 [Accessed 11 August 2006].

Rojas, O. (2005) "Corporate blogging (external) – Spain". International Association of Online Communicators (IAOC) [blog], June. Available from: www.iaocblog.com/blog/_archives/2005/6/15/942131.html [Accessed 8 July 2006].

Rosenstiel, T. (2006) "The future of news: sense-making and other strategies for survival". Poynteronline, 9 June 2006. Available from: http://poynter.org/content/content_print.asp?id=102671&custom= [Accessed 12 June 2006].

Sassen, S. (2004) "Local actors in global politics". *Current Sociology*, 52(4): 649–670. Available from: Thomson Gale Academic, ref. 14000511, Winthrop University Dacus Library [Accessed 11 August 2006].

Schwartzman, E. (2006) "On the record: interview with Dan Irvin, public relations director of Mitsubishi Motors of North America". 24 June 2006. Available from: ipressroom.com [Accessed 24 June 2006].

Scott, A. (2006) "Crack down". *PROMO*, May: 12–13.

Slaughter, R. (2000) *The Knowledge Base of Futures Studies*, Vols 1–4 on CD-ROM. Brisbane, Australia, Foresight International.

Strategic Communication Management (2006) "Fast forward: future trends in corporate communication". December 2005/January 2006. Available from: http://www.allbusiness.com/periodicals/article/922079-1.html [Accessed 14 July 2006].

UA Center for Computer & Professional Education (2006) "Business communication program". Available from: www.ceao.arizona.edu/comped/bus_comm.html [Accessed 9 July 2006].

Unilever (2006) "The campaign for real beauty". Available from: http:campaignforrealbeauty.com [Accessed 26 June 2006].

Wilbert, C. (2006) "Coca-Cola secrets plot foiled: three under arrest: Federal prosecutors say a Coco-Cola employee and her accomplices tried to sell documents and a new drink sample to Pepsi. The original formula was not at risk". *The Atlanta Journal-Constitution*, 6 July 2006: A1. Available from: Thomson Gale InfoTrac Custom Newspapers, Winthrop University [Accessed 7 August 2006].

Glossary

abstract words   the opposite of concrete words, these pertain to ideas and concepts; they are harder to comprehend and usually require more explanation; these are words like truth, honesty and love

accountability   the new global definition of accountability is communicating to others that you have been responsible in everyday tasks, both large and small

acting as a primary communication agent   public relations professionals communicate information to the public, employees, media and other interest groups to create awareness, build brand image, gain publicity and achieve other communication goals

advertising   information from an identified entity that pays for media time, space or sponsorship; advertising as a communication tool has expanded and matured into a billion dollar industry since its rise to importance in the 1930s and 1940s

"arrow" approach   grounded in authoritarianism, this approach views communication primarily as a one-way process based on the skills of the sender or leader; feedback is unnecessary, as the arrow leader believes that he or she is speaking with absolute credibility and authority

audience	a fourth element added by modern persuasion theory to Aristotle's three components of rhetoric (ethos, pathos and logos) – the mindset of the public, its culture, educational level, biases, interest in the subject and its power to make a difference
authoritarian leaders	believe employees need direct supervision because they feel workers left on their own will be unproductive
body	in a formal business letter, the body of the letter is where you place your information
boundary spanners	public relations departments are the connectors of companies to the outside, particularly to the media, and as such they act as boundary spanners between an organization and its publics
branding	the process of branding involves creating a product that resonates with customers; brand management is a crucial function of integrated communication and involves a continued financial commitment as well as consistent policy efforts
captive audiences	are those required to be in attendance – they may be physically in attendance (or required to read a report), but mentally they may be a million miles away; you will have to do something significant to get them to listen to you; you will have to be engaging and accommodating
cause-related marketing	according to Pringle and Thomson, a strategic positioning and marketing tool that links a company or brand to a relevant social cause or issue, for mutual benefit
channel	how information is being sent: face-to-face, email, phone, fax, text messages, advertising, group presentation, etc.
chronological pattern	material presented according to a time line

"circuit" approach	this approach might be called the democratic leadership model; the circuit manager is a networker who stresses feedback over process; managers who practise this leadership style believe in total openness and that, if employees are satisfied and trusted, effective communication will occur
closing	in a formal business letter, the closing is a phrase that signals the end of the letter
cocooning	coined by American futurist Faith Popcorn in 2004, this term is used to describe the phenomenon whereby, when busy people get home in the evening after a hectic and stressful day, they retreat into their homes, or cocoon; this trend continues to characterize American culture
communicasting	refers to the merging of media and community for the purpose of empowerment and engagement; the concept was pioneered by Donald Mains, at Johns Hopkins University, and has broadened to include using media to cast public views and opinions to, and through, a community of people with like interests
communication audit	a review of all company communication efforts to external target publics and internal audiences; it serves to identify a company's communication strategies and provides the opportunity to evaluate effectiveness
communication management	the deliberate attempt to construct, organize, frame and deliver messages to specific audiences
communication objectives	these are developed to help understand how communication planning helps achieve goals
concrete words	refer to tangible objects such as a table, a car or a computer program, and are easily defined and understood

connotation	this meaning of a word depends largely on the subjective message within and surrounding the word
consumer sales promotions	seek to encourage customers to try a product they don't currently use or normally purchase; promotions aimed at building brand images may include coupons, sampling, price deals, sweepstakes and contests
context	refers to the occasion, time and place of a communication – it comprises all the underlying and overarching factors that impact a message; the concept of context in conversation, as introduced by Hall, is the information surrounding an event that helps determine its meaning
controlled medium	a medium over which a company has complete control; advertising, one of the most useful and common persuasive communication tools, is a controlled medium as the sponsor determines when and where an ad runs, unchanged and unedited; this is a benefit over an uncontrolled medium like a media release where a company relinquishes control of its story to gatekeepers – reporters and editors
cultural relativism	implies that an organization first accepts local values before considering how corporate actions might affect others, its brand or its international reputation
customer relationship management	the process of gathering information and feedback and using that information to achieve customer satisfaction and loyalty; at the core of this process is a variety of communication tools, from direct mail to electronic billing to call centre services
"dance" approach	the most effective management communication style; this leadership style, much like a positive laissez-faire approach, combines the positive quality of direction in the authoritarian approach and the relationship building of the democratic approach; communication, like dance, involves many patterns and movements, and thus no single approach or movement fits every performance

datacasting

the transmission of data as a secondary service on digital broadcasting networks; datacasting efficiently and effectively communicates with large audiences, using Internet protocol to distribute digital content

date

in a formal business letter, the date contains the day, month and year of the correspondence

democratic leaders

value group participation and are supportive of this process; they believe others have opinions worth considering

demographic

an attribute or trait that can be measured or verified

denotation

the standard definition of a word

deontological approach

this approach to ethics judges all actions by whether they are morally right or wrong

direct marketing

direct marketing through print or electronic media enables the customer to order and purchase a product by phone, electronic media or the Internet

disfluencies

the "not fluent" words or sounds that we intersperse in informal conversations, such as "ah", "um", "like", "you know", "well" and "okay"; they make a speaker seem natural and spontaneous when used in moderation; however, in the business world, using too many disfluencies makes the speaker appear unprepared and unprofessional

disinterested audiences

will need an attention-getter to get them to listen and a listener relevance component to make them want to listen to what you have to say

eager receivers

are audiences that want to hear what you have to say and will actively try to understand your points; they are easy to reach

effective message

a message that is received in the manner in which the sender intended; effectiveness depends on the overlapping areas of the worlds of the sender and receiver

Eiffel Tower organizations	are task-oriented organizations that are also hierarchical in nature
ethical imperialism	says that organizations follow their home customs in conducting business; this precept fails to recognize different cultural beliefs or to acknowledge that there is a global standard for ethical behaviour
ethical trust	centres on integrity, honesty and fair play
ethnocentricity	the opinion that one's own world is superior to that of another's
ethos	according to Aristotle's study of rhetoric, the power of speakers, including their credibility, expertise, trustworthiness, sincerity and above all charisma
evaluation of external organizational performance	public relations professionals also make an evaluation of external organizational performance by monitoring public perception of company activities
external noise	physical activity, external to the source, that inhibits the communication process
external publics	present and potential customers, the local community, suppliers, bankers, media, government agencies, environmental and consumer advocacy groups and any other entity with whom an organization wishes to do business and for whom they want to present their best image
family-centred organizations	are more person centred and hierarchical
feedback	the verbal and non-verbal messages sent back and forth between sender and receiver as communication proceeds; it may or may not be noticed, heard or understood, but it exists nonetheless and often determines the future direction a message will take

focus groups a qualitative research tool designed to gather information about receivers of communication messages through small group feedback

goals plans that are long range in scope and indicate what action or behaviour the organization/unit ultimately wants to achieve; leaders set goals and managers set objectives to accomplish those goals

guerrilla marketing focuses on the use of low-cost alternative media to reach targeted small groups of consumers; it is based on the premise that all organizations, no matter their size, can and should develop marketing programmes

guided missile organizations are task oriented and equalitarian

heading in a formal business letter, the heading is the return address of the individual or company sending the letter; for most businesses the information contained in its letterhead serves as the heading

hearing the biological process of sound waves striking the inner ear bones and turning the waves into vibrations that the brain can decode

idioms sayings that mean more than the actual words

image the aggregate perception people have about the company, its employees and its products or services

importance pattern presents information by starting with the most significant projects or facts and continuing to the least significant; this format can also be reversed as a report goes from the least important to the most important information

incubator organizations businesses that foster and encourage new ventures and entrepreneurial efforts; they are person centred and equalitarian in nature

individualism–collectivism	relates to whether a society emphasizes individual achievement or group identification
innovation	the process of applying creative ideas in a practical way to improve an organization
inside address	in a formal business letter, the inside address is the receiver's courtesy title (Dr, Herr, Mme, Mrs, etc.), name, position in the company and address, including the postcode
integrated business communication	the process of planning, executing and evaluating unified messages that create stakeholder relationships and build brand recognition
intellectual property rights	involve ownership of intellectual activity in the literary, artistic, industrial and scientific arenas
interested receivers	are ready to listen to your message; it will take little work to get their attention
internal noise	found in the mind of the receiver and how he or she reacts to the message as well as to the messenger
internal publics	employees in the office, in the field or working from home, in corporate headquarters or around the globe, and also the families of the employees; effectively communicating with employees builds solid employee–company relationships
issues management	the process organizations use to anticipate, analyse, respond to, evaluate and take control of complex issues that affect their business; it can involve legal disputes, environmental concerns, community awareness issues, product recalls, labour actions, natural disasters and other developments
laissez-faire leaders	may offer guidance and support but generally stay out of the decision-making process

listenability	ease of aural comprehension
listening	making sense of the messages that the brain is receiving; it involves analysis, evaluation and judgement based on individual capacities
logos	according to Aristotle's study of rhetoric, logos is the power of logic
marketing	a function that researches and develops strategies to answer the needs, wants and desires of the consuming public and uses these findings to design, package, promote, distribute and sell a product or service; traditionally, this is called product, price, placement and promotions
masculine versus feminine	describes the emphasis in a society on characteristics of a particular gender, such as male assertiveness or female nurturing
mass customization	a marketing trend that manufactures for the masses but offers individual product customization to its customers
measurability	the ability to produce quantifiable data
media relations	involves establishing a symbiotic relationship with media outlets
metaphors	verbal and visual shortcuts to understanding and comparing a complex subject to a simpler image
mission statement	articulates the goals and objectives of the company and concisely states why the organization exists
monitor of institutional policies	as monitor of institutional policies, it is the responsibility of public relations to ensure that organizations do what they say they will do

narrowcasting	another way of looking at the receivers of your business messages, whether individuals or a customer database; the term was first used by the mass media industry to mean the opposite of broadcasting – it references information, programming or advertising cast out to highly selective audience-specific segments; the term has also been used by other industries – it applies to defining your audience using narrow terms rather than broad characteristics
niche markets	smaller segments of the market that share common interests, such as contact lens wearers
noise	interference with the transmission of a message – it can be external (a sudden loud noise, a sneeze, a power shortage, etc.) or internal (lack of education, prejudice, stubbornness, etc.); it is also defined as any physical, semantic or contextual action that detracts from or distorts the receipt of a message – often referred to as static, noise comes from both external and internal sources (in the workplace, noise may take many forms, from Intranet information overload to poor lighting)
non-verbal communication	includes facial expressions, eye contact, tone of voice, body posture and motions and hand gestures; it also may include physiological elements such as blushing, twitching, shaking, stuttering, etc.
non-verbal language	body language – tells as much about speakers as the words they choose to use
objectives	how the organization/unit plans to meet established goals; as they are short term in scope, they should be audience specific, measurable and date/time specific and designate desired outcome
open system	appealing to global customers means managers must learn to function in an open system, a system that affects and is affected by various stakeholders and subject to change from a wide range of external factors; communicating with these entities requires synergy, efficiency and expertise

organizational communication	a mature discipline that provides much of the framework for effective management and employee communication; it includes such concepts as formal and informal communication methods, the flow of communication up, down and across all levels of employees and power structures
paralanguage elements	rate of speaking, silence, volume, pitch, stresses on words, accents, disfluencies and vocalizations – tools we can control and use to our advantage when trying to formulate an effective message
pathos	according to Aristotle's study of rhetoric, the emotional appeals of a speaker; some people are moved first by emotion before considering the credibility of the speaker or the facts
pausing	gives listeners the time to absorb what the speaker is saying and to internalize the message and make it their own
permission marketing	seeking customer agreement to accept promotional material from a company
pitch	the high or low tonal qualities of your voice: high-pitched, squeaky voices are generally read as weak and unimportant; very low voices can be read as slow and dim-witted; you can change the pitch of your voice by working to raise or lower the vocal tone; variations in pitch keep listeners interested and engaged
power distance	refers to the range and degree of acceptance of the distribution of power within a culture
proxemics	an individual's use of space in a cultural context
practical trust	develops because of leadership competency and successful behaviour over time
precision listening	in-depth evaluation and processing of the material one is listening to rather than merely engaging in surface listening

primacy — one of the two terms to know (the other being recency) in the context of the importance pattern; primacy means putting first the most important information, such as the most expensive commodity or the most urgent issue, etc.

proactive trendwatching — is picking up on early trends in unrelated industries and adapting them to your industry

profiling — a systematic way to look at all the information gathered about an audience, evaluate it and make a composite picture of audience members; profiles are used in databases to identify target consumer characteristics

psychographics — segment groups and individuals by their values, attitudes, interests and opinions

public affairs — a public relations function that works with and communicates to governmental bodies; to be successful, multinational companies must develop positive working associations with government representatives in all consumer markets

public relations — addresses four primary functions in a business organization: anticipation of social change, monitoring of institutional policy, evaluation of organizational performance and acting as the primary communication agent

rate of speaking — too slow or too fast can undermine an effective message

reactive trendwatching — identifying trends that have already entered the outer fringes of an industry

receiver — decoder of a message to give it meaning; judgements have to made on the basis not only of the actual words the person is hearing but also of an infinite number of subtle cues, such as tone of voice, a smile, a handshake, a furtive eye, ambiguous word usage, etc.

recency

one of the two terms to know (the other being primacy) in the context of the importance pattern; recency means putting the most important information at the end of your message, so it is the most recent point your audience hears or reads before they turn their attention to another matter

resistant receivers

are hard to reach mentally – they are wary of you and what you have to say; developing an opening that warms them to your message is sometimes crucial; you have to show that you understand their wants and needs and are sincere about imparting your message

salutation

in a formal business letter, the salutation is the greeting to the receiver of the letter, and varies according to country; using the proper salutation helps to ensure that your reader will be receptive to your letter

secondary publics

groups that are not primary stakeholders but that may be crucial to a company's reputation

selective alteration

as we move further away from an event, the information we have remembered undergoes increasing alteration; we immediately begin to use selective alteration to alter and adjust what we saw or heard

selective attention

people give selective attention only to those messages or communications that they are interested in or that are in agreement with their values or belief system; they tune out those messages that conflict with their beliefs

selective exposure

individuals look for information that reinforces existing values or beliefs and therefore selectively expose themselves only to certain material

selective perception	in 1958, Donald Broadbent, the British cognitive psychologist, identified the concept of selective perception when he noted that our human perceptual system has limitations; each individual perceives messages diferently
selective retention	the tendency to remember information consistent with our values and beliefs; psychological factors inhibit our retention and block out unwanted information
semantic noise	the meaning and value of words that affect understanding; this differs according to the sender's or the receiver's perspective
sender	also called the encoder – the sender's mission is to compose a message embedded with meaning from his/her world, while considering the interpretative resources the receiver will use to decode the message
signature	in a formal business letter, the signature block includes the writer's name written out, either by hand or electronically, above the writer's printed name and title
silence	accomplishes two ends: firstly, it can be interpreted as non-response in different ways – not interested, too busy, still thinking about it; secondly, it can be interpreted as "your turn to respond", which also has various decoded meanings – give me an answer, provide me more information, prompt a response from me
simultaneous and continuous	describe actions in the communication process: many messages are sent simultaneously in the guise of a smile, toss of the hair, accent, nod, furtive eye or yawn; messages are also continuous – even though words have a starting and an ending point, non-verbal messages do not, they never stop

situational approach developed by therapist Fred Fiedler in the 1950s, this approach is based on a self-assessment measurement scale called the least preferred co-worker scale; Fiedler believed that identifying co-workers with whom one does not like to work provides valuable information on leadership styles: leaders identified as easy to work with tend to be more relationship oriented, while those less easy to work with are more task oriented – these orientations influence leadership and communication style

social change function this requires public relations professionals to be aware of social, economic, cultural and political changes that could affect the livelihood and reputation of an organization

social media a term applied to digital media that enable customers to control content

sociographics characteristics that have to do with what activities people do in society with others

spatial a spatial outline groups events, facts or problems according to location, such as where it happens, where it will take place, the region of the country, etc.; rather than a time line, it is like a snapshot, and is generally used for descriptions

stakeholders individuals or entities that have an interest in your company: government, customers, employees, financial institutions, media, scholars, industry leaders, interest groups, communities, distributors, trade and professional organizations and competitors

stereotypes short cuts for identifying people, places and things; they are often a compilation of information received from what individuals consider reliable sources such as books, newspaper articles or friends

stories help people feel connected to an institution and its history and are important to maintaining institutional culture

strategic management	the planning process used by managers to balance the mission of the organization with what the environment will allow or support
stress	the uncertainty an individual feels when confronted with a serious opportunity, problem or demand for which the perceived outcome is in question
tactics	specific ways and means of achieving objectives
teleological approach	measures how much gratification will be produced by a certain action; advocated by utilitarians
theory of cognitive dissonance	introduced in the 1950s by psychologist Leon Festinger, who recognized that individuals seek out or readily accept information that conforms or reinforces their attitudes or beliefs; they do not seek out dissonant information, which results in uneasiness or doubt
theory of equilibrium	states that there is an inverse relationship between mutual gaze, a non-verbal cue signalling intimacy, and interpersonal distance and space
think globally, act locally	refers to the concept that, to succeed in the modern marketplace, companies must expand beyond national borders yet act responsibly by considering the wants and needs of the countries into which they move
timewarping	the alteration of time; people want things faster than ever before, faster than thought possible
trademark	a trademark differentiates a company's product or services from another's
trade promotions	offer incentives to retailers, distributors, dealers or salespersons to increase sales or to stimulate excitement

trait approach the trait approach suggests that, for an organization to be effective, its leaders must have certain characteristics; however, this approach tends to be highly selective, focusing primarily on the leader, not on the influence of followers or situations in determining leadership traits

transformational leadership involves developing communications that motivate and nurture the values of both leaders and followers; the theory focuses on charismatic leaders who motivate and move followers; such leaders are master communicators

transactional leadership occurs in everyday communication with others; transactional leaders are concerned with satisfying physiological, safety and social needs

transparency a new buzz word that means everything done in the company's name is above board and, when appropriate, open for public inspection; it has become a means of garnering public trust, a vital component of doing business in an increasingly scrutinized world

trendwatching a telescopic view that detects emerging issues; it requires awareness, insight and thinking in new ways and is not the realm of staid managers, uncomfortable with supposition or prediction

tryvertising a term coined by trendwatching.com, tryvertising means offering customers the ability to try various products at minimal cost and effort

two-way open communication a dynamic exchange of information that effectively conveys a message from sender to receiver as it was intended with the expectation that feedback, offered without fear of repercussion, will be considered

uncertainty avoidance	describes the willingness of a culture to accept or reject change and take risks
uncontrolled vehicle	medium over which public relations professionals have little say about how the message is used; the primary PR tool for disseminating information is the media release, an uncontrolled vehicle
usergraphics	define how customers use a product
vision	an organization's vision is a guideline for long-term success, a blueprint for the future; if a company cannot define its vision, it will never reach its potential
vocalizations	occur when you imitate a sound or laugh, moan, cry, etc.; they can be useful when we want to add drama or understanding to a message
volume	how loudly or softly you speak
voluntary audiences	want to hear what you have to say – they are listening (or reading) of their own free will, but this does not mean they will continue to stay focused if your message is not clear and relevant; however, you don't have to work too hard to get their attention
webographics	include information about a user's Internet system and speed, software use, format choice for receiving content, frequency of Internet access, etc.

Index